AMU

Advance Praise

'It was like serving two warring masters simultaneously: the British colonialists and the orthodox co-religionists. And there was another problem – the need to address the fears of a significant and socially backward minority without annoying the majority. In a desperate attempt to meet both challenges, Sir Syed slipped. The resultant intermixing of the conflicting goals of learning and identity led Aligarh Muslim University (AMU) to a path where secular learning was destined to take a back seat and champions of identity were to lead the institution to a blind alley.

This brilliantly researched ethnographic-cum-political history of AMU is a tour de force that starts at the beginning and leads up to the present times. In doing so, they walk us through a verifiable minefield. On the one side is an up-close account of Muslim identity politics – the force that created the university. Although conceived as a vehicle for modernising the Muslim mind, in recent decades, AMU has veered towards becoming a Muslim (intellectual) ghetto. Inbreeding, illiberalism and Islamic revivalism are threatening to remove it from the mainstream of Indian and international academia. On the other side stands an aggressive and militant Hindu right wing that perceives every assertion of Muslimness with jaundiced eyes. In between the two is the steadily narrowing path of secular knowledge and universal truths. For a Pakistani who wishes equally well for Indian Muslims and Hindus, the facts related in this book are deeply unsettling. Suppose Indian Muslims are to avert further marginalisation. In that case, they must take heed of this dangerous situation and recall AMU's foundational principle as articulated by the great Sir Syed – retain your identity but move with the modern world, understand and absorb its changing ways and cheerfully accept the duties and responsibilities of citizenship.'

Pervez Hoodbhoy, columnist, Pakistan

'The book takes a critical view of the chequered history of AMU since the very birth of the idea. The authors' meticulous research and constant touch with ground reality will be self-evident to the reader. Interspersed with insightful anecdotes, the book from a notoriously independent authors is interesting.'

Prashant Kumar, journalist

'Within the hallowed halls of Aligarh Muslim University, history whispers. In this captivating exploration of AMU, we embark on a journey through the institution's intricate tapestry, where each thread reveals a nuanced story, defying stereotypes.

Born as a beacon of modernity in pre-Partition India, AMU rose to become a prestigious intellectual and cultural haven. Yet, its legacy is woven with paradoxes. The Maheshwaris masterfully unravels them, revealing how AMU transformed from a catalyst for Muslim renaissance into a contested battleground for political ambitions.

Within these pages, leading intellectual and political leaders traverse the shifting sands of nation-creating debates, shaping AMU in profound ways. We grapple with the institution's enduring challenges – political entanglements, ideological clashes and the perpetual struggle to balance religious identity with modern education.

The Maheshwaris invite us to encounter diverse perspectives, from nostalgic reverence to contemporary critiques. The book delves deep into AMU's dilemmas, offering a thought-provoking analysis of its impact on the socio-political landscape of Indian Muslims.

This timely and insightful book is an invitation to ponder the intricate interplay of education, religion and identity within one of India's most iconic institutions. Prepare to be captivated by the Maheshwaris' engaging prose and the enduring complexities that have shaped AMU's legacy.'

Nikhil Kumar, literary critic

'This opus is a remarkable collection of history, anecdotes and insights. The arsenal the writer harnesses in describing AMU does not illuminate just its career but exposes the bare bones and deep underbelly of Indian academia. The book is an intimate biography of India's most controversial bastion of learning that was born in a churning time and remains to this date a churlish experience. It is a comprehensive chronicle of Aligarh Muslim University's arduous journey from its inspiring inception to its somewhat languid present. The number of varied dimensions it covers, the loving gaze it throws on various things, ideology, infrastructure and individuals included, the critical discussion over things that plague this great institution with a deep past and long future, the academic corruption, the financial irregularities, the nepotistic recruitment, the reign of family cartels, the self-debilitating inbreeding, not so unique to AMU but sufficiently strong here to mar its potential. The authors have covered a whole range of sweet-sour issues. What had started with the unstinted support from the colonial masters, in due course became an *ashrafia* bastion from which sprang forth battle troopers of the Muslims League torch bearers, and now has settled down to being an institution that caters mainly to India's aspirational class of students. The book gives interesting anecdotal insights into institutional politics in one of the modern yet conservative universities. The authors have brought out numerous back and side stories regarding events and individual idiosyncrasies that entertain and engage the readers. The book is very pacy and engaging.'

Prof. Rahul Ramagundam, Jamia Milia Islamia

AMU

Institution of Learning or Identity

Anil Maheshwari and
Arjun Maheshwari

ISBN: 978-93-92209-68-0

First published in India 2025
This edition published 2025

BluOne Ink Pvt. Ltd
A-76, 2nd Floor, Sector 136, Noida
Uttar Pradesh 201301
www.bluone.ink
publisher@bluone.ink

Printed and bound in India at Nutech Print Services - India

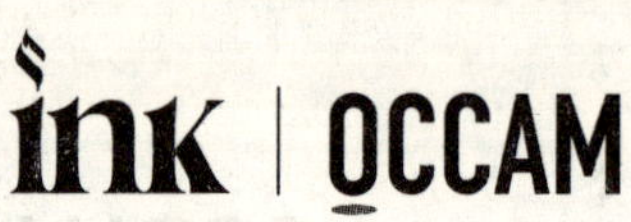

To Prof. V.S. Rekhi and Dr Rahat Abrar

CONTENTS

FOREWORD

Once institutions come into existence, they don't often die. In India, they generally fade away. Every institution, at some point, faces change and resists it for sure. Change, whether it is good or bad, affects the character of an institution: either overwhelmed by a tidal wave or adapting naturally to it. In India, AMU has perhaps faced more blows than any other institution in the country, both pre-and post-Independence, more from a good number of AMU alumni – who claim an extreme emotional attachment to it forming the ranks of Muslim politicians of all sorts – than from its adversaries. AMU has survived all such attacks and has in fact thrived for a number of reasons, chiefly and paradoxically ideological contradictions that have been present since its inception. It is also not necessary that history has presented the correct perspective on AMU. New schools of thought come up frequently, presenting things differently, each according to its own ideological predilections. In saying so, I do not mean that on the occasion of the centenary celebrations of AMU, all those who are in any way associated with it should not introspect. On the contrary, its vast network of alumni spread across the world must necessarily conduct this exercise.

Every institution is the product of a particular time, and its relevance must be analysed in that backdrop. Therefore, each institution must be measured on different standards, and employing a one-size-fits-all approach will inevitably give chaotic results. Having said this, I must note that there are only a few objective academic works on AMU, and it has always been almost impossible to analyse any aspects of the university or its founder, Sir Syed Ahmad Khan, based on those accounts. Anything that does not heap encomiums on the institute or its founder has been regarded as blasphemous. Therefore, every writer has been careful while writing about either, leaving one unaware of a number of uncomfortable truths about Syed Ahmad Khan, who has over time gained an almost-mythological persona. It is shameful that despite AMU receiving one of the largest government grants in the country and a huge alumni network, it has been unable to publish the collected works of its founder in their original Urdu, let alone their translations. I shall not delve much into the university's role before Independence nor the founder's allegiance to the British government, but will only note that it played a decisive role in the formation of Pakistan with its alumni having a role in running this new country and also in paving the way for the formation of Bangladesh, one of the initial catastrophes that Pakistan had to deal with.

Without commenting on Sir Syed's British loyalties one way or the other, it is worth considering that an anti-British organisation could never have thought of establishing an institution in the 19th century. Nor would it have been possible for it to be alleviated to the status of a university from a college – in this case, Muhammedan Anglo-Oriental (MAO) College, established by Sir Syed Ahmad Khan in 1886, a refined version of a madrasah ul-uloom (school of knowledge). The British government granted it the status of a university through an Act in 1920, twenty-two years after the founder's death, against a fee of two crore rupees funded mainly by Muslims. The moot point remains that simply alleviating its status to a university did not alleviate its mindset towards higher knowledge. This quest has always been missing from the ethos of AMU. Academically it has never been a centre of excellence in post-Partition India.

Independence altered the character of every institution earlier run by government fiats. After its adoption on 26 November 1949, all institutions came within the purview of the Indian Constitution thereon. The Constitution allowed minorities to establish and run their institutions without any monetary contribution. However, the minority status of AMU posed a problem because of the perks and privileges granted by the Government of India on par with the staff of central universities. While it enjoyed every privilege, when it came to answerability and excellence, it took recourse to the emotional plea of a minority institution and the overall backwardness of Muslims in India. The first case relating to AMU's minority character was decided by a constitutional bench of the Supreme Court of India in Aziz Basha vs Union of India. While it was in the court, neither the then vice-chancellor enjoying all privileges nor the alumni nor any other Muslim, a Muslim organisation, or politician intervened, that is, requested the court to hear their case because the party concerned either had a stake or wanted it to be heard in the broader public interest, a request which is generally granted by the relevant bench. A case is still pending in the Supreme Court in an appeal in which the Allahabad high court questioned the minority status of the university. While not commenting on the case's merits, I cannot resist mentioning that it reached the high court due to the inept handling by the then vice-chancellor, Naseem Ahmad, who, ironically, was a trained lawyer. In later years, he was booked by the CBI; but according to sources, the agency could not move to prosecute him due to an outdated law requiring a presidential nod for prosecuting a member of the Indian Civil Service. In his case, the CBI was denied permission by the president's office. The pending case in the Supreme Court of India is not the last, and the university will have to face many such cases in the coming days with more challenging competition. Hopefully, however, it will survive till Articles 29 and 30 of the Indian Constitution are not abolished.

While appointing a vice-chancellor of AMU, five potential candidates are chosen randomly by the University Executive. A candidate's consent is not necessary, so one can lose the election without any intention of contesting for the post. Of them, the University Executive votes for three candidates, who are thereby elected by the University Court, the highest body, and these three names are then sent to the President of India, who selects any one candidate. Due to the university's minority status, a candidate for vice-chancellorship faces only mild competition for many reasons, including the convention that only a Muslim can be appointed to the post. Moreover, patriarchy has also never allowed a woman to lead the institution. Owing to such prohibitions, the vice-chancellorship of AMU is not open to the brightest minds in the country, regardless of community and gender.

The vice-chancellor of the university is, however, a compelling person. He can nominate 20 per cent of students to any course save medical studies. According to Clause 19(3) of the university laws, which bestow a prerogative that not even the prime minister of India enjoys, the vice-chancellor can take any decision in the name of emergency, and a study would find every AMU vice-chancellor has taken recourse to this clause for 90 per cent of their crucial decisions.

AMU has witnessed extreme religious orthodoxy and sectarian strife among different religious groups and bitter rivalry among the followers of the Wahabi school of thought, whose leading proponents in AMU are Deobandis and followers of the Jamaat-i Islami. Deobandis have monopolised the institution from Sir Syed's time, so it can be said that AMU is more an orthodox madrasa than a university. AMU, during Saiyid Hamid's tenure as vice-chancellor (1980–85), was the first Indian university to recognise the degrees of *dini madaris* formally. After 1980, the university ethos has been dominated by a madrasa mentality, giving anti-Muslim forces a boost.

Having grown up in a Muslim family in a small town in western Uttar Pradesh, I am well aware of the obsession of Muslim parents in north India with sending their wards to AMU. I do not recall any educated neighbour or relative who did not attend the university or at least tried to get admission into its hallowed portals. Still, somehow, I decided not to follow this tradition. I have, therefore, been a keen observer of the university's functioning to assess whether my decision was wrong. The answer is undoubtedly a 'no', but the reasons why next-generation Muslims either did not join AMU or moved elsewhere after receiving one degree is vital for evaluating its current status and importance.

AMU does not value books. If it is not interested in making the works of its founder available, as explained earlier, it cannot be expected to value other books on its history. The first book on the history of MAO College by S.K. Bhatnagar could only be published due to the interest of the then provost of Sir Syed Hall through the donations of the residents of the hall. The university press recently republished it, I am told, or by Sir Syed Academy; both are redundant, so despite my best efforts, I could not get a copy of the book.

Nevertheless, after a long time, we have an informative book on the university that will undoubtedly fundamentally advance our understanding of the phenomenon named AMU. The Maheshwaris belong to the heart of western Uttar Pradesh and have spent their childhood with Muslim friends. These are the two requirements crucial for closely understanding and studying AMU historically and Muslims in contemporary India.

I conclude with what should have been stated in the beginning. When the All India Muhammadan Educational Conference (AIMEC) merged with the Muslim League in 1906, or, succinctly, when the conference gave birth to the Muslim League, the movement spearheaded by Sir Syed Ahmad Khan stopped being educational. Partition came as a boon for AMU to bury its past, but it did not convert it into an opportunity. Since then, the university has become a sanctuary for backwards-looking Muslim leadership and survived on emotional issues, thereby increasing the sufferings of Indian Muslims on the one hand and depleting the university's standard on the other.

Ather Farouqui
General Secretary, Anjuman Taraqqi Urdu

1

INTRODUCTION

Aligarh Muslim University (AMU) lost its status as an institution of higher learning even in pre-Partition days; it instead transformed into a movement. However, it has remained the most prestigious intellectual and cultural centre for Indian Muslims for over a century. Little wonder, it is a singular symbol of Muslim life in India.

Member of Parliament G.M. Banatwala (Indian Union Muslim League) said the AMU represented the hopes and aspirations of Muslims in India.[1] In the debate in the Rajya Sabha on the AMU Amendment Bill (1965), B.K.P. Sinha said, 'Aligarh is the microcosm of the great Muslim community of this country. What a seed is to a tree, Aligarh is to the great Muslim community.'[2] It can be considered an index of the status of Muslims in the country.

Mohammad Ali Jinnah, the founder of Pakistan, once hailed the AMU in pre-Partition days as 'the arsenal of Muslim India'.[3] Though it may not have remained the only centre of Muslim politics after the Partition of the country in 1947, it still has tremendous importance in Indian politics and in defining its contours as well as in terms of social and political mobilisation. AMU has also been listed as an institution of national importance in the VII Schedule of the Constitution of India.

However, it would be misleading to suppose that 'the Aligarh spirit',[4] as the Aligarh College movement came to be labelled, has always been confined exclusively to Islamist interests.[5] It inspired new generations of Muslims to realise that knowledge, not merely faith, would be the guiding principle of life and progress. During World War I, the Indian rebels who had formed a government-in-exile at Kabul chose Raja Mahendra Pratap, an Aligarian (also involved in the Silk Letter Conspiracy), as their president. The Ali Brothers; Maulana Hasrat Mohani; Muslim Leaguers Liaquat Ali Khan, A.R. Nashtar and Qayyum Khan; Congress leaders T.A.K. Sherwani, Rafi Ahmad Kidwai, Khan Abdul Ghaffar Khan, Dr Syed Mahmood of Bihar and Dr M.A. Ansari; Communist leader Kunwar Mohammad Ashraf; and a host of others on both sides of the political divide were the illustrious products of Aligarh during the pre-Partition period.

Professor M. Mujeeb, the biographer of Dr Zakir Husain, aptly observes:

> The common man who raises the question of the value and significance of Aligarh Muslim University would, after the kind of enquiries he can make and the answers he elicits, conclude similar to what the Russian poet Tyutchev said about his country:
> Russia cannot be grasped with the mind,
> Or measured with the common yardstick;
> She has her peculiar quality,
> In Russia – one can only believe.[6]

Almost all those educated at Aligarh or in service there long enough share this belief. Others wonder. Reverence for the university was reinforced by institutions like the All India Muslim Educational Conference (AIMEC), now virtually defunct and a sizeable number of old boys' associations in various cities across the globe besides the Duty Society. These bodies continue to nurture the emotional bond between the alumni and the university. The degree of reverence for the institution is reflected in the peculiarity that anyone making even mildly unpleasant remarks is often accused of bias and seen as ill disposed towards Muslims or branded anti-religious, at the very least. Objectivity becomes a casualty in such a charged atmosphere.

Sir Syed launched a Muslim modernism that sought to reconcile traditional Islam with modern needs.[7] However, there is no denying the fact that the Muslim University Movement (1898–1920), after the death of Sir Syed Ahmad Khan, represented concerted efforts to create an all-India Muslim constituency and to carve out a decisive piece of political power for it. AMU lost its status as an institution of higher learning even in pre-Partition days; it instead transformed into a movement.

Even today, Muslim leaders search for a constituency in Aligarh and do not refrain from using students for this purpose. Political leaders, particularly those who profess to be secular, see Muslims as little else than a minority vote bank. They conveniently forget Dr Zakir Husain's caution that Aligarh's participation in the various walks of national life would determine the place of Muslims in India's national life and the way India conducted itself towards Aligarh would largely determine the form our national life would acquire in the future.[8]

The lofty ideals of Sir Syed Ahmad Khan to establish a Muhammadan Anglo-Oriental (MAO) College, which later blossomed into the university, were undermined by mass politics and drives to raise funds in the institution. Coupled with them was the rise of populist electoral politics, including Muslim politics, different from the nationalist politics dominated by the majority community during India's struggle for freedom.

The idea of MAO College later transformed into the Aligarh movement in the course of Sir Syed's stout defence of the Urdu cause, resistance to the introduction of the Devanagri script in official business, opposition to the demand for a ban on cow slaughter, and demand for proportional representation as well as weightage for Muslims in representative bodies. In the founding of the AIMEC in 1886 as a forum for Muslim intelligentsia to process, articulate and press for their demands and grievances, as well as his strident opposition to the Indian National Congress (INC), Sir Syed initiated educational, cultural and political trends that laid the groundwork for the Muslim renaissance in India, one offshoot of which resulted in the demand for, and creation of, Pakistan. Transitional anxieties and ambiguities would be accentuated by the upsurge of nationalism on the one hand and the assertion of Hindu revivalism on the other. Sir Syed's vision demanded a much smoother context to actualise itself, the most primary condition being the non-intrusion of politics in education.

In all this, Sir Syed, a product of the cultural and ideological traditions of his day, and the influences that he had absorbed from the historical part of the country (itself shaped and moulded by history), left a lasting impact on the history of the subcontinent. Central to the historical legacy that Sir Syed and the Muslim intelligentsia received was a romantic version of Muslim rule in India. In the disastrous aftermath of the 1857 rebellion leading to the decimation of the Mughal Empire, Islam was in a vulnerable position for the first time in about a thousand-year-old encounter with India. The crushing of the Muslim elites and the inertia and fatal defeatism that engulfed the community led Sir Syed to ponder ways to rescue the sinking community. He saw the panacea in modern education and scientific approach, as he knew that his modernity project could not find traction among the Muslims. His call of reconciling reason with faith, Islam with science and logic with theology was bound to raise the hackles of the ulema, who considered themselves the arbiters of Islam. Sir Syed said, 'Let Muslims reinvent themselves by adapting to a new epitome and evolving a new Weltanschauung of reason-religion reconciliation.'[9] Peace was an ineluctable imperative and had to be practised as a conviction of conscience rather than a mere expedient. The Muslims had to abjure hostility to the new dispensation. In an obituary reference, a London newspaper described Sir Syed as the apostle of education to the Mohammadans of India.[10] It added that he stood as an interpreter between them and their (British) rulers and between them and the British people.

At the close of the 18th century, Indian Muslim society presented a sad spectacle of inertia and degeneration. In the twilight of the Mutiny, by and large, the Muslims in much of North India had been politically and economically ruined. The rude jolt of the shift from power to powerlessness, from Bengal and Lucknow to Mysore and Madras (now Chennai), had left Muslim society shrouded in a time warp, unable to comprehend the present and fearful of the future. A dread of the unknown prevailed as the sudden decline was hard to bear, made worse by the ignorance, conservatism and traditionalism among Muslims. The lack of modern education further weakened the foundations of their identity and brought Muslim society to the verge of collapse.

A highly revered figure among Indian Muslims today, in his time, Sir Syed Ahmad grappled with an extremely reticent and sceptical Muslim community. He laid the foundations of modernism but could not guard or isolate these foundations from the onslaught of Muslim separatism. However passionately Sir Syed might have wished to insulate Muslims in general and the Aligarh project in particular from politics, politics could not have been kept away in the late 19th and early 20th centuries. Against this backdrop of inevitability, politics permeated Aligarh on a note of exclusion, with a tinge of parochialism and in the spirit of potential separatists. Sir Syed would not have approved of this contamination of politics and religion. Therefore, from a movement for modernity, Sir Syed's mission degenerated into a vehicle for asserting identity along primordial lines. For Aligarians and Muslims (from North India in particular), the AMU remains a symbol of Muslim independence and self-reliance.

However, MAO College, as an educational institution, had its limitations. Those joining MAO College in its incipient phase came from the elite sections (*ashraf*) of the Muslim society, whose stakes lay not in change but in the persistence of the status quo ante. This was a limiting factor of the capacious vision of Sir Syed. The discrepancy between his progressive ideas would run into the retrogressive pull of the conservative section of Muslim society. They would bide their time before mounting a backlash. At no time did the majority of Muslim graduates, even of the North-Western Province, belong to it. Of the 1,184 Muslims graduating in India between 1882 and 1892, Aligarh produced only 220, compared to 410 from the University of Allahabad. What Aligarh did was to produce a class of Muslim leaders with a footing in both Western and Islamic cultures, at ease both in British and Muslim society and endowed with a consciousness of their claims to the aristocracy. Educated in a residential college that imitated the English public schools of the time, with an emphasis on character, leadership and prowess in games and not just scholarship alone, with debating societies and old boys' association to engender college esprit de corps, the Aligarh student was encouraged to work for the welfare of the Muslim community in India. Success in examinations and individual achievement was at a discount.

Sir Charles Hawkes Todd Crosthwaite (1835–1915), lieutenant-governor of the North-Western Provinces, advised Muslims: 'It is better for the future of your race that ten men should be sent out than that a hundred able indeed to satisfy the examiners but otherwise imperfectly trained.'[11] The boys at Aligarh were not exhorted to nurture an unhealthy anxiety about the fate of their souls or, indeed, to an individual investigation of God's demands upon them in the modern world. Islam, for them, was a matter of cultural rather than religious conviction. Whatever the founder's real intentions, Aligarh became an institution for coming to terms with the British-created world on a footing of equality rather than for questioning that world from a burning religious conviction. Colonialism, with all its ambiguities and contradictions, was itself a limiting factor as it did not allow leeway for an ambitious vision to take off, take wings and take the world by storm.

Sir Syed, like any thinking and growing person, contradicted himself often. At one place, he would insist on being called a Hindu, and at another, he would spill his bile against them. This is neither hypocrisy nor dissonance. He struggled in his soul between his ideals and his community's immediate interests. He did not retract his ideas. All he did was to stop highlighting them with similar militant activism as he did earlier. He did so in the hope that the institution he was building would take forward the ideas it was built on. Had he known that the college would censor, ban and bury the very ideas on which it was founded, he would indeed have had second thoughts about its establishment.

Precisely 90 years after the 1857 revolt, Muslims who opted to remain in India after Partition were in more or less the same predicament, though the colonial masters had granted independence to India in 1947. There was no reason for the people on the Aligarh campus to be alarmed as communal harmony more or less prevailed. Moreover, the university was accorded the status of an extraordinary institution and dubbed as the living symbol of the *millat's* survival in independent India, in addition to being well protected by Article 30 of the Constitution of India. The seemingly unambiguous terms of the Article read:

> All minorities, whether based on religion or language, shall have the right to establish and administer educational institutions of their choice. The State shall not, in granting aid to educational institutions, discriminate against any educational institution on the ground that it is under the management of a minority, whether based on religion or language.

Notwithstanding the large-scale exodus of the faculty and alumni to Pakistan, the university has retained its predominant role of nurturing Muslim ethnicity in north Indian states, Uttar Pradesh and Bihar in particular. Though the catchment area for attracting students has shrunk with the mushrooming of new educational institutions and universities in almost every nook and corner of the country, Aligarh retains a special significance. No wonder it has attracted friends as well as foes.

Which university in the country can boast of such illustrious names on its Court (Senate) and Executive Council (Syndicate) as the AMU? Finding a place in the university's decision-making bodies is part of political embellishment.

However, a distinct change has occurred in the post-Independence era so far as the social milieu of the students is concerned. The nouveau riche among the socially backward sections of Muslims have discovered in Aligarh the path to social recognition. This class has succeeded economically, edging out the older wealthy Muslims. It naturally seeks upward social mobility. While denominational and sectarian divisions are not alien to the ethos of Islam, deep social divisions based on caste are peculiar to Indian Muslims. Islam does not allow a caste system. In principle, there is no place in Islam for *telis*, *julahas*, *kasais* or *nais*. But the ground reality in India is different.

With the nouveau riche getting admission to the university in sizeable numbers, it has undergone a cultural metamorphosis. Moreover, in the wake of the economic liberalisation of the 1990s, most students are no less career-conscious than their counterparts in other universities. It is no surprise that one finds the Maulana Azad Library, the library of the Careers Guidance and Coaching Centre and the professional seminars in various departments always crowded.

While students from the university are more aspirational today, can it provide Muslim youth with the much-needed fillip to climb up the political and social ladders? Anyone willing to leap finds all avenues open in Aligarh, a promise doled out to Aligarians by Jawaharlal Nehru and Maulana Abul Kalam Azad in 1948 and 1949, respectively.

Several generations of Aligarians have been sacrificed by the machinations of power-hungry politicians in the Muslim community and the Hindu chauvinists who persist in demanding proof of Muslims' loyalty to India. Two generations of Muslims have grown up in an independent India where they are often perceived as the Trojan horse. At the same time, Pakistan tries to use Indian Muslims, or Muslim Indians, as leverage. Politicians on the other side of the border continue to justify the decision by Muslims to migrate to Pakistan, citing the alleged plight of their co-religionists in India. Hemmed in at both ends, Muslims too are becoming 'ghettoised'.

When Sir Syed founded MAO College, he was aware of the burgeoning problems of his community. He also foresaw with extraordinary clarity that if left unguided, Muslims would slip into the mire of ignorance, oblivion and backwardness. Hence, his experiment later came to be called the Aligarh movement. But unscrupulous elements among Muslims, masquerading as established leaders (the majority sans constituency), could never allow his endeavour to succeed.

Established Muslim leadership is unwilling to let this symbol or springboard of Muslim sub-nationalism slip out of its hands. Few Muslim leaders recognise that contemporary India has come a long way. It is a secular and pluralistic society in which different sections of people can live together and understand one another. Besides, the basis on which the groups of people are recognised has changed. Sociologically, Hinduism, Islam or any other religion is an identity. The days of religion as an organising principle are over. In contemporary India, a principle other than religion is needed for organising groups sustainably. The kind of religiosity prevalent in the 19th and early 20th centuries is irrelevant in the modern world. For example, Arabs are fighting for a national identity, not a religious one.

When Sir Syed talked about modern education for Muslims, he did not envisage a religious university. Otherwise, he would have established a *madrasa*. His agenda was straightforward. To have a distinctive place in the socio-economic order of the day, it was necessary for Muslims to acquire modern education.

What was supposed to be the very basis for the existence of Aligarh has, therefore, been subverted? If Aligarh, in search of religious identity, fails to educate its students to cope with modern life and outlook, it will no longer fulfil its role as a university. The trouble arises when the religious question masquerades as an academic one, and outsiders with ulterior motives start dictating the academic programme of the university.

To continue performing the function its founder Sir Syed had dreamt of, the AMU must prepare its students to take a quantum jump in modern secular India. This does not mean that an Aligarian should only aspire to become a member of Parliament or a legislative body, a minister, or an administrative or police officer. The problem confronting this great seat of learning is that a section of vocal and ambitious Muslims wishes to exploit the university platform to advance its personal political ambitions. In the process, students lose an opportunity to become responsible citizens of 21st-century India.

However, a sizeable section of the university community is still preoccupied with a distinctive Muslim identity, which, if carried to excessive limits, can threaten Indian nationalism. The traditionalists refuse to realise that the separation of religion from state is desirable for all communities, particularly minorities.

In a pluralist society, students from both communities would have made attempts to understand each other with exposure to each other's culture. If Muslim and Hindu boys and girls were to meet in the same classroom and study together, they would cultivate mutual respect, instead of turning into ignorant fanatics in their later life.

Despite the ups and downs of the 20th century, Aligarh has flourished and continued to cherish its fundamental values. An integrated life has survived, and the educational-cum-residential system has acquired a flavour of its own.

The 'unknown Indian', as author Nirad C. Chaudhuri described himself, was a detractor who became an admirer.

> From my boyhood, I had a dislike for Aligarh ... I thought that Aligarh was the cradle (we preferred to regard it as the hotbed) of Islamic revivalism in India. Under the teaching of Bankim Chandra Chatterji and Vivekananda, most of us had become Hindu revivalists. Still, we were not, on that account, prepared to concede to the Muslim the right to his revivalism because we regarded our Hinduism in its revivified form as nationalism and reformed Islam as anti-national. As between the Hindus and Muslims of India, it has always been an ethics of double standards ...
>
> The AMU is trying to retain the socio-cultural distinctiveness of the Muslims only as a contributory factor in creating a multicultural society in India. It is remaining Islamic without sacrificing modernisation or the absorption of Western influences.

> I found its Islamism to be far less reactionary than the Hinduism of an organisation like the Jana Sangh.[12]

All, however, is not well within the AMU. It is necessary to take a critical view. An *Economic and Political Weekly* (EPW) editorial in 2010 lamented:

> The Aligarh Muslim University, which had the potential to become the premier provider of higher education to the Muslim middle classes as well as to help generate knowledge about India's largest minority, has reduced itself to being a small-time distributor of patronage and corruption. While government policies and interference must bear a large part of the blame for this trend, the culpability of the 'university community' cannot be denied either.[13]

Writes Neyaz Farroquee in the *Hindustan Times*,

> It's a university of world repute; it's a university in decline. It's a progressive centre as any; it is a conservative university. Its founder was a proponent of the two-nation theory; its founder was a votary of Hindu-Muslim unity. It has failed its founder's vision of providing Indian Muslims with a modern education; it has given India, and the subcontinent, Muslim intellectuals. It's doomed beyond repair; it's the only hope. Aligarh Muslim University (AMU) is many things to many people, but for now, the only certainty is that it's walking a thin line.[14]

Such a dialectical approach to the truth about AMU may help its students, teachers, and administration to take this institution of learning (not identity) to great heights.

Frank Islam says candidly: 'If Muslims succeed, India will succeed. And just as I am part of the American fabric, Muslims are part of India and must use opportunities created by India's inclusiveness.'[15] Long before Fakhru Islam, hailing from Azamgarh, became Frank Islam at the suggestion of a teacher at the University of Colorado from where he did his M.Sc. in Computer Sciences, he, along with his parents had moved to Varanasi, from where he went to the AMU and where a visiting American mathematician arranged a fellowship for him in the US. He donated US $ two million to his alma mater.

Messiahs and prophets have their moments, but posterity often uses them in ways they could have never envisaged. One of the recurrent ways this happens is by attributing words and statements to them that they never uttered or championed in the first place. Sir Syed would have preferred substance to symbolism.

Najmul Hoda, an Aligarian, rues that Sir Syed was not a narcissistic 'smart' like Jinnah. He was a wise man. Above all, he was a pragmatist, while Jinnah was an adventurist. Like every thinking individual, he displayed contradictions but was not disingenuous. There is a dire need to rehabilitate him as a thinker and reformer. He was not a mason who built the Muslims a college, which they, with their pious ingenuity, turned into a (intellectual) ghetto. Aligarh's Sir Syed is an eviscerated and sanitised non-thinker – a lifeless idol for only ritual homage. I don't think any other institution ever buried its founder's thoughts like Aligarh did his.

Sir Syed did create a paradigm shift – but it was a complex paradigm, not always without contradictions: for instance, he was an 'anti-dissenter' in politics but a 'pro-dissenter' in theology.

Aligarh betrayed Sir Syed in politics, too. Had his successors heeded him, and had they not jumped into politics, Aligarh wouldn't have earned the dubious distinction of rendering the Indian subcontinent asunder and the community into three. Perhaps the two worst calamities to have befallen the Muslims are Aligarh and Pakistan. They have a cause-effect relationship. Nothing better could be expected of an institution built on the grave of its founder's ideas and dreams. From a movement of modernity, it would degenerate into a vehicle for asserting identity along primordial lines. Sir Syed would have preferred substance to symbolism.

Another Aligarian laments that MAO College was a very limited embodiment of all that Sir Syed stood for. The establishment of the college and his need to see it flourish made him compromise on his ideas as a reformer and his insights as an exegete. The college killed the religious thinker and the social reformer in him. In Aligarh, Sir

Syed, the founder, is worshipped, but Sir Syed, the thinker and the reformer, is ignored as an embarrassment.

Sir Syed's importance lies in his pursuit of evolving a sound methodology for engaging with the world and ideas and how they work. His words and his works were epistemology and hermeneutics. Moreover, experiments like Aligarh Muslim University came very late in the day; even then, it remained too mired in the religious glory of the past.

AMU has been caught in a time warp. The Muslim world is already stuck in a time loop, their world of ideologies pushing them back backwards. Syed Ubaidur Rahman forewarns,

> Despite the great achievements of AMU, it is a sad truth that Muslims have abysmally failed to live up to the vision of its founders. Instead of building more such institutions, the community leaders sat still, eulogising Sir Syed and trying to protect the institution he had built 145 years ago. New institutions modelled on AMU's vision would have greatly benefited the community and the country. Perhaps Muslims were in a time warp for a long and focused on religious education imparted at madrasas until they awoke just a few decades ago to find themselves boxed in and outclassed in a changed society. Now Muslims are emerging from their inertia and trying to focus on modern education again – hopefully, it is still not too late.[16]

Ibn Khaldun Bharati, perhaps a pseudonym, writes:

> The acronym AMU stands for Aligarh Muslim University. Still, to all intents and purposes, it stands for Allah Miyan's University, that is, a divinely ordained sanctuary where the mere thought of reform is considered sacrilegious. Understandably so, since it is effectively a Succession State of the Mughal empire, much on the lines of Oudh, Bengal and Hyderabad. The descendants of the Muslim conquerors, the thousand-year-old ruling class – the Ashrāf – have been endowed with a principality of their own to wallow in the nostalgia of their imperial past and to fantasise about its revival. These lotus eaters are maintained by the Indian

> State, which pays for their reverie from the Consolidated Fund of India.[17]

He suggests that to integrate Indian Muslims, the totem of separatism, Muslim Personal Law, needs radical reform. And the process must begin with an overhaul of AMU's power structure. Came a prompt repartee on the post, 'AMU stands for Ashraafia (Elites) Muslim University.' Noted scholar Tabish Khair tweets: 'A significant 19th- and 20th-century difference between upper-caste Hindu leaders, secular and religious reformers, is that they faced up to caste-class among Hindus. Ashraf Muslims evaded this issue among Muslims.'

2

ALIGARH TOWN

Aligarh gets its name from Prophet Mohammad's cousin and son-in-law, Ali, after the storming of its fort by Shia commander Mirza Najaf Khan and his lieutenant, Afrasiyab Khan, in 1775. It was also known as Ali Gur. *Pierre Cuillier-Perron or Cuellier* (1755–1834), a French military adventurer who changed his name from Pierre to *Perron*, and another military adventurer, Benoît Leborgne (1751–1830), better known as Count *Benoît de Boigne* or General Count de Boigne, built many buildings and extended the fort at Aligarh. British Generals Gerard Lake and David Ochterloney conquered the fort during the Anglo-Maratha wars.

Benoit De Boigne is not a name one would typically think of as a jagirdar in the Doab region in Uttar Pradesh. And yet the Frenchman and another who succeeded him were among the men who ruled the Doab from Aligarh. In the 1780s, the Doab, the fertile alluvial plain between the Ganges and Yamuna rivers, came under the possession of Maratha chief Mahadaji Scindia, who had become the virtual ruler of north India by then. He had employed several European mercenaries in his army to train his troops in the latest military techniques.[1]

Aligarh city consists of two distinct townships separated by the rail track, a sort of Bosphorus Line. (The line of defence built by the French against German invasion. However, the Germans outflanked it during World War II and entered France through Belgium.) With its congested lanes, the old city radiates to all sides. The Civil Lines, where AMU was established, is, by contrast, a much more airy and green area.

The post-Babri Masjid demolition period has affected a change in the pattern of localities, already fissured with communal tension. During riots in the 1980s, residents of Civil Lines faced an acute shortage of essential commodities. Therefore, a market grew around Dodhpur, an area sandwiched between the university and the Civil Lines. Within a short period, Dodhpur registered a building boom.

Jamalpur, on the fringes of the university, too, has seen unplanned development in recent decades. There is hardly any known criminal in the city today without a hideout in the new localities. The area between Lal Diggi and Marris Road also turned into a concrete jungle.

Earlier, nobody would have bothered to curfew restrictions in the Civil Lines area as it remained least affected by riots. But the riots of the early 1990s reversed the scenario. This area now has a mixed population of the elite from both communities. However, the right side of Marris Road has a predominantly Muslim population.

Attitudes have been changing remarkably over the years. A Muslim doctor from the Maldives was doing his MS in Ophthalmology at the AMU in the early 1990s. He and his wife initially stayed in a rented accommodation in a predominantly Hindu locality but after some months shifted to a Muslim locality. Later, his wife told her friends that during the riots, a few shots were fired in the air. Somebody suggested that all the womenfolk be sent to one house for safety. After that, the women were herded into a big room. It was a 100 per cent Muslim locality and, therefore, there was no threat from the other community. Yet, fear prevailed.

Though Aligarh is not a Muslim-majority town, it has a Muslim image because of the university. Notwithstanding its plural character, AMU embodies Muslim culture and remains a symbol of Muslim identity in India. However, AMU has often been portrayed as a bastion of Muslim separatism. Around 13,000 to 16,000 Muslims migrated from this town to Pakistan, most belonging to elite groups. Those who remained (metal workers, butchers, agricultural labourers, weavers, etc.) had to bear the burden of the legacy of

Partition. Pratinav Anil quips, 'The Muslims of Aligarh town and gown, too, were chalk and cheese.'[2]

Irfan Ahmad reveals what Aligarh meant to the Muslim child:

> I first heard of AMU when I was a student in a village madrasa. The madrasa administration asked us to get 'Aligarh pyjamas' and 'kurta' to wear at an upcoming function. Later, after moving to a government school, I heard more about the university from some rich relatives who studied there. As students of AMU, they felt superior to me. Studying at AMU meant not only getting a degree but also embodying 'Muslim culture'. Such was the AMU's place in the Muslim imagination![3]

Etiquette (*adab*) remains a crucial element of the daily life of students at AMU. Studying here offers a Muslim environment and a guarantee of security and morality, which are missing in metropolitan cities. It has become the preferred option for educated Muslim families in India, who move to Aligarh in significant numbers to get a job at the university or to ensure their children get an education there. After retirement, many choose not to return to their native places.

The Muslim identity is often referred to as a stigma leading to spatial relegation by those in the old town, while in Sir Syed Nagar (SS Nagar), the 'intelligentsia colony' of South Asian Muslims, the 'Muslimness' of the residents is a matter of pride and prestige. An agglomeration of AMU professors and Muslim graduates of modern India have gathered in the large pucca houses surrounding the university. It is hailed as the most educated colony in Asia. However, it does not represent the local Muslim population of Aligarh. While they hardly visit other parts of the city, SS Nagar residents often travel to foreign countries. They work for the university, want their children to study at the university, live near it, have friends, and fight for the university. The university indeed bounds its world in an enclave mentality. It is altogether a different matter that the Municipal Corporation poorly serves the area. Narrow roads and newly constructed small flats that have mushroomed recently, besides lacking civic sense, have become hallmarks of this locality. The locality is, however, swamped by sewage. The Muslim *mahol* (atmosphere) of the neighbourhood is praised by its residents. The AMU evolved as a habit of ideology, where culture is not taught but lived. If you ask someone from the university, they will say it's a 'feeling'. Every door and wall of the university has a story attached to it, waiting to be told by someone living thousands of miles away. Unlike big metropolises, Aligarh is considered a safe and friendly town with a higher morality. SS Nagar is peopled with local avatars of *Homo academicus*, an expression borrowed from Pierre Bourdieu's study on French academics.[4] It is an elite ghetto. Muslim residents here are insular and inward-looking, and a ghetto mentality prevails. Communal feelings run high, and the need for security is exaggerated.

Self-segregation has played a part in forming Muslim enclaves where Muslims have regrouped for physical and cultural protection. Mixed areas are becoming rare. Clusters of Muslim settlements are scattered around the university. The mosaic of Hindu-majority and Muslim-majority localities leads to ghettoisation of the residents. These clusters are virtually hermetically sealed to each other as communities are more polarised in this age of fanaticism. The segregated urban structure of Aligarh city, therefore, appears to be the product of past communal tensions. The social and spatial gap that separates elite and non-elite Muslims is vast. Little wonder, the communal segregation of the town is coupled with a social one, both being equally inseparable.

Though the city continues to expand, there has been no concomitant upgradation of the sewerage system. The drains are generally choked, leading to a sluggish flow of wastewater, which in turn spills onto the roads, leaving holes and potholes. During the rains, sewage overflows and spreads, leading to slow but steady groundwater contamination. The drainage system gets clogged with salt at several points leading to periodic outbreaks of diseases like cholera and malaria.

The city is also pockmarked with garbage dumped along roads and lanes. At times, vacant plots serve as waste dumping sites in the middle of residential areas. Rotting garbage, scavenging dogs and swarms of flies and mosquitoes have made several localities hotbeds of disease and filth. At Lal Diggi, a few metres from the university's administrative block, the stench as one approaches the university from the railway station negotiating a road, which is permanently submerged in dark black water, makes one gag. Naked children merrily cavort around. Of course, these conditions are not peculiar to Aligarh alone, they hold true for most north Indian towns.

Sir Syed had never seen Aligarh before his transfer to that town from Ghazipur in 1864. That was the year the railway line was opened up, connecting Delhi (now New Delhi) with Calcutta (now Kolkata), the then capital of British India. Aligarh was on the main line. In Aligarh, Sir Syed found an enthusiasm for his educational efforts that he had not encountered previously. Khwaja Mohammad Yusuf, a prominent town citizen, was keen to have the proposed college at Aligarh. There were well-to-do Muslim landlords in the vicinity, some of them newly created in return for backing the British in 1857. They had good relations with the colonial rulers. The Scientific Society, founded by Sir Syed, also flourished here.

Perhaps remembering the distractions of his youth, Sir Syed wanted to avoid major old cities such as Delhi and Agra for his dream project. He preferred a small town – accessible but isolated. He wished to keep students away from pigeon fights, kite flying and courtesans. Another attraction of Aligarh was the availability of revenue-free land. In 1869, the military camp was abandoned at Aligarh because of the perceived threat of endemic and the absence of adequate water. Some villages adjoining the camp had already been confiscated and demolished in retaliation for the 1857 mutiny. Several British residents of the Civil Lines were leaving and selling their private living quarters. With adequate open land and many vacant (though old) buildings around, it was an excellent site for starting a college. The barren land of Aligarh turned into a lush green campus, producing thousands of earners.

Sir Syed did extensive research before deciding the site for the college he visualised. He consulted doctors and many other reputed persons regarding the various issues related to the mental and physical well-being of the wards he was intending to nourish at the college. A detailed account, writer Huma Khalil notes, was sent to Khan stating that Aligarh's '*aab-o-hawa*' is 'perfectly suitable' for the intellectual and physical well-being of an individual.

'Aligarh is in the Doab region of north India. Its topography is bowl-shaped and is situated in between two mounds, making it a highly fertile region. The water levels and the quality of water was reasonably good,' she says.[5] Moreover, the Aligarh sub-committee contributed more money (and gave firm assurances) than any other sub-committee. Therefore, the central committee requested the secretary to proceed with the school's foundation at Aligarh.

Life in and around the university remains more or less what must have been in the time of Sir Syed. The milieu is perfect, and one could wonder whether one had stumbled into a time machine that catapulted one to this education town. The air and the pace of life in the university are somehow years behind the fast-paced, materialistic life of the metros. From the moment the first rays of sunshine herald a new day to dusk, the topic of discussion is one: What did the vice-chancellor say? Who did he meet? What will be the implications of his policies?

In the wake of the smart city project, an ambitious scheme of the government, changes in Shamshad Market and Dodhpur areas in the vicinity of AMU is discernible. Eating joints have replaced old shops and roads have been widened, making the areas crowded.

Elisabeth Mann, in her seminal study,[6] identifies 24 Muslim *biradris* in the city, among which the most 'prominent', socially, economically and politically, are the Qureshis (*the meat-sellers*), the Ansaris (*the weavers*), the Saifis (*the ironsmiths*) and the Pathans.

The first three would fall in the Pasmanda category, whereas the last would fall in the Ashraf category. Of these, the Qureshis are supposed to have undergone 'rapid economic growth'. The Qureshis have often been at loggerheads in electoral politics with the Saifis, who are comparatively backward in this part of the country.

The vice-chancellor of the university is the king and the newsmaker. More than 30,000 students and officials are his subjects, functioning under a near-perfect democratic setup. Nobody cares about whatever is happening outside the university. Even the market boom and liberalisation era has failed to shake AMU and its leisurely lifestyle. On 5 November 2023, the Aligarh Municipal Corporation passed a resolution to rename Aligarh as Harigarh. The recommendation has been sent for approval to the Yogi Adityanath-led Uttar Pradesh government in Lucknow.

This name-change business has been under the civic body's active consideration since at least 2019. Calls for new names emerged after Allahabad was renamed Prayagraj; the Mughalsarai Railway after Deen Dayal; and Faizabad district was renamed Ayodhya district in 2018.

However, the idea of Harigarh was birthed in the early decades of Independence, possibly in the 1960s or 1970s, when some Hindu organisations had begun to raise the demand for it.

Whether Aligarh was ever known as Harigarh? The answer is a categorical *no*. Did the Mughals or pre-Mughal Muslim rulers name the town as Aligarh? The answer is again, *no*.

Aligarh was once called 'Kol' or 'Koil'. In fact, a part of the town, a tehsil (lower administrative unit), and a legislative assembly seat is still known as Kol.

The earliest written reference to Kol may be traced back to the 12th century. Prior to that, the Jain community possibly populated the area, and the existence of the Jain temples before the 12th century is testified by archaeological evidence.

'From the 13th century onwards, it gained some commercial importance and is repeatedly mentioned in Sultanate sources as "Kol", or "Koil", probably an older name, which continued to be used by the Delhi sultans and their officials.'

'The origin of this name "Kol" is obscure. In some ancient texts, it has been referred to as a tribe or a caste, the name of a place or mountain, and the name of a sage or demon.'[7]

According to the myth recorded in the colonial District Gazetteer of 1879, the name Kol was given to the city by Balarama, who slew the great Asura (demon) known as Kol and, with the assistance of the Ahirs, subdued this part of the Ganga–Jamuna doab.

In another account, Edwin T. Atkinson points out a 'legend' that Kol was founded by the Dor tribe of Rajputs in 372 AD. By the time Mahmud of Ghazni came, Hardatta of Burn or Baran (Bulandshahr) was the chief of Kol.

From the period of Qutbuddin Aibak (1194 AD), Kol acquired, so to say, the status of a 'province'. Ghiyas ud din Balban erected a minaret with engraved inscriptions in 1252 AD, which the British destroyed in the 19th century. Later, Sir Syed Ahmad Khan collected its remnants and fixed them on the wall of the Nizam Museum within the MAO College complex. This is now preserved in the Aligarh Muslim University Museum.

During Alauddin Khilji's reign, it became known as Iqta (an administrative unit, possibly akin to a province) Kol. According to the 14th-century traveller Ibn Battuta, Kol was a 'fine town surrounded by mango groves'. These lush orchards are also why the place became known as 'Sabzabad'.

According to Professor Syed Ali Nadeem Rezavi, recorded history suggests that by 1524-25, Ibrahim Lodi's governor built the fortress (or re-built?). Sources from Mughal emperor Akbar's period identify Kol as a part of the province (*suba*) of Agra. Jahangir, in his memoirs, refers to Kol as a site for his hunting.

In the 18th century, the fortress, for a brief period, became known as 'Sabitgarh', named after Sabit Khan, a governor. The fortress, having become a prized possession for all rulers, was even captured by the Jats with the help of Jai Singh, the raja of Jaipur.

'In 1757, Surajmal, the Jat leader, changed the fort's name to Ramgarh, after a governor called Ram.'[8]

Perhaps it is worth questioning why some Hindu organisations began raising a demand in the 1960s or 1970s to rename Aligarh as Harigarh. Why not Kol, which goes with the politics of nativity while having 'sound' historical justification or Ramgarh, which was briefly its name in the 1750s?

3

SIR SYED WALKS THE RAZOR'S EDGE

The Muslim intelligentsia in India has followed its Hindu counterpart in all stages of social development during the last two and a half centuries. The only difference has been the time lag. Raja Ram Mohan Roy initiated a movement for reform and rationalisation of Hindu thought coupled with the absorption of the West in education by founding the Brahmo Samaj in the early 19th century. Almost half a century later, Sir Syed Ahmad Khan launched a similar movement known as the Aligarh movement. It was different in some of the superficial aspects, but in inner purpose and content, it was essentially identical to the movement started by the Hindu reformer.

In their emotional response to history, the two revivalisms stimulated each other, competed with each other and became more and more different in outlook. Religious neutrality and political expediency prevented the British government from attempting to guide or harmonise them. After a preliminary effort to suppress the extreme manifestations of the Islamic revival, it accepted and adjusted itself to both Hindus and Muslims alike. It began to give up many practices that they had imbibed from each other and which had formed bridges between the two communities. Revivalism prompted organisation on communal lines and often assumed an aggressive tone, bringing the different communities into the acrimonious debate over theological and other matters.

Both Ram Mohan Roy and Sir Syed considered Western education as the means to uplift their respective communities.

Roy's attempts at social reform met with opposition from orthodox Hindus, but he enjoyed the enthusiastic support of his people in promoting Western education and loyalty to the British government. In contrast, Sir Syed faced a stiff challenge in every sphere of his ambitious programme.

Some scholars even trace the 'two-nation theory' to Sir Syed's policies and pronouncements. They forget that 'nationalism' as a consciously held idea was a mid-to-late 19th-century phenomenon even in Europe, from where it migrated to India. The spirit of 19th-century India was different. During that period, Muslims and Hindus lived in equal subjugation under British rule, devoid of any 'national' feeling or identity. As Anil Seal points out, there were not two nations, there was not even one nation, there was no nation at all.[1]

The Aligarh movement, which found its material expression in the establishment of MAO College, was inevitably motivated by a complex set of impulses. It claimed to be a movement of reinterpretation and revival of Islamic culture, but it attempted only social reinterpretation, not a religious one. The Aligarh movement was primarily rooted in the economic necessities of the Muslim middle class. Moin Ahsan Jazbi, a prominent Urdu poet and a faculty member in the Urdu Department of Aligarh Muslim University, in his doctoral thesis '*Hali Ka Siasi shaoor*' (Political consciousness of Khwaja Altaf Husain Hali) said, 'There are different opinions about Sir Syed's movement. Some consider it religious, some social and some educational. Personally, I think this movement was largely political, created by the general social conditions of Muslims. It is usually deceived by the veil of religion, society and education.'[2]

Dr Masood Alam Falahi, an Islamic scholar who claims to be concerned with the plight of Dalit Muslims, alleges that Sir Syed was a casteist. He opened the AMU only for the upper-caste Muslims and Hindus. He specified categorically that his college was not for weavers. Even in 1947, the character certificate given to students mentioned that the certificate holder belonged to a *sharif khandaan* (literally 'a good clan', which means the upper caste/class) of his district.[3]

Sir Syed's influence was most substantial in north India. The credit for encouraging the Muslims of Bengal to take to Western education belongs mainly to scholar–jurist Ameer Ali and Nawab Abdul Latif, a founder of the Presidency College and fellow of Calcutta University. But their achievement paled before that of Sir Syed.

Whereas the Hindus took advantage of English education and the intellectual emancipation that it spread, Muslims sought refuge in fundamentalism after the first war of Independence in 1857. This parting of ways between the two communities served the British interests well. The Muslim community reeled under historically enforced political isolation, socio-economic backwardness, spiritual atrophy and psychological sullenness, helplessly licking its wounds, looking back all the time with nostalgia for their glorious past in India.

Sir Syed desperately aimed at drawing his reticent, sceptical and sulking community out of the despair it had sunk into. He also desired to set it on the road to modernisation by attempting to initiate the middle class in Western education and science. He declared that Western education was neither forbidden by Islam nor dangerous to Muslims. He advised Muslims to

> The blind prejudice of Muslims is preventing them from emulating (Western) education, sciences and technology; Muslim society erroneously admires the blindness of those who are stubborn and haughty and considers all nations except their own inferior. There is not a single nation in the world which acquired excellence, material progress, and spiritual happiness entirely by virtue of its own efforts. Nations always benefit from each other; only bigots deny themselves the fruits of their fellowman's labour. They are like wild animals, happy in (the narrow life of) their flock, and are deaf to the sweet melody of the nightingale and the chirping of little sparrows, and know not how the garden (i.e. the world) was laid out and what makes the flowers bloom. Prejudices and progress will never mix.[4]

Though Sir Syed preferred the vernacular to the English language earlier, he confessed later: 'I am the person who had first entertained the idea that the acquisition of the knowledge of European science through the medium of vernacular would be more beneficial to the country ... But I could not help acknowledging the fallacy of my opinion at last.'[5]

He recognised Western education as an imperative since Hindus were taking full advantage of the educational facilities provided by the British and thus were virtually monopolising whatever crumbs of political and economic advantage were offered to Indians by the British masters. Muslims stared at a new order. 'The truth is', wrote William Wilson Hunter in 1871, 'that our system of public instruction, which has awakened Hindus from the sleep of centuries, and quickened their inert masses with some of the noble impulses of a nation, is opposed to the traditions, unsuited to the requirements, and hateful to the religion of Mussalmans.'[6]

Sir Syed foresaw that Muslims had to come to terms with the present. They could not afford to rot. The educated Indians first began thinking and organising on a national scale through quasi-religious societies. Sir Syed and his associates wished to enable their co-religionists to overcome their despair. However, he refrained from donning the mantle of a saint. The British Indian government, too, shared with Sir Syed the impression that the cataclysm of 1857 had made the Muslim population withdraw into purposive cultural isolation. In a monograph published in 1858, Sir Syed listed the causes of the Indian revolt under five heads:[7]

> (I) ignorance on the part of the people, by which I mean misapprehension of the intentions of government; (II) passing of such laws and regulations and forms of procedure as jarred with the established customs and practices of Hindustan, and the introduction of such as were in themselves objectionable; (III) ignorance on the part of the government as to the condition of the people, of their modes of thought and life, and of grievances through which their hearts were becoming estranged; (IV) neglect on the part of our rulers of such points

> as were essential to the good governance of Hindustan; and (V) bad management and disaffection of the army ... that the leading cause of disaffection was the ignorance of the government of the feelings of their subjects.

Spurred by his convictions and strengthened by his observations during his visit to England, Sir Syed took the initiative in 1870 to objectively assess the situation before adopting a remedial policy. His initiative coincided with Lord Mayo's policy (formulated in 1871) of distributing an equitable share of opportunities in education and government among neglected Muslims. Containment of the influence of the modernised and articulate Hindu middle classes that virtually monopolised government jobs and modern professions available to Indians probably inspired Mayo's sense of distributive justice. Moreover, the Punjabi Muslims' eager collaboration with Sir Syed offered widespread acceptance to the Aligarh movement.

Sir Syed wanted Muslims to reach a *modus vivendi* with the British and to take advantage of Western education. He wanted the gulf between the Muslims and the British to be bridged. In another monograph *Risala Khair Khwahan-e Musalmanan-e-Hind*, he tried to establish that Muslims were 'loyal' subjects of British India. He did not deny that some Muslims had created problems for the British rule. However, he insisted,

> ...if in Hindustan there was one class of people above another who, from the principles of their religion, from habits and associations, and kindred disposition, were bound fast to the Christians, in their dreaded hour of trial and danger, in the bounds of amity and friendship, those people were the Mohammadans.[8]

He stressed that Christians and Muslims were the followers of revealed religions and, therefore, had much in common. The British, too, saw the Muslims as sharing the same values and having been in the same position as conquerors of India, but, at the same time, they were apprehensive of Muslims on account of the revolt of 1857.

Sir Syed challenged William Wilson Hunter's contention that Muslims were bound by their religion to rebel against their Christian rulers. Explaining that *jehad* was incumbent on Muslims only if they were denied peace and could not practise their religious tenets, he argued. Since this was not the case, Muslims needed to be 'loyal' to the British rulers. Besides, Muslim 'revival', he believed, was inexorably tied to cooperation with the British. There was no other way Muslims could secure 'honour, prosperity and high rank' under the changed circumstances.

In the late 19th century, those who wished to improve their position or to protect it against the effects of change were not powerful enough to do so by their efforts. They could achieve their ends only with the approval and assistance of the government. But if their efforts to gain the government's aid and imprimatur were to succeed, it was vital that they represented interests that the government believed to exist, that it imagined needed help, and which, for political or other reasons, it wished to help.

There was a tendency, therefore, for leaders of such groups to mould themselves into shapes that they thought their rulers wished to see. Ram Mohan Roy and the early leaders of the Indian National Congress (INC) were no less vocal in their assurance of loyalty to the British Raj and in singing praises of the benefit conferred by British rule. Sir Surendranath Banerjee, for example, said in his speech in Aligarh in 1884:

> We appeal to England gradually to change the character of her rule in India, to liberalise it, to shift its foundations, to adapt to the newly-developed environments of the country and the people, so that, in the fullness of time, India may find its place in the great confederacy of free states; English in their origin; English in their character; English in their institutions, rejoicing in their permanent and indissoluble union with England.[9]

Besides the pull of modernity and rationality coupled with the quest for scientific temperament, the lure of monetary gains in return for loyalty and a desire to preserve religiosity punctuated the approach of the Muslim leaders, though they were only a handful. The establishment of MAO College, the forerunner of the AMU, modelled on the Oxbridge residential and tutorial system, which brought generations of young Muslims gravitating towards Western science, moral philosophy and the dual virtue of loyalty to the empire (referred to in Anglo-Indian jargon as the 'British Raj'), as well as to Islam.

Observed Jawaharlal Nehru in his autobiography:

> Hindus, half a century ahead in Western education, could indulge in the pastime of criticising the government, but he [Sir Syed] had counted full cooperation of that government in his educational undertakings, and he was not going to risk this by any premature step.... Sir Syed's decision to concentrate on Western education for Muslims was undoubtedly the right one. Without that, they could not have played any practical part in building up Indian nationalism of the new type, and they would have been doomed to play second fiddle to Hindus with their better education and far more robust economic position. Muslims were not historically or ideologically ready then for the bourgeois nationalist movement as they had developed no bourgeoisie, as Hindus had done. Sir Syed's activities, therefore, although seemingly very moderate, were in the right revolutionary direction.[10]

Sir Syed, who, contrary to the family tradition, had hitched his wagon to the coattails of John Company rather than the now decrepit Mughal rulers, as the Raj rewarded him handsomely. Apart from a knighthood, he was nominated twice to the Viceroy's Executive Council. Sir Syed reckoned British help indispensable for Muslims, his antipathy to the Congress and its functioning axiomatic. Muslim participation in its nationalist activities would retard his reform movement. For, as former rulers of the subcontinent, they had – he reasoned – been unjust 'victims' of history and insofar as Hindus had stolen a march in education as well as employment, Muslim youth must be educated *separately* under their community's auspices. British rule was necessary to achieve this and was preferable to Hindu domination. Sir Syed's

> assumptions were to become the dogmas of Muslim separatism in the half-century following his death in 1898.[11]

Muslim nationalism in South Asia did not exist till the end of Muslim rule here. The decline of the Mughal Empire, the rise of British colonialism and the political reassertion of Hindus in India were the factors that began to shape what is called Muslim Nationalism. Dr Mubarak Ali has insightfully noted one very important (but often ignored) element that helped create a sense of nationhood among sections of Muslims in India – how Urdu began to replace Persian as the preferred language of Muslims in India. As Mughal rule began to fall, Persia and Central Asia immigrants stopped travelling and settling in India because now there were few or no opportunities left for them to bag essential posts. The Urdu language began to form in India in the 14th century. Spoken mainly by local Muslims (most of whom were converts), by the early 19th century, Urdu had already begun to make its way into the homes of the Muslim elite. This helped the local Muslims climb the social ladder and fill positions that were once the exclusive domain of Persian and Central Asian immigrants. This initiated the early formation of a new grouping, mostly made up of local Muslims now enjoying social mobility.[12]

The concept of Muslim and Hindu nationalism, says Ayesha Jalal, was essentially the result of British social engineering after the 1857 mutiny for which the British held Muslims primarily responsible. The project began when the British introduced the idea of conducting a census. Much emphasis was placed upon an individual's faith in the census. Religion and caste were its basis rather than economic or social status. The outcome was the rather abstract formation of communities based on faith, constructed through an overwhelmingly suggestive census, undertaken not only to comprehend the complex nature of Indian society but also to devise a structural way to control it better.[13]

However, the fact remains that rural-agricultural sections of both Hindus and Muslims lived below the subsistence level. They were inhumanly exploited and deprived of all opportunities in life.

Heavily indebted, their existence was at a subhuman level and was, hence, altogether without a voice. They were indeed children of a lesser god. The upper strata of the hierarchically stratified Hindu and Muslim societies mattered in the given context.

For nearly five centuries, Muslim rulers – the nobility, *ulema* in particular – saw India as three regions: India north of the Vindhyas was *Hindustan*, in which they were directly and primarily interested. The Vindhyas range, along with the Sahyadri region extending roughly to the borders of Mysore, was the Deccan, which was of commercial importance because of the western coastline and of strategic interest in the Aurangabad–Daulatabad region. South of the Deccan lay the Dravidian region, where they were only peripherally interested. It lay, for all practical purposes, beyond their vision and imagination.

The north Indian Hindus, too, mainly from the region extending from Bihar to the westernmost extremity of Punjab and right up to the Hindukush, came to regard *Hindustan* as the region that constituted the real India. The Vindhyas region and the Deccan did figure in their imagination, but only because of the interest of the rulers in the region and later because of Shivaji and the Marathas. The Deep South hardly registered as a part of India with them.

The Ganga–Yamuna Valley – the region between south Bihar in the east and the easternmost tributaries of the Indus and east Rajasthan in the west – is the hinterland of the Indian subcontinent. North to south, it extends roughly from the foothills of the Himalayas to the forests and uplands of the Vindhyas, that is, up to the Narmada river.

The Muslim community faced a complex crisis. Its manifestations and consequences were often contradictory and bewildering – the British wrested political authority from the Muslims, who had been in power for centuries. Islam had already consolidated itself in India by the middle of the 13th century. By the time Muslim political authority was overthrown, the subcontinent had a sizeable Muslim community with a distinct social and cultural identity, notwithstanding substantial internal differentiation.

With Hindus, the advent of the British and their emergence as the ruling power and authority was merely a matter of changing one master for another. For them, the British and Muslims were both conquerors. The penetration of modern Western education and learning, and ideas and institutions into India, were welcomed in specific regions and among certain sections of the Hindus, particularly an upwardly mobile middle class.

The Hindu *Bhakti* movement had already drawn strength from Sufism. The concept of *Sulah-kul* (universal peace), propounded by Akbar, the greatest Mughal emperor, was the essence of *Deen-e-Elahi* or Divine Faith, a syncretic religious belief system. It did not encounter any opposition from Hindus. Akbar (1542–1605) was a contemporary of Queen Elizabeth I (1533–1603). Like her, he had to deal with the problem of religious strife among his subjects; his solution was more profound than the Elizabethan compromise. Though born into a royal family of orthodox Muslims, Akbar provided India with the first Muslim dynasty to receive the free allegiance of Hindus and Muslims, whose claim to rule was accepted for reasons other than the possession of superior force. In fact, the Mughal dynasty faced no problem so long as it did not drift away from the principle of *Sulah-kul* in the time of Shah Jahan. Despite evidence of cooperation and service extended to the authorities in Delhi, Agra and other seats of central and provincial power during the Muslim rule, the overall attitude of the Hindus towards Muslim domination could be described as one of sufferance, if not positive hatred.

Muslim invaders were ferocious in establishing their hegemony over an alien land, terrorising the people into subjugation and converting many of them to Islam to create acceptance for their rule. The conversions were, therefore, more political than based on any tremendous religious conviction. The forced conversions drove Hindus to see Islam as a religion of the sword, whose central impulse was proselytisation. After Muslim rule had been established in north India and the Mughals had created a stable empire, the proselytising zeal dampened. The inherent strength of Hinduism and the weakening of Islamic bigotry ensured that Hindus remained a large majority.

However, there was a lot of assimilation, and culturally, Hindus and Muslims grew closer together as the former adopted the manners and habits of the conquerors seeking court positions. In contrast, the Muslim conquerors adopted local mores and customs. Inter-marriages and other relationships also caused different ethnic bloodstreams to merge, even if religious differences were assiduously maintained. Hindus and Muslims in India not only have centuries of experience living together (or apart) but have also developed methods for managing their relations.

Indo-Muslim synthesis was visible in architecture, music, painting, philosophical thought, jurisprudence, food and dress habits and ways of living. The militant affirmation of Islam and an infinite eclecticism of Hindu thought coexisted, coalesced and coordinated creatively. In the late 19th century, many Muslims and Hindus had more in common with each other than their co-religionists. The political connections which mattered were based on the common outlook and interests of Hindu and Muslim landlords and government servants.

The British masters brought with them a militant occidental Christianity, which looked at all non-Christians as heathens and Hindus as pagans and worshippers of false gods. The new Hindu urban middle class, however, welcomed the British's political and economic subjugation of the country. It cherished the illusion that the historical function of the British was to wipe out the last vestiges of Muslim political authority, after which Hindus would again become the ruling power. Muslims too fondly nursed hopes during the revolt of 1857 that once the *firangis* were driven away, their political authority would be restored to its pristine glory.

It was only after the British rulers had firmly entrenched themselves in India and shattered the illusions of both communities that both Hindu and Muslim upper classes allowed themselves to be used as cat's paws. The leaders in both communities then embraced another delusion. They regarded the British rule as unshakeable and irreplaceable. They argued that if the Mughal Empire could last about three centuries, an immensely better organised and vastly more efficient regime would have no chance of being uprooted at any conceivable time in the future. Expediency demanded that each community look after its interests and not care about the other. The British rulers encouraged discord between the two communities. The Governor of Bombay, Lord Elphinstone, openly confessed in a minute in 1859 that *Divide et Empera* should be the motto of British rule in India. Later, Maulana Mohammad Ali commented, 'It is an old maxim of divide and rule. But there is a division of labour here. We (Indians) divide, and you (British) rule.'[14]

The embers of 1857 limped back to cold ashes. During the height of Muslim rule in India, the *ulema* were only allowed to play a marginal role in the state's work. But as this rule receded, the *ulema* gained strength in the Muslim community. They blamed the decline of the Mughal Empire on their inclusive policies, which strengthened the Hindus and extended patronage to Sufi saints and orders, resulting in the corruption and weakening of Islam. This perception caused several clerics to get drawn towards a radical puritanical movement, which had mushroomed 2,000 miles away in Arabia (present-day Saudi Arabia) in the 18th century and had begun to take root in India.

The movement's most influential exponent was Shah Wali Ullah of Delhi in the last quarter of the 18th century and his son, Shah Abdul Aziz, at the turn of the century. In fact, a section of Muslim leaders had always faced a dilemma while defining Islamic culture and the limits of its interaction with Hindu culture. Whereas the Hindu culture was assimilative and willing to synthesise with other religions, Islam has been prickly about preserving its distinct identity.

Following the crushing of the 1857 mutiny and the dismantling and annihilation of the Delhi Muslim court, the Indian Muslims themselves followed two opposing paths. One, led by Sir Syed, looked to the West and believed that Indian Muslims could revive their fortunes only by embracing Western learning. With this objective, Sir Syed founded MAO College (which later blossomed as the AMU) and tried to recreate Oxbridge in the plains of Hindustan. The other approach, taken by survivors of *Madrasa i-Rahimiyya*, was to reject the West altogether and to attempt to return to what was regarded as the pure Islamic path. For this reason, disillusioned pupils of the *madrasa*, such as Maulana Muhammad Qasim Nanautawi (who in 1857 had briefly established an independent Islamic state at Shamli in the Doab region) founded an influential but depressingly narrow-minded Wahhabi-like *madrasa* at Deoband, about 100 miles north of the former Mughal capital. With backs to the wall, they reacted to what the founders saw as the degenerate and rotten ways of the old Mughal elite; the Deoband *madrasa* went back to Koranic basics and rigorously stripped the curriculum of anything seemingly Hindu or European. However, it was by any means a total divide, though religious education at Aligarh, for example, was in the hands of Deobandis.

The followers of the Wahabi movement established *Dar-ul-Uloom* at Deoband in western Uttar Pradesh after the collapse of the revolt of 1857 to organise, preach and propagate its puritanical version of Islam. The mission was transferred from the battlefield to the seminary. Deoband Seminary's founder, Maulana Mohammad Qasim Nanautvi, and MAO College's founder, Sir Syed, were pupils of the same master. Both were equally concerned about the fate of Muslims in the changed situation, but there was a world of difference between their approaches. Deoband tried to achieve this objective through traditional Islamic learning; its curriculum of studies is based on what was prescribed by the *Dars-i-Nizami* and a continued policy of non-cooperation with the British government. In contrast, Aligarh endeavoured to proceed towards the same goal through a symbiosis of Western education and religious teaching and a cooperation policy with the British.

Deoband was primarily a centre preoccupied with religious puritanism without considering worldly affairs. Still, Aligarh positioned itself as a modern educational institution that trained its students to take their rightful place in society. The Deoband

Seminary found itself in accord with the views and aspirations of Jamaluddin Afghani and his pan-Islamic movement.

Rashid Ahmad Gangohi, the successor of Mohammad Qasim as the head of the Deoband Seminary, believed Indian Muslims could, according to the *shariat*, cooperate with Hindus in their nationalist endeavours. Gangohi refrained from joining the INC because he was firmly in favour of complete political independence and absolute severance of connection with the British.

The leaders and workers of the Deoband Seminary were a dedicated group committed to asceticism. They were held in high esteem by a large section of Indian Muslims. Under ordinary circumstances, Gangohi's interpretation and his unequivocal statement about the Indian Muslim position should have considerably helped the contemporary nationalist movement, till then led mainly by Hindus. But it did not.

The socio-religious attitude of the Deoband Seminary was traditional, conservative and inward-looking. Intellectually, the Deoband leaders were closely fettered by unquestioning acceptance of scriptural authorities. Their anti-British and anti-foreign attitude was not political but more ethnic and religious, hence somewhat circumscribed. At that time, nationalism was increasingly taking a realistic political and economic turn. Deoband could not bridge the gulf that separated the Muslim leadership from the Hindu, nor could the latter. The Deoband leaders, except for Maulana Husain Ahmad Madani, distanced themselves from the national movement and dedicated themselves solely to religious pursuits. Therefore, their role in the history of the struggle for independence is not mentioned even in the footnotes.

Maulana Shibli Nomani (1857–1914), a profound scholar of Arabic and Persian and a well-known Urdu writer, was a teacher at MAO College till 1898, the year Sir Syed died. But he did not share Sir Syed's political views. On the contrary, he was a great supporter of the Deoband Seminary. He was a far greater scholar than any of the European teachers in the College but (being an Indian) did not command a place of honour in MAO College.

Even at college functions, Maulana Shibli was accorded a lower place than even the least qualified white. On a visit to Aligarh in 1908, he delivered a short speech in Strachey Hall and read out some of his verses. There was nothing controversial in what he said. But the next day, Maulana Sulaiman Ashraf pronounced a *takfir* (ex-communication) of Maulana Shibli in his Friday *waaz* (sermon). Some students went with the news to Maulana Shibli, who gently stroked his white beard and said, 'Subhanallah, There was a time when outside Muslims used to excommunicate Aligarh, now Aligarh excommunicates outside Muslims.'[15]

A confirmed democrat, anti-imperialist and pan-Islamist, he was an admirer of the INC and had sympathy for the political aspirations of the Indian nationalists. He sincerely believed that Muslims were citizens of India and, hence, owed loyalty to their motherland. He was convinced that Muslims and Hindus could join hands in working out their common political destiny and forge a nation-state in which both could live together happily and with honour without transgressing the dictates of their conscience and respective faiths. No one was, however, interested in such lofty ideas.

The Wahabi movement carried a tremendous desire for re-establishing a *Dar-ul-Islam* (a state in which Muslims will be the sovereign rulers) in India. This limited the movement to Muslims and led to their political awakening in certain parts of the country, for instance, Bengal.

Before 1856, the Mohammedan Association had been established in Calcutta, followed by the Mohammedan Literary Society in 1863 and the National Mohammedan Association in 1877. Thus began the history of Indian Muslims forming separate and exclusive socio-cultural organisations of their own, away and apart from those of Hindus. The 'two-nation theory' was a natural corollary.

Badruddin Tyabji (not to be confused with his grandson Badruddin Tyabji, ICS, who became vice-chancellor of the AMU in the 1960s), a successful barrister of Bombay and a leading member of the Muslim community, pleaded in vain to Sir Syed to join the INC against the British. A month before the second session of the INC, Sir Syed had condemned that body as 'seditious' in an editorial in the *Aligarh Institute Gazette*. A.O. Hume, the Scotsman who, after retirement from the ICS, had founded the INC, told Sahibzada Aftab Ahmad Khan in London in 1892: It was after reading Sir Syed's book *The Causes of the Indian Revolt* that I first felt the need for having a forum of public opinion in India, and eventually, the INC came into existence. But the fantastic thing is that when it was started, Sir Syed was the first to oppose it.[16]

Indeed, from what Sir Syed said and did in 1886, it seems that he had already come to accept the theory that the political destinies of Hindus and Muslims lay in two altogether different directions. The expression 'two antagonistic races' had already been used by him in *The Causes of the Indian Revolt.* Initially, he believed that the 'two races' could cultivate friendly relations on an equal footing. However, the Hindi–Urdu controversy convinced him that Indian Muslims must take the necessary steps not to be overwhelmed by the majority community.

Historian Dr Ishwari Prasad writes:

> In his political philosophy, Syed Ahmad was a liberal and a believer in Hindu-Muslim unity at the beginning of his career ... He held that all those who lived in *Hindustan* were Hindus, "just as the Aryan people are called Hindu". And yet Sir Syed died as a leader of his community rather than the nation. This transformation of his mental attitude resulted from British manoeuvres and his love for the institution of his dreams. MAO College, whose welfare he had at heart, made him a handmaid of British politics lest government support be withdrawn.[17]

On the social plank, however, Sir Syed pleaded for amity and friendship right till the end of his life. Between 1897 and April 1898, shortly before his death, he wrote a series of articles arguing that, 'Just as the difference of religion which exists between Mussalmans and Hindus ought not to prevent social dealings, mutual affection, love and sympathy between them, so also differences on political questions ought not to prevent social dealings, mutual affection, love and sympathy.'[18] He did not realise that social relations don't grow and thrive in a vacuum or isolation from other relations in life. Neither can mutual ties of love, affection and sympathy subsist in conflicting political and economic interests and objectives.

Sir Syed believed in the historical perspective that a reformist movement could not be set in motion in the contemporary situation without the help and cooperation of the British rulers since they were the judges and dispensers of all professional opportunities. No wonder he wanted the Muslim community to pledge loyalty to the British. In the process, he lost the sympathy and cooperation of leading contemporary co-religionists like Jamaluddin Afghani (not an Indian), Maulvi Samiullah Khan, Maulana Shibli Nomani and the members of the influential Deoband school, all of whom were anti-British, but orthodox, purist and traditional regarding their religious attitudes. Political expediency had seemingly dictated the approach of Sir Syed.

Sir Syed and Jamaluddin Afghani were two intellectual giants of the Muslim world in the 19th century. Despite a shared obsession and desperate concern with regaining the past glory and power of Muslims, they had divergent views and approaches. Sir Syed was a pragmatic leader, concerned with the particular and the concrete, whereas Afghani was a theorist, concerned with the general and the abstract. It was for this reason that the latter's pan-Islamic movement remained unable to solve the real problems confronting Muslim countries that differed from one another. According to the poet–philosopher Iqbal, it would have been much better if Jamaluddin Afghani had devoted his entire life and tremendous intellectual capabilities to establishing that Islam was a perfect code of conduct for life. Had he done so, 'the world of Islam', says Iqbal, 'would have been on much more solid ground today'. Iqbal expressed great admiration for Jamal-ud-din Al-Afghani in his prose and poetic writings.

> Maulana Jamal, Sayyid of all Sayyids, whose
> eloquence gave life to stone and shred.

behold, that world lies within your own heart;
now I will tell von of its firm foundations.[19]

Sir Syed, being a practical man, achieved his goal. A revolution had taken place, which beckoned a bright future.

Even in the 1930s of the 20th century, Inayat Ullah Khan-al-Mashriqi, popularly known as Allama Mashriqi, a Cambridge-educated member of the Indian Educational Service, founded the Khaksar movement. He resigned at 40 as Principal of Islamia College at Peshawar in 1930. He adopted austerity in his living, donned a khaki dress and began organising Muslims on military lines. Members swore loyalty to the *quaid* (leader), wore khaki uniforms, carried *belchas* (shovels) on their shoulders, and proclaimed *khidmat-e-khalq* (social service) as their proximate and *ghalba-e-Islam* (Islamic supremacy) as their ultimate aim. Many lower-class Muslims, who had great nostalgia for an imperial past, responded eagerly. Some from the middle class joined him.

Allama Mashriqi praised Sir Syed for advocating English education but censured him for not invoking *jehad* against the British and Hindus, as Afghani had rightly done. In the words of Akhtar Hameed Khan, an Indian Civil Services officer whose paternal and maternal grandfathers were Sir Syed's contemporaries:[20]

> In his fantasies, Mashriqi saw himself leading Muslims to regain their lost empire in India. Social service was only a means, a camouflage. However, at the end of World War II, the Khaksar movement was in shambles, having destroyed the lives of hundreds of good men for the sake of pan-Islamic fantasies and nostalgia. At least Sir Syed had no destructive nostalgia or bewitching fantasies. His message was a vivid, rejuvenating one.

To deal with the increasingly strident (essentially) Hindu demand for self-determination, the British sought to play upon the existing fault lines, determined and conditioned by history, between Hindus and Muslims on more counts than one. They emphasised that the interests of Hindus and Muslims differed and that the emancipation of Indian Muslims lay in safeguarding their sub-national interests against those of the Hindus. Sir Syed unwittingly got trapped in this manoeuvre.

The die was cast by 1898 when Sir Syed died. The upper class urban and semi-urban Muslims, by and large, followed the lead of Sir Syed and not of Deoband or any other individual or group. The Muslim elites opted for modernisation through Western education and to give up anti-British hostilities. By the last decade of the 19th century, the Aligarh movement had gathered immense momentum. Originating in Uttar Pradesh, it became an all-India movement with enthusiastic support everywhere. In the social situation of *Hindustan,* Sir Syed had hardly any base to work upon except the one provided by the *zamindars* and *taluqdars* of the United Provinces (renamed Uttar Pradesh after Independence in 1947). He was already friendly with some of them, as he had been posted in several districts as an officer of the British Indian government.

After the death of his father in 1838, Sir Syed had been advised by his friends and relatives to follow the family tradition of serving the Mughals. But he was intelligent enough to foresee the finale of the Mughal drama. Therefore, he decided to start his career as *sheristadar* (court clerk) under the East India Company. The following year, he was promoted to the post of *naib mir munshi* under Robert Hamilton, Commissioner, Agra Division. Two years later, he qualified for the post of *munsif* and was posted at Mainpuri. When transferred to Fatehpur Sikri in 1842, Emperor Bahadur Shah Zafar bestowed on him the hereditary title of *Javvad-ud-Daula Arif Jung*. He worked at different places: Delhi (1846–54), Bijnore in Uttar Pradesh (1855–58); Moradabad as *dar-us-sadar* (1858–62); Ghazipur (1862–64); Aligarh (1864–67); Benares as Judge of the Small Causes Court (1867); and back to Aligarh (1876), from where he sought premature retirement to devote himself to his project. At the time of retirement, he was working as a subordinate judge under the British government with the title of Companion of the Order of the Star of India, which had been conferred on him in 1869 in London, where he had gone to study the English method of education and also to collect material from the British Museum and other libraries for a book on the life of Prophet Mohammad. He was later conferred the title of the Knight Commander of the Star of India on his retirement from active service.

Soon after, Sir Syed occupied himself in formulating what he considered his life's mission: (a) to rid his community of its irrational and puritanical attitude, (b) to bring about an understanding between his community and the British ruling authorities and (c) to work towards the spread of English education and Western ideas, institutions, practices and even patterns of dress and behaviour.

All his initiatives were opposed in the name of religion. Describing his dilemma, Sir Syed said: 'We were keen to avoid any discussion of religion, but the problem is that our behaviour, social practices and religious beliefs are so mixed up that no discussion of social reform is possible without provoking a religious controversy.'[21] Frustrated with the clergy, he added, 'When urged to give up something harmful, they say it has religious merit, and when asked to do something positive they assert it is prohibited by religion. So, we have no options but to discuss the religious context to push our agenda forward.'

Enlightened by secular Western education and thought, Sir Syed wanted to apply reason and intellect to understand and interpret the creed and dogma of his religion. His attitude and approach had been sharpened by his sojourn in England in 1869. He had to sell his house at Aligarh to raise money to accompany his son, who had bagged a scholarship in England. From what he saw and learnt there, he could not help comparing the social situation of the English with that of his fellow Indians.

Cordial relations with the British rulers and a decisive shift in the British attitude towards Muslims offered the best opportunity for rapprochement between the British and Muslims to complement the second aspect of his programme.

It was the third aspect wherein Sir Syed's heart lay. The massive advance of popular education and self-improvement was the significant intellectual development of the century. It was one of the objectives, as well as the outcomes of the working class movement. The rationalism of 19th-century science, the presiding spirit of education and enlightenment, proof and guarantee of progress and emancipation of the lowly was widely imbibed.

The masses in Europe were on the move and getting educated. No wonder the number of primary school teachers grew by leaps and bounds, ranging from about one-third in well-schooled countries like France, and seven or even thirteen times its 1875 figure in formerly ill-schooled ones like England.

In 1847, when *Asar-us Sanadid* first came out, Syed Ahmad Khan, 30, had had six publications to his credit. *Asar-us Sanadid* (variously translated as 'The Remnant Signs of Ancient Heroes', 'Vestiges of the Past' or 'Traces of the Notables') is a book on pre-1857 Delhi, its main buildings, monuments and people. Two book versions were published: the first in 1847 and the second in 1854. A third version was perhaps in the works but for the Uprising. *Asar-us Sanadid* today is a canonical text. When first published, it was considered most impressive for its contribution to the knowledge of the history and archaeology of Delhi. But this monumental book had a share of controversies, never leaving Sir Syed in his life.

Scholar Nikhil Kumar writes,

> In the writing of *Asar-1*, we see a reflection of Syed Ahmad's earlier interests, that is, before he became a social reformer and developed an antipathy towards Delhi, its culture and its literary traditions. At this time, he is undoubtedly a rational man with antiquarian interests but is not encumbered by practicality or bereft of aestheticism.

He adds,

> The most significant change in *Asar-2* is the language. Many portions of the first book are written in highly ornate and Persianised Urdu, while the second is in a factual and much more concise style, which came to be later recognised as the style of 'Sir Syed'. C M Naim and others have suggested that much of the

> first was written by Syed Ahmad's senior friend and collaborator on *Asar-us Sanadid* -Maulvi Imam Baksh Sahbai – to whom the ornate style is attributed. Sahbai, who taught Persian at Delhi College from 1840 till his tragic death at Yamuna near the Rajghat *darwaza* in 1857, had a reputation for ghostwriting.[22]

The existence of this manuscript in the British Museum and Library catalogue raises pertinent questions, particularly concerning the originality of *Aasaar us-Sanadeed*, given the incorporation of identical *katbaat*, sans acknowledgement of either the *katbaat* from Hafizuddin Ahmad's manuscript or *Sair ul-Manazil*, or both. It is improbable that Sir Syed or Imam Baksh Sehbai directly copied these *katbaat* from the inscriptions on the buildings. One can also reasonably infer that the *Aasaar* may have been inspired by either Hafizuddin Ahmad's collection or *Sair* itself, and either Syed Ahmad or the author of the book's inaugural edition, Imam Buksh Sehbai, benefitted hugely from the inscriptions/*katbaat*/ chronograms available in Ahmad's or Sangin Baig's manuscripts, comfortably copying them without any effort to collect them, and delightfully without any acknowledgement of either of the texts. Their collection is the most arduous part of the labour involved in writing a book like *Aasaar*, and their availability in both the Hafizuddin manuscript and *Sair* seems to prove that neither Sir Syed nor Sehbai undertook this!

The bare fact that Sehbai is the author of *Aasaar*'s first edition is supported by Hali's unequivocal statement in *Hayat-I Javid*, which remained uncontested by Sir Syed despite the publication of the biography during Sir Syed's lifetime. Hali wrote on the authorship of *Aasaar*:

> *Aasaar-us Sanadeed ka pehla eDeeshan jis ki ibaarat mein kuchh saakhtagi aur takalluf paaya jaata hai, vo jaisa ke khud Sar Saiyed iqraar karte hain, Maulaana Sehbaai ka likha hua hai*
>
> [The language of the first edition of *Aasaar us-Sanadeed* is somewhat contrived and extravagant; as Sir Syed has himself admitted, it was written by Maulana Sehbai]

I don't think this simple statement can be interpreted in any other way than to attribute authorship of the first edition of *Aasaar* to Sehbai![23]

In his travelogue *Musafiran-e-London* (Travellers to London),[24] he mentions that during his sojourn in Bombay on his way to London, he met an old gentleman named Ashraf Ali at a bookshop at Bhendi Bazar. When Ali found that the visitor was from Delhi, he asked if he knew one Syed Ahmed, who had written *Asar-us Sanadid.* Ali was pleasantly surprised to hear, 'By God's grace, he is very well and is sitting before you.'

When Sir Syed Ahmad Khan was going to visit the universities of England, his friend Maulvi Imdad Ali was also going to Mecca for Hajj. On this occasion, Akbar Ilahabadi composed his couplet in his famous humorous and satirical style: *Sidharen Shaikh kaabe ko hum inglistaan dekhen ge; Wo dekhen ghar khuda ka hum khuda ki shan dekhen ge* [25](loosely translated: Let the shaikh depart to Makkah, I would rather go to London; for he intends to see God's home, I God's glory.)[26]

On his return from England in 1870, Sir Syed started active public life as a socio-religious reformer. He started an Urdu periodical called *Tehzib ai-Akhlaq* (manners and individual culture). The magazine contained articles aimed at social reforms. Through its columns, he attempted to substitute reason for authority in interpreting the *Quran*. 'Reason alone,' he said, 'is a sufficient guide.'[27] He aimed to create an Islam that was thoroughly compatible with progress. He also published two books in Urdu: *Khutbat-i-Ahmadiya* and an incomplete commentary on the *Koran*. His articles in the periodical and these two books reveal Sir Syed as a confirmed rationalist and non-conformist. He argued, among other things, that there was nothing in the *Koran* that stood in the way of Muslims taking to English education, Western learning, science and thought for their advancement.

Earlier, a bi-annual journal *Risala Khair Khawa Musliman* (Loyal Mohammadens of India) was published in 1860. In the first issue, Sir Syed gave a detailed account of many Muslims who pledged their allegiance to the British government. In the second issue, the Islamic concept of jihad, besides pleading fraternal treatment to the British, on account of being the People of the Book. The third and last issue came out in 1861. It contained an agreement between the Prophet of Islam and Christians in Medina.[28]

Not surprisingly, Sir Syed incurred the organised wrath and opposition of the orthodox Muslim *ulema*. The forces of tradition were still overwhelmingly powerful. Attacks and diatribes against Sir Syed corkscrewed into a profitable industry for the obscurantists. The leading *alim* of Firangi Mahal, Maulana Abdul Hai, denounced him as a follower of Satan. At the same time, *fatwahs* (religious decrees) were issued by the *maulvis* declaring him a *kafir* or a heretic in every town and village of north India. He was excommunicated. Threats to his life were frequent. One man told him, 'Sher Ali, who assassinated Lord Mayo, was an idiot. Had he killed you, he could have reserved a place in Paradise for himself.'[29] Ali Baksh Khan, a sub-judge at Gorakhpur, travelled to Mecca to secure a *fatwah* against Sir Syed. The Imam of Mecca was happy to oblige. He issued a *fatwah*, which said: This man (Sir Syed) is erring and causes people to err. He is instead an agent of the devil and wants to mislead Muslims. It is a sin to support the college. May God damn the founder! And if this college has been founded, it must be demolished and its founder and his supporters thrown out of the fold of Islam. The hostility and opposition of the Muslim clergy to Sir Syed continued till he died and persisted in certain quarters.

In 1923, Maulana Mohammad Ali Jauhar, the then President of the Indian National Congress, remarked in his presidential address to the Kakinada session:

> Be it remembered that the man who enunciated this policy was at the time persona non grata to the major portion of the people he sought to lead. He was hated as a heretic because of the heterodoxy of his aggressive rationalism in interpreting the Koran and his militant opposition to popular superstitions believed in the bulk of the orthodox and to the shackling customs consecrated by time, though wholly unauthorised by Islam. He was abused and vilified

> by hundreds of thousands of his co-religionists, and for long, the college he had founded at Aligarh was the bete noire of the pious Muslim. It is you (Syed Ahmad Khan) that had taught the community its mischiefs;
> If we are its culmination;
> you are its commencement.3[0]

Within less than a decade of his demise, Sir Syed's followers strayed far from his agenda. They founded the Muslim League in 1906 at the behest of the British. It had a far-reaching symbolic value. Education was no longer a priority for Muslims; politics was. This had disastrous consequences, cutting India into three, with Muslims becoming a trunk without limbs.

To Sir Syed, the Muslims of India had lost political power because they had lost their ability to rule.[31] He castigated the *ulema* for forcing the Muslims to reject science (because it was Western); he warned that such an attitude would keep Muslims buried under the weight of superstition and dogma. When the *ulema* responded by accusing him of creating divisions in a community which they were trying to unite, he wrote that since he was a reformist, his job was not to unite but to jolt members of his community by questioning established (but corrosive) social, intellectual and political norms. The Greeks, he argued, learned from the Egyptians; the Muslims from the Greeks; the Europeans from the Muslims. So, what calamity will befall the Muslims if they learned from the British?

His initial work was primarily analytical and pedagogic. Though he did not have the platform of mosques and *madrasas* that his detractors had, he believed that the changing reality would eventually subscribe to his point of view. He wanted them to overcome their cultural and theological inertia and embrace modern education. There was to be no meeting point between the *ulema* and him simply because both were viewing the Muslim condition in India through different lenses. However, Sir Syed did try to meet them by dissecting their theological critiques of modernity. He wrote that a man's spiritual and moral life could not meet his material needs.

Kerala Governor Arif Mohammad Khan recalls:

> The intensity of opposition can be understood from the comments of Maulana Abul Hasan Ali Nadwi in his book *Islamist Aur Maghribiat ki Kashmakash* written more than 60 years after Sir Syed's death. Maulana Nadwi said: The education mission of Sir Syed and his advocacy of Western civilisation became correlatives and caused apprehensions and doubts in people's minds. A wave of opposition took hold of the religious circles, and his movement met with a simultaneous call for its boycott.[32]

First, Sir Syed was targeted when he shared food with the British and defended his action in a signed article. The opposition became fierce during his stay in London. Sir Syed responded through a memorandum saying:

> The terrifying call of Kanpur, the lyrical satire of Lucknow, the idle tattle of Agra and Allahabad, the *fatwas* of Rampur and Bareilly and the snide remarks of holy men of Delhi grieve me not. My heart is overflowing with the idea of the welfare of my people, and there is no room in it for any anger or rancour.[33]

Conscious of the hostility of the *ulema,* Sir Syed offered to have no role in matters of religious instruction in MAO College and invited leading clerics to prepare the syllabus. Maulana Qasim Nanautvi and Maulana Yaqoob of Deoband opposed the proposal saying they could not associate with an institution with Shia students on the campus.

In his biography of Sir Syed, Maulana Altaf Husain Hali comments:

> 60 *maulvis* and *ulema* had signed *fatwas* accusing Sir Syed of disbelief and apostasy. There was a total consensus among the Indian clerics. Only divine approval was missing. Sir Syed took the development calmly. He quoted a line from the 14th-century Iranian poet Hafiz Shirazi:
>
> Behold how blessed is my temple of idols.

That it becomes the house of God when it is demolished.[34] No storm of opposition could either dampen his spirits or daunt him. He carried on his mission with greater zeal and enthusiasm. The *mullahs* and pretenders stumbled and grumbled as their denunciation of Sir Syed rebounded against themselves when literate and educated sections of Muslims began hailing the interpretation of the doctrines of the Koran in the *tafsir* (exegesis) enunciated by Sir Syed. However, in this hostile atmosphere, Sir Syed was obliged to give up the cause of socio-religious reforms. For the rest of his life, he confined himself to spreading English education and Western learning and leading Indian Muslims towards political advancement.

Sir Syed was no ordinary man. In 1885, an intimate friend, Colonel G.F.I. Graham[35] described him as being of middle height and massive build: he weighed 19 stone. He was a 'born orator', independent of mind and argued 'with a freedom of tone and language which natives seldom use'. He possessed 'untiring energy', an incredible breadth of view and an uncommon eye for detail. There was little in which he was not interested and had no opinion; his table talk moved quickly from religion and metaphysics to politics and Persian poets. Few who met him – Europeans or Indians – failed to fall under his spell.

During his sojourn in London, Sir Syed saw that Islamic expansion faced a continuing, silent, piecemeal, but irreversible process, though not backed by organised missionary endeavour or forcible conversion. Yet the pan-Islamists sought not merely to return to the original purity of the time of the Prophet but also to shun Western innovations. Religious revivalism was likely to take the form of some new emotional cult, miracle-performing saint or pilgrimage within the accepted framework of the religion. But this return to 'pure' religion required the creation of social and sometimes educational and political institutions in an environment that provided none, and among politically undeveloped people, it gave primitive expression to their discontentment and aspirations.

Sir Syed and the Muslim society in Delhi were already exposed to modernity by their contact with the tiny British society and the renamed Delhi College, established in 1828. The British rule had not only introduced Delhi's citizens to a new culture but also initiated a period of social mobilisation, which prepared Indian Muslims, especially after 1857, to accept the change from traditional to modern ways of life. Asadullah Khan alias Mirza Asadullah Nausha (with 'Ghalib' as his *nom de plume)* had intuitively grasped the spirit of modernity, which he considered the secret of British power. He welcomed the achievements of his times as they beckoned the future. Regarding the idolisation of the past, Ghalib remarked: 'Were there no fools in the past?' or 'Every line that is old is not a straight line.'[36] He welcomed and admired the new machinery of administration set up by the British.

Sir Syed grasped and appreciated the challenge of modernity and explored its possibilities for Muslims after he visited Britain in 1869. During his formative years (1817–1857), primarily spent in Delhi, he remained a traditional Muslim, essentially seeking validation of his convictions and behaviour regarding generally established Islamic norms. Most of his historical and religious treatises, particularly trivia on Sufism – such as *Namiqa* (1864), *Kalmat ai-Haq* (1850) – and the biographical sketch of Prophet Mohammad, *Jilal-qulab bi dhikr ai-Mahbub* (1842), reflected traditional views on mysticism and the Prophet. Most of these views disappeared later under the scrutinising glare of rationality.

In 1859, he founded the *Moradabad Panchayat Madrasa*. The medium of instruction was Persian. The first batch of this school included 72 Hindus and 103 Muslims. In 1863, he established the Scientific Society, the first to develop a scientific temper among Muslims. It translated English works on science into Persian and Urdu and made them accessible to Muslims. A year later, in 1864, he established an English High School in Ghazipur, later named Victoria High School. Its foundation was laid jointly by Raja Dev Narayan Singh and Maulana Mohammad Fasih.

Since 1884, Sir Syed's approach underwent a dramatic change. Addressing a gathering at Meerut in 1888, Sir Syed asked: 'If the British withdrew from India, who would rule the country? Is it possible that under these circumstances, the two nations

– Mohammadans and Hindus – could sit on the same throne and remain equal in power? Most certainly not! One of them must conquer the other.'[37] Earlier, in December 1887, opposing the one-man-one-vote principle of election for the Viceroy's Legislative Council, Sir Syed had said,

> The demand of the National Congress is that the people should elect a section of the Viceroy's Council. They want to copy the English House of Lords and House of Commons. Now let us suppose that we have universal suffrage, as in America, and that all have votes. And let us first suppose that all Muslim voters vote for a Muslim member and that all Hindu voters for a Hindu member and now count how many votes the Muslim member will have and how many the Hindu. We can prove by simple arithmetic that there will be four votes for the Hindu to every one for the Muslim. Now, how can the Muslim guard his interests? It will be like a game of dice in which one man had four dice and the other only one.[38]

The same year, the United Indian Patriotic Association (UIPA) was founded by Theodore Beck with the active support of Sir Syed. The primary aim of the association was to persuade the British that the Congress's demands were not representative of India as a whole. Camping at Nainital (August 1888), Sir Syed urged Indian Muslims to join the UIPA instead and convince the British parliament that the Congress's claim of representing all communities in India, including Muslims, was a false pretension.

The UIPA received support not only from the majority of Muslims but also from those Hindus who disapproved of Congress's position on representative institutions and 'democracy'. Within a few months of its formation, however, the UIPA disintegrated. Its Hindu and Muslim supporters fell apart. Five years later, in 1893, Sir Syed founded the Mohammedan Anglo-Oriental Defence Association of Upper India, an exclusively Muslim body, to bolster his anti-Congress campaign. The declared objectives of both these organisations were to oppose all that the 'liberal' INC had been claiming to stand for and, by implication, to keep Muslims away from all kinds of agitational political activities directed against the British.

Says Dr Abid Husain, a contemporary of Dr Zakir Husain, that the Mohammadan Defence Association was the sickly child of Sir Syed's old age and expired in 1900 with the death of Theodore Beck (a few months ago).[39] Still, the seed of communalism that had been sown was to sprout six years later in the form of the Muslim League at Dhaka.

Even in the early 1870s, when Sir Syed was posted at Benares, he had requested the then Commissioner of Benares that the new move to replace the common language, Urdu, with Hindi convinced him (Sir Syed) that Hindus and Muslims could no longer work and live together as one nation.

Sayyid Tufayl Ahmed Mangalori stated that it was because of his opposition to the Congress, especially after the Lucknow session of the Mohammedan Anglo-Oriental Educational Conference in 1887, that the British Government knighted Sir Syed.[40] The proceedings of the fifth session of the Congress, which convened at Bombay on 26 December 1889, roused particular anxiety in the mind of Sir Syed. It was presided over by Sir William Wedderburn, who had come from England, particularly for the purpose. Together with William Digby, Wedderburn had been promoting Congress demands in England. An even more critical guest at the meeting was Charles Bradlaugh, MP, who had earned the sobriquet of 'member for India' because he often spoke for India in Parliament. He had prepared and circulated a bill embodying the views of the Congress as known till then and had come to India to ascertain their latest opinions so that these, too, could be included in the bill.

From its very first session, the Congress had been demanding the expansion of the Governor-General's Council as well as the Provincial Councils by the admission of elected members and also the conferment on them of the right to discuss the budget and 'interpellate the executive regarding all branches of the administration'.

Since Muslims had no agency in England, Sir Syed feared that the Congress lobby would ensure the success of Bradlaugh's bill. To show that most Muslims opposed the Congress's demands, he caused a petition, signed by 49,000-odd Muslims from about seventy cities and towns, to be presented to the House of Commons in April 1890.

The petition emphasised that Muslims were not a tiny minority; they numbered 50,000,000 strong. It stated further that the demand for introducing an elective system proceeded from English-educated Hindus, a class that is exceptionally well able to make its voice heard both in England and India. At the same time, the Mohammadans, being very backwards in English education, have been unable to give equal prominence to their views. Theodore Beck drafted the petition. In the last period of the Mughal Empire, when the British officers had to issue some proclamations, it was announced, 'Public is of God, Country is of King, Order is of Company Bahadur. Unfortunately, during Sir Syed's old age, the same applied to the Aligarh College with some modifications: "Nation is of God, College of Sir Syed, Order of Beck".'[41]

Bradlaugh agreed to withdraw his bill, but the government-sponsored Councils Act of 1892 granted some of Congress's demands. It expanded only the provincial councils and granted them the right to discuss the budget and question the executive on administrative matters. Still, it denied them the right to vote on them. Direct elections were also not conceded. A few non-official members were still to be nominated. Still, for the majority, 'recommendations' were to be invited from local bodies or corporations such as religious communities, municipalities, universities and chambers of commerce. The concession that religious communities could recommend their candidates meant that Muslims had won the right to separate representation. This first step, little noticed then, was to develop into a system of separate electorates with momentous consequences.[42]

After Sir Syed's death, Muslim leaders succeeded in obtaining a guarantee from the British government on communal or separate representation, which later became the principal cause of the evolution of a separate Muslim nationalism.

However, Sir Syed had, by and large, followed a politically eclectic approach towards Hindus till 1884, notwithstanding reservations on some issues. He often described Hindus and Muslims as one *qaum* (nation), arguing that 'the word *qaum* is used for the inhabitants of the country, even though they have characteristics of their own'. Once, he said, 'By the word *qaum*, I mean both Hindus and Muslims.'[43]

He, however, did harbour a Muslim nationalist strand. Sir Syed wanted the Muslims to steer clear of political agitation given their poverty and educational backwardness as well as the British suspicion of them owing to 1857. Nor could Muslims, in their perilous state of educational and economic backwardness and numerical inferiority, compete with Hindus in elections. Moreover, Sir Syed's educational effort was mainly for the *shurfa* (genteel, literally meaning upper crust), an elitist bias inherited from Victorian public schools.

From his statements and speeches during the Punjab tour in 1884, it appears that Sir Syed was a social reformer, a person committed to social, cultural and intellectual emancipation and the broadening of mental horizons.[44] He believed in the dynamism of thought and ideas, and it seems unjustified to place his ideas within the rigid framework of any narrow political ideology. Judging from his speeches and statements during his Punjab perambulations, he emerges as strongly secular despite being a devout Muslim and a learned scholar of Islam. In Jullundur, the welcome address presented to him by the Anjuman-e-Islamia pointedly said: 'You have been equally mindful of the interests of Hindus and Christians, who are not debarred from reaping the benefits of the institution you have established. They (Hindus and Christians), too, are grateful to you for your non-prejudicial feeling of benevolence towards them.'[45]

At Lahore, almost the first to call on him (without making an appointment in advance) was a 50-member delegation of the Arya Samaj. Lala Sangam Lal, welcoming him on behalf of the Arya Samaj, said, inter alia:

> Although your visit may be connected with your interest in the affairs of Muslims, it has also been a source of honour for us, Hindus... Although you are not a Hindu, we consider it a matter of pride that one of the greatest reformers of our age is today present amongst us.

The Lala then recalled some of the honoured guest's services to the Hindu community as a member of the Legislative Council. He mentioned the benefits of Aligarh College to non-Muslims and the unbiased attitude of the College towards Hindus and other non-Muslims.

Sir Syed underwent a rather dramatic personal evolution to the extent that by the time he established MAO College, he firmly believed that his community needed to be protected from the majority, preferably with help from the British. The sahibs did not take the initiative, but the natives took it and just recognised the opportunity.

Sir Syed was able to collect sufficient funds to construct MAO College. However, the intensity of opposition from co-religionists forced a postponement.

On 8 January 1877, the Viceroy and Governor-General of India, Lord Lytton, laid the foundation stone of the first building on the intended campus of MAO College at Aligarh. Mukhtar Masood (1926–2017), a renowned Pakistani Urdu writer and bureaucrat, visualised it as a fun event.[46] Two roads were built up to the location of Stretchy Hall. Two hundred trees, brought from Banaras, were planted. One thousand *gamlas* (earthen pots) were prepared. The tent was raised for the guests' accommodation. Ride Bags, flags and rugs for decoration, carpets, and makeshift bathrooms were hired from Agra for convenience. At the same time, uniforms for workers from Allahabad and silver knives and forks for food and drinks were provided by Ms Khelnar & Co. from Calcutta. Those who came from outside to attend the foundation ceremony, cattle and humans alike, were guests and enjoyed the hospitality of Sir Syed.

He made elaborate arrangements for making the foundation-stone laying ceremony a grand one. Sir Syed's letter of 25 October 1876 to Messrs G F Khelnar & Co (head office: 4, Esplanade Road, Calcutta) is relevant:

> His Excellency Lord Lytton is expected to reach here on the coming 7 or 8 January, at the College Committee's request,

> to lay the college's foundation. The committee will organise a breakfast or lunch or both for his staff and on the same day, a dinner will be organised in honour of the European gentlemen who will be invited to the occasion. About 50 or 60 persons would be invited, but the number may considerably increase if Lt Governor Sahib accepts the invitation for dinner. The Viceroy is not expected to be present at the dinner. Therefore, we hope you inform us what would be your terms and conditions if you are asked for a complete supply of wine to entertain these gentlemen. Everything should be of excellent quality. You have to supply the wine too. Our committee would only arrange for the furniture.[47]

In his address, Lord Lytton described the event as 'an epoch in the social progress of India'. About eight decades later, Sir Hamilton Gibb characterised MAO College as 'the best modernist institution in Islam', while looking back at the Muslim transition from the medieval to the modern way of life in his book *Mohammadanism*. MAO College was an affiliate of Calcutta University, but in 1888, it was affiliated with Allahabad University, which was set up the same year.

The welcome address, in honour of Lord Lytton, candidly pointed out the objective as:

> To educate Muslims to dispel those illusory traditions of the past which have hindered our progress, to remove those prejudices which have hitherto exercised a baneful influence on our race; to reconcile Oriental learning with Western literature and science, to inspire in the dreamy minds of the people of the East the practical energy which belongs to those of the West; to make Mussalmans of India worthy and valuable subjects of the British Crown.[48]

If the expectations above came true, Sir Syed hoped:

> From the seed which we sow today, there may spring up a mighty tree, whose branches, like those of a banyan, shall strike firm roots into the earth and themselves send forth new and vigorous saplings; that this college may expand into a university whose sons

> shall go forth throughout the length and breadth of the land to preach the gospel of free enquiry, of large-hearted toleration and pure mentality.[49]

Sir Syed did not forget that the Maharaja of Patiala had made a generous contribution of Rs 58,000 towards the college fund. He said, 'The Maharaja of Vizainagram and The Maharaja of Benares head the list, which includes the names of many liberal-minded Hindu gentlemen, whose philanthropy forbids them to recognise distinctions of race and creed.' The contribution from the Nizam of Hyderabad was Rs 90,000.[50]

Sir Syed's views in this regard remained unaltered. In a letter to his mother on 2 March 1888, Theodore Beck, the second principal of MAO College, recorded the conversation between Sir Syed and Maulvi Imdad Husain, 'the most influential Mohammadan of Allahabad'. The Maulvi was against English education because educated Muslims became less particular about religious duties. Sir Syed politely tried to persuade him, saying, 'Let a few men go to Hell if the *qaum* (nation) is improved.'[51]

Akbar Ilahabadi, the great 19th-century Urdu poet of 'tanz o mazaah' (satire and humour), was a contemporary of the great social reformer and scholar Sir Syed Ahmad Khan. Initially, Akbar Illhabadi opposed Sir Syeds's vision of promoting English education among Muslims, and he used to express his feelings through his satirical couplets:

Dil mera jis se bahalta koi aesa na mila
But ke bande mile Allah ka banda na mila

Syed utthe jo gajatt le ke toh laakho laaye
Sheikh Quraan dikhaata phira, paisa na mila

(No one I found who could divert my heart;
I found servitors of idols but not of Allah.
Syed got up, flaunting gazette and got millions;
The sheikh showed the Quran and got nothing.)

Hazir huya main khidmat e Sayyad mein ek raat
Afsos hai ke ho na saki kuchh ziyaada baat

Bole ke tum pe qaum ki islaah farz hai!
Main chal diya ye kah ke aadaab arz hai

(I showed up to Syed's service one night,
but regretfully, we could not talk much.
He said it's incumbent on you to reform the qaum.
Please accept my aadaab arz, said I, and left.)

Later, Akbar realised Sir Syed's vision and the importance of his work in promoting Western education and started supporting him.

Noted Urdu critic Professor Rasheed Ahmad Siddiqi has waxed eloquent about Sir Syed's versatile genius. He says,

> Had he so desired, Sir Syed could have retired to a Khanqah (monastery) and would have become the source of guidance and rectitude for the world; had he gone into politics, he would have been the leader of one of the political parties; had he cared for high office, the highest office would have been his; had he chosen to be a writer or a poet, his excellence would be universally acknowledged; had he taken to historiography, he would have been considered an authority on the rise and fall of nations; had he strayed into the valley of philosophy and religion, he would have made his mark; had he concentrated on architecture, he would have brought to life the period of Shahjahan; had he dedicated his energies to law, he would have been a great jurist; had he attended exclusively to education, he would have founded a new system.[52]

The catch-22 situation of Sir Syed has been poignantly summed up by Urdu writer Shamsur Rahman Faruqi, who, discussing a letter of Sir Syed, remarked,

> Syed Ahmad Khan wrote his letter after 1891, perhaps in 1892. But it wasn't Javed-ud Daulah Arif Jang (a title conferred on Sir Syed by the last Mughal ruler Bahadur Shah Zafar) who was looking at Delhi then; it was Sir Syed Ahmad Khan Bahadur, K.C.S and he

never wrote a word about old buildings or cities or their citizens, past or present.[53]

It was sea change in Sir Syed's perception of composite nationalism that Allama Shibli Nomani, his associate for more than 15 years, was forced to write about in the Muslim Gazette, Lucknow: That strong hand, holding powerful pen, which wrote the book Asbab-i-Baghawat-i-Hind (The causes for Indian Revolt) at a time when the horrendous heat of Martial Law was raging at its highest peak; that brave man who had shredded into pieces the arguments advanced by Lord Lytton against the Punjab University Bill; that knowledgeable person who pressed for the individual rights in the form of three articles in a language that the literature produced by the INC could not match; that fearless man who walked out of the Agra Darbar because the sitting arrangements of Indians and the British were not at par; that justice lover who stood alone in support of Bengalis and bore witness saying that Bengalis are the only *qaum* in this country on whom Indians can justifiably take pride, the surrounding situation and turn of events forced that every man to stop Muslims from taking part in politics. Why did this happen? What were the reasons behind this? To discuss and debate the questions and answers of what brought about this sudden change and differences in him would not only be irrelevant, but harmful as well.[54]

Recording it, Maulana Hussain Ahmad Madani says:

Thus, the magicians of Britain entrapped a politically conscious and wise man (of Sir Syed's nature) and not only used him to oppose composite nationalism but also to prevent Muslims from participating in politics and constitutional struggle to alienate them from politics forever. It would not be surprising if the same enchanting spell is cast on Mohammad Iqbal too.[55]

Sir Syed (Sayyid Ahmad), Nomani (Shibli) and Abdul Halim (Sharar) created and shaped historical consciousness for the Hindustani public in the late nineteenth century. Their works are important interventions into what was until then a purely colonial project of writing history.[56]

4

Web of History

The first student at MAO College was Hamidullah, the son of Maulvi Samiullah Khan. An 11-year-old kid, he was introduced to potential donors in Punjab during fundraising campaigns as an example of the kind of person the proposed institution would serve. Some students were wards of relatives and friends of Maulvi Samiullah and Sir Syed from Delhi. Others were wards of subordinates in various courts. Though Aligarh was founded primarily for Muslims, it warmly welcomed Hindu students. The boarders were lodged in separate Hindu bungalows. In the first year, the student body was an all-Muslim one, but thereafter, it always included a significant number of Hindus.

In keeping with Sir Syed's frequently proclaimed principle of fellow feeling between the two communities and as an expression of gratitude for financial assistance to the college from Hindus, their number was increased. The tablets in Strachey Hall, installed at the time of the establishment of the college, bore testimony to people, irrespective of religion, coming forward to support the venture. In the very first list, two of seven members of the college staff were Hindus. Even a British teacher was appointed to teach Arabic. The 22-member managing committee included six Hindus. Amba Prasad, who later joined MAO College as a teacher, was the first student from the College to pass the high school examination.

H.G.I. Siddons, a 23-year-old Englishman, was appointed the first headmaster and principal. He worked selflessly without harbouring a complex of White supremacy, but Theodore Beck, the second principal, played an important role in the College's history. During his time, European teachers started encroaching on the trustees' privileges.

A tussle between the principals and managing committees characterised the state of affairs in the various colleges of Uttar Pradesh in the 20th century, and MAO College was no exception. Even trifles aggravated the strained relations between the two.

The development of Muslim Cricket (in India) got an enormous boost with the setting up of MAO College in 1875, where a Brahmin teacher of Mathematics, Rama Shankar Mishra, sponsored a cricket club. A Brahmin teacher began cricket at Aligarh, and it was an Englishman who was most energetic to promote it. He was Theodore Beck.[1] Shaukat Ali, the elder among the Ali Brothers of Khilafat Movement, loved cricket. A fiercely nationalist Syed Mohammad Tonki was also a good cricketer. He later retired as principal of STS (Minto Circle) High School, AMU. His cricket, drama and teaching (Maths and History) have been lauded by all, including Saeed Jaffery, Mushirul Hasan and K.M. Ashraf.

The interest of Aligarians bordered on fanaticism. Ramachandra Guha mentions a recollection:

> A one-day match against a visiting team was going the way of the visitors. The home team had a massive total to chase and ran out of time. Everyone was visibly upset. I, Inayutullah, was a spectator. I was heartbroken and turned away to head for my room. Suddenly, I noticed Aftab Ahmed Khan running from the field towards the Boarding House. Since the building was still under construction, it comprised only a platform with a corner covered by tiles, which used to serve as our Masjid. Aftab Ahmad Khan ran into this masjid. I went closer and found him to be facing West and praying hard. After several supplications, he ran back towards the field...[2]

Like every other old city, Allahabad, a culturally rich city, also has many tales to tell, in particular concerning Nehrus. One of them, given currency to by the Muslims of South Asia, especially the Aligarians, is about Anand Bhavan, which served as the Nehru residence.[3] One part of which, Swaraj Bhavan, was later dedicated to the INC. Instead of two parts of one museum, both are now museums run by the Nehru Memorial Trust. The legend is that Anand Bhavan originally belonged to [Sir] Syed Ahmad [Khan] – 'Sir' and 'Khan' were titles given by the British and the Mughals, respectively. Distorted oral history is responsible for the inaccurate fact mentioned on a plaque at the entrance of the Anand Bhavan. In reality, the house briefly belonged to Sir Syed's son, Justice Syed Mahmood, a judge in the High Court, who was one of the finest legal minds of his time. He sold the house to Raja Jai Kishan Das, an old friend and colleague of Sir Syed, in 1894, and Motilal Nehru purchased it from him later. Sir Syed never had any direct connection with the house, and he never lived there with his son.

The first showdown between the college trustees and principal was recorded when Beck, who was ex-officio president of the students' union known as the Siddons' Union Club, wanted his nominee, Mohammad Husain, son of Sir Syed's old friend, Maulvi Mohammad Shaheed Khan, to be elected vice-president of the union in 1885. A group led by Aziz Mirza opposed the move. The principal's candidate was not elected even to the cabinet of the union. Beck summoned the newly elected cabinet to express his displeasure and even ordered the cancellation of the election. In protest, the elected members resigned en bloc and thus compelled the principal to rescind his order.

The visit of Sir Surendranath Banerjee, president of the Indian Association (forerunner of the INC), a year earlier proved to be a turning point in the attitude of European teachers led by Beck. Sir Surendranath addressed a meeting chaired by Sir Syed in the building of the Scientific Society. Sir Syed praised Sir Surendranath, who dwelt eloquently on the wrongs done to Indians by the British. This development alarmed Beck and his group.

After gaining de facto control over the publication of the *Aligarh Institute Gazette* from Sir Syed, Beck used the journal to launch a campaign against the freedom movement. On 1 November 1890, an article commented: 'MAO College differs from most other colleges in being the expansion of a political rather than a purely educational impulse.'

Meanwhile, students wished to manage the mess in the boarding house themselves. With Sir Syed's approval in 1886, they elected a committee headed by Mazharul Haq. The mess manager resented this. Soon after, the committee was changed at the instance of the manager. The ongoing tussle between the manager and the students snowballed into a major controversy in February 1887.

The bearers, under the direct control of the manager, were arrogant while dealing with the students. Once, tempers flared, and a student, Mohammad Husain, nicknamed Bangroo (meaning rude or hillbilly), hit a bearer for an act of negligence. A complaint was made to Sir Syed, who rusticated Bangroo. The students, in turn, held a meeting in the room of Aziz Mirza, secretary of the Siddons' Union Club, and submitted a petition to Sir Syed, stating that the drastic action against Bangroo would embolden the subordinate staff. Sir Syed rejected the plea and stuck to his stand. He could not tolerate such rude behaviour towards servants because, in his teens, he had himself been punished by his mother for ill-treating a servant.

Aziz Mirza called for a strike in which more than 60 per cent of students participated. They packed their belongings and left the boarding house for a building called Kacchi Sarai. The striking students sent a telegram to Maulvi Samiullah Khan soliciting his help. On the students' easy relationship with the Maulvi, Mir Wilayat Husain, who was associated with the college in its formative years, first as a student and then as a teacher, records in his autobiography:

> Sir Syed was like a father to the students and Maulvi Samiullah Khan like a mother. Students generally had no access to Sir Syed, but the latter used to visit the boarding houses at times and meet each boarder. Some students used to visit his residence to unburden themselves frankly.[4]

The Maulvi arrived from Raebareli and asked the students to call off the strike. Meanwhile, Principal Beck drafted an apology and said that the students could be allowed to come back only after they signed it and repented for their actions before him and Sir Syed separately. The Maulvi failed to resolve the issue and left Aligarh. Aziz Mirza, Mazharul Haq and a few others were named as ringleaders and refused readmission. Others submitted their apologies and were taken back.

Beck emerged victorious. The relations between the Maulvi Samiuulah and Sir Syed were further strained in 1888. Sir Syed's son Syed Mahmood married a girl who had earlier been betrothed to Hamidullah Khan, son of Maulvi Samiuulah and the first student of MAO College.

Beck took advantage of the strained relations between the two. The European staff manipulated Mahmood to urge his father, Sir Syed, to nominate the former as his successor and end uncertainty. They were supported by some trustees in this endeavour. Sir Syed agreed. Arthur Strachey, a barrister at Allahabad, drafted the lengthy trustee bill naming Sir Syed as honorary secretary for life and his son Syed Mahmood as joint secretary for life to succeed as secretary after his father's death. The new bill was passed despite the opposition of Maulvi Samiullah, Khwaja Mohammad Yusuf and others. The Maulvi, who had been considered the natural heir, responded with a pamphlet accusing Sir Syed of making the college his personal fiefdom. He added that Syed Mahmood was not adequately pious, that the boarding house had been handed over to Christian management, and that excessive power was given to the British government. He recalled that Aligarh College existed to transmit English education through reliable Muslims. Samiullah and his group severed their relations with MAO College, again a significant victory for Beck. Sir Syed was now totally under the spell of Beck.

A rapprochement between Sir Syed and Maulvi Samiullah ensued through the intervention of Viqar-ul-Mulk of Hyderabad. (Maulavi Mushtaq Husain of Amroha had been given the title of

Viqar-ud-Daula Viqar-ul-Mulk Jung Bahadur while he was in the service of the Hyderabad state.) Maulvi Samiullah and his friends were again inducted into the board of trustees. Beck feared Maulvi's active intervention in the institution. He, therefore, suggested setting up a board of management consisting of staff members and trustees in place of the old committee to manage the affairs of the college. Maulvi Samiullah sensed something underhand in the scheme, as it would be difficult for the trustees, living in distant places, to attend every board meeting. The truncated presence of the trustees in any meeting would benefit Beck and his team. The maulvi decided once again to sever his relations with the college. Widely publicised, the tussle between Sir Syed and Maulvi Samiullah resulted in animosity. The maulvi and his friends focused on establishing a Muslim boarding house at Muir Central College, Allahabad.

A former bureaucrat Naved Masood recalls:

> Mushtaq Husain (1841–1917) – known more widely by the title conferred on him by the Sixth Nizam of Hyderabad viz. Viqar-ul-Mulk has carved a niche for himself in the history of the Aligarh movement as Sir Syed Ahmad Khan's close confidante and the Secretary of the Board of Trustees of MAO College from 1907 to 1913 during a turbulent phase of the history of the institution. He also played a role in shaping far-reaching political developments as one of the founders of the All India Muslim League, of which he was the first Joint Secretary. To many alumni, of course, his claim for being remembered is as someone after whom "V.M. Hall" is named!
>
> By all accounts, he was a very stern, uncompromising person not given to levity and humour so characteristic of the Muslim elite of the age. Someone writes of him as someone "who commanded respect and fear rather than affection." Mushtaq Husain resigned from his position as Tehsildar in UP as his Collector was not agreeable to his taking a few minutes off for the Zuhr prayers. It was after this confrontation that Sir Syed helped him get employment in Hyderabad, where he made a long-lasting contribution to the Revenue administration and was instrumental in making Urdu

– instead of Persian - the official language of the largest princely state in British India.[5]

In *Khutoot-i-Viqar-ul-Mulk*, it is stated,

> His eldest son, Mohammed Ahmed (1868–1896), went to England to qualify as Barrister. There, he married a young lady, 'Shelly'. The couple settled down in Bangalore while Viqar-ul-Mulk was still serving in Hyderabad. Mohammed Ahmed died in Bangalore at 28 after a brief illness, leaving a young widow and a one-year-old daughter called 'Hameeda'. By then, Viqar-ul-Mulk had left Hyderabad and returned to his native town Amroha in UP. The widowed daughter-in-law and the granddaughter joined him there. The family's misfortunes did not end; Hameeda was claimed by cholera at the age of five. Following the death of the daughter, Shelly decided to return to her native England and Viqar-ul-Mulk, despite financial difficulties – after all, he was only the 'title holder' of Nawab but was otherwise a pensioner – ensured that the daughter-in-law received regular remittances for her upkeep. This arrangement continued for several years until she wrote to him on 6th January 1906, informing him that she had received an inheritance of more than 10,000 pounds and requested him to stop the financial assistance instead quaintly called 'Pin Money'. The following excerpt from her letter is worth quoting:
>
> 'Let me in the fullness of my heart again express my loving gratitude for the fatherly care you have taken of me ever since you knew of me and during my widowhood. I am thankful beyond words to you, especially now that you are relieved from the extra expense you have so generously given and continued uninterruptedly.'
>
> In reply, Viqar-ul-Mulk wrote her that for a long time, he wanted to tell Shelley something but had so far refrained from doing so lest she misconstrue as intended to relieve his financial burden. Now that the situation has changed, he would suggest that she seriously consider getting remarried.
>
> Viqar-ul-Mulk wrote, 'Let me assure you that if one of my daughters had faced a similar situation, I would not only give her similar advice but also try to see that my advice was acted upon…

If you heed this advice, let me assure you that our relations will continue as before. If Khuda blesses you with an issue (from the second marriage), my affection for that offspring will be the same as with the child of my daughter. My hand of friendship will extend towards any family with whom you may choose to establish such relations. All this is on account of the affection which I have naturally for you and which shall always remain thus. My greatest satisfaction, if you act on this advice, will be that when my time comes, I can leave this world unencumbered with the painful thought of your troubled life.'

The reply of the doting daughter-in-law is as interesting: 'It is a highly kind one and shows great delicacy in that you never mentioned the subject of my re-marriage whilst I depended on you for support.

My dear *Mian*, to be perfectly candid with you, I have no wish to marry again – there is no man who can take my dear husband's place. Probably, there are plenty of men who would not object to having me now that I have some money and those I would scarcely marry. But under any circumstances, I would prefer to die the widow of Mohammed Ahmed.'

To this, the father-in-law replied on 17th May 1906, 'I realise that it is not appropriate on my part to write further in the matter; Nevertheless, with apologies, I would like to submit that the matter will bear reconsideration at a future date.'

The last word on the matter was said by the daughter-in-law, who wrote: 'I shall always think with loving gratitude of your care of me during all these long years of my widowhood. No English woman ever had a better father-in-law than I, although some are perfect.'[6]

Shelly did not remarry and passed away at a relatively advanced age.

It is interesting to note what Sir Syed wrote of Viqar-ul-Mulk, 'I believe that Mushtaq Husain would not change his opinion even if God revealed Himself against it'.[7]

Sir Syed was isolated. The transformation of Sir Syed's attitude from indifference towards the INC to opposition was crucial in the early history of MAO College. The initial activities of the AIMEC coincided with the students' strike, poor examination results and the trustee bill controversy. With declining enrolments and the withdrawal of some significant grants, the College relied more and more on the backing of the British government. Sir Syed had no hesitation in soliciting such support by claiming a role for Aligarh as an outpost of 'loyalty' to the Raj.

The mid-1890s was a time of renewed internal crisis for the College and renewed public activity in the outside world. In 1893, Syed Mahmood was forced to quit the Allahabad High Court under unsavoury circumstances.

Enrolment at Aligarh declined further. The very existence of the College seemed to be in danger. When Syed Mahmood returned to Aligarh to gain control of the College, a bitter quarrel ensued between father and son in which Sir Syed opted to desert the house. For several days, Sir Syed actually became a resident of the boarding house. Family emotions had been foisted on to a public institution with a vengeance. In March 1898, the incident was repeated. Sir Syed now moved to the house of his friend Ismail Khan Sherwani, the *raees* of Datiavali. This house was famous as *bibi wali kothi*. There, he died within a few days, a bitter and utterly frustrated man.

Describing the scene at the time of Sir Syed's death, Sheikh Abdullah (not to be confused with the Kashmiri leader with the same name), a first-generation convert, wrote in his autobiography that he heard the news of the death of Sir Syed at the Aligarh railway station while returning from Delhi.[8] It appeared that the news had just reached the station since an *ayah* from the ladies' waiting mom rushed out and said to the waiter in the men's waiting room, 'Gosh! I hear the elder *Syed Sahib* has passed away. Will his head now be cut off and sent to London?' 'No, Syed Mahmood *Sahib* has said that we will not allow his head to be severed or sent to London,' said the waiter. This conversation between these two was occasioned by the rumour leading ordinary Muslims of India to believe that some doctors of London had agreed to give a large sum in exchange for the head of Sir Syed so that they could examine it and find out what made him so intelligent.

Abdullah did not see Syed Mahmood or Syed Mohammad Ahmad (nephew), or any other relative in the friend's house where Sir Syed had died. The funeral would start in the morning, but there was no information about the burial place. He was shocked to know there was no money for Sir Syed's burial. The time for the funeral was set at four in the evening. Around one o'clock, Abdullah, accompanied by two friends, went to Syed Mahmood and told him about the time of burial. Abdullah wrote,

> Upon seeing us, Syed Mahmood, hand upon his head, started sighing heavily and said, 'Alas! My father is dead. I did not even have sacks in my house to seat visitors.' When he quieted down a little, we told him his presence there was necessary. College students, staff members, English and Indian officers, residents of Aligarh close to Sir Syed, and many city people accompanied the funeral procession. On nearing the mosque, it was decided that the *namaz-e-janaza* (funeral prayer) be read in the cricket pavilion. The bier was kept on the cricket ground. Meanwhile, Syed Mahmood also arrived there, wearing Arab attire.
>
> The *namaz-e-janaza* was led by Maulvi Abdullah Ansari, Dean of the College. After the burial, when the final sod of earth was put in place, Nawab Mohsin-ul-Mulk sat on a chair on the ground and roundly castigated the family of Sir Syed. He said they did not contribute even Rs 50 towards the burial of the person responsible for any standing these people may have.
>
> Sure, I am a friend of Sir Syed, but I am not his heir. It was the responsibility of his heirs to bear this expenditure, but they did not do so.[9]

The most notable of Sir Syed's admirers was Altaf Husain Hali, who preceded Mohammad Iqbal as the national poet of the Indian Muslims. He came under Sir Syed's spell from the moment he saw the latter and described their first meeting in graphic terms: 'All of a sudden, I saw a man of God, a hero among men, going ahead on a hazardous path… I was drawn to him, almost within an instant.'[10]

Hali's best-known poem, *Musaddas*, written at Sir Syed's instance, first appeared in *Tahzib al-Akhlaq*. It poignantly portrays the past glories and the contemporary decline of Muslims. Iqbal paid due tribute to Sir Syed and Hali for inspiring the Indian Muslims and giving them confidence:

> The Tulip of the Desert (the Muslim nation) Encountered autumn and withered away.
> Syed (Ahmad) gave it a new life,
> With the dew of his morning tears,
> And Hali did not cease his heart-warming melodies,
> Until the bedewed tulip had once again got its shining spot.

Akbar Ilahabadi wrote this as a tribute to Sir Syed:

> *Hamaari baaten hi baaten hain,*
> *Syed kaam karta tha*
> *Na bhoolo farq jo hai,*
> *kahne aur karne waale mein*
> *Koi kuchh bhi kahe hum to yehi kahte hain*
> *Khuda bakshe bahut si khoobiyan thi marne waale mein*
>
> We Indulged in empty talk while Syed worked;
> See the difference between a talker and a doer.
> No matter what others say, I always say this:
> The deceased had many qualities; may God forgive him.[11]

In 1895, the college and school at Aligarh had 595 students on its rolls. At the time of Sir Syed's death, the number had fallen to 323. Later, it plummeted to 189. Financial grants stopped coming. Some faculty members, including Maulana Shibli Nomani and Thomas Walker Arnold, left. Later Arnold joined a college in Lahore. Aligarh's loss can thus be said to have been Iqbal's gain. He was a student of the college Arnold joined. An unseemly struggle for power between Beck, Mahmood and Mehdi Ali Hasan

(Mohsin-ul-Mulk) on one side and Maulvi Samiullah on the other followed. Mahmood went on drunken escapades even in the college boarding house, once calling in the police to arrest a member of the staff for hitting students, and writing strange, long-winded legal briefs for every trivial piece of business. With his abetment, there was almost a repetition of the 1887 student strike.

Maulvi Samiullah Khan once again emerged on the scene. The Nawab of Rampur promised to bail out the college from its desperate financial position on the condition that Maulvi Samiullah should be appointed honorary secretary. As a countermove, Beck, supported by Aftab Ahmad Khan, a former student of the college and then a trustee, put forward the name of Mehdi Ali Hasan. Anthony McDonnell, Lieutenant Governor of North-Eastern Provinces and Oudh, came out with an offer of more financial assistance if the college management could restore order and provide the government with new supervisory powers. At the same time, the government exerted pressure on the Nawab to distance himself from Samiullah. The government denounced Samiullah's demands publicly. Mehdi Ali Hasan was nominated honorary secretary in place of Syed Mahmood, and Beck guaranteed tenure for life. Students gathered to see the founder's son tearfully embracing his 'uncle' Mehdi Ali Hasan on the steps of Strachey Hall. At last, Syed Mahmood left the college for good and followed his father to the grave at a cousin's house in Sitapur in 1903. His son, Syed Ross Masood, whose public *bismillah* in the lap of Raja Jai Kishan Das, a Hindu friend of Sir Syed, had marked the high point of Aligarh's mixed brotherhood credo, remained at the college under the guardianship of Theodore Morison, deputy to Beck.

Following Sir Syed's death in 1898, Beck whipped up all his organisational and rhetorical skills to save the sinking ship by leading a campaign on a large scale to revive the old dream of an independent university for Muslims of India. Aftab Ahmad Khan, Shaukat Ali and other friends joined. In 1899, Beck led a group of Aligarh students to Delhi to sit at the main gate of Jama Masjid on Friday noon and collect signatures for an anti-Congress petition to

Parliament. Such practices did not continue because the lieutenant governor of Punjab declared that student agitation against Congress was just as improper as the one in favour. Exhausted, Beck died in Simla on 2 September 1899 at the young age of 40.

Beck thought Hindus and Muslims would be unable to work together because of their essential 'attitudinal' difference. 'The difference between the burning plains of Mecca and snowy heights of the Himalayas' is not more significant than 'the difference in thought and feeling between Mohammadan and Hindu worlds'.

'They cannot unite,' said Beck, 'because the glory of one is the humiliation of the other.' He continued, 'The growing hostility of the newly educated Hindus towards Muslims is not an amiable feature of the times', and therefore, Muslim participation in the Congress movement would be suicidal for that community. Indeed, 'they have no intention of putting a rope around their necks and placing themselves at the mercy of those who have hold of the other end'.[12]

Theodore Morison, guardian of Syed Ross Masood, succeeded Theodore Beck as principal of the college. After Beck, the onus of keeping communalism, anti-nationalism, conservatism and obscurantism alive at Aligarh College fell on his shoulders. He tried to convince Aligarh students that democracy in India would reduce minorities to the position of hewers of wood and drawers of water. Mehdi Ali Hasan had already succeeded Syed Mahmood as honorary secretary of the college. He preferred to surrender to Morison the last vestiges of power in the college. Morison ignored the trustees completely. The college alumni led the effort to regain control over Aligarh from the British hands. The tussle resulted in Morison's resignation in 1904.

Morison's successor, W.A.J. Archibald, proved even more autocratic and clashed with the honorary secretary Maulvi Mushtaq Husain (Viqar-ul-Mulk), who had succeeded Mehdi Ali Hasan in 1907 following a students' strike reportedly engineered by Mohammad Ali, later the legendary hero of the Khilafat

Movement. Lord Minto had become the Viceroy of India. During his predecessor Curzon's regime, due to the partition of Bengal, there had been widespread agitation throughout the country. Britain wanted to assuage discontentment in India by introducing some reforms. During the summer vacation in 1906, Archibald went to Shimla. Anticipating the introduction of reforms, he contacted the private secretary of the Viceroy and pressed upon him the desirability of granting exceptional representation to Muslims on a communal basis.

At Archibald's instigation, a delegation headed by Aga Khan met the viceroy and presented him with a memorandum on 1 October 1906. The petition, ghost-drafted by Principal Archibald, demanded the right of communal representation in all administrative bodies all over India. The British government was already anxious to accept the demand. A jubilant British officer sent a letter that evening to Mary Minto, the Viceroy's wife, which said, 'Huge thing has happened today; a work of statesmanship that will affect India and Indian history for many long years. It is nothing less than the pulling back of 62 million people from joining the ranks of the seditious opposition.'[13]

Three months later, on 30 December 1906, the All India Muslim League was born in Dacca. In a speech before the students of Aligarh, three months after the formation of the League, Viqar-ul-Mulk declared, 'God forbid, if the British rule disappears from India, Hindus will lord it over; and we will be in constant danger of our life, property and honour.'[14]

In April 1908, an anonymous article was published in one of the most prestigious Urdu journals of its time, *Urdu-e-Mualla*, headed by one of the most celebrated literary giants, then a towering leader of the freedom struggle in India, Maulana Fazlul Hassan, commonly known as Hasrat Mohani. The article was abrasively critical of the British policies in India in general and the British occupation of Egypt in particular. In this, the author most blatantly highlighted the deceitful and cunning tactics of the British Crown in waging proxy wars in the name of alleviating poverty and liberation of humanity to subdue and invade weaker and underprivileged countries.

This was the time when MAO College had become a honeypot of freedom struggle. *Urdu-e-Mualla*, which he started in 1904 from Aligarh, was no ordinary journal but was the best literary-cum-political weekly to which celebrated writers of the country would contribute. The said article proved to be a catalyst in the already furious situation. The stir created by the article drew the attention of the British authorities, who found it illegal and seditious and therefore approached the journal's owner. The Indian government asked Maulana to disclose the author's name or face charges of instigating revolt. Despite all intimidation and an imminent prosecution, the Maulana refused to divulge the author's name. Resultantly, he was convicted and put to prison for two years. The Maulana was perhaps the first political prisoner in British India convicted under the press laws. Instead of being treated as an 'A' Class prisoner, he had to undergo rigorous imprisonment with scanty miserable clothes – a khaki shirt and knickers, a cap, a piece of jute cloth and a rough dirt-laden blanket as his bedding. During the initial period of his stay in jail, he was repeatedly cajoled to give away the name of the author as the British authorities felt uncomfortable having had a man roaming around freely, capable of producing rancorous literature that could help trigger yet another storm of freedom struggle they had been so ruthlessly keeping under the watch.

However, the Maulana did not budge an inch from his stance. The British authorities then, to squeeze the author's name, turned more precise in their tactics, brutish enough to break any man, let alone a man of letters. He was then slapped with a massive fine. When he couldn't pay the fine, the magistrate confiscated his most treasured possession – his books and rare manuscripts and auctioned them for a paltry sum. He was shifted into solitary confinement and was made to grind one mound of wheat on a stone hand mill daily, which required extraordinary labour to which Maulana was not accustomed. Maulana, in later years, wrote in his *Urdu-e-Mualla* that in the beginning, he was much perturbed and distressed by the rigour of jail life, miserable clothing and lack of water to perform ablution for prayers. But by and by, he became habitual to this sort of life. Nevertheless, despite his trials and tribulations, the Maulana remained steadfast and never revealed the author's name. A great deal of his literary work, especially the Ghazals, he owes to his imprisonment.

He was released from jail in 1910. Much later, on repeatedly being asked about the name of the author who caused him so much trouble, he revealed his name and identity and said that the article was penned by a minor student of MAO College of no more than 12 or 13 years. The British, then, were following a ruthless policy without discrimination of capital punishment for anyone found guilty of instigating, abetting or arousing fissiparous tendencies. The article was not anonymous, but Maulana, by his foresight, expunged the name of the author. If he had revealed the boy's name, he would have been rounded up and executed.[15]

As far as the administration of the Aligarh College was concerned, its history was one of continuous conflict between the principal and European staff on the one hand and the trustees on the other. Principal Archibald, too, had to resign in 1909. The percentage of Hindus in the college had declined from 15 per cent in 1901 to 4.5 per cent in 1909 due to multiple factors. Meanwhile, in 1914, five new trustees were elected, of whom Mohammad Ali Jinnah and Dr Mukhtar Ahmad Ansari were prominent political personalities.

The power struggle between the principal and trustees continued till 1919 when J.H. Towle, the last of the British principals, resigned en bloc along with the European staff. Earlier in 1911, differences had arisen between the *ihrar* (independents) and *stibdadi* (reactionaries) among the trustees of the college and the Aligarians. The government suggested the names of two proposed universities at Aligarh and Benares as Aligarh University and Benares University, which evoked a strong reaction. When Harcourt Butler, member education, Government of India, informed the promoters of both the universities that the Secretary of State did not agree to use 'Hindu' or 'Muslim' in the names of the universities, both communities (Muslims and Hindus) opposed it. The Maharaja of Darbhanga, President of the Hindu University Society, wrote to Harcourt Butler that 'the new name will not appeal to the Hindu public at large'.[16] Viqar-ul-Mulk said:

> It is a wrong policy which has pained the hearts of 350 million subjects. Much of the constitution we have presented to the honourable member of Education (Sir Harcourt Butler). We have very clearly stated therein that the doors of the university shall be open to all communities and (followers) of different religions, with only this difference that we would not be able to provide for religious education in the university except for the Mussalmans.[17]

Maulana Shibli Nomani poignantly summed up the feeling when he said, 'This system of our education should be in our hands', to which Akbar llahabadi sarcastically retorted: 'provided that your hand is (really) your hand'. Maulana Shibli Nomani, who lived in a small bungalow within the compound of Sir Syed House, rarely met Sir Syed (at the fag end of the latter) because of Syed Mahmood's presence. In fact, after coming back to Aligarh, Syed Mahmood often went to the Maulana in the early mornings to kill time. But that was precisely the time when the Maulana did his writing and research work, which thereby greatly suffered. He hinted this to Syed Mahmood one day. Syed Mahmood felt quite offended and stopped meeting the Maulana altogether. That was possibly why, soon after Sir Syed departed, the Maulana quit his residence in the compound of Sir Syed House and shifted to Ismael Khan's kothi. A few days later, he resigned from the college and returned to his hometown, Azamgarh.[18]

5

SIR SYED'S POSTHUMOUS BABY FACES PANGS OF BIRTH

Establishing a Muslim university had been mooted during Sir Syed's lifetime. However, the actual campaign for its establishment began after his death. The required reserve funds of Rs 3 million were collected. Aligarh's case for a university with the power to affiliate colleges received a severe blow with the passing of the Benares University Act in 1915, which provided a university with a residential character.

However, Sir Mohammad Shafi steered the passage of the AMU Bill, on the lines of the Benares Hindu University Act, in the Viceroy's Council, and the AMU Act eventually came into force on 1 December 1920. The inaugural ceremony of the university took place 17 days later, with Her Highness Sultan Jahan Begum, ruler of Bhopal, appointing Sir Mohammad Ali Mohammad Khan as its first Chancellor, the Raja of Mahmudabad (a principality in Oudh, Uttar Pradesh) as the first vice-chancellor and Syed Mohammad Ali the first treasurer.

In the first meeting of the Executive Council on 26 March of the following year, Dr Ziauddin Ahmad was appointed the first pro-vice-chancellor. He had been the principal of MAO College since the unceremonious and abrupt exit of J.H. Towle and his team two years earlier. He tried to soothe and persuade British officials to release those grants that had been held up and simultaneously assure Muslims that the government did not look upon the college with disfavour.

The pro-vice-chancellor's job was indeed challenging. He had to win over the government and Muslim opinion without appearing to give precedence to either. He was also supposed to ensure jobs for students and opportunities to satisfy the ambitions of his colleagues. Besides, he had to possess academic distinction and the ability to stimulate intellectual activity and win recognition for the university as a centre of learning in the world of scholarship. While the pro-vice-chancellor, Dr Ziauddin, was invested with international fame as a mathematician, combined with his enigmatic personality, making him appear ideal for Aligarh, he also generated opposition, and his methods of responding to it became less and less effective. While his supporters identified him with the university and pinned their hopes on him, his opponents believed the university could be saved only if he was removed from office. The result was three decades of conflict.

The AMU Act had virtually vested all power in the pro-vice-chancellor, the principal academic officer while reducing the vice-chancellor to an ornamental cypher.

The university started with 15 disciplines and 261 students. However, the total number of students, including those of the intermediate college, the university school and the city school, stood at 966.

In February 1923, vice-chancellor Sir Mohammad Ali Mohammad Khan resigned, following differences with Dr Ziauddin. In December, the University Court elected Sahebzada Aftab Ahmad Khan as the new vice-chancellor. He was already a member of the Secretary of State's Council. He assumed office on New Year's Day. Relations between him and Dr Ziauddin, which were already strained, worsened. They differed on several issues. Aftab Ahmed was a stickler for rules and regulations, whereas Dr Ziauddin had scant regard for them. One of Dr Ziauddin's favourite maxims was 'Rules are made for students; students are not made for rules'.[1] For Aftab Ahmed, principles took precedence over practicality, whereas Dr Ziauddin interpreted rules in the light of expediency. Dr Ziauddin followed a 'liberal' admission policy, waiving certain restrictions as and when he wished. He also introduced the scheme of private examination, which was discouraged by the government. The introduction of supplementary and compartmental examinations system was yet another area of much controversy.

Aftab Ahmed and Dr Ziauddin also differed about their powers. The former asserted that it was his duty as the vice-chancellor to ensure that the provisions of the Act, statutes, ordinances and regulations were duly observed. As such, he had the right to look into the academic affairs of the university. On the contrary, Dr Ziauddin felt that as the principal academic officer, all academic matters fell within his domain. Their relations continued to deteriorate, and in April 1925, Dr Ziauddin submitted his resignation, which was not accepted. Sahebzada Aftab Ahmed persuaded him to continue.

Dr Ziauddin was re-elected pro-vice-chancellor in 1926. The Uttar Pradesh director of education, A.H. MacKenzie, expressed his reservations over the declining standard of education in the university due to flagrant violations of rules and regulations. News regarding this negative development appeared in the *Leader* of Allahabad. The sahebzada not only resigned but also issued a pamphlet explaining his difficulties in continuing as a vice-chancellor and pointed out shortcomings and irregularities in the university administration. Copies of the pamphlet were freely distributed and sent to members of the University Court and the central and provincial governments. According to A.A. Suroor, a contemporary student, the pamphlet was a bombshell.[2] It became the subject of animated discussion in university circles.

In his capacity as Rector, the Governor-General of India instituted an inquiry into the university's affairs in 1927. In her capacity as Chancellor of the university, Sultan Jahan Begum was also in favour of a commission of enquiry. She paid Rs 18,000 towards its expenditure. The committee, headed by Sir Ibrahim Rahimtoola, noted that the main trouble lay in dividing powers between the vice-chancellor and the pro-vice-chancellor. Under the prevailing system, the vice-chancellor was the executive head, and the pro-vice-chancellor was the academic head of the university. The framers of the Act had obviously in mind the provision of two posts generally corresponding to that of the secretary to the Board of Trustees of MAO College, who was for practical purposes the executive head, and to that of principal, who was its academic head. That system worked satisfactorily during the lifetime of Sir Syed and for a short period afterwards. In Beck and Morison, Sir Syed had found men of remarkable ability, inspired by his ideals and endowed with the capacity to implement them. He also realised that interference would wreck his scheme. But, after the departure of Morison, all hell broke loose, resulting in numerous resignations.

The committee recommended consideration of the division of financial, executive and administrative powers and duties of the vice-chancellor and pro-vice-chancellor at par with other educational institutions in the country. It made several recommendations and noted:

> Given the close association of Dr Ziauddin with recent troubles (on the campus), his continuance in the university's service is inconsistent with the new spirit of harmony and progress which is essential for the future success of Aligarh. Perhaps the best course would be for Dr Ziauddin to take leave preparatory to retirement.

Consequently, on 26 March 1928, Dr Ziauddin resigned. But he wielded so much clout that his resignation was accepted after about a month. Dr M.M. Sharif was elected to replace Dr Ziauddin as pro-vice-chancellor.

Sir Ross Masood, who was in the service of the Nizam of Hyderabad, was elected vice-chancellor. This appointment fulfilled his long-cherished desire to head the institution in the building where his father, Syed Mahmood, and grandfather, Sir Syed, had played leading roles. In 1919, following the resignation of J.H. Towle, principal of MAO College, Sir Ross, who was then drawing Rs 2,000 per month as an employee of the Nizam, had expressed his willingness to come to Aligarh on Rs 1,000 per month plus free residence and Rs 140 per month as his pension contribution. But his request was not conceded to.

Sir Ross's tenure was comparatively peaceful. In 1933, when he learnt about Jawaharlal Nehru's visit to Aligarh, he invited the latter to address a meeting at Strachey Hall. He introduced Nehru as the son of his friend, Motilal Nehru. The British government viewed this move with disfavour. Correspondence ensued between Sir Ross and the lieutenant governor of Uttar Pradesh on this issue in which the vice-chancellor asserted his right to invite Nehru, a prominent political personality.

Sir Ross enlisted the services of Khan Bahadur Fakhruddin Ahmad, who was in the Bengal Educational Service, for the registrar's post. Alarmed at Sir Ross' rise to power, a committee was appointed by the University Court to suggest cuts in expenditure. The committee suggested the abolition of the post of pro-vice-chancellor. It also recommended that the term of appointment of the registrar not be extended. This suggestion involved an increase in the burden of work for the vice-chancellor. The proposal of Sir Ross to retain the services of the registrar was turned down by the University Court, which started bypassing the grandson of Sir Syed on several other important matters as well. The message was loud and clear. Sir Ross resigned in October 1934.

Andre Weil, the French professor of mathematics, whose services had been hired by Sir Ross, commented: the university had begun to bear a strong resemblance to the princely courts that the English had taken pains to preserve in India.

In the court in Rampur, a princely state, Andre Weil remarked, 'Everything hung upon the whims of the prince and plots were constantly being spun and unravelled around him. The same was true in Aligarh, with countless intrigues revolving around the person of Sir Ross, the VC.'

Citing an episode in this regard, Weil said, 'I was seen as Masood's creature. A pamphlet in Urdu was circulated criticising me for importing French mathematics into India: according to the pamphlet's author, only English mathematics was suited to the Indian mind.'[3]

However, he sounded optimistic when struck by the eagerness and openness of mind evident among the younger generations, in sharp contrast with their elders.

Offering a further glimpse into the messy state of affairs, Andre Weil added:

> Sir Ross considered it quite a coup for AMU that he had obtained from the Nizam of Hyderabad (under whom he had served as a minister) funds for two richly endowed chairs, in physics and chemistry. To the chemistry chair, he appointed a young Englishman whose merits I could not appreciate but whom I found friendly and who became my neighbour. In physics, Sir Ross thought it a triumph when he pushed through the appointment of a German whose only qualification was a letter of recommendation from Einstein and whose merit in Einstein's eyes could only have been that he was an unemployed Jew – for he never displayed any other quality. At that time, many European scholars thought any European was good enough for a colonial country. To make this appointment official, the procedure required that an ad hoc committee be convened with the participation of an outside specialist. It was a 'mistake' to invite the celebrated Sir C.V. Raman, a Nobel laureate, who himself had a student seeking a position at that very time. I believe this student was not without merit. In any case, this student was, without a doubt, superior to Sir Ross's candidate. I was also a member of the committee. Sir Ross was in Europe and cabled his orders. To contravene him would have touched off a severe crisis, and my fellow committee members, who were utterly unqualified to judge the substance of the issue, would never have taken such a risk. Sir C.V. Raman, justifiably outraged, threatened to cry foul and create a scandal. I tried to dissuade him from doing so. An outcry would only have exacerbated an already highly uncomfortable position.[4]

However, Tariq Hasan writes, 'Dr Rudelph Samuel, whose name had been recommended by Sir Einstein, was immediately appointed.

Another prominent European scientist Dr R.F. Hunter, was appointed in the chemistry department.'[5]

Andre Weil later lost the confidence of Sir Ross. He writes that in November 1931, the university administration picked a trumped-up quarrel with him. He had neglected to seek official authorisation to go to Allahabad to attend the inaugural meeting of a provincial academy. Adding insult to injury, he refused to help tabulate votes in an election held by the students' club. The quarrel rapidly turned bitter. In January 1932, while he was writing his resignation letter, the university informed him that his contract had been terminated. In his naivete, he had never asked to see the contract. Nevertheless, the whole episode was premeditated, he felt.

Meanwhile, Dr Ziauddin had already sown the seeds of a nefarious game. He was instrumental in sabotaging the attempts of the Ali Brothers (Mohammad Ali and Shaukat Ali) to convert MAO College into a national university instead of a statutory one. The power structure within the college was remarkably similar to that of Muslim society. Rajas and nawabs dominated the management, whilst the students, particularly the scholarship boys, were often attracted to more radical politics. The Ali Brothers, both former scholarship pupils, had their most vital links with the students and old boys, and their chief aim in college politics was to democratise the board of trustees in such a way as to gain a position of greater prominence for themselves and their followers.

By then, Mahatma Gandhi had emerged on the political scene. He realised that religion remained the only language in the subcontinent, whereby one could communicate with people. Religion mobilised men and women for purposes that could not be entirely translated into secular idioms. Religion was ideologically omnipresent before MAO College was converted into a statutory university. Gandhi, who had been invited to speak to the students, tried to find the right words, but 'his accent seemed droll to his "pseudo-sophisticated" audience who did not agree with him, for their political and economic background and affiliations did not predispose them to accept his radical new doctrine of non-cooperation'.[6] The first shot misfired. He then appealed to the trustees of MAO College to decline any further government grant, disaffiliate the institution and reject the charter of the Muslim university.[7]

Brought up in the tradition of sturdy loyalty to Pax Britannica, the trustees did not heed Gandhi's earnest plea. They had already decided to run their college on 'old established lines' and make their Muslim brethren 'worthy and useful subjects of the British Crown'. Most trustees rallied around the principal, Dr Ziauddin. They agreed to isolate the pan-Islamists and the Anjuman-i-Khuddam-i Kaba, co-founded by Maulana Abdul Bari and Mohammad Ali's younger brother Shaukat Ali. Mohammad Ali had been fiercely opposing the move to convert MAO College into a government (statutory) university. He was then spearheading the Khilafat Andolan, revolting under the banner of Allah against the British because of the fall of the Turkish Sultan, who had been ex-officio *khalifa*, or head of all the Muslim faithful. He did not need any persuasion. Maulana Bari was apprehensive that secular education would undermine religious allegiances, and he saw the Balkan wars as fertile ground for the extension of the influence of the *ulema*.

In October 1920, a meeting was again held in the students' union hall in the afternoon. At that time, the principal used to be the ex-officio president of the union. Abdul Aziz, barrister and an alumnus of MAO College, asked what the students would do after leaving college. The answer was that they would support the Khilafat movement. When asked about a scheme of constructive work, Maulana Shaukat Ali (elder of the Ali Brothers) replied that, even without such a scheme, Muslims should not hesitate to sacrifice their all for religion. Aziz posed another question: What would happen to Benares Hindu University? Maulana Mohammad Ali replied that the question was irrelevant because Khilafat was a religious duty of Muslims.

Gandhi supported the Khilafat Movement because if Islam was in danger, he said, Hinduism could not be safe. He announced that, despite Madan Mohan Malaviya's opposition, he would go to

Benares to urge students to boycott classes. Abdul Majid Khwaja, a barrister who supported Gandhi and the Ali brothers, said he realised his duty but would not urge others unless he abandoned his law practice.

The Aligarh Institute Gazette, a college weekly, carried on a vigorously anti-non-cooperation campaign. However, there were dissenting notes too. M.A. Husain, an undergraduate student, Nurul Hasan, a student from Azamgarh, and some others were influenced by leaders of the non-cooperation movement like Maulana Abul Kalam Azad and Azad Subhani. Amidst fiery and passionate speeches, resolutions, promises and assurances, many more responded – estimates ranging from 200 to 700 – to the call of non-violent resistance against the colonialists and enrolled themselves in the newly-founded Jamia Millia Islamia.

The Khilafat contingent, led by Dr M.A. Ansari, Azad Subhani, Maulana Abul Kalam Azad, Hakim Ajmal Khan and the Ali Brothers, returned to Aligarh on 23 October and addressed numerous meetings. On 10 November, 100 boarders attended, one of whom was a Hindu. Most of the other Hindu college students were day scholars, and they had indicated their intention to join the new university. The boarders, who joined the Ali Brothers, left the college to stay in a nearby building, leading to the birth of Jamia Millia Islamia, a national university at Aligarh, which, after some months, was shifted to Delhi. Dr Zakir Husain was among the teachers who left MAO College to give direction to the nascent institution.

The Ali Brothers and their friends had earlier decided to open a college in Dehradun under the name of Sultania College, with Mohammad Ali as principal. They intended to provide education even to those who could not afford to study at MAO College with its 'very high' fees.

It was to be an institution where teachers and students enjoyed complete freedom and were bound by a healthy academic relationship. The group, endeavouring to establish the model college at Dehradun, professed emotional allegiance to the

Ottoman Turks. In contrast, the British government vehemently opposed the latter due to their close relations with the German Emperor, Kaiser Wilhelm. And the proposed Sultania College died even when it was born.

The AIMEC had, in 1910, invited the 'progressive' *ulema* and modernists to national seminars to 'enlighten' them on Muslim cultural orientation. Five years later, an unusual suggestion was made to establish teachers' training schools for *ulema* in every division of the Indian provinces and to provide them special incentives for enrolment. The trained *ulema* would then be employed in Islamic schools. A large section of *ulema* equipped to teach only in elementary schools would thus find secure employment. This conciliatory stance elicited a positive response from the higher echelons of *ulema*.

6

CLOUDS OF SEPARATISM HOVER OVER AMU

In March 1937, Maulana Husain Ahmad Madani of Deoband's well-known *Dar-ul-Uloom* suggested establishing symbolic relationships between *ulema* and modernists. In the 72 years of its existence, Dar-ul-Uloom had educated about 13,000 scholars. Besides, numerous Arabic–Islamic seminaries in the country produced several thousand *ulema* yearly, though there were no visible employment means. Maulana Madani's approach was a cry in the wilderness. Three years later, in 1940, the Muslim League adopted the 'Pakistan Resolution', completely transforming the Indian political environment. The traditional *ulema* of the Deoband seminary supported the INC, while the modernists opted for Pakistan through the Muslim League. A unique opportunity to harmonise traditional Islamic educational values with modernism was lost.

In Aligarh, Dr Ziauddin, in league with Aftab Ahmad Khan, continued his efforts to insulate students from the Congress movement. Khan, an old student of MAO College, was among those who had arranged the first meeting of the Muslim League in December 1906, just after the meeting of the AIMEC in Dacca. Mohammad Ali wrote the minutes of the meeting. The 56-member committee included 15 young Aligarh alumni. Mohammad Ali's polished oration, involving analysis of British politics, impressed everyone. He argued that 'the lines of cleavage' in India were primarily on religious lines and that those divisions were political and spiritual. No matter how good the faith of some of the Hindu leaders was, the primary conditions of India could not be changed, and an effort had to be made through the new political system to secure the protection of specific Muslim interests.[1]

Until 1910, the Muslim League had remained an appendage of the AIMEC, but later it was decided to separate the two organisations and move the League headquarters from Aligarh to Lucknow. Aziz Mirza, leader of the 1887 students' strike at MAO College, was the League's Secretary.

In 1912, the Ali Brothers met Maulana Abdul Bari of Firangi Mahal in Lucknow. Soon, they became his religious disciples and political allies. They discarded their fashionable British attire for flowing robes, grew beards and prefixed Maulana to their names in preference to Shaukat Ali resigned from a senior government post and became secretary of Anjuman-i-Khuddam-i-Kaba, Mohammad Ali had made unsuccessful attempts to clear the ICS examination in London. In the following years, the Ali brothers rose to prominence in Indian politics. Still, their political actions were dictated by a total commitment to Islamic devotionalism from their discipleship to Abdul Bari.

Until the Ali brothers rediscovered the inspiration of Islam as a living guide to a total social order, Aligarh politics remained a rear-guard action. Sir Ross Masood was succeeded by Nawab Ismail Khan, who remained vice-chancellor for about a year only, from April 1934. Meanwhile, Professor of Mathematics Dr Ziauddin, popular among the students for allowing laxity in admissions, was emerging as a follower of the cautious 'loyalty' line. In April 1935, he not only staged a comeback but also got himself elected as vice-chancellor by the University Court. The British government strongly favoured his election, and it is a wonder that as many as 23 persons with the title 'Sir' gathered in Aligarh to elect Dr Ziauddin as vice-chancellor. They included Sir Firoz Khan Noon and Sir Sikandar Hayat from Punjab. It was felt that no one could suit the British interests better than Dr Ziauddin. A.B.A. Haleem, Dr Ziauddin's trusted lieutenant, took over as pro-vice-chancellor.

Ziauddin Ahmad was a brilliant student at MAO College and had been selected as Deputy Collector. Clutching the joining letter, he rushed to Sir Syed, expecting a pat on his back. Seeing the letter and the radiant glow on his face, Sir Syed pointed to a lock in the room, saying, 'Go, lock the college. If brilliant students like you leave the campus, who will run it?' Ziauddin Ahmad preferred to stay to study and serve the college and later university.[2]

Dr Ziauddin remained vice-chancellor for over three years. In April 1938, he was succeeded by Sir Shah Muhammad Sulaiman, a judge of the Federal Court, who was a stickler for rules. Dr Ziauddin was keen on another term, but Nawab Ismail Khan also threw his hat in the ring, and M.A. Jinnah suggested the name of Sir Shah as a compromise candidate. Born in Azamgarh, he did his B.A. Honours in Mathematics in 1906 with a first class, which earned him a scholarship to pursue higher studies at Cambridge. After he was appointed vice-chancellor, he framed new rules of service and superannuation and obtained a large grant for the university from the government.

In a requiem for Sir Shah Mohammad Sulaiman published in Nature, one of the most reputed scientific journals in the world, on 20 September 1940, the Nobel laureate Sir C.V. Raman writes,

> Sir Shah Mohammad Sulaiman studied mathematics and physics at Cambridge, taking Part II of the Mathematics Tripos in 1909. During his subsequent career as a practising barrister and as a judge at Allahabad, he continued to retain a general interest in the progress of physical science. Later in life, the stimulus of contact with the university staffs at Allahabad and Aligarh led him actively to undertake the study of theoretical physics as a subsidiary pursuit. Sir Shah's high position in public life secured for his writings and lectures scientific topics the widest publicity in India, also sympathetic, though critical, reception from his academic friends and colleagues. His published papers indicate marked reluctance to accept the ideas of the newer physics as expounded by the leading authorities on the subject. They largely consist of attempts

> to explain the facts of the newer physics on the basis of classical semi-classical ideas aided by special hypotheses. It could scarcely be hoped that work on such lines would find general acceptance. Sir Shah was the recipient of honorary doctorates from the Universities of Allahabad and Aligarh in recognition of his eminent public services and his deep interest in the cause of education and science.

The death of Sir Shah on 13 March 1941, however, once again brought Dr Ziauddin to the fore. He played a crucial role between April 1941 and December 1946. Notwithstanding the escalation of Hindu–Muslim violence and the growing rift between the Congress and the Muslim League, Aligarh remained unaffected until the mid-1930s. In general, campus politics was not marred by religious polarisation. In 1931, Tufail Ahmad Manglori, a distinguished Aligarh old boy, criticised the Muslim demand for a separate electorate, arguing that the real cause for the communal tangle was the recognition of special interests, 'which appears to have dimmed the national outlook'. He proposed a constitution to safeguard minorities by 'correct redistribution of India with compact homogenous zones, autonomous in character and with a few central subjects as circumstances permit'.[3]

Support for Indian nationalism sat comfortably with socialist commitment. Thus, the refrain of capitalist exploitation, class conflict and revolt against imperialism figured in the writings of former Aligarh graduates like Hasrat Mohani, Sajjad Hyder Yaldarim, Wilayat Ali 'Bambooq', Qazi Abdul Ghaffar and A.R. Bijnori. Political debates were conducted in and around the hostels. Revolutionary poems of Josh Malihabadi, Asrarul Haq Majaz and younger poets resounded in Aftab Hall, the focal point of much radical activism and venue of public lectures delivered by local Congress stalwarts like Maulavi Abu Bakr Mohammad Shish (chairman of the Sunni theology department from 1925 to 1940).

Then campus politics underwent a dramatic change. Emboldened by a spate of successfully organised League conferences in Delhi and its neighbouring districts, the All-India Muslim Students' Federation (A-IMSF) arrived on the scene to counter the growing influence of the All India Students' Federation, a frontal organisation of the Communist Party of India. They placed a strident demand for removing teachers holding 'socialistic' and 'atheistic' ideas. As a result, some progressive and radical teachers were dismissed, some were told to fall in line, while others were eased out of administrative positions to be replaced by the Leaguers.

Criticism of the League in the *Aligarh Magazine* was suppressed with an iron hand. No wonder an article by Khwaja Ahmad Abbas, a law student, was not published. A.B.A. Haleem, the pro-vice-chancellor, stated,

> Pakistan has been adopted as a creed by the great bulk of the Muslim community in India, and the publication of Abbas's article in the *Aligarh Magazine* would surely be exploited by critics of the university and the opponents of the movement'. Mukhtar Masood of Pakistan recalls Professor Haleem's welcome to Jinnah, stating, 'Mr. Jinnah, we are teaching history and you arc making it.[4]

The idea of the partition of India was officially adopted for the first time in March 1940, when the Muslim League, at its Lahore session, passed the famous 'Pakistan Resolution'. The Aligarh students played a vital role in achieving the desired objective of the League.

The atmosphere in Aligarh, as W.C. Smith noted that in the mid-1940s, was 'one of mystic frenzy'. Young students 'began to pour their idealistic zeal into the emotionalism of Pakistan and discussed rational arguments with the contentment of religious authoritarianism, and its scorn'.[5] The Lahore Resolution inspired new hopes and excitement besides stimulating League politics in Aligarh. Inspired by the lectures of Jinnah and Liaqat Ali Khan, another alumnus of AMU, in the summer of 1940, students gravitated towards the League in large numbers. The students' union adopted the Lahore Resolution as its 'official creed'. A jubilant union official declared that 'the Pakistan scheme was shaped and crystallised by Aligarh men' and that Aligarh again had the 'privilege of expressing the hidden feelings of the Muslim nation'. It was a sign of the changing times that an organisation established for secular education was now under the total influence of the League Former student and retired Aligarh University professor of English Masood ul Hasan described the allure of the League; he remembered, 'The Congress volunteers had their Young Men's Corps. Even the Khaksars had theirs. The ordinary young student, the ordinary young man, was left out. The League seemed to present an opportunity to fulfil the students' desire for 'self-manifestation.'[6]

The new energy displayed by Aligarh students trapped them in a politicised identity. Associations and debating societies were formed to discuss the idea of Pakistan. The A-IMSF launched a quarterly journal, *Awakening*, in English and *Biradari*, in Urdu, from Aligarh. The *Aligarh Magazine,* too, carried articles in support of the Pakistan movement.

Interestingly, the Aligarh students, who had rebuffed Jinnah's early initiatives and heaped scorn on his constitutional style of politics, were now turning towards his leadership. The 5 May 1937 issue of the Aligarh Muslim University Gazette explicitly took up the university's role in politics. Addressing the university's role in students' lives, the editorial evokes the separate nature of the university itself and the dangers of the temptations of the outside world. While in the university – an enclosed space, apart from practical life and strictly bounded – students were being prepared for life outside, but they were not in it yet, and to become involved would mean a dangerous distraction from the priorities of the student. Thus, the editorial reminds students that 'the Muslim University allows fullest liberty to the students to discuss all social political and economic problems of the day and form into groups on that basis provided that the rules of discipline are scrupulously maintained and the strictly academic nature of these activities is not violated'.

A distinct transformation occurred in The Muslim University Gazette by the end of 1937. The Muslim University Gazette in its issue of 24 December 1937 described the majority rule as 'despotic'. It went on to attack Aryan Hindu claims of Indian nativity that would exclude Muslims. It argued aggressively for an inclusive system that would recognise the Muslim contribution to the Indian nation. The Muslims may have been in the minority, this argument suggested, but they were not separate from the Indian nation. Part and parcel of this argument is the demand that Urdu be recognised as the national language. The piece concluded with a jab at the majority community – calling it communally minded – and beckoned a leader 'of vision and imagination' who could transform the political environment.

From the examination of The Muslim University Gazette above, however, it is clear that discontent grew quickly in 1937 both in the university and outside of it. Controversy erupted over the actions and agendas of the Congress ministries.

Considering the repeated and zealous involvement of Aligarh students in political activities, the 'traditional' separation seems flimsy at best, but it is frequently invoked as a critical pillar of Aligarh's identity. The university was drawn into the politics of the Muslim League to the extent that in late 1938, Vice Chancellor A.B.A. Haleem went so far as to estimate that 'about 90% of the students of the university have strong Muslim League sympathies and it is no exaggeration to say that out of 114 members of the staff, about 100 at least are Muslim Leaguers'.[7]

Communal consciousness generated by pan-Islamism during the Khilafat Movement of 1920 eventually fed into Jinnah's movement. The notion of Muslim solidarity made the community more susceptible to communal propaganda in the 1940s. Aligarh-based scholars, many of whom had invoked the theme of a separate Muslim identity in their controversial defence of the Khilafat cause, found it intellectually convenient to defend the two-nation theory. Likewise, the community consciousness of the students, which 'was far more secular than religious' when Mohammad Ali was a student, expressed itself in a vigorous movement of 'Muslim nationalism'. Most leaders of the Muslim community were in the grip of pan-Islamic feelings in the late 1930s and early 1940s.

Jinnah's endeavours to gain a foothold in the university were no less significant. He sedulously cultivated the vice-chancellor Dr Ziauddin, who, in turn, maintained regular contacts with the Muslim League. According to Athar Parvez, then a student at Aligarh, Jinnah was virtually worshipped in Aligarh around 1941. In April 1942, the University Court conferred upon Jinnah the *honoris causa* of Doctor of Law. Jinnah, however, refused to accept the honour on the plea that 'I have lived as plain Mr Jinnah and I hope to die as plain Mr Jinnah. I am very much averse to titles or honours and I would be happier without a prefix to my name.'[8]

Jinnah's visits to Aligarh were always marked by fanfare. Large crowds used to gather at the otherwise sleepy railway station, and crackers would be laid on the track so that when the engine of the Kalka Mail passed over them, it seemed like a gun salute to welcome him.

His last visit to the university in 1943 was observed as 'Jinnah week'. It formed an important event in the political itinerary of Jinnah. His efforts were bolstered by some Aligarh 'old boys' from among the professional and landowning classes. By winning them over to his side, Jinnah could dictate his will to his newly found Aligarh constituency and guide the progress of the Pakistan movement with a free hand. The atmosphere was charged with tension. Dr Matin Zuberi, a contemporary student, recollects: One day, I was sitting in my room. Suddenly I heard the shouts *Qaid-i-Azam zindabad, zindabad,* (Long live Zinnah) from a nearby room in the Aftab Hall. I thought some meeting was going on in that room. Full of curiosity, I rushed to that room. To my utter astonishment, I found the sole occupant of that room raising slogans all by himself. Such was the admiration for Jinnah.

Aftab Hall became the headquarters of the League activists in Aligarh. The students were asked to read only *Dawn* and *The Statesman*. Nationalist papers such as *The Hindustan Times* were disliked by League activists, whose diktat no student dared defy.

However, even amid the tumultuous welcome accorded to Jinnah during his visits to the AMU, some dissenting voices could still be heard. Rashid Ahmad Siddiqui and Mohammad Habib adhered to the notion of a plural Indian nationality. They favoured a political solution to the communal tangle within the framework of a united India. Similarly, the socialist and communist groups (a label still often used in Aligarh for those who hold liberal and progressive views) too represented an important strand in university politics. The communists openly came out to distribute party literature and enlist new members. Reacting sharply to these developments at Aligarh, Jinnah wrote to Jamiluddin Ahmad, lecturer in English and a leading protagonist of Pakistan, 'I should have thought that Aligarh is now strong, well-knit and organised enough to resist any mischief that may be created against us' and exhorted him to oppose any attempt to disrupt the 'Aligarh solidarity'.[9]

The League machinery got rapidly into action. The Uttar Pradesh State President of the League, Liaqat Ali Khan, helped set up as many as 14 libraries in various hostels to propagate his party's message. The AMU unit of the League published pamphlets on the Pakistan movement. National guards were raised to demonstrate Aligarh's solidarity with the 'Muslim cause'. A camp of the League was organised in October 1944 with the help of the Raja of Mahmudabad. The *Aligarh Magazine* published a 'Pakistan Number' in 1945 to silence detractors and opponents of the Pakistan idea. Earlier in March, the A-IMSF, at its conference in Aligarh, had passed a series of resolutions demanding the creation of Pakistan.

The role played by Aligarh students in the 1945–46 elections to the central and provincial legislative assemblies revealed their intense involvement in the League politics. For them, much was at stake in these elections, regarded as a rehearsal for the bigger fight later on. Fundraising groups fanned out all over the subcontinent. They were advised to stay only in mosques, shun their relatives in the towns they visited, grow beards and offer *namaz*.

The British Islamic activist Kalim Siddiqui, reminiscing about those times, wrote:

> One of the author's earliest memories is of the arrival in our ancestral village in northern India of three young men carrying the Muslim League flag – the Islamic crescent and star on a deep green

> background. The three were students from Aligarh university. They planted the flag in the village square and a crowd of little boys gathered around them… Within an hour our quiet village had been turned into Pakistan village…. Every piece of green material our mother could find was made into Muslim League flags…A few months later they [parents] all walked in their bare feet and some carried their aged and sick parents on their backs to the polling booth four miles away to vote for the Muslim League and Pakistan. This was repeated all over India. Seldom in History have so few inspired so many with so little effort.[10]

It was claimed that the students' efforts were rewarding for the League as in several constituencies of Uttar Pradesh in Aligarh, students succeeded in tilting the balance in favour of the League candidates. Jinnah remarked, 'I have been following the wonderful work that the Aligarh boys have done…. You have proved that Aligarh is the arsenal of Muslim India.'[11] Not only did students but the AMU administration headed by the vice-chancellor Dr Ziauddin and his two influential colleagues, A.B.A. Haleem, chairman of the history department, and Obaidur Rahman Khan Sherwani, treasurer of the university and a member of the Uttar Pradesh legislative assembly, too was an integral part of the 'arsenal of Muslim India'.

In 1936, Dr Ziauddin denied admission to the organisers of a student strike – Ali Sardar Jafri, Jalil Abbasi, Khalil-al-Rab and Zamir Siddiqi – in order to suppress nationalist and patriotic elements in the camps. Students with progressive social and political views also met the same fate. In September 1938, Dr Ziauddin, backed by the Uttar Pradesh government and Aligarh landlords, rusticated a few more student agitators. Some years later, Dr Ziauddin boasted that Congress activists were lying low in Aligarh. Some senior teachers also supported the vice-chancellor.

Dharam Veera, a distinguished political administrator, who served as a joint magistrate in Aligarh, recalls in his autobiography,

> Aligarh, the seat of the Muslim University, was an exciting posting to have (in 1930). The university was the hotbed of Muslim

> communalism and provided the bulk of leadership to the Muslim League. The late Sir Syed Ahmed established it under the inspiration of the British to combat the rising Indian nationalism on the pretext of safeguarding Muslim culture in India and protecting the interests of the Muslim community. While the general outlook of the university was markedly communal, one could not help being impressed by the cultural outlook and sophistication of most of its teachers.[12]

The bureaucrat also found nationalist dissenters on the same campus. Professor and Mrs (Mohammad) Habib, Professor Haider Khan and Ashfaque Hussain were, he wrote, staunch nationalists in this fort of communalism. Despite the troubles of Hindu–Muslim relations, they never swerved from the path of nationalism.

Recalling his discussion with Dr Ziauddin, Dharam Veera said that the vice-chancellor confessed that Pakistan was only a bargaining chip and that there could never be any question of the Muslims desiring Partition of India.

British politicians and Muslim civil servants, he observed, used this opportunity to fan communal flames. The League's demands grew more and more exacting and onerous while the Congress leaders continued to advocate idealism. To them, democracy, in reality, meant majority rule.

American political scientist Paul R. Brass observed that the Muslim elite, which had been in danger of losing power in north India, chose divisive rather than composite symbols as focuses of political action.[13] Aligarh attained new heights of practical and symbolic prominence in the 1940s as a centre for mobilising a robust Muslim response to the Pakistan movement.

In the words of the Aga Khan: 'We may claim … that the independent, sovereign nation of Pakistan was born in the Muslim university of Aligarh.'[14]

In January 1944, the faculty system was introduced in the AMU. Maulavi Habibur Rehman Khan Sherwani (Theology), Dr Babar Mirza (Science) and Dr Zafrul Hasan (Arts) were appointed deans. The post of pro-vice-chancellor was abolished.

Falling victim to his machinations, the vice-chancellor Dr Ziauddin was prompted to resign after a significant student agitation. Dr Zahid Husain was elected the new vice-chancellor on 20 April 1947. In the intervening period, Obaidur Rehman Khan Sherwani worked as acting vice-chancellor. But Dr Zahid Husain resigned after a few months, and Nawab Ismail Khan took over as the acting vice-chancellor (October 1947–November 1948). Dr Ziauddin died a broken-hearted man in London on 23 December 1947. His body was brought to India and buried beside the grave of Sir Syed, the founder of the university. He had come to the university as a student in 1887 and stayed there for 60 years. Interestingly, neither Dr Ziauddin, nor Dr Babar Mirza or Obaidur Rahman Khan Sherwani migrated to Pakistan.

Dr Ziauddin had also been successful in securing jobs for students. Old-timers recall that every season he would visit Nainital, the summer seat of the Uttar Pradesh government. He would carry a list of graduates and return with appointment letters for them in the provincial civil services. Sometimes, he would return early to get supplementary lists to fill the vacancies. Perhaps, this consistent approval of the list provided by Dr Ziauddin prompted Akbar Ilahabadi to comment on the later careers of Aligarh's graduates:

> *Ham kya kahein ahbaab kya kaar-e-numayan kar gaye;*
> *B.A. hue, naukar hue, pension mili, phir ma gaye.*
> (What words of mine can tell the deeds of men like these, our nation's pride? They got their B.A., took employment, drew their pensions, and then died.)

'We worked for Pakistan and played our part in making Allama Iqbal's dream a reality under the guidance of Quaid-e-Azam.' This is how a woman member of the Uttar Pradesh State unit of the A-IMSF summed up the role of students in creating Pakistan.[15]

In October 1939, the AMU Students Union (AMUSU) passed a resolution condemning the 'fascist' policies of the Congress government in the provinces. Two years later, the AMUSU passed another resolution that the best way to achieve India's freedom and bring about lasting peace in the country was to strive for the establishment of independent states as regions of Hindu and Muslim majorities. The idea of Pakistan, the AMUSU felt, represented the universal faith of the Musalmans of India. Addressing the students on 31 August 1941, Liaquat Ali Khan declared: We look to you for every kind of ammunition to win the battle of independence of the Muslim nation.[16] In 1945, *Aligarh Magazine* published a Pakistan number.

In the 1945 elections, students of the AMU fanned out through Uttar Pradesh, Bihar, Punjab, North-West Frontier Province (NWFP), Sind and Bengal provinces to canvass for the Muslim League, strengthening its *ulema* in Punjab. The students also mobilised support for Pakistan in the referendum held in 1947 in the NWFP and the Sylhet district of Assam. Kasim Razvi, the fanatic communal leader of Hyderabad state, was an alumnus of the AMU.

Being dissatisfied with the working of the provincial autonomy under the 1935 Act, the AMU Muslim scholars suggested the alternative of British India being divided into three independent sovereign states: (a) a Muslim state of north-west India comprising Punjab, Sind, NWFP and Baluchistan, to be known as Pakistan; (b) a Muslim state of Bengal, Sylhet district of Assam and Purnea district of Bihar, to be known as Muslim Federation and; (c) the rest of British India to be called *Hindustan*. Delhi and Malabar (Kerala) were to be autonomous provinces, and Hyderabad (including Berar and Carnatic) was a sovereign Muslim state under this plan. In short, the Aligarh scheme envisaged partitioning British India into four states – three Muslim and one Hindu. Little wonder, *Quaid-e-Azam* M.A. Jinnah paid handsome compliments to the AMU students for their role in the campaign for Pakistan.[17]

AMU students were perceived to be foot soldiers for the League during its campaign in the 1945–46 elections that became a sort of referendum on Pakistan. Was there overwhelming support for Pakistan among the Muslims in undivided India? No. But scholar after scholar conveniently overlooked the inconvenient truth.

Aligarians smugly boast about the university's role in the creation of Pakistan. However, while it is true that Aligarians branched out to villages of Uttar Pradesh and Bihar to garner support from the Muslim masses. By sporting beards and skullcaps to win the hearts of Muslims and staying in mosques, they had no appeal for influence over the Muslim elites (*ashraf*), who were the only ones who had the right to vote in the 1946 polls.

M.A. Jinnah visited Aligarh regularly, as did the top League leadership from all parts of India. These visits became more frequent after the 1940 Lahore Resolution. Jinnah delivered some of his most important speeches on the developing political situation in India, the League's politics and Pakistan in the students' union hall. During the 1940s, the League moved quickly to capture the AMU by electing its men to the AMU Court and Executive Council. The vice-chancellor Dr Ziauddin was the secretary of the League in the Central Legislature. At the same time, the pro-vice-chancellor A.B.A (Abu Bakr Ahmad) Haleem, hailing from Bihar, was a League notable. He would go on to head Sindh University after Partition.

Some of Jinnah's earliest and most ardent supporters who played a significant role in fashioning the Qaid's public persona included Jamiluddin Ahmed, a lecturer in the English department of the AMU, who edited the bestselling two volumes of *Some Recent Speeches and Writings of Mr Jinnah*,[18] which remain a major primary source for scholars working on Jinnah, Partition and Pakistan. Ahmed also produced several other topical pamphlets during the 1940s, published from Lahore as part of the League's propaganda on Pakistan.

The A-IMSF, founded in 1937, was headed by Mohammad Nauman, an Aligarh student. Later, its president was the young Raja of Mahmudabad, a member of the League's Central Working Committee and its treasurer. The League had a separate unit for the university, much like a district unit. University news formed a regular column in *The Dawn*, the League's flagship newspaper.

About 400 AMU students worked for Liaquat Ali Khan's campaign in the Meerut constituency during the first round of elections for the central assembly, especially since Congress had pulled out all stops to defeat him. He publicly thanked the students for his victory. The AMU students' usefulness in this round of elections prompted Jinnah to draft them for the polls to the provincial assemblies and also handsomely fund their campaign in Punjab, Sindh, Bengal, NWFP, Assam, Central Provinces and Uttar Pradesh. The Aligarh staff also aided the students.

Many scholars refer to statistics from the 1946 provincial assembly elections in which the League captured about 4.5 of 6 million Muslim votes. This seemed to suggest that 75 per cent of Indian Muslims voted for the League and its demand for Pakistan.

This claim glosses over the crucial fact that the 1946 elections, based on the Sixth Schedule of the Government of India Act of 1935, had a limited franchise, which means that only a tiny percentage of adults – those with money and property – were eligible to vote. In fact, only 3 per cent of the population could vote for the central assembly, and only 13 per cent could vote for the provincial assemblies. Hardly 30 million people could vote in assembly elections out of a total adult population of 120 million.

The League's demand for Pakistan was a cause embraced by the Muslim elite. The same people were allowed to vote and were likely to gain economic and other opportunities from the creation of Pakistan. Therefore, the claim of 75 per cent support would appear to be a gross over-representation. This is a fact that India's British rulers clearly understood. '[A] vote of the whole adult population or the enfranchised population would be unlikely to provide the result that Jinnah requires,' wrote Viceroy Lord Wavell to Lord Pethick-Lawrence, Secretary of State for India, on 20 November 1945.[19]

Limited franchise meant that only people with property or money and educated professionals had the right to vote. The large mass of people of all communities was disenfranchised. Such an arrangement created elite leaders such as Jinnah, who otherwise would not have had mass electoral appeal under a genuinely democratic franchise. It's no accident that Nehru, Jinnah and other leaders of both the Congress and the League were wealthy anglicised lawyers, landowners, merchants or princes.

If Pakistan indeed had mass support, there would have been large-scale migration from Uttar Pradesh and Bihar. Yet, there's no evidence of such an exodus. Census data tells us that the Muslim population of those provinces dropped by one to two percentage points between the 1941 and 1951 censuses. Even if one assumes that all these people went to Pakistan, it hardly qualifies as a mass exodus. The overwhelming majority of Indian Muslims in these un-partitioned provinces remained in India, whether by choice or by default.

An interesting Aligarh story of those days concerns Salman Rushdie's maternal grandfather, Dr Ataullah Butt.[20] He was appointed the first principal of AMU's Tibbiya College in 1927. An ophthalmologist by training, he had earlier been in charge of the university's health services and chief medical officer. A Kashmiri, he was a prominent Ahmadiyya or Qadiani by faith. He was a member of the executive committee (*shura*) of the Qadiani community. He used to organise *manazirah* (religious debates) with adherents of other Islamic sects and other religions in Aligarh, his adherence to the Qadiani sect being no hindrance in his relations with followers of other sects. Even Sir Syed and Sir Iqbal had been impressed with the knowledge and oratory of Mirza Ghulam Ahmad Qadiani, founder of the Ahmadiyya sect. Still, they parted ways with him when he proclaimed prophethood. The elder brother of Sir Iqbal, Atta Mohammad, remained an Ahmadiyya. Iqbal even appointed his nephew, Sheikh Aijaz Ahmad, an Ahmadiyya by faith, as one of the guardians of his children – Javid Iqbal and Munira Salahuddin.

Dr Butt was so devoted to his sect that he asked a Shia student Zarghaam Ali Khan (of 1927 batch who graduated in 1932) from Salon town in Raibareli, who had topped the first batch in Tibbiya College, to join the Ahmadiyya sect if he wished to become a lecturer in the college. Unrelated to his devotion to the sect, but giving a further insight into his character, is the fact that he got an undertaking from Zaigham Ali Khan that *Kitab-ul-Ain*, a book penned by him, would be published under the name of Dr Ataullah Butt by the University Publication Division. As a concession, Dr Butt mentioned the name of his student (author) in the acknowledgement.

In 1949, when Dr Ataullah Butt superannuated, Zarghaam Ali Khan lost no time in returning to the Shia fold after convincing others that there was a provision of *taqiyya* (to lie for a cause), and he had merely resorted to that to get the job. Dr Ataullah's son, Mahmood Butt, later became Chief Secretary of Uttar Pradesh. He was the first Muslim Chief Secretary (1975–76) in the state. Little information is available on Zarghaam Ali Khan in the university town. It is believed that he migrated to Pakistan in the early 1960s.

Aligarh still remembers Dr Butt's son-in-law, Mohammad Shaghil, the first husband of Salman Rushdie's mother. Mohammad Shaghil was appointed lecturer at the university in 1936, but a few years later, he went to the United Nations Organisation (UNO) when it was established in 1940. He returned in the 1980s and died in the university town in the 1990s. He is remembered as a gentle soul and never talked of his first marriage or Salman Rushdie.

Dr Ataullah Butt's brother, Abdullah Butt, was also a professor of mathematics at AMU. His son, Mahmood Butt, sold the house at the famous Marrice (Marris) Road of the university town after his father migrated to Pakistan in the mid-1960s. The house was named *Butt Kada*. Rasheed Ahmad Siddiqi, a legendary professor at the AMU, equally well known as a humourist, in a lighter vein, suggested to Ataullah Butt that the house should be renamed *But-kada*, literally a temple, since '*but*' is a metaphor for the beloved's indifference in Urdu poetry. It is difficult to differentiate in English between Butt, the surname, and *but*, an idol; however, the two are pronounced quite differently in Urdu. Additionally, the pun on Butt could have also referred to what male university students felt about Ataullah Butt's beautiful and very modern daughters who were, unlike most young Muslim women, very visible but unattainable. Little is known about Mahmood Butt's days in Aligarh. The wife of R.A. Siddiqui has recalled the friendship between her family and Dr Butt's family.

In his autobiography *Anton Joseph*, Salman Rushdie has chosen to reveal things with a purpose and in a way that it has a fictional aspect, evoking readers' interest. He has been somewhat economical with stories about his mother's family background, and whatever he has stated falls in the category of convenient truth. Though Rushdie loves controversy more than any other formidable writer of the 20th century simply because it has selling potential, he somehow ignored Aligarh, a phenomenon with a lot of potential to sell anything related to it and whose ethos is part of Rushdie's DNA in many ways. His close connections with the university town did not find sufficient space in the book. Since Mohammad Shaghil, as his mother's first husband, did not figure in his scheme of things, he has almost ignored him, though he does not spare his mother from what is crudely called 'bitching'. What is apparent but finds no mention in Salman Rushdie's autobiography is that it was pretty unlikely that his maternal grandfather Dr Butt had married his daughter to a non-Ahmadiyya Muslim. Salman Rushdie is not alone in forgetting Aligarh. Basharat Peer, a young writer who graduated from AMU, did not mention the university's name on the jacket of his famous book *Curfewed Night*.

7

A New Beginning

After Partition and the creation of Pakistan, Aligarh began to be viewed with suspicion. Its new vice-chancellor Nawab Mohammad Ismail Khan, the erstwhile President of the state unit of the Muslim League , pledged its loyalty to the Indian state and its Constitution. He laid out the tasks the university and its denizens had to fulfil in the new India:

> We shall have to create an atmosphere of goodwill and fellowship so that the doubts and suspicions about our aims and objects may be dispelled. It is my firm conviction that politics should be altogether divorced from this university, and it should now revert to its primary role as a seat of learning, pure and simple. Not many students who will pass out from here can hope to secure employment under the government. The abolition of weightage may not be an unmixed evil. Still, it may, on the contrary, be a blessing in disguise if it thereby makes our students more self-reliant and enterprising and ready to explore other fields and direct their hopes and aspirations from stagnant careers in government services to channels more productive material goods. We must now learn to stand on our fate.[1]

Barely 45 days after Partition, in September 1947, the Pakistan Adjutant-General's office sent a letter to Obaidur Rahman Khan Sherwani, the then acting vice-chancellor of AMU, who, in turn, marked the letter to Captain S.M. Ali, a university officer for necessary action. It was a request to hire officers for the Pakistan

Army (regular commission) from the university's alumni. Captain Ali invited written applications. The request from Brigadier N. Raza of the Pakistan Army was for 'a complete list giving full names, age and qualifications of the shortlisted candidates'. The matter was brought to the knowledge of the then deputy prime minister Sardar Vallabhbhai Patel by the then Uttar Pradesh chief minister G.B. Pant.[2]

Wo chehchehati bulbulen jane gayeen kahan;
Ay, katib-e taqdeer mujhe etna bata de;
Kyon mujhse khafa hai,
kya maine kiya hai

(Whither have those warbling nightingales flown, O' disposer of my fate, tell me? Why are you annoyed with me? What wrong have I done?)

A student cycled past, humming these lines from an immortal song sung by K.L. Saigal. A group of students inside a hostel room in the AMU heard the song and cast melancholic looks at one another. They lacked the words to express their feelings so appropriately reflected in the couplet. The lanes of the university were deserted. The university was facing one of the worst crises in its chequered history. India had been partitioned, and the AMU had played a crucial role in that eventful development. Partition was followed by the large-scale exodus of its students and faculty to Pakistan.

Recalling those days, Dr Matin Zuberi, a senior political science teacher, recalled:

> A deceptive calm prevailed on the desolate campus. Inwardly though, anxiety loomed large. Students in groups would not talk to one another, even when going for a stroll in the evening. They failed to understand what Partition meant to them. A few months earlier, Sheikh Rashid, the proctor, used to make the rounds of the campus in a jeep in this volatile atmosphere. A searchlight was

> fixed atop the Science Faculty. Once, the warden of Aftab Hall summoned some of its boarders and expressed his apprehension about a mob attack. He advised students to collect bricks on the roof and prepare red chilli powder to face any eventuality. The rumour mills were grinding over time.[3]

Recalling Partition days, Riaz-ur-Rehman Sherwani, a nonagenarian, retired professor of Arabic who taught at Aligarh Muslim University and later at Kashmir University before superannuation, confided in Eram Agha, a journalist,

> Around Partition, my brother, sister and I were in Kasauli, Shimla, then in Punjab. I was a master's student in Aligarh. My sister was being treated for TB in the hills. We were stuck. We couldn't return to Delhi or Aligarh and had to cross to Pakistan with only a little money.[4]

His father was the Muslim League leader Obaidur Rahman Khan Sherwani.

> On their way to Pakistan, they spent nine days at Kalka Refugee Camp, starting August 15. 'It was tough, raining heavily and the shed was provided to sick, women and children, while young and healthy sought shelter under a tree. There was scarcity of water and we could wash our face only once in a day, we were provided with ration but we never had any way to cook in the rainfall. At that time some people brought food for us but we declined thinking it would be poisoned. But hunger is such a thing that people later ate it, and it was not poisoned,' he said.
>
> Later, they got into a coach for refugees guarded by Gurkhas and finally reached Lahore. Sherwani had no idea he would be stuck there for a long time. His sister died in January 1948. After that, his father, who was a member of the UP legislative assembly, made efforts to get his sons back. By then, Sherwani had taken a good look at the new country that was being given shape and didn't like what he saw. 'The government gave us a place to stay because my family back here was influential, but I did not want to stay in a

country dominated by a single religious identity. I wanted to come back to the plurality of India,' he says.

...

And to carry on with his education in the meanwhile, he was admitted to Oriental College, Lahore. 'I found the new nation to be in disarray. People were not welcoming towards migrants except those from Punjab. They only behaved a little better with me when they found out I was there temporarily,' the retired professor added. The migrant experience was significant. 'Those who went from India to Pakistan were called "Mohajir" and were distinct in appearance and culture. Those who went to India were quickly assimilated,' he points out. In March 1949, his family arranged a flight to bring him back.[5]

Arif Mohammad Khan asserts that there were plans to swap AMU with DAV College Lahore at the time of Partition, but Maulana Azad defused such moves.[6] In this situation, when uncertainty loomed, the Government of India 'nominated' Dr Zakir Husain to head AMU after Independence. Dr Zakir Husain left MAO College in 1920 at the call of Mahatma Gandhi and the Ali brothers to establish Jamia Millia Islamia. The state of affairs at AMU tormented him. The university remained under the influence of the League, and he had even been deprived of membership of the University Court at the instance of Dr Ziauddin.

Dr Husain was not willing to take charge as a government nominee. At a meeting of the University Court on 28 November 1948, Nawab Mohammad Ismail Khan, the acting vice-chancellor, resigned and proposed the name of Dr Zakir Husain, who assumed charge two days later.

'The way Aligarh participates in the various walks of national life will determine the place of Muslims in India's national life', said Dr Husain on the occasion of the visit of the then President of India, Dr Rajendra Prasad. 'The way India conducts towards Aligarh will determine largely the form which our national life will acquire in the future.'[7]

Dr Zakir Husain was reappointed after three years under the AMU (Amendment) Act 1951. The vice-chancellor's term was now fixed for six years or the date of superannuation, whichever was earlier. The amendment was the first since 1920.

The important changes it effected were (i) non-Muslims could also become members of the University Court; (ii) theology was not to be taught as a compulsory subject; (iii) the composition of the University Court, the Executive Council and the Academic Council was to undergo changes following the university's new statutes. But implementing the changes was not an easy job as there was opposition to the first two.

Lok Sabha member from Bihar, Hussain Imam alleged that even the limited liberty the British gave was being snatched away.[8] Maulana Abul Kalam Azad regretted that the autonomy of MAO College had already been curtailed by the AMU Act of 1920.[9] He quoted Theodore Beck (one of the British principals of the college), who had advised the students 'to act upon the Viceroy's words'. Biswanath Das sounded a note of caution 'you cannot have abstract freedom of thought inculcated in the students unless you engender freedom in the university'. He pleaded for the independence of the universities as well as for the utilisation of universities for ends that are greater, nobler and more helpful than what they had been.

According to Professor M. Mujeeb, the changes in the University Act were not liked by many Muslims who would, nevertheless, have cheerfully admitted that compulsion had throughout failed to make religious instruction either religious or instructive in any, except a farcical, sense.[10] The change in the Act to make non-Muslims eligible for the University Court also evoked strong reaction. It was feared in some quarters that such a change would result in the Muslims being crowded out of the Court. Many insinuations were made against Dr Zakir Husain, who was sincerely in favour of both changes – of having created a 'new' Aligarh of the kind the government of independent India wanted. His endorsement of the amended Act proved correct as Chief Justice of the Supreme Court of India S.R. Das firmly stated at the time of the Kerala Education Bill

(1958): 'So long as the Constitution stands as it is and is not altered, it is, we conceive, the duty of this court to uphold the fundamental rights and thereby honour our sacred obligation to the minority communities who are our own.'[11]

Dr Zakir Husain, who came to Aligarh at a time when the country was rocked by communal violence following India's partition, accepted the challenge to save the university from persistent onslaughts on account of its dubious record of having secured as 'an arsenal of Muslim India'.

He ensured the university's survival during a period of uncertainty. As a contemporary student leader Ahmad Saeed described him as 'a sort of a "screen" which almost saved the University from adverse days that it was expecting to see after partition'. Mohammad Amin reiterated that 'it was primarily Nehru and his choice of sending Zakir Husain Sahib as vice-chancellor that saved Aligarh University from extinction'.

Any secular national government would have had to devote adequate attention and resources to its maintenance and development for the sake of its prestige as well as the expansion of education and advancement of learning. But again, specific objectives and standards of judgement were almost automatically expected of the AMU. It was meant to showcase the satisfaction and loyalty of an entire community to the state.

Dr Babar Mirza and T.A. Khan Sherwani, two trusted colleagues of Dr Ziauddin, were still active in the university. Dr Mirza was nursing a grudge as he considered himself the natural successor of Dr Ziauddin. Partition had depleted the strength of senior staff in the university to a considerable extent. At the end of 1948, there were only three professors at AMU, including Dr Mirza, a zoology teacher. Among the junior staff members and the students, there were not many who had remained unaffected by the communal epidemic. Dr Zakir Husain's first task was to alleviate fear and suspicion. He looked around for fresh blood and brought in teaching faculty from other universities.

The impact of Partition on the Aligarh Muslim University was severe. Several staff members left for Pakistan. The university's financial resources dwindled, and for a while, its future looked bleak, recorded Dr Piara Singh Gill, a renowned physicist who was inducted as Head of the Physics Department, in his memoirs. He added that Dr Zakir Husain set about finding the best scholars. He sought the best students in post-graduate classes, regardless of caste, creed or sex. Brilliant physicists like P. Venkateshwarlu, an expert in spectroscopy and microwaves, and A.N. Mitra, a theoretical physicist, joined the university as readers, strengthening the department.[12]

Dr Zakir Husain introduced the practice of sending senior faculty members abroad for higher studies. Perhaps it was meant to eliminate troublemakers who were at the forefront of Muslim League politics on the campus and did not migrate to Pakistan even when their political aims were met. The vice-chancellor introduced several courses to make the university a real centre of learning. He took interest even in minor matters to satisfy faculty members he had drawn to the university. Once, he asked the wife of Dr Piara Singh Gill:

> if they needed anything. She said they were pleased to be there, but one basic requirement should be introduced. Despite city water running through the university (round the clock), sanitation required upgradation. The VC assured Mrs Chambeli Gill that their house would be the first to have sanitary fittings. As soon as the work was completed, the distinguished professor of Zoology, Dr Babar Mirza, complained to the VC that his wife was born to German parents, yet his house had no sanitary fittings.[13]

The vice-chancellor was embarrassed at not having flush toilets when he had to put up an American guest at his house, but he selected Gill's house as the first to be upgraded.

The AIMEC was revived, and the Old Boys' Association was reorganised. The reorganisation of the association was, in a way, an attempt to re-establish contacts between the university and the north Indian Muslims after Partition. But the task of rebuilding the university was not an easy one. Abdullah Ghazi, who joined the university in July 1951, told Dr Mujeeb that among a section of students, Dr Zakir Husain was considered an intruder, foisted on

AMU by the government for the *shuddhi* (conversion to Hinduism) of Aligarh. They believed that Dr Babar Mirza or Professor Habibur Rehman, Principal of the Teachers' College, would have been better suited for the post. Ahmad Saeed, who gave himself the nom de plume of *jarrah* (the indigenous surgeon) and whom the students nicknamed *anda* (egg) was secretary of the students' union and on occasion, made caustic remarks in speeches while welcoming the vice-chancellor.

Dr Abidullah Ghazi (later President of the Students Union AMU in 1959) hailed from Ambeta town in Saharanpur district. He was the great-grandson of Maulana Abdullah Ansari (the head of Deeniat at MAO College and who performed Sir Syed's Namaz Jenazah) and grandson of Mohammad Miyan Ansari (a freedom fighter, member of Reshmi Roomal Tehreek and one of the members of the Government of India in Exile at Afghanistan). His father, Maulana Hamid-ul-Ansari Ghazi, was also one of the freedom fighters and editors of the *Madina*, Bijnor.[14]

When Liaqat Ali Khan, prime minister of Pakistan and an Aligarian, was assassinated in Rawalpindi on 10 October 1951, some AMU students insisted that the siren be sounded, as was usual on occasions of general mourning.[15] There were some dissenting voices, but one dissenter was even beaten up. A rowdy group came to the vice-chancellor lodge and insisted that he give the order to sound the siren. He tried vainly to make them resist pressing their demand, but they broke the lock of the room where the siren was kept and sounded it.

During the debate on the AMU (Amendment) Bill of 1972 in the Rajya Sabha, Joachim Alva (Congress) recalled: 'Perhaps in 1953, I posed a question to the then minister of education, Maulana Azad, in the Lok Sabha "Is it true that the AMU students are going to demand a corridor to Pakistan?" Maulana Azad cupped his ears and said, "I can't hear you".'[16]

In his convocation address on 20 February 1949, Maulana Abul Kalam Azad, the first education minister of independent India, told the students:

> I want to speak to you without any reservation. Perhaps you hope so from me. Before 15 August 1947, the country was, unfortunately, reeling under the impact of poisonous communal politics. Had I felt that the influence of those forces still punctuated the affairs of the university, I would have said without reservation that I do not see a bright future for you … I am happy to find a new awakening in the atmosphere of the university. You have sensed the reality without wasting time. You have responded to the demand of the changed times without delay. You have accommodated yourself in the new environs. I think that by doing so, you have not only served your institution but also rendered yeoman and timely services to Indian Muslims. I congratulate you for the same. You can expect in a secular and democratic setup that all the doors are open to you … The free atmosphere in the country must help you in broadening your horizons. You have to come out of the old mindset and find your place by your ability in independent India. If you can adjust yourself to the requirements of a secular and democratic country, I am not in doubt that there will hardly be any avenue where you would not be able to reach.[17]

However, Azad's fond hopes were dashed when, in the afternoon, in the customary address in the Students' Union Hall, he was welcomed by Hasan Raza, a student from Lucknow, with a few selected *ayats* (verses) from the Koran, referring to traitors. The message was loud and clear to the Maulana, a profound scholar of Arabic. His face flushed with anger, to the dismay of vice-chancellor Dr Zakir Husain. Even as marigold petals were being lowered from a window overhead the podium to cascade around him, the Maulana stood up. He said he had been at fault while delivering the convocation address that morning. 'No door is open for those who refuse to correct themselves in the wake of developments in secular India,' he said before abruptly leaving the meeting in disgust.

Perhaps the incident reminded him of the day, a few months before Partition, when he was derided by AMU students at Aligarh station during a train journey from Simla to Calcutta. Several thousand students of Allahabad University were at the Allahabad railway platform to greet the Maulana. But the train had been detained by the Aligarians and they had roundly abused him.

A few months after Independence, before Dr Zakir Husain had assumed charge as vice-chancellor, Prime Minister Jawaharlal Nehru said in the AMU convocation address:

> Do not think that you are an outsider here, for you are as much flesh and blood of India as anyone else, and you have every right to share in what India has to offer. But those who seek rights must share the obligations also. Indeed, if the duties and obligations are accepted, rights flow themselves. I invite you, as free citizens of free India, to play your role in the building up of this great country and to share your way. The present, with all its unhappiness and misery, will pass. It is the future that counts, especially to the young, and it is that future that beckons you. How will you answer that call?[18]

There were not many at the AMU willing to answer Nehru's call.

Professor Irfan Habib recalls an old incident. He was sought to be denied a government scholarship because of his links with leftist groups. He applied for a government scholarship to study abroad in 1954–55. Still, his passport was denied by the Government of India because of his connections with the Communist Party of India. He wrote a letter to Nehru, asking him that in future, whenever the Government of India issues an advertisement for any scholarship, there should be a caveat that 'Communists need not apply'.

This letter created a furore in the Prime Minister's Office (PMO). Nehru enquired about this episode from vice-chancellor Zakir Husain. On Husain's intervention, Habib was asked to meet Prime Minister Nehru. Nehru wrote:

> Irfan Habib came to see me this morning, and I had a talk with him. When you mentioned his case to me, you gave me the impression that while he was a young man of leftist sympathies and ideas, he was not a regular member of the Communist Party.
>
> ...

The purpose of giving a government scholarship is to train a person who might be of service to the State in some capacity or other in the future. If a person could not be relied upon to serve the State with discretion and integrity, then obviously, this primary purpose would not be served. No State could be expected to go out of its way to give a scholarship to a person on whom it could not rely or who was likely to indulge in activities which were harmful to the State. I use the word 'State' broadly and not as applicable to a particular government. Also, I realise that it is rather difficult to draw a hard and fast line. Anyhow, it is not a question of differing views, political or other, but rather of a basic faith in a person's integrity.

My own experience of communists has been that it is exceedingly difficult to rely upon their word or their basic integrity in this sense. Their loyalty to their party overrides all other loyalties and, therefore, they are often prepared to function in a way which cannot be reconciled with my standards of personal behaviour. Again, I repeat, this is not a question of difference in idea. Personally, I have had no animosity against the communists at all, but I have come to feel increasingly how out-of-date communist parties in non-communist countries are. As I told Irfan, they are like the Jesuits belonging to the strict order and not over-scrupulous in their dealings with others, provided they carry out the dictates of that order to whom they owe their primary loyalty. I see no reason why the Government should go out of its way to offer a scholarship to a person who is so tied up with an order of this kind, whether it is the communist party or some other.

I recognise, of course, that one must not judge young people too strictly and youthful enthusiasm must not be ignored.... Anyhow, in the balance, we should decide in favour of Irfan Habib as a special case. My main reason for thinking so is that he is a young man of intelligence and, I believe, integrity, and these qualities will undoubtedly influence his future growth.[19]

By mid-1955, Dr Zakir Husain decided to quit. He confided his decision to some close friends. His relations with Maulana Azad were no longer cordial. Perhaps, Azad had not forgotten the insult heaped on him at Aligarh. At the fag end of his innings in Aligarh, there were occasions when opposition to Dr Zakir Husain was vocal and bitter. He had become unpopular for reducing Moharram holidays from ten to two and making Sunday the weekly off instead of Friday. He was equally stern against the practice prevalent among some students of gaining seniority by continuing their stay on campus. A few days before he left Aligarh, he made a speech expressing more plainly that he had lost hope of achieving anything worthwhile at the university.

Dr Zakir Husain left Aligarh in 1956, a year before the expiry of his term. For his friend, Rashid Ahmad Siddique, it was a symptom of Aligarh's failure to reconcile with its role in history. 'Its group hostility, the conservative-radical dichotomy which invariably surfaced in terms of "government lackeys" and "devil's advocates" has continued to sap its energy since independence,' observed Salman Khurshid, a former union minister and grandson of Dr Zakir Husain.[20]

By the time Dr Zakir Husain left Aligarh, academic standards had been restored, and the university was functioning like any other in the country. However, there were some disquieting trends, which later on were to surface dramatically. First, there was a yawning gap on the campus between groups with leftist sympathies (labelled as 'communists' by their opponents), and the more traditional elements soon to be branded as 'communalists' and 'obscurantists'. Second, there was unrelenting pressure from the old city of Aligarh and degree colleges, where people were unprepared to tolerate what they described as a 'Pakistan outpost' at their door.

Even in 2020, hitting back at the Union Government panel that suggested the word 'Muslim' be dropped from the name of AMU, the university, in its formal response to the University Grants Commission (UGC), called the proposition 'preposterous' for ignoring the institution's long history and unique character. Criticising the panel for going beyond its mandate, AMU registrar Javaid Akhter wrote to the government,

> The name of the university gives us an idea about its history, purpose and character and preserving the same is our bounden Constitutional duty. The Panel incorrectly draws the conclusion that renaming AMU as Aligarh University would instil secular values. One must recall that in India, the concept of secularism arises more from the discourse of justice and equality than from an anti-religious position mostly practised in the West.[21]

There is an umbilical relationship between the two.

Dr Zakir Husain was succeeded by Col. Bashir Husain Zaidi, who completed his six-year term. To quote Zaidi's successor Badruddin Tyabji, during that time Aligarh had acquired 'a sullied image'. Fights among student groups had become common.

There was, as usual, much speculation on who would succeed Col. Zaidi. The pro-vice-chancellor Dr Yusuf Husain (Dr Zakir Husain's brother), a historian and notable scholar of Urdu literature with a doctorate from Sorbonne University (France), was a natural choice. But he had not got along well with Col. Zaidi, despite the latter's close friendship with his brother, Dr Zakir Husain.

In his autobiography, Tyabji remarked:

> Dr Yusuf Husain's conservative views about how the university should be run and on Muslim education contradicted the current secular trend in politics and social life in India. They were also out of keeping with the objectives of a university that was almost entirely dependent on the bounty of the government. He seemed to underrate that this bounty could only be sustained if the university responded to the sentiments of the bulk of the Indian people, not only the Muslim community.[22]

The outgoing vice-chancellor proposed Tyabji's name in the Executive Council of the university. A section in the Executive Council led by an influential local figure opposed the name of Tyabji on the principle that a serving officer of the government should not be appointed as vice-chancellor as it would set a wrong precedent. The Urdu press also opposed his candidature, alleging that it was an obvious method employed by the government to deprive the premier Muslim educational institution in the country of its independence. According to the rules, two other names – those of Dr Yusuf Husain, the pro-vice-chancellor and Professor Mohammad Habib – were also bracketed with his. The visitor obviously chose Tyabji.

If Col. Zaidi, in the flights of Urdu poetic hyperbole in which Aligarh students excelled, was often likened to Shahjahan, a Mughal ruler known for his building, Tyabji was likened to Firoz Shah, the only recorded Indian medieval ruler who had made it a point to restore and repair the buildings constructed by his predecessors.[23]

Vishnu Sahay, an ICS colleague of Tyabji, had advised the latter before he joined the university as vice-chancellor that he would have to deal with many bearded people with *tasbihs* (rosaries) in their hands.[24] Still, he should not be alarmed by them. If he cultivated them, he would find them amenable to reason and persuasion. The persons about whom he had to be careful were those who grew beards but shaved off their moustaches. They were the tough nuts to crack, warned Sahay.

Tyabji later observed that though Sahay's hirsute classification of the old orthodox representatives of the Muslim gentry and theologians on the Aligarh campus was not wholly exact, it was a fair enough indication of the two distinct types to be found there. Both types were prominent and influential in university affairs. They were well represented on the various statutory bodies of the university, such as the Court and the Executive Council as well as its associated organisations such as the Old Boys' Association and the AIMEC, etc. They directly or indirectly exercised a powerful influence on the campus and the university's relations with the town, if not the rest of the country. They had, through their long personal or family association with the university, acquired almost a proprietary right in its affairs.

Tyabji ran the university with a firm hand. Recalling his stay on the campus, he said considerable change was required in both the working of the university and the manner of conducting its business. Hitherto, this had been carried out on the pattern of an old feudal principality, with the vice-chancellor functioning more or less as its *rajah* or *nawab*. Reforms he initiated were viewed with suspicion, and the initial unpopularity, if not hostility, that the vice-chancellor had to face was not easy to bear. But gradually, most people, especially the students, began to appreciate the merits of the new working system. It resulted in quicker and more purposeful disposal of business. It also succeeded in creating a feeling of confidence in everyone.

Tayabji was amazed when he was about to take over as the vice-chancellor at the quality and scale of entertainment proffered by some provosts of halls as a farewell gesture to his predecessor and incidentally also to welcome him. Initially, he thought the provosts were exceptionally generous and rich individuals imbued with a real Harun-al-Rashid spirit. Later, when he found that all the expenditure incurred had to be borne by the hall students and had a crippling impact on their mess bills, he was disgusted.

He took immediate steps to stop this practice. To improve catering arrangements and management of the halls, he made drastic changes in their administrative personnel. Hitherto, provosts had been selected from among the most senior teachers. The appointments were considered an official favour and recognition of their social eminence. The special allowance was treated as a part of the other perquisites that went with the post, such as disposition and utilisation, for the benefit, of the considerable domestic staff of the halls. In Tyabji's view, the discharge of such administrative chores was below the dignity of professors. Therefore, he decided to appoint readers in their place. He claimed that the change in the system brought about a marked improvement in the management of the halls and their catering.

Tyabji regretted that not a single non-Muslim had been elected to any students' union post following the communal riots that engulfed several towns in west Uttar Pradesh in 1962, notwithstanding his strong plea in his Sir Syed Day speech to impress on the students the need for making Aligarh what he called 'the spearhead of national integration'.

He was a stickler for rules. Recalling the days of Tyabji as vice-chancellor, Basir Ahmed Khan, president of the AMUSU in 1964, said that when Prime Minister Nehru arrived to attend the Sir Syed Day function, Tyabji and his wife reached the helipad in their personal car to receive the guest. Tyabji always followed the rules he framed for others. Even the security men could not follow the prime minister in uniform because Tyabji was averse to the presence of policemen on campus.[25]

On another occasion, the then district magistrate of Aligarh requested the vice-chancellor to postpone the elections to the AMUSU as the town was reeling under communal tension. Tyabji refused, saying, 'The town is your problem. If you cannot maintain law and order, hand over the town to me. I will deal with the problem. But I do not seek your opinion in running the university.' And he went ahead with the elections as scheduled. There was no problem whatsoever.

Ali Yavar Jung succeeded Tyabji. When Professor A.A. Suroor (Urdu) asked Tyabji in his last meeting of the Academic Council about the new vice-chancellor, Tyabji said, 'You people will forget me'.[26] But destiny had decreed otherwise. The tenure of Jung proved a landmark in the chequered history of AMU. A minor incident blew into a murderous attack on the vice-chancellor on 25 April 1965, tarnishing the fair name of AMU forever and leading to an unending quest for the minority character of the university.

8

An Ugly 'Aberration'

'Why do you want to take my life?' pleaded suave vice-chancellor Ali Yavar Jung in a trembling voice as a student armed with a knife pounced upon him in room number 132 of the then Sir Syed Hall (East). The boy wanted his resignation. The vice-chancellor readily conceded. He asked P.V. George, then assistant registrar, who was accompanying him, to arrange for a pen and scribbled on a paper, 'I, Ali Yavar Jung, the VC of the AMU, hereby resign'.[1] The stone tablet outside the room, a mute witness to the incident, silently proclaimed that Jung's maternal grandfather made donation to construct the room. The resignation was handed over to Basir Ahmed Khan, Convener of the Action Committee and former president of the AMUSU, who was waiting outside along with university officials and students.

Earlier, the vice-chancellor had to run for his life from a meeting of the University Court in the students' union hall when rampaging students entered the hall. The meeting had been a stormy one, as one of the items on the agenda was the election of the university treasurer. Obaidur Rahman Sherwani had lost the election by a wide margin to Kunwar Ammar Ahmad. His nephew, Anisur Rahman Khan Sherwani, came out of the meeting hall and signalled the news of his uncle's defeat to his supporters. Already restive, the sizeable number of students outside the hall mistook it for losing the case before the University Court for enhancing the percentage of internal candidates in admissions to various courses and became more agitated. Later, senior court members and university dons pacified the students.

Meanwhile, Iqbal Ahmed Khan, nicknamed Barula, senior proctorial monitor, slapped a student who wanted to drink the iced water in an earthen pitcher outside the meeting hall. After a few minutes, a group of students gatecrashed into the meeting hall, chasing Barula, who had rushed there to save his life. When confronted by senior teachers, the students said they wanted to teach Barula a lesson for the incident. Justice Bashir Ahmad Sayeed (a retired judge of the Madras High Court and an eminent educationist, reverentially known as 'Sir Syed of the South'), who was a nominee of the visitor on the court, asked a university official to call the police. Accordingly, the proctor's office was contacted. As luck would have it, the usually unreliable internal telephone system was working at the crucial time, and the Superintendent of Police S.K. Shanglu, an upright officer, was requested help.

Post-haste, the officer mobilised reserve forces from the police lines and reached the university. The vice-chancellor had already expressed apprehension of trouble that day. On sighting the police, the students became unruly and began stone pelting. A stone struck a constable. In retaliation, a policeman fired. Two boys were injured. None was a student. They were passers-by. The teachers exited the meeting hall and asked the police chief to withdraw. The police had come through the Victoria Gate. M.M. Siddiqui, registrar, and Dr Abdul Bashir Khan, Professor of Zoology and a member of the Uttar Pradesh Legislative Assembly from Aligarh City constituency on a Republican Party of India ticket, rebuked the police chief for entering the university portals without permission. They were not aware that police assistance had been sought. The police chief ordered his force to retreat but had to pay a price. The state government later asked him to explain his retreat without ensuring adequate protection for the vice-chancellor.

In the melee, Jung ducked beneath a table. The court members, including the Nawab of Chhatari, were manhandled by the students. Even senior teachers, including Professor Yusuf Husain

Khan, pro-vice-chancellor and younger brother of Dr Zakir Husain, Proctor Nasir Ali, A.A. Suroor and Nurul Hasan were not spared. In the meantime, someone switched on the university siren installed on the rooftop of S.S. Hall. Students began assembling from other hostels too.

The vice-chancellor left the meeting hall for his lodge, but he inadvertently turned towards S.S. Hall. As he had joined the university only a few days earlier, he was unfamiliar with its layout. Registrar M.M. Siddiqui tried in vain to stop him from turning in that direction. A student swung an iron rod at Jung's head. Instinctively, Jung had placed his hands on his head. His fingers broke as they bore the brunt of the blow. He also received as many as 30 stitches on his head. A few minutes later, he resigned under threat to his life.

He was taken to his residence in an ambulance. His predecessors, Col. Zaidi and Badruddin Tyabji, arrived from New Delhi to get him admitted to a private nursing home there. Jung narrowly escaped from the jaws of death. He returned to the university in August to continue for less than three years, mainly operating from his residence. The murderous attack led to the arrest of Justice Bashir Ahmad Sayeed (retd), the university's registrar, besides several student leaders. Shamshad Ahmad, a court member, who was district magistrate of the neighbouring Bulandshahr district, was reprimanded by the government for failing to discharge his duties as a government official present on the incident site.

Something unprecedented had taken place. Jung's predecessor Badruddin Tyabji had increased reservations in admission for internal candidates from 50 to 75 per cent. Beneficiaries belonged to both communities. At that time, the number of Hindu boys in science courses was almost half the total strength. The new vice-chancellor decided to revert to a reservation of 50 per cent, leading the students to go on the warpath. They were already sceptical because Jung, as vice-chancellor of Osmania University, Hyderabad, had changed the medium of instruction from Urdu to English. The decision received an adverse reaction from the Muslim community.

Two days earlier, on 22 April, a delegation of student leaders had gone to the guesthouse (now the old guesthouse) to apprise Justice Sayeed of their demand. Incidentally, the vice-chancellor had been at the guesthouse when the students emerged from Justice Sayeed's room. This meeting was construed as a part of the conspiracy hatched to assault the vice-chancellor.

Dr Abdul Jalil Faridi, a reputable medical practitioner in Lucknow, who later emerged as a front-rank Muslim leader demanding restoration of the minority character of the university, was also staying in the guesthouse. He was at the university to attend a meeting of a selection committee to which he had been invited as an expert. He was a member of the Uttar Pradesh Legislative Council as the Praja Socialist Party (PSP) nominee. He was resting on a chair on the veranda. The student leaders approached him for help to resolve the issue, but he refused point blank to intervene in the internal affairs of the university. He withdrew into his room, saying, 'It is time for *maghrib* prayers'. Later, however, he did not shy away from using the AMU issue to incite Muslims.[2]

The president of the AMUSU had managed to leave the university under the pretext that his *phuphi* (paternal aunt) was ill. Some self-appointed supporters of the university administration had assured the vice-chancellor that the issue would be resolved amicably. Senior proctorial monitor Barula was prominent among those who sided with the administration on this issue. Later, during the regime of Professor A.M. Khusro, he was rewarded with a teaching job in the Theology department.

Dr Mohsin Raza, President of the AMU Students Union 1966–67, has given slightly different versions of the ugly incidents and held the vice-chancellor responsible for the behaviour of unruly students.[3] He blamed outsiders and non-students for inciting the violence. He has given room no. 135 in his version. According to him, the issue of reducing reservation percentage was not on the agenda of the meeting, but the students had gathered in large numbers, thinking that the crucial issue would be taken up.

A deceptive lull descended on the campus. On 27 April, pro-vice-chancellor Yusuf Husain Khan called Basir Ahmad Khan to inform him that the police were looking for him. Basir Ahmad Khan surrendered and was lodged in the district prison in the company of the registrar and Justice Bashir Ahmad Sayeed (retd). During the identification parade inside the prison, the benevolent vice-chancellor refused to identify the arrested persons, including students. Later, speaking on the AMU Amendment Bill (1979), Rasheed Masood (Janata) described the incident as a minor one and alleged that on this pretext, the university had been deprived of its minority character by the then government.[4] Dr Pratap Chandra Chunder, the then education minister, intervened to state that the university's autonomy was curbed in 1965 and 1972 by education ministers who were Muslims by faith. Masood retorted that the then-dictator (referring to Prime Minister Indira Gandhi) used to take away the rights of communities by putting members of those communities in the forefront.

The attack on the vice-chancellor turned out to be a turning point in the university's history. It was for the first time since Independence that the police had entered its portals. (Earlier, the police had entered the university only once to arrest Maulana Mohammad Ali, the veteran freedom fighter, and that too, during the struggle for Independence.)

The union government took the incidents seriously, and an ordinance suspending the University Court was issued on 29 May. Subsequently, the AMU (Amendment) Bill was passed in Parliament. The main amendment was brought about in Section 23(2) of the Act, which provided for the composition and powers of the court. Until then, the court had been the supreme governing body, with only one essential modification introduced in the 1951 amendment: the dropping of the clause providing for exclusive Muslim membership. Under the new rules, the court practically became a body nominated by the visitor (the President of India is the ex-officio visitor of the university), with merely an advisory role.

Recalling the incident in his autobiography, the then education minister M.C. Chagla stated that Badruddin Tyabji, the vice-chancellor, was a senior ICS officer of undoubted ability who had earned a reputation for himself in the External Affairs Ministry.[5] But, unfortunately, he was too impersonal and perhaps too rigid to keep friendly contact with students. Aligarh harboured a section of students who were bitterly communal and fanatic. There was also a section that was ultra-radical. Due to an eternal conflict between these two, most students uninterested in politics or ideology suffered adversely.

Chagla came to the conclusion that the AMU needed a change in leadership and also in the atmosphere prevailing there. This could only be brought about with a vice-chancellor who was forward-looking, flexible, and knew how to handle not only affairs but also people. He immediately thought of Nawab Ali Yavar Jung, the ambassador of India in Paris, who was a staunch nationalist and a man of progressive views. He was not acceptable to the bigots and communalists in the student community and also to those who represented this section in the court and the executive council of the university.

Chagla had reason to believe that students alone were not responsible for the attack. Others were hiding behind them. Some court members sympathised with the attackers and, instead of going to the rescue of the vice-chancellor, looked the other way. Chagla thought the vice-chancellor couldn't function in the existing set-up of the university. He, therefore, got the cabinet's approval for the promulgation of an ordinance by which the existing Executive Council and the court were dissolved, and the government was empowered to set up nominated bodies. He took pains to see that the persons nominated were sympathetic to the vice-chancellor and held similar views concerning the policy to be adopted in running the university.

A bitter raging campaign was started in the country by fanatical elements. Chagla was charged with being a dictator and interfering with the university's autonomy. It was alleged that Chagla was a

Khoja Muslim. A demand went up for the administration to be left to the Muslim community, which had a unique interest in its well-being, and for the ordinance to be revoked. Chagla reminded the agitators quietly but firmly that the AMU was not a minority institution as defined in the Constitution – that it was neither established nor maintained by the Muslim community, that it was a national institution in which the whole nation was interested, and that though it undoubtedly had a particular purpose to serve, namely the advancement of Arabic and Islamic studies, that did not change its essential character because even non-Muslims might have an interest in such studies.

Chagla recalls that during the agitation, he received hundreds of letters threatening him with assassination. Meetings were held to denounce him. A body called *Majlis-e-Mushawarat* was established to defend the 'cause', as the organisers saw it, of the university's autonomy. It convened many meetings where fiery speeches were delivered, arousing communal passions. An Aligarh Old Boys' Convention was called at Lucknow, inaugurated by Dr Syed Mahmood, a Bihar politician and Congressman of the old days. M. Nurie, who had many years earlier been a minister in Bombay and had then gone into retirement, resurfaced for the specific purpose of targeting Chagla and presided over the convention. He suggested a programme of action, which, he probably knew in advance, would remain only on paper. Having performed 'a noble and public duty', he returned to retirement and was not heard of again.

In the whole controversy, what was most painful and revealing to Chagla was the spectacle of the so-called 'nationalist Muslims' of the old days appearing in their true colours. Chagla had always believed that the Congress, in its eagerness to appease the minorities, had supported many Muslims who were communal at heart and had set them up as nationalist leaders before an unsuspecting public. He was glad these so-called 'nationalist Muslims' had been fully exposed during this controversy. Chagla clarified that the ordinance was intended to eliminate a minor, fanatic, obscurantist and reactionary section in the university, that it only dealt with the administrative set-up and that the Academic Council had not been affected.

As many as 22 members of the Academic Council of the university issued a statement condemning the agitation as being fomented by misguided people and emphasising the fact that a deliberate attempt was being made to gloss over the events that culminated in the attempted assassination of the vice-chancellor.[6] The express purpose was to prevent the public from focusing on the serious issues arising from this incident. They warned that the agitation would not only jeopardise the fundamental interests of the university but also impair the cause of national integration. They pointed out that the ordinance had in no way changed the character or academic life of the university.

The injured vice-chancellor was laid up in a hospital in Delhi for many days. Chagla prevailed upon him to resume his duties after he had fully recovered, and to his eternal credit, Jung did resume his duties. The minister described his decision as an act of faith and courage. After he took charge of his office, the vice-chancellor wrote a letter to Chagla in which he defined the true character of the university. He said,

> The AMU is intended to be a university which must maintain and promote high academic standards. It must be open to all, attract all-India talents, and at the same time remain designated as a Muslim University in the sense that it specialises in subjects connected with Muslim culture and is expected to have due regard for the claims of deserving Muslim students.[7]

Chagla replied that the government had not the slightest intention of changing the essential and basic character of the university.

The bill to replace the ordinance came before the Lok Sabha on 27 August 1965.[8] The atmosphere was heated and charged with emotion. Objections arose immediately that the bill went against the fundamental rights granted to religious and linguistic minorities in the Constitution. The Speaker refused to give a ruling, saying that the constitutionality or otherwise of an Act of Parliament should be decided by the Supreme Court, which upheld the view that the AMU was not a minority institution. Chagla asserted that AMU was not a theological convent but a national university.[9]

Chagla disclosed that he had received a letter from Dr Syed Mahmood asking him to consider the repercussions the ordinance would have in Pakistan.[10] His reply to this letter was that he was not worried about the reaction in Pakistan, which was always hostile to India. He also read a letter from the vice-chancellor, which said, 'It is largely due to the ordinance that we have been able, despite obstacles, to reopen the university under conditions of comparative calm.'

Law minister A.K. Sen piloted the bill in the Rajya Sabha on 14 September.[11] He quoted at length from the report of the vice-chancellor, who had pointed out that through years of maladministration, the university's management had become thoroughly inefficient and 'untrustworthy'. Delays in constituting selection committees for the appointment of teachers resulted in a large number of posts being usurped through temporary postings to create a coterie connected with those who were occupying the seats of power in the university. Close relatives of those in power filled up various posts. There was no financial adviser officially appointed to check and scrutinise the disbursement of funds, and so, on innumerable occasions, cheques issued by the university bounced. Accounts were in a hopeless state of confusion. It transpired vested interests had succeeded in rousing the passions of some of the student leaders, sometimes in the name of religion, sometimes in the name of Muslim interests.

One of the student leaders who had taken a prominent part in the violent agitation, the vice-chancellor informed, held a Pakistani passport.

It is painful for me, regretted Col Zaidi,

> to find that Muslims should be talking in terms of exclusiveness, of separatism. They want to shut themselves up in a sort of ivory tower. And we fall back upon Article 30 or various legal enactments

for our protection. I, for one, feel, and I am sure every sane, right-thinking Muslim will be with me, that the biggest guarantee for the prosperity, well-being and progress of Muslims in this country is not the provisions of the law but the goodwill and affection, the trust and friendship of the majority community. We, as a minority, cannot prosper unless we win for ourselves a niche and corner in the hearts of Hindus and the other communities of our country.

When the British, who were supposed to be in love with Muslims of India, left, what was the annual grant to the AMU? It was a paltry Rs 3 lakh. What is the annual recurring grant to the university today? I believe it is over Rs. 80 lakh. I can say before man and God with perfect truth and sincerity that had I been the VC of the BHU instead of the VC of the AMU, I could not have received greater help.[12]

Dr Tara Chand (nominated) observed:

The word 'communalism' has been overworked. It has been used inadvertently in different significances. In one meaning, communalism is vicious. I regard that attitude of mind that identifies the interests of that group exclusively and without considering the interests of the other groups in the country, that narrow outlook that creates suspicion or apprehension against other groups of citizens of this country I regard this as vicious communalism. Unfortunately, in both communities, such communalism does exist. There is another kind of communalism which I regard as harmless. There are many people among Muslims as well as among Hindus who think that they have their traditions, they have their own rules and laws, they have their own culture and ways of looking at the world and things. They desire that these traditions should be continued and that their young men and women should be trained in these traditions. How can we take exception to such an attitude of mind? There are conservative people all over the world in every nation. These conservative people also have their contributions to the life of the country. Such communalism exists in Aligarh Muslim University, as it exists outside the university. This communalism is not hostile to patriotism, love of the country and loyalty to the state. It would be a falsification of history if it were

> asserted in any quarter that AMU was not established by Muslims and primarily for the educational advancement of the Muslims in India.[13]

Agreeing with the minister that the attempt on the life of the vice-chancellor was a concerted and planned one, M.R. Masani (Swatantra) said there was nothing communal about it.[14] He declared that it was obscurantist, it was reactionary, but it was not communal. He said:

> The issue was between local people, people domiciled there and Indians from other parts of the country. There is no quota for Muslim students in this institution. The quota of 50 per cent was for people domiciled in Aligarh, whether Muslims or Hindus and 50 per cent for the rest of India, whomever they may be. The previous vice-chancellor shifted the proportion to 75 for local people and 25 for outsiders. The present VC attempted to change it back to enhance the standard of learning.

The Rajya Sabha passed the amendment bill on 16 September 1965. At least two cases were filed before the Supreme Court of India challenging the amendments of 1951 and 1965. The repeal of the Act was demanded by its opponents because Muslims were no longer represented in the management and administration of the AMU. On the other hand, Professor Nurul Hasan, M.C. Chagla's successor, was in favour of restoring the historic character of the university. Brought up and educated in liberal traditions and cosmopolitan environs of Lucknow and Allahabad, Nurul Hasan spelt out the historic character of the AMU. He thought that Sir Syed had founded the AMU with the mission of modernising Muslims in India.

The supporters of the 1965 Act pointed out that it was wrong to think that Muslim interests could be represented by Muslims alone in modern India. Even the Constitution did not subscribe to this view.

The first managing committee of MAO College, the forerunner of the AMU, had six non-Muslim members out of 22 on its executive committee. However, the first Act of the university, framed in 1920, specified that all members of the University Court should be Muslims. It subscribed to the British thesis that only Muslims could represent their interests. The thesis was rejected in the 1951 Amendment Act, necessitated by the constitutional mandate. Muslim leaders described the Act as a part of the sanitation programme to clean the debris left by the British rulers. Nobody vocally resented the changes in the Act.

By the time the 1965 Amendment Act was introduced, the political atmosphere in the country had begun to turn against Congress. Anti-Congress leaders propped up the image of Muslims as an amazingly reticent and sceptical community, compared to the time of Sir Syed following the 1857 Revolt. The attempts by the union government to bring AMU into the mainstream of central education were deliberately misconstrued by opponents in a bid to organise Muslims against Congress.

The Congress had been replaced in several north Indian states by coalition governments after the 1967 elections, and its strength in the Lok Sabha reduced drastically.

The electoral verdict evoked sharp reactions from Muslim leaders. Prime Minister Indira Gandhi appointed a cabinet subcommittee, which, in turn, recommended the constitution of the eight-member Beg Committee to look into the grievances of Muslims, which came out a few months later with a document to be hailed from all sides within the Muslim community. The Beg Committee indeed declared in unambiguous terms: 'Notwithstanding any judgement, decree or order of any Court or tribunal to the contrary, AMU shall be deemed to have been established by the Muslim minority of India as an educational institution of its choice. It shall be administered and managed as provided for in Articles 29 and 30 of the Constitution.'

However, Mrs Gandhi did not budge from the official stand. She asked her Minister of State for Education, Professor Nurul Hasan (earlier professor of history at AMU), to table the bill[15] to replace the 1965 Act with the AMU (Amendment) Act of 1972 towards the fag end of the Lok Sabha session. It was tabled on 31 May and passed the next day. After three days, it was tabled in the Rajya Sabha and passed the same day.[16]

Vocal sections among Muslims criticised the bill on two main grounds. First, it amplified the measures initiated in 1965 denying the AMU's minority character. Second, it concentrated too much power in the hands of the vice-chancellor, thus violating the principle of autonomy. Nurul Hasan said the bill had been designed to democratise the structure and functioning of the university by giving a more incredible voice to teachers and associating students in its administration. It would then liberate the university from the clutches of 'feudalists' and 'obscurantists', and make it a 'progressive' (and modern) institution.

Most Muslim leaders wanted to keep the issue alive to gain political mileage. Dr Faridi, who had refused to come to the rescue of students in 1965, emerged as the leader of the action committee for restoring minority character of the university. Assailing the 1972 Act, he said care had been taken not to give any representation to the Muslim community as such.[17] Class representation had been made the basis of representation in the court. The experts of Muslim culture and learning, Faridi continued, the AIMEC and the donors, had been denied representation in this great seat of Muslim culture, and representation had, instead, been given to trade unions, agriculturists and industrialists, and the number of nominated members increased.

The Beg Committee had recommended that, to give it an all-India character, 16 Muslim legislators, four from each zone, should be included. This recommendation, too, was not accepted. Representation to members of Parliament had increased to 10, but the recommendation of the committee that they be Muslims (which was in accordance with Article 16(5) of the Constitution) had been rejected. Thus, there was no guarantee that Muslims would remain in the majority in the University Court. Still, it was being loudly proclaimed by the Congress Party that the university would remain a Muslim university.

The fact was, in July 1971, the report of the Gajendragadkar Committee on University Education, constituted at the request of the UGC, was submitted. The AMU Act had to align with other universities in the country to implement the Committee's recommendations.

In some respects, the AMU Act of 1972 was unique. It reduced the role of the University Court to an advisory one but, at the same time, it gave representation to the teaching community on the Executive Council. This privilege was not extended to the non-teaching staff, which outnumbered the teaching staff. Professor Nurul Hasan, who piloted the bill and incurred the wrath of the Muslim orthodoxy, sold an ideology. For the first time, the AMU Students Union was made a statutory body. Before this Act, it was an organisation with voluntary membership. Moving the bill, Professor Nurul Hasan mentioned the demand for the restoration of the minority character to the university. He said it was a demand that was neither in the national interest nor in the interest of the university itself, nor of any section of the population, including the Muslim community.

S.A.H. Haqqi, the then head of the political science department in the university, wrote:

> If the AMU (Amendment) Act is indicative of New Delhi's new philosophy of education, nothing can perhaps be more revealing than the restructuring and staffing of the university's academic bodies and the involvement of the teachers therein ... One wonders whether it is an unmixed blessing for the VC to have been vested with an almost dictatorial position and to expose him, without a shield or buffer, to the vagaries of student power. [18]

Aligarh resounded to conservative slogans once again. The movement against the 'black law' of 1972 was launched under the aegis of the AMU Action Committee, comprising Aligarians. AMU became, both for Aligarians and ordinary Muslims of north India, a symbol of Muslim independence and self-reliance. The leaders of the action committee succeeded in whipping up emotions. The intensity of feeling and area of impact of the agitation extended beyond the traditional catchment area of the university in Uttar Pradesh and Bihar. Soon it was transformed into a national issue.

In 1973, amid a deepening crisis, a delegation of leading academicians and members of Parliament impressed upon Prime Minister Mrs Gandhi the need to reconsider the 1972 amendment. The education minister himself stated that he was not opposed to minor adjustments. Some statutes were eventually democratised. The main issue – the 'minority character' of AMU – was not touched and, over the years, it was to become an obsession. The AMU Action Committee carried on, never despairing, benefiting here and there with the help of some vigorous advocates and nawabs of Marris Road in Aligarh, who (having enjoyed their grip over the AMU and its forerunner, MAO College, since the beginning) were able to reactivate the crusade and press the Muslim demands.

Emergency was imposed in 1975 following widespread agitation against Mrs Gandhi and her party. In the 1977 elections, the Congress, led by Mrs Gandhi, received a severe drubbing. In several north Indian states, it was wiped out. Mrs Gandhi herself lost the Lok Sabha election. Soon after the announcement of the crucial Lok Sabha elections in January 1977, Arif Beg, a Janata Party leader from the Jana Sangh faction, said in Hyderabad: 'The Janata government will soon take steps to restore the minority character of AMU.'[19] During the election campaign, Morarji Desai, who later became the head of the first non-Congress government at the Centre, told Muslims that 'their interests, including the restoration of the original character of AMU, would receive the utmost priority of his government'.[20]

There was much discussion about the amendment to the AMU Act during the short-lived Janata regime. In a meeting at the residence of Union law minister Shanti Bhushan, where several representatives of Muslims were present besides education minister Dr P.C. Chunder, it was decided, in principle, to restore the minority character of AMU. However, both ministers expressed apprehension that if the demand for restoration of minority character were conceded, there would be a demand for reservation in admissions for Muslims. The Muslim representatives unanimously assured the ministers that no such demand would be raised. They maintained that their sole concern was that AMU should provide modern education to Muslims.

In a meeting with university educators and representatives of the Muslim community, a joint secretary to the government of India asked: 'Do you think that the suggested legislation will settle the problem?'[21] A non-Muslim participant replied, 'At least, it would resolve the present imbroglio'. At this juncture, the joint secretary quipped: Muslims have three problems. One is the issue of Urdu. With a place for Urdu in the three-language formula, it has been solved. The second is the Muslim Personal Law. The Government has iterated that it is not in favour of interfering in the Muslim Personal Law. The third problem is the AMU. Even if this problem is solved, Muslims will invent another problem.

In January 1978, The Minorities Commission was constituted by the Janata Government, the first non-Congress government at the Centre. It took up the AMU case as its first task. The Commission (comprising M.R. Masani, M.R.A. Ansari and noted educationist V.V. John), in its report to the government, regretted that the amendments to the 1920 Act by the AMU (Amendment) Act 1965 not only affected rights under Article 30 but also wholly undermined the autonomy of the university.[22] The Act provided for an immense concentration of power in the hands of a nominated vice-chancellor. This was entirely against the universally accepted principle of autonomous administration of universities.

The commission also commented: If the view taken by the Supreme Court in Azeez Basha's case is correct, it would mean that a religious or linguistic minority is debarred from establishing a university, which can only be established by an act of the central or state legislature. We cannot but share the regret of Hormasji 'Home' Maneckji Seervai (a leading constitutional lawyer), which he expressed before the Minorities Commission in the following terms:

> It is the first case in which the Supreme Court has departed from the broad spirit in which it had decided cases on the cultural and educational rights of minorities ... It is submitted that the decision is wrong and productive of grave public mischief, and it should be overruled.[23]

However, Minoo Masani, the first chairman of the Minorities Commission rued, 'The Government at that time, the Janata Government, behaved in a partisan manner and refused to accept the fact that Aligarh is a Muslim Institution, though our Commission, after proper research and study, concluded that the Aligarh Muslim University is a Muslim Institution.'[24]

Moving the AMU Amendment Bill (1979) on 3 May 1979, Dr P.C. Chunder cited the opinion of the Minorities Commission to which the Bill had been referred for consideration.[25] The Minorities Commission had opined that the 1979 Bill was a welcome step towards the restoration of the autonomy of the university with the power to make statutes. Additionally, the compositions of the court, Executive Council and Finance Committee of the university were to be restored to the pre-1951 Act of statutes. These changes fully met the criteria of an autonomous institution.

The education minister said:

> The various committees that have been set up could not agree on what could be the definition of the word 'university' in the statute. The Beg Committee thought there should be a special provision that the university should be 'deemed to have been established' by Muslims of India. The word 'deemed' was used, meaning thereby that the Beg Committee was not entirely satisfied that Muslims of India established the university. The word 'deemed' meant that something untrue is taken to be true.

The university set up another Committee, headed by the then vice-chancellor Professor A.M. Khusro. It stated that 'University' meant the university (AMU) established by Muslims of India.

The Minorities Commission also dealt with defining the word 'university'. 'University means the educational institution of their choice established by Muslims of India, which was incorporated and designated as Aligarh Muslim University of 1920.' G.M. Banatwalla (Muslim League) introduced a private member bill in which he reiterated that 'university' meant the educational institution of their choice, established by Muslims of India.

Participating in the debate, Banatwalla said the definition of the word 'university' should be in accordance with the suggestion of the Minorities Commission, which gave the university protection under Article 30(A) of the Constitution. Saugata Roy (Congress) pointed out that while resigning as Chairman of the Minorities Commission, M.R. Masani had alleged that the Commission was not taken into confidence while drafting the amendment bill.[26]

Somnath Chatterjee of the Communist Party of India (Marxist) forewarned:

> It has been a sad experience in this country that wherever or whenever the strict minority character has been conceded in an educational institution, democratic functioning has been hampered, which Muslims would not tolerate or accept. He warned against any institution which may give rise to coteries coming into power and control in the name of maintaining a particular character and called for efforts to protect the great institution of learning from falling into the control of a handful of persons representing vested interests.[27]

The bill was adopted unanimously by the Lok Sabha on 3 May 1979. Still, the government was reluctant to take it to the Rajya Sabha, where the Congress, then in opposition, was in the majority. Before the impasse could be tackled, the Janata Government fell in July 1979.

In December 1979, every political party mentioned AMU issue in its election manifesto. The Congress maintained that the minority character of AMU would be assured. The Janata Party stated in unambiguous terms that it would give priority to enacting appropriate legislation for restoring the autonomy and original character of the university as an institution for oriental and Islamic studies and for the promotion of educational and cultural advancement primarily of the Muslim community. The Lok Dal (of Charan Singh) said that amendments by legislation governing the university during the days of Indira Gandhi would be annulled and the university's minority character restored.

Muslims, on account of excesses during the Emergency, had turned against the Congress in the 1977 Lok Sabha elections. The established Muslim leadership in Congress successfully sold the theory that Muslims drifted away from the party, which cost it dearly regarding electoral permutations and combinations. Mrs Gandhi was desperate. Then came the 1980 Indira–Congress victory. Muslims had not been hostile to her party this time. However, the community leaders persuaded her that she should reward Muslims and presented the case for restoring the 'minority character' of AMU as a first move in a politically expedient manner.

The Congress cleverly passed on the blame for the 1972 bill to her then-education minister Professor Nurul Hasan who was portrayed as the villain. He was suitably rewarded later for saving Mrs Gandhi's skin and for owning responsibility for bringing in the 1972 Act. Arif Mohammad Khan, one of the leaders of the action committee and a survivor of political games, had deserted the Janata Party to join the bandwagon of Mrs Gandhi in 1979. The same year, Triloki Singh of the Congress moved a private member bill in the Rajya Sabha. His definition was that the AMU should be 'deemed to have been established at the instance of Muslims in India'.[28]

Shankaranand, the then education minister, moved the 1980 Amendment bill in the Lok Sabha.[29] It was a 'single clause' bill that limited itself to seeking to amend the definition of 'university' in the AMU Act 1920. It would hold that Muslims of India established the university. Later, the education minister withdrew the bill. In 1980, the Congress government brought in one bill, withdrew it and brought in another and then withdrew it again.

The issue caused embarrassment to successive central governments. No less than four times, amendments turned abortive. The simple matter developed into a constitutional and political confrontation antagonising the minorities. Challenges and stakes were portrayed as dangerously high before the *millat*, an incredibly diverse population. Mrs Sheila Kaul, education minister in the Indira Gandhi government, successor of Shankaranand, rushed the AMU (Third Amendment) bill through Parliament on 22 December 1981 at the fag end of the session. There were no severe objections to any provision of the new document.

The ensuing debates in both Houses lent colour to the issue. Dr Subramaniam Swamy (Janata) pointed out that until then, the academic, appointment and faculty have been dominated by two or three families which showed a particular affinity for the CPI(M).[30] About 35 relatives of one family happened to be employed at the university. One so-called Marxist academician lived in a 40-room mansion, drove a Toyota car, and so on. This structural change would mean the loss of power of this oligarchy.

Chitta Basu (Forward Block), on a special discussion in the Rajya Sabha, said:

> The House should not remain in the oblivion of the existing state of affairs in the university, and it has to be examined as to what extent the present bill can rectify the malady which exists today. One of the maladies is deliberate encouragement given by certain quarters within the university campus to communal forces. Another malady is the violation of the rules of academic appointments. I am told that even research degrees are awarded by proxy. Somebody does the research work, and a doctorate degree is conferred on somebody else. This is a very extraordinary malady. It is also seen that certain sections within the administration want to convert the administration as an instrument of their self-aggrandisement.[31]

Syed Shahabuddin said:

> This bill is the culmination of a long struggle, which began 15 years ago when the rights and functions of the university were distorted by two successive enactments of 1965 and 1972. Since then, national politics has had its Aligarh movements and Muslim politics, of course, has been completely hypnotised by the Aligarh trauma ... We have been talking about the various characters of AMU. This poor university seems to be rather 'characterless'. We talk about its minority character, its historical character, its secular character, its democratic character, its autonomous character, its national character, its communal character ... perhaps its Congress character, its Islamic character, its feudal character, but nobody talks about its character as a university. Nobody talks about its character as a centre of learning, a centre of education, or a centre of excellence in a minority institution.
>
> We have to look at the functional aspects of the matter. What is a university if not a cooperative venture, a cooperative undertaking between the teachers, the students and the management? The question is who teaches, who is taught and what is taught, and who manages it?
>
> The AMU has to provide facilities for modern, secular education in all its complexities and diversities. It is not to produce *mullas*, but young men who will stand up with confidence and march shoulder to shoulder with the rest of the country in building the nation. I, therefore, believe ... that even doctrines, political, economic and social, inconsistent with Islam should and must be taught in the university; there should be no doubt about it. But we do not like the university to be a fundamentalist university.[32]

Dr Swarup Singh (former vice-chancellor of Delhi University) said:

> Aligarh is a political constituency ... Has anybody bothered about Muslims? And non-issues become issues. Aligarh has become an issue. Then (several) thousand Muslim boys are there. But what about the hundreds of thousands of Muslim boys who cannot get a chance to get an education? What about their jobs? Everybody is

> bothered about Aligarh ... We have driven Muslims of India into a corner to such an extent that they say, "Give us minority character." Minority complex is a complex of self-pity ... If a Muslim feels self-pity, it is a judgement of all of us.
>
> Everybody has been saying that the minority character has to be restored and is being restored. I would say that the 1965 Act, the 1972 Act, etc. have not taken away the minority character. And you may condemn Dr Nurul Hasan as much as you like. But the fact is that he had tried to perform a very excellent service to AMU. What had happened was that the powers of the Court had been taken away. Throughout the country in all the universities, the powers of the Court have been taken away. And there is a reason. At one time, the Court could elect the VC.[33]

Professor Rasheeduddin Khan (Nominated) observed:

> The whole ethos of Aligarh is an attempt to develop a certain personality, particularly among Muslims. This was not, if I may say so, a minority character. This was not even an exclusive character. It was a most positive revolutionary character that Sir Syed wanted to restore to the people of India, particularly the educationally and economically backward Muslims of India ... The number of Muslims in the University of Calicut and my impression of Osmania University is much more than the number of Muslim students on the rolls of the AMU. It is, therefore, one of the universities where Muslims also come for education or higher education. One must remember the all-India spread of the Muslim people and the regional variations. When discussing Muslim education, we are not only talking about Aligarh. Aligarh's importance is there, but it should not be confused with Muslim education. Therefore, whatever you do to Aligarh, you are not doing to the whole mosaic of Muslims who account for 13 per cent of the total population of India ... You are looking for Muslims in Uttar Pradesh, that too of the five or six districts from which 70 to 80 per cent of Muslim students come to Aligarh. The AMU Court is a very unwieldy one. In all the other central universities, it is tiny. It was not wise to include as large a number as this ... Secondly, it is just not possible to give such supreme governing

> power to the court. In every university in India today, the powers should be restored to the executive committee and the VC, which are answerable to the court on one side and the academic council on the other. Under the present circumstances, the VC can't run the institution ... Thirdly, it should have been a deliberative body, as originally it was meant to be, to have a larger outlook about the policies and review the principles of the university and not act as its governing body.[34]

The bill was also passed in the Rajya Sabha. However, violence rocked Aligarh on 23 December. A bus of the Uttar Pradesh State Road Transport Corporation was torched by the agitating students of two local post-graduate colleges of Aligarh, who were demanding affiliation to the AMU.

When the great moment came, said Salman Khurshid, to reward Aligarh for its 15-year struggle to preserve its independence, there was no fanfare or celebration.[35] Almost as though the government did not know what it had done, it did not expect any public show of gratitude. For 15 years, a meaningless battle had been fought with transitory 'saviours' and 'savages' healing and drawing blood periodically. The real issues were lost soon after the battle began. The victory seemed hollow as a spate of stay orders from the Allahabad High Court virtually paralysed the implementation of the Act.

A large chunk of 25 seats remained unfilled due to the court case. The University Court functioned without it. In 1999, the court case was settled as the parties resolved the issue amicably out of court. However, 25 seats for the AMU Old Boys could not be filled because the AMU Old Boys Association, and its Aligarh chapter alone, insisted on sending a list of its representatives. Former vice-chancellor Saiyid Hamid, too, supported the old boys in this regard. The university administration wanted to hold polls among the old boys for filling these seats, at par with the standard practice in other universities.

Strange is the university's functioning, like any other institution in the country. Piquant is the story of the Art Gallery, which Professor Iftikhar Alam Khan, museologist has investigated:

> The majestic building of AMU, at an important trisection of roads inside the campus, is an Art Gallery named after Moinuddin (1877–1932), who hailed from a reputed family of Meerut. He taught oriental languages at the Bombay's Wilson College. In 1924, he wrote a letter to AMU asking it to take away all his paintings and preserve them in a hall constructed out of the money he would provide to the university. He also instituted an endowment. On June 30, 1924, in the Executive Council meeting of AMU, Moinuddin's proposal (letter of Moinuddin to AMU, dated June 2, 1924) was discussed at length, which reveals that an amount of Rs 8,000 for the building, and Rs 20,000 endowment, was offered. Eventually, in January 1926, an agreement between Moinuddin and AMU was signed. By October 1928, the building for the Art Gallery was ready, and the paintings gifted by Moinuddin were displayed in the Gallery by 1929. Moinuddin made a further donation of Rs 25,000 for the upkeep of the Art Gallery. A total of 299 paintings (out of which 261 were oil paintings), including the Italian, French and English ones, were there.[36]

Qayyum Husain was appointed as the curator, and in the early 1930s, a few more paintings were added to the gallery. By mid-1930s, however, AMU appears to have begun to neglect the Art Gallery. In May 1936, a proposal emerged to use the Art Gallery as a cinema hall. Instead, the gymnasium hall was proposed to be used as a cinema hall. It was proposed that The Art Gallery (also called Picture Gallery) be used for technology classes. Around that time, another proposal was mooted to use the Art Gallery as a radio broadcast house for the next few years. Attached to this very building, AMU's automatic telephone exchange also began to run in 1937.

Around 1938, it was found that out of 376 paintings, only 321 could be traced. Rest was lost. By April 1940, more big-size paintings were lost. By 1942, this Gallery came under the Engineering College. Thus, the art and paintings suffered gross negligence, but the building meant for that became more critical. By 1945, when the Muslim League gained strength inside the campus, and correspondingly, art and paintings kept losing importance to the extent that the paintings of the Art Gallery had to be shifted into another building. So much honouring the will (*wasiyat*) of the donor, Moinuddin! As if this was not enough, by the 1950s, the Art Gallery came to house a canteen. Its upper section was the Archaeology Section of the Dept of History. The canteen contractor, Rampur's Javed Kamal, also ran a club of poets and writers in the canteen. In 1987, Syed Hashim Ali, the then vice-chancellor, renovated the building for the purpose of running the canteen on a bigger scale. The wife of Hayatullah Ansari, Editor Quami Awaz and a Congress member of the Rajya Sabha, was the niece of Moinuddin Ahmed. She happened to have visited the AMU around 1987. She sternly objected to the violation of the will of the donor. She was assured that once the UGC sanctions and releases an amount for the canteen building, the Art Gallery would no longer be used as a canteen. The hundreds of the paintings lost are yet to be traced and retrieved. These might be costing several millions now. In 2004, the renowned writer Shamsur Rahman Faruqi (1935–2020) wrote a letter to the then vice-chancellor, Nasim Ahmad, asking him to trace the paintings. This is where the story of the tremendous loss of the paintings remains suspended. AMU's attitude towards art and painting and its wilful, brazen dishonour to the donor's will is evident.

9

HINDU AND MUSLIM BIGOTS JOIN HANDS

Following the 1965 Amendment Act, troublemakers shifted their theatre of action from Aligarh to Delhi following a tough stand taken by both the union and state governments. Professor Abdul Aleem, a senior faculty member, succeeded Ali Yavar Jung. For the first time since Independence, a professor of the university was elevated as its vice-chancellor.

With a good knowledge of Arabic, Abdul Aleem found an old manuscript on Aijaz-ul Qurân (Miracle of Koran) in Germany. He wrote his PhD thesis at Berlin University, editing it critically with notes and a covering article. He had taught at Lucknow University before he was appointed Professor and Head of the Arabic Department in Aligarh during the reign of Dr Zakir Husain. He was a convinced Leftist, a member of the undivided Communist Party of India (CPI); he served as the secretary in the first conference of Progressive Writers of India at Lucknow in 1936. Most young men at Aligarh followed his advice in academics and ideology. But as the vice-chancellor of AMU, he enacted a strictly neutral policy; despite that, he and the university remained a constant target of harassment from his Rightist opponents who never spared any opportunity to foment troubles. Teacher politicians encouraged some student leaders to challenge his religious faith publicly, tutoring others to shout their complaints outside his official residence past midnight. He would wake up, dress, and emerge out to listen to them. Sometimes he would weep, only to postpone all morning appointments on health grounds. Shamim Ahmad Khawaja, a reader in civil engineering at that time, when asked why he had built his house two furlongs farther from the utmost reach of Dodhpur on Zaheer Manzil Street (Nagla Road), replied, 'to buy night peace, and not to hear anything from the University until a big cannon is fired'.[1]

Three immediate predecessors of Professor Aleem were non-Sunnis, Colonel B.H. Zaidi was a Shia, Badruddin Tyabji was an Ismaili Bohra and Ali Yavar Jung was a Shia again. Shia–Sunni politics played out in the university, although there was nothing in common between Colonel Zaidi and Tyabji. Professor Aleem was a Sunni by faith, and had the qualities to satisfy both the union government and the Muslim community. His professed inclination towards the Left never created any problems with the government, while it endeared him to the liberal and progressive groups. When he felt his Leftist leanings were obstructing the smooth running of the show, he brought in Professor K.A. Nizami and Nawab Hasan Khan, who were believed to be in the right conservative group, at the helm of affairs.

Professor Aleem is remembered for being the most non-communicative vice-chancellor of AMU. More than 60 of his relatives worked in the university at that time. He embarked on a purging exercise and superannuated as many as 27 persons, including some senior teachers such as Hafizur Rahman, a professor of law. Later, he roped in Rashid-ul-Zafar, son of Hafizur Rahman (a friend of Justice Bashir Ahmad Khan, retd, and a Jamait i-Islami activist, who had been arrested on the charge of hatching a conspiracy to assault Ali Yavar Jung). Aleem's term, too, was not free of turbulence. Once, he was forced to walk from the office to his residence barefoot before a hostile crowd of more than 5,000 students who booed and abused him. Later, he was appointed chairman of the Urdu Board by the union government.

He relinquished the charge on 3 January 1974, just three days before the end of his five-year term. He handed the charge to the pro-vice chancellor, Khaleeq Ahmad Nizami, Professor of History. A. Aleem went on indefinite leave days before he was to submit his papers. This stratagem, many vice-chancellors followed later on for the sake of continuity until their successors were formally appointed. A. Aleem had appointed Professor Shafi of the geography department pro-vice-chancellor after Fazl-ur Rahman had left, who was to officiate as vice-chancellor. However, Nurul Hasan, Professor of History, got the decision altered in Nizami's favour. Nizami managed the university efficiently for about a year up to the winter of 1974, running three consecutive semesters in a year by suppressing the summer vacations under the approval of the Academic Council, which brought the university sessions to perfect order. On that performance, he should have been appointed regular vice-chancellor for the entire term, but perhaps for the controversy he provoked in his own department.

Professor Ali Mohammad Khusro joined the university as vice-chancellor on 20 December 1974. Professor Nizami was in the race for vice chancellorship, but some teachers opposed him. His detractors had the ear of Mohammad Yunus Khan, the visitor's nominee on the Executive Council, who convinced Mrs Gandhi that it would be catastrophic were Professor Nizami to be elevated as vice-chancellor. Professor Nurul Hasan, the then union education minister, was pleading Professor Nizami's case. A compromise was, however, worked out, and Professor Nizami was shunted out as Indian ambassador to Syria.

Khusro's case was pleaded by P.N. Haksar, the then advisor to Mrs Gandhi. He was also a favourite of Mohammad Yunus Khan. Besides possessing academic credentials, he was also a fixture at all *mehfils* (social gatherings) in Delhi.

When Professor Khusro joined the university, students were again on the warpath. There had been communal riots in and around Aligarh. Confronted with the problem of restoring peace on the campus, the new incumbent constituted a joint committee of representatives of students, teachers, old boys and non-teaching staff. It was left to this committee to evolve a defusing mechanism to contain the students' agitation for repeal of the 1972 Act. What came about in the form of the AMU Act 1981 was, to a great extent, the outcome of deliberations in this joint committee, although the constitution of the University Court, as stipulated in the AMU Act 1981, was not per its recommendations.

Professor Rais Ahmed told some newsmen, and rightly so, as evidenced after the storm, that he thought most students wanted to concentrate on their studies, unconcerned with politics. However, his statement caused unrest. The university closed down sine die in consequence, and two senior Professors, namely Rasheed uz Zafar of civil engineering and Shah Mashood Aalam, head of the zoology department, got suspended. Rahman Ali Khan, the Staff Association President, was there to keep the movement alive.

Khusro had been a Distinguished Professor at the Delhi School of Economics. In that capacity, he continued advising not only the concerned ministries in the Government of India but also several embassies in Delhi, particularly that of Thailand, often even after joining Aligarh. Son of a reputed Hyderabad family ascending to Sufis, he was polite, highly cultured, democratic and proud of leading the Students Union at Oxford. He had become vice-chancellor at an age younger than usual for this post. On his arrival, he was so popular that student leaders wanted to carry him from the railway station, all three kilometres long, to the vice-chancellor's lodge on their shoulders. Welcome ceremonies for Khusro's arrival were numerous; various unions and associations in the university invited him to their gatherings one by one, often reading an address in the versified eulogy.

In his acceptance speeches, he was charmingly fluent either in Urdu or English, quoting at ease choice verses of literary Masters, particularly of Mir Anees. Since then, Khusro continued to charm his listeners with his excellent oratory, even when he was invited after his term. On one occasion, Naseem Qureshi of the Urdu Department, himself a spell-bound orator from pre-Independence Muslim League times, paid him a tribute on his face: 'There are some whose eyes spell magic, here it's in thy tongue!'[2] At the cultural evenings of song and music, he would preside over in Kennedy Hall; the charm of his wife Tayeba was overwhelming.

Khusro soon appointed Professor M. Shafi of the Department of Geography as the pro-vice-chancellor to shoulder the bulk of internal administration. He spent morning office hours in his department engaging in teaching activities and noon to late night hours in the pro-vice chancellor's office. Khusro invited noted teachers of the university to a simple dinner in groups convenient enough to talk with informally. Occasionally, Khusro casually walked over to the staff club, adjacent to his lodge, for a decent chat. In the meeting room of this very Club, Ja'afar Reza 'Shailesh' Zaidi spoke one evening so eloquently against him as if to dethrone him. Replying at the end, Khusro did not only satisfy the listeners but also silenced everybody, including the disgruntled lot.

The honeymoon was soon over, and everybody indulged in open bargaining. On one such occasion, Khusro recalled an old maxim aloud: 'Everyone has a price, only if you can pay it.'[3] With demands, movements, picketing and hunger strikes, Khusro faced every attack from students, teachers and other employees. He reacted with the logic and understanding of an economist, saying the main problem of Aligarh consisted of cut-throat competition for the limited facilities that existed locally. As a remedy, he persuaded individuals to seek jobs outside Aligarh in the country or abroad instead of everybody rotting in the alma mater. Several countries in Africa and West Asia, besides Pakistan, had opened their doors to Indians, who had availed of those facilities for quite some time. Khusro granted long leaves without pay but with a lien to the teachers and other employees to take advantage of the opportunities for up to three years. Many of them overstayed, affecting the university adversely later.

During A.M. Khusro's period, the appointment of some Urdu Professors followed an exceptional line. Upon A.A. Suroor's retirement in 1973, Khursheed-ul Islam took charge of the Urdu Department as the solitary Professor and Head of the Department. His tenure would not have ended in a few years, and Khalil-ur

Rahman Aazmi was the next man in waiting, after which Qazi Abd-us Sattar would have followed. The former was a known scholar, critic and poet, and the latter a well-known fiction writer of Dara Shikoh's reputation and recipient of Padma Shree. Soon the struggle of succession warmed up, and Qazi, an informal Department Secretary looking after timetables, etc., accompanied Islam all the time in the office and at his house after office hours. Then at the eleventh hour, Qazi announced his candidature on the insistence of friends. In the selection committee, Islam pleaded as the Head of the Department to postpone the appointment as the two candidates were of equal merit so that, after the necessary UGC approval for an additional post of Urdu Professor, both of them would simultaneously be promoted in the next meeting of the committee. So, it was done, and the UGC obliged the university on the request in a year. But Khalil, suffering from leukaemia for years, succumbed to it before the meeting, bringing a sea change in the atmosphere of the department. Khalil's untimely demise was lamented for quite some time, but it provided the interested parties with the occasion for complex personal politics. Amidst these developments, intense lobbying started for and against Qazi, as the only qualified candidate according to the confidential proceedings of the earlier selection committee, and as the cruel intriguer against Khalil and the cause of his mental agony and death. One or two days before the interview, Islam told his colleagues in the department, 'He would support and appoint a Mediocre who knows just enough to fulfil his job, and not the wicked though a genius.'[4] Both the posts got filled, leaving the 'wicked' behind.

Khusro's term lasted five years. On account of his leadership qualities, this period remained comparatively tranquil. According to Salman Khurshid, Khusro was a brilliant economist and, in public relations, a diplomat par excellence.[5] Affable by temperament, Khusro approached the university with a highly accommodating attitude that permitted immense liberties to student leaders. Aligarh has a peculiar tradition of students acquiring 'seniority' by pursuing as many different courses as are available. Each time one course is completed, another form is submitted with the admission office. The influx of students from Bihar and Uttar Pradesh and the increasing pressure of volatile student leadership strained the university facilities and discipline. Still, Khusro was allowed to complete his term in relative peace.

There was another dubious tradition in Aligarh. The vice-chancellors have been in the habit of blaming their immediate predecessors for harbouring unwanted elements. Tyabji's successor, Ali Yavar Jung, was beaten up within three weeks of joining the university. Did Tyabji bring in unwanted elements? Did Jung encourage the unwanted elements that humiliated his successor Professor Aleem? Students' agitation, backed by unwanted elements, became a perennial problem. Turbulence is natural on any campus with more than 15,000 boarders.

Another significant contribution of Professor Khusro was that the students of the AMU were selected in large numbers in various competitive examinations during his tenure. Significant and substantial research work was undertaken with the return of peace. It is also a fact that two years of his tenure fell in the Emergency period. But he had taken charge a year before its imposition and continued for two years after the dreadful days were over. He protected those elements in the university who could have become victims of the Emergency. There was peace on the AMU campus compared to other universities in north India during those years. Barring two teachers, who were on the rolls of the banned *Jamait-i-Islami*, no one was arrested in Aligarh. They, too, were released shortly following Professor Khusro's intervention.

Professor Khusro had some great predecessors, including Dr Zakir Husain and Colonel Zaidi. Tyabji was a ruler in his own right, but Khusro ushered in an era of dialogue to resolve every issue. He believed in a modern, rational method of discussion and communication in the administration. He manoeuvred students towards the discussion table. He introduced the element of persuasion while dealing with the university community. Even then, his period was not trouble-free.

Once, students took to the roads protesting against an assault on some students by commuters on a train at Dadri on the Aligarh–Delhi route on 9 May 1979. The district administration ordered the university's closure and posted the Provincial Armed Constabulary (PAC) and Central Reserve Police Force (CRPF). Some shops in Shamshad Market and Zakaria Market were set ablaze. The police opened fire. Two passers-by were injured. Mediating between the students and police were some five-odd persons, including a barefoot Khusro, the proctor, and some deans.

Later, on 17 May, in a special discussion in the Rajya Sabha, CPI, Congress and Muslim League members on one side, and Jana Sangh members (who had merged with the Janata Party) on the other, traded allegations in a verbal duel. It was alleged that the district administration had posted the PAC on campus without the consent of the vice-chancellor. Initiating the discussion, Bhupesh Gupta (CPI) assailed the Uttar Pradesh chief minister for issuing a statement accusing students of attacking commuters.

However, Khusro managed to defuse the tension. At the same Shamshad Market, students clashed with police and several lives were lost during the subsequent tenures of Saiyid Hamid, Hashim Ali and later Professor M.N. Faruqui. Professor Khusro's tenure is described as the only one in the university when the administration was willing to listen to criticism. His administration was open, though this caused his successor, Saiyid Hamid, trouble. The latter became unacceptable to students who had become used to openness and resolving issues based on dialogue and consensus, a policy that was anathema to Saiyid Hamid.

After Professor Khusro relinquished the charge in December 1979, Professor Mohammad Shafi, pro-vice-chancellor, took over as acting vice-chancellor and continued till May 1980. He was succeeded by Professor Q.H. Farooquee and Dr J.N. Prasad for brief periods before Saiyid Hamid, a retired bureaucrat, took over in June 1980. Hamid said he was like a disciplinarian 'father to Aligarh students but was not willing to act as a mother'.[6]

Trouble erupted again on the AMU campus, which remained closed for several weeks. Hostels wore a deserted look. Relentless whisper campaigns began doing the rounds. The clash was portrayed effectively by a group as one between Muslim obscurantists and 'entrenched vested interests' in the university administration on one side and progressive and secular elements on the other.

The Hamid camp's followers alleged that to run their fiefdom, these vested interests required the help of anti-social elements to run their clique, who, in turn, demanded their pound of flesh for services rendered. No wonder in the preceding caretaker regimes, rules were flouted flagrantly, merit lists for admissions were tampered with, and corrupt practices were adopted to appease them. Some of these toughs were listed as part-time workers in the building section. But it was merely on paper to help them pocket a substantial amount as none of these beneficiaries ever performed his duties; the less lucky ones were rewarded from the funds of the Medical College in connivance with corrupt sections of teachers and employees of the university.

Understandably, whenever any vice-chancellor or any other important functionary attempted to put the university on dialysis to flush out the toxic elements or to put teaching work back on the rails, trouble erupted in one form or the other. Sometimes, ideological issues were also used as a smokescreen.

The same happened with Saiyid Hamid, a civil servant with distinguished innings in Uttar Pradesh. The situation in the university had deteriorated to such an extent during the preceding academic session that it required firm handling to tone up the administration. Though the vice-chancellor had the powers to nominate a sizeable number of students for various courses, barring medical, Professor Mohammad Shafi, as acting vice-chancellor, had exceeded all limits. Blank admission slips in lots were reportedly issued to student leaders. Sometimes, the slips were issued in advance for the next academic session. With bright academic credentials, Professor Shafi had the image of a strict administrator. It is a mystery why he acted as he did while discharging his duties as acting vice-chancellor.

Changes in the structure of courses and examinations to suit vested interests had been a little too frequent, even arbitrary. The university administration had flouted statutes with impunity on such matters as admissions, appointments, keeping of accounts and other administrative rules. Obviously, the laxity in examination rules led to falling standards. Favouritism and nepotism were rife on campus. Allegations abounded that the erosion of authority and discipline, which had crept in during the time of Professor Khusro, had increased manifold.

Even before the new vice-chancellor assumed charge, Professor Q.H. Farooquee and Dr J.N. Prasad, acting vice-chancellors in the absence of Professor Mohammad Shafi (who had proceeded on leave), had tried vainly to improve the situation. Dr Prasad was even roughed up in his office when he refused to dance to the tune of student leaders who were pressing for acceptance of their illegitimate demands.

The new vice-chancellor was considered a devout person, sympathetic to the cause of Islam, but not one to give in to Muslim obscurantism. His deft handling of the case of Jamalur Rehman, the acting registrar who was also a candidate for the post, made this evident to one and all. Jamalur Rahman's case was placed before the Executive Council, which met after a long gap on 12 July 1980. Professor Habib had been appointed dean of social sciences by being senior-most in the faculty. As an ex-officio member of the Executive Council, he pointed out the distortion in bio-data, suppression of facts and other irregularities in Rahman's application form. The civil servant in Hamid took strong exception to this bungling, and Rahman was asked to proceed on leave preparatory to retirement. Heartburn ensued in the circle of vested interests of which Rahman was stated to be the kingpin. Three days later, an emergency meeting of the Executive Council was held again to reconsider its decision, but the vice-chancellor refused to budge.

By being the dean, Dr Habib was an ex-officio member of every selection committee in the Faculty of Social Sciences. The vested interests saw a danger in it as Dr Habib was considered a stickler for rules. Their apprehension proved correct. In the selection for the post of a temporary lecturer in the Department of Psychology, Dr Habib insisted on adhering to merit as the sole criterion for appointment.

Three posts of readers in the History department were advertised in August 1980. Professor K.A. Nizami was the Head of the Department. Mrs Azra Alvi and Rafiq Alvi, daughter and son-in-law of Professor Nizami, were lecturers in the same department and had applied for the posts. Professor Nizami was apprehensive that Dr Habib would not let his relatives corner these posts.

The departments of Islamic Studies and West Asian Studies were also under the purview of the Faculty of Social Sciences. Entrenched old-timers knew that as long as Habib remained dean, they would not be able to resort to nepotism and favouritism in appointments. The dean carried weight in granting extensions to retiring teachers in the faculty. The unscrupulous elements mustered the strength to have Habib removed from their path by using ideological issues as a smokescreen. Syed Nasir Ali, a professor in the political science department on the verge of retirement, was stated to be a keen aspirant for the coveted post of dean. He was the next senior-most professor in his faculty. In the eventuality of Habib being eased out, he would have been elevated as the dean of the Faculty of Social Sciences.

Meanwhile, Hamid became a thorn in the flesh of the hooligans among the students because of his zeal for conducting examinations in a fair manner. As many as 256 students were caught cheating in the examinations conducted from July to September 1980 in the Faculty of Social Sciences alone. Manzar Safi, a notorious character, was one of them. Safi was admitted to the graduation course with political science (main) in the academic session 1977–78, and that too after the date of the last admission was over. After a gap of 20 years, he was readmitted. In early March 1980, he threatened Dr I.D. Pant of the Geology Department and told him that he had sent 20 Hindus to hell and would not mind adding a 21st to the list. Dr Pant reported the matter to the authorities, but no action was taken against Safi. Dr Pant resigned in protest. Later, he was persuaded by the authorities not to press for its acceptance and was assured of stringent action against Safi. A fine of Rs 50 was imposed, and Safi was asked to tender an unconditional apology, which he never did.

Safi faced several criminal charges concerning the infamous Sambhal communal riots of 1978. The district magistrate of Aligarh confirmed the charges after contacting his counterpart at Moradabad. Safi was a proclaimed offender as declared by the district administration but had been successfully evading arrest.

In the examinations on 5 July 1980, Safi was caught red-handed copying. The disciplinary committee, in its meeting five months later, decided to expel him from the university. But inexplicably, that decision was never communicated to him.

Three days before the meeting of the disciplinary committee, Dr Irfan Habib was attacked by a hockey-wielding group of hooligans near the vice-chancellor lodge while returning with his colleague Professor Athar Ali after research work in the late hours. Professor Athar Ali bore the brunt of the attack and sustained bruises on his right hand and palm while defending the feeble Habib. The guards at the vice-chancellor lodge rushed to the scene after hearing the cries of the victims. The professors went to the proctor to lodge a complaint, but the latter refused to leave his residence.

The matter was reported to the police, who arrested Waliullah Faridi, identified by Professor Habib as one of the assailants. A university student for 14 long years, he had been expelled earlier. Threats to Habib's life continued. The following day, armed policemen were posted at his residence. However, Professor Habib politely declined to have armed guards while discharging his duties on the campus.

On 17 December, Habib was mobbed in the dean's office. He was chased even as he fled to the Department of History in the same block. Had his colleagues and some saner students not come to his rescue, he would have been severely assaulted.

On the same day, Dr Habib and the vice-chancellor's effigies were paraded. A bitch, with the nameplate 'Irfan Habib' around her neck was dragged around by the processionists. Slogans like 'The VC is a snake in the grass' (*aasteen kaa saanp*) and 'The VC is a serpent in the bosom' rent the air. The university's walls were splattered with slogans like 'AMU is not Poland', 'Down with Communism', 'AMU is for Islam' and 'Habib is a Russian agent'.

The dean of social sciences had permitted a meeting of the All India Students' Federation (AISF), a frontal organisation of the CPI, on the faculty's premises sometime in late December. He was within his rights to grant such permission, and nothing was wrong with it. Other student organisations had earlier used the premises for holding meetings. Still, the vice-chancellor intervened and asked the proctor to stop the meeting. The action encouraged rowdy elements in their drive to hound out secular forces from the university.

The university reopened after the winter break on 5 January. Three days later, the vice-chancellor convened a meeting of senior students to introduce K.M. Bahauddin, the new pro-vice-chancellor. However, the meeting broke up in chaos when several students unleashed a virulent, scurrilous verbal attack not only on the vice-chancellor but also on the new incumbent. This was an indicator of the troubles in the offing. On 14 January 1981, several administrative transfers occurred, displacing entrenched interests from essential positions. Thee disgruntled elements were further alienated.

On 25 January, students carrying knives and country-made revolvers mobbed the vice-chancellor inside his residence. They demanded his resignation following his failure to suspend Professor Habib. The vice-chancellor tried in vain to pacify the agitators by announcing that the Executive Council had decided to hold a judicial enquiry into the charges levelled against Dr Habib. Finally, at the insistence of the enraged students, it was decided to ask Dr Habib to refrain from discharging his duties till the enquiry was completed.

The vice-chancellor remained a prisoner for three days inside his residence. With the situation seemingly out of control, the university authorities sought the district administration's help.

Police swung into action to get the hostels vacated. The university was closed sine die. The CRPF men remained unprovoked even amid slogans raised by a section of students against the authorities.

The scene could have become worse than in 1965 when vice-chancellor Ali Yavar Jung had been assaulted and university furniture burnt. The troublemakers had summoned bullies from neighbouring towns. Arson and murder would have followed had the administration not taken stringent measures to deal with the worsening situation.

This was not the first time secular and progressive forces were hounded out of the university. Under similar circumstances, Dr Rais Ahmad, the then dean of the science faculty, was forced to leave the university after he dared to remark that the students' union did not represent all students.

The venom spewing against secular forces continued. In a pamphlet, Shaukat Husain, President of the AMU unit of the Students Islamic Movement of India (SIMI), a frontal wing of the *Jamait-i-lslami*, urged the vice-chancellor to gird his loins to do something.

The atmosphere of the university was vitiated to the extent that scholars preferred to stay away. Dr Nurul Hasan, Vice-President of the Council of Scientific and Industrial Research (CSIR), was in town on 24 January when Dr Abdus Salam, the Nobel Laureate, was awarded an honorary degree. Dr Salam was visiting the country at the invitation of the CSIR. The vice-chancellor personally requested Dr Hasan to be present, but the latter politely declined as he was not prepared to be insulted by some students for his known secular views.

A section of students and teachers pointed out that out of three appointments made in the History department during the three-year tenure of Dr Habib as its head, two were Hindus. He was criticised for being close to the 'enemies' of Islam and Muslims. His support for the candidature of Dr K.P. Singh, instead of a Muslim, for membership of the Executive Council from the teachers' constituency was also questioned.

Another significant feature of the trouble during Hamid's reign was that Hindu reactionaries had joined their Muslim counterparts. A Rashtriya Swayamsewak Sangh (RSS) sympathiser, Professor R.C. Gaur (ancient Indian history) was perceived to be the leading advisor of Professor K.A. Nizami in departmental politics. Professor Nizami, head of the same department, was on the editorial board of *Manthan*, a research journal published by the Deen Dayal Historical Research Institute, an RSS outfit.

Dr B.P. Mitthal, a reader in the mechanical engineering department, known to have RSS links, sided with Muslim communalists against Dr Habib. No wonder Dr S.S. Gupta, another RSS fellow and the then principal of D.S. College, a local postgraduate college affiliated to Agra University, who had authored a book, *AMU in the National Context*, remarked at a public function that students of AMU were disciplined and justified in demanding the resignation of Dr Habib for his interview to a daily newspaper, which had brought a bad name to the university.

Several students with proven RSS track records, like S.K. Mishra, an engineering student, Suresh Kumar Sharma and S.K Bisaria, a medical student, sat on *dharna* demanding Habib's resignation. It was not a coincidence that Bisaria's father was a prominent RSS functionary in Delhi. Both the reactionary groups joined hands, claiming that they were devout. *Hum dono deen imaan wale hain* (We are both devout).

An interview given by Dr Irfan Habib to V.M. Qaiser, the *Indian Express* staff correspondent based at Aligarh, on the university affairs, forced Saiyid Hamid into isolation, which he could not shake off during his entire term. Dr Habib mentioned the presence of criminals inside the university and its hostels. No one bothered to take note of the observations made in the April 1981 issue of *Khair-o-Khabar*, an Urdu fortnightly, by the then office-bearers of the AMU Students' Union about the deteriorating conditions in the university.

Anwarul Yaqin, a lecturer of law at AMU pointed out the gradual deterioration in administrative efficiency, academic standards and moral discipline.

> The by-products are harassment and victimisation, favouritism and nepotism and manipulation in the selection of panels of experts and examiners; in the constitution of selection committees, in appointments and promotions and the award of scholarships and grants. Long delays in advertising posts, forming selection committees, filling vacancies, awarding scholarships and utilising grants are part of the mess.[7]

On 28 May, the police fired at a mob near the vice-chancellor lodge. One student was killed, and another was injured. The government instituted a judicial enquiry. Matters finally came to a head, resulting in the suspension of several student leaders from the university for six years.

Following the firing, the vice-chancellor resigned but was persuaded by the government to continue. Salman Khurshid's allegation that the victim, Aftab Mufti, was dragged 50 yards into the vice-chancellor lodge was far from true. According to independent eyewitnesses, the victim was only taken there by some boys and not dragged.

Analysing the AMU crisis during the reign of Sayyid Hamid, noted historian Professor Romila Thapar writes:

> Academic freedom in our society today is confined to or delimited by pressures of two kinds. The first is that academics themselves do not exercise the freedom which they can legitimately claim. To this extent, we academics tend to subordinate ourselves even where this is not necessary. The second pressure is political or governmental interference which seems to be on the increase judging by a large number of occasions when such interference is apparent.
>
> Indian universities were not established as they often were in Europe either as support to theological seminaries or later as centres of dissident opinion. Indian universities, when they were started in the nineteenth century, functioned as schools for producing professional groups to service British institutes in India. They also incidentally became a channel for access to middle-class status. Basically, they still perform the same function, and contrary or dissident opinion is not encouraged as part of the system.

> Added to this were the post-independence problems. The expansion of university education became part of economic development and the consequent spread of education. But this expansion was not centrally geared to the function and role of higher education since universities were often established from other considerations in which political factors were prominent.

Referring to the AMU crisis in particular, Professor Thapar stated that it was not merely over a newspaper interview given by one of the faculty members, Professor Irfan Habib, but had deeper roots in the conditions at AMU in terms of its relation with local political parties and the government. It was also a clear example of political parties using the students' union and pressurising the vice-chancellor in a show of strength. The events that led up to the crisis involved trouble over admissions of students who did not qualify or those involved in criminal activities as well as over students caught cheating in university examinations.[8]

In a letter to the AMU vice-chancellor, the president of the SIMI stated,

> We want that every teacher of the University should be loyal to the Islamic faith and community. He must not do anything detrimental to the interests of Islamic culture, community and this University. Not only the present statement of Irfan Habib but his attitude in the past as well was always inimical to Islam and the community.
>
> Therefore, in this case, taking advantage of loopholes in the law, we have to throw him out of the University. This question cannot be decided conclusively based on apparent legal principles. This action is a necessity for which we will have to find ways of circumventing the law.

Such sentiments expressed by multiple organisations on the AMU campus and elsewhere can only be described as Muslim communalism on the rampage. Academic freedom cannot be circumscribed by the needs of a particular group within a particular community. The right of individuals to hold and express diverse views on any aspect of life cannot be denied, especially in an academic institution. The attacks on individuals in universities should not be treated as isolated instances affecting the particular university but as trends that may further damage a deteriorating situation.

Throughout his reign, Saiyid Hamid remained opposed to those considered close to his predecessor, Professor Khusro and embarked on a witch-hunting expedition. He relinquished the charge on superannuation in March 1985.

His successor, Syed Hashim Ali, ruefully remarked:

> The vested interests within the university have always tried to keep it unstable. From Dr Zakir Husain till today, there was not a single V-C in whose term there was peace throughout. Anyone who tried to improve academic standards or follow the correct path was opposed because the moment it is stable, many things in which hard work is involved would become necessary for those who are not used to it.[9]

Professor N.M. Faruqui, deputy director of IIT Kharagpur, succeeded Hashim Ali. He tried his best to computerise the functioning of the university. It was the timely impetus at the right time. However, he was a pushover who could never say no to anyone and his nature was exploited to the hilt. Ms Najma Akhtar, controller of examinations, was the most powerful educator during his reign. A few months before the end of his term, Faruqui resigned.

In an article, Professor Mohammad Sajjad asked: Why are all the AMU troubles sine die?

> If assured of anonymity, significantly a large number of the insiders would share the "secret" that the student agitation at the AMU is an outcome of the fierce rivalry between the "warring" groups of teachers
>
> Is there a link between the "discomfiture" of the teachers/officers and those of the students? … In an unpublished brilliant essay on AMU, 1909-65, Prof. Hameeduddin Khan (1893-1974?), informs

> that the void (created by the teachers who migrated to Pakistan), was largely filled by the Left-leaning teachers, whose influence in the power structure of AMU enhanced particularly with the Amendment Act of 1965. Could they help "radicalising" the orientation of campus life? How and why did the Islamist outfits emerge on the campus?
>
> The teacher-officer-student nexus often forces the VCs to resort to populism, yet they feel helpless in dealing with the turmoil. The VCs depend upon the various internal lobbies for local support.... Even an upright V-C of impeccable credentials and capabilities can face enormous resistance, hindering him/her in confronting the lobbies (persistent centres of power whose support is so crucial for the VCs to complete their tenure) head-on and breaking the networks of kin-clan-faction-region-sub-region ties.[10]

M. Rahman, a career bureaucrat who succeeded Faruqui, did his bit to replace the prevailing anarchy with order. Unsurprisingly, he encountered tremendous opposition. Rahman's singular contribution was his relentless drive to free the AMU land of encroachment. It may be said that it cost him his desperate bid to get a second term because his drive had hurt vested interests, who ganged up against him. Prime land adjacent to the riding club faced a severe threat from land-grabbers who had already occupied a portion. The encroachments were removed, and about 100 acres of land were retrieved. In this vulnerable area, on 27 July 1995, the land-grabbers murdered Dr Rajiv Sharma, an innocent lecturer in the Department of History. He was president of the riding club.

The area was near Abdullah Hall and Women's College, known as *Kankarwali Kothi*. A Working Women's Hostel has been built on the property recovered from the encroachers. An open plot now fully protected by a boundary wall around the Nadeem Tareen Hall, Sir Syed Nagar, is worth crores. About 100 acres of land adjacent to the Institute of Agriculture have been recovered and enclosed by a boundary wall. Some shops at Shamshad Market have been recovered after evicting trespassers.

A plot of land opposite *Kankarwali Kothi* was also recovered from the land-grabbers. Construction of a boundary wall along the open land at Shamshad Market was started with fencing valuable land and property.

The university has an area of 55 lakh sq. metres. Out of the 72 land-related cases decided by the courts during Rahman's tenure, the university lost only two. Still 152 cases were pending when Rahman quit. Rahman's predecessor, Professor Faruqui, had also written to the Uttar Pradesh chief minister on 6 June 1994, 'The case of forcible occupation of land belonging to the university by unscrupulous people in collusion with undesirable and criminal elements has been a very thorny problem for us.'[11] He had also enclosed a list of such land.

Rahman was cool, which was good for him as the man in the hot seat he came in for a lot of flak during his tenure. His detractors alleged that he gave the university community the cold shoulder, and that he was aloof, dictatorial, given to using foul language, indulging in violence and shielding the corrupt. They thought that if there was a hell on this earth, it was here and the vice-chancellor was the devil who had destroyed the peace in the Garden of Eden.

Rahman, however, believed everybody was well cared for and happy. He used to say, 'I was hurt even if one student was hurt.'[12] He faced virulent propaganda and was accused of shielding corrupt vested interests. But he ensured safeguards for a foolproof examination system. He also successfully lambasted the well-entrenched left lobby among the teachers. Still, he lived in a fool's paradise if he did not realise the discontent brewing.

Rahman's successor, M. Hamid Ansari, should have been grateful to his predecessor for having cleansed the campus of many undesirable elements. Rahman had expelled several notorious students from the university. In one case, he himself lodged a report with the police against two notorious characters and succeeded in persuading the district administration to book them under the National Security Act.

Professor H.A.S. Jafri, who had joined AMU as a teacher and rose to become pro-vice-chancellor, recalls that when he joined during the reign of Syed Hamid, politics was at its peak in the university with one camp demanding the removal of Professor Rais Ahmad as the dean of science faculty, resulting in the rustication of Arif Mohammed Khan and later the suspension of two senior professors from the zoology and civil engineering departments. As he was against the demand for the removal of the dean of science faculty and against the suspension of the two teachers, Jafri faced the wrath of both camps. He soon discovered that the teachers and students were divided among Rampuris, Badayunis, Azamgarhis, Bihari, etc.[13]

Professor Jafri said one could easily discern the hidden hand behind most agitations in halls/hostels or against the vice-chancellors. To check this menace, one vice-chancellor liberalised the leave rules and sanctioned EOL (leave without pay) to a record number of teachers and thus completed his term more or less satisfactorily. Still, his successor, who took a severe view of this practice and terminated the services of more than 40 teachers, had to spend his entire term of five years dealing with agitators resulting in the sine-die closure of the university and the loss of life of an innocent student. The problem has since continued unabated.

Despite all opposition, outgoing vice-chancellor Syed Hamid had got the panel for the new vice-chancellor prepared well in advance and prevailed upon the government to immediately announce the name of his successor, who was already the vice-chancellor of another university at Hyderabad. The new appointee wanted some time to relinquish his existing charge and join. Still, the then union minister of education asked him to proceed to Aligarh immediately and hold simultaneous charge for both universities until his successor was appointed in Hyderabad.

The vice-chancellor was new to Aligarh but had vast experience as a distinguished bureaucrat and vice-chancellor of Osmania University, Hyderabad, where he was said to have carried out the same task of 'cleansing' the university. He called two prominent persons behind the agitation against his predecessor and had a closed-room meeting with them. Against one of them, an enquiry regarding his involvement in the agitation had been conclusively completed, and disciplinary action against him was on the anvil. The other person had some correspondence with the student agitators in his handwriting and could face severe disciplinary action. The vice-chancellor showed them their files and told them he would not initiate action if they promised not to bother him or get involved in dirty politics. Failing that, he would immediately take action. The trick worked, and both of them remained dormant during his tenure.

The following vice-chancellor, Professor N.M. Faruqui, considered getting Professor Jafri removed from the Academic Staff College job. Jafri's resignation letter under a forged signature was submitted to the vice-chancellor, who began its acceptance process. Professor Jafri learned of this and met the vice-chancellor, protested and asked for an enquiry. The enquiry was never set up, but he was told to continue. The matter ended there.

His tenure was all trouble. His successor appointed Professor Jafri as registrar. Most of the vice-chancellors that headed the AMU came with ideas and plans to improve the functioning of the institution, but they soon got disillusioned. The system of the search committee for selecting a vice-chancellor had already been dispensed with.

In a university system, the senior professors as principals, deans, heads of the various departments, or members of forums like the Academic Council, Syndicate (Executive Council) and Senate (Court) are required to make policy decisions. Sub-committees like the admission committee, discipline committee and examination committee consist of none other than the university teachers. The task of the vice-chancellor is basically to implement the decisions of these bodies. In practice, however, the vice-chancellor assumes the role of a decision maker and the teachers act as no more than mere courtiers. All actions of the vice-chancellor taken on behalf of these committees are not only endorsed but in some cases, he is authorised to take future decisions. When the time comes to attack a vice-chancellor for irregularities, he comes out clean with the approval of the various university bodies. So why not let this be a privilege of the teachers to adorn the highest executive office by rotation?

The tenure of Naseem Ahmed, a no-nonsense IAS officer from Haryana cadre and an Aligarian, was disastrous. He had enjoyed the esteem of all the three Lals in Haryana – Devi Lal, Bansi Lal and Bhajan Lal – a difficult feat, but in his alma mater, he could not insulate himself from the clique. In a particular case, the examiner report was summoned via telegram to appoint the person concerned as a professor in the law faculty. In another case, apprehensive that his hand-picked appointee would not appear to advantage against a meritorious candidate, he conveyed the message to a talented staff member also in the running not to appear before the interview board. Several years after his superannuation, he had to face the Central Bureau of Investigation (CBI) for favouring a candidate in recruitment to the finance department.

Professor P.K. Abdul Azis joined the university on 11 June 2007 as its 21st vice-chancellor. It was a time when there was a complete breakdown of the rule of law, and everyone was constantly threatened with assault and humiliation. Azis claimed to have brought the university back to normal with firm and well-thought-out initiatives.

His singular contribution was a massive expansion programme with a target to establish five special centres of the AMU at Murshidabad (West Bengal), Katihar (Bihar), Bhopal (Madhya Pradesh), Pune (Maharashtra) and Malappuram (Kerala) at an estimated cost of Rs 2,000 crore. The Government of India allocated Rs 50 crore for the centres at Murshidabad and Malappuram. The state governments came forward to allocate land.

He shall be remembered for his off-the-cuff remark that the AMU was a sleeping one as almost the entire faculty retired for a siesta in the afternoon.

He was succeeded by Lt General (retd) Zameer Uddin Shah. Even a minor issue of suspending an associate professor based on his Facebook posts snowballed into a big issue in 2014 during his tenure. Associate Professor (History) Dr Syed Nadeem Ali Rezavi was suspended on 22 July after describing the vice-chancellor as '*be-aqal*' (brainless) and former vice-chancellors as '*lutiya chor*' (a colloquial term for a petty thief).[14]

Within the next few days, several prominent historians from all over India and academics threw their weight behind Rezavi. In a signed statement, historians Professor Romila Thapar, Professor B.D. Chattopadhyay (also President-designate of the Indian History Congress that year), Professor S.Z.H. Jafri (Secretary, Indian History Congress), Professor B.P. Sahu (former secretary, Indian History Congress), Professor D.N. Jha, Professor Mridula Mukherjee and others demanded that Rezavi be 'reinstated forthwith'.[15] Questions were raised about whether military officers should be expected to run academic institutions and about freedom of expression on university campuses.

The academicians said the treatment meted out to Rezavi,

> including the withholding of his order of appointment as professor for the last two years, suggests the pre-existence of much personal prejudice against him. His suspension avowedly on the grounds of some criticism he levelled against the VC on the Internet betokens an extreme intolerance of dissent.[16]

Shah justified the suspension as not just because of the '*be-aqal*' comment but a culmination of things Rezavi had continuously been saying on social media from September 2013. He said,

> In a slanderous mail on September 2, 2013, Professor Rezavi accused me of inaction during the Gujarat riots 2002. He writes, '*Ek kam aql fauji jiske under Gujarat 2002 me jalta raha aur fassad badhte rahe, uski lagaane ka kya matlab? Yeh wahi to hain jinko Atalji ne Gujarat dange rokne bheja tha aur dange Army hone ke bawajud hote aur bhadakte rahe! Sherwani pahanke aur dua me haath uthhake nek niyati nahi aati!*' I summoned him to my office on September 16, 2013, and told him to find out from the Muslims of Gujarat the good work done by the army, of which I was general officer commanding.[17]

The vice-chancellor alleged that because the university had decided to scrutinise the accounts of the Aligarh Historians Society, historians are now 'on the back foot'. Shah also described Rezavi as a 'protégé' of Professor Irfan Habib, who, in turn, asserted he thought of Rezavi as a historian with 'promise and potential and the suspension as "wrong, an overreaction" which must be revoked immediately'.[18]

In 2016, in an initiative to seek 'wider' consultations to appoint his successor, Shah wrote to all the Supreme Court judges, chairpersons of the Union Public Service Commission and the UGC, former AMU vice-chancellors and all vice-chancellors of the central universities to recommend names for the post.[19]

This 'unprecedented' move drew criticism even from Vice President of India M. Hamid Ansari, a former AMU vice-chancellor. He was of the view that the AMU Executive Council should constitute a search committee of eminent Muslims or non-Muslims and request it to suggest, within 30 days, a panel of five names to the AMU court for further action, 'as per the relevant provision of the statutes of the university'.

The five names shortlisted by the Executive Council for Shah's successor were Javed Usmani, Tariq Mansoor, Seyed Ehtesham Hasnain, S. Ahmed Ali and Furqan Qamar Hasnain. Two of them, Dr Tariq Mansoor and Brigadier S. Ahmed Ali, were disqualified after a few days because of conflict of interest. Both of them had participated in the meeting and voted in which the names had been shortlisted. Eventually, Tariq Mansoor won the race. But his selection was not without unsavoury controversy for which AMU has earned dubious distinction.[20]

A UGC report said the AMU did not have a national character. The AMU authorities said the panel had said the same thing for the past 33 years, and other universities like Banaras Hindu University (BHU) and Jawaharlal Nehru University (JNU) had been included in the list in the past.

Vice-chancellor Professor Tariq Mansoor countered by claiming that students from 29 states studied at AMU: 'How anyone can say that there is no diversity here.'[21] He said the university had a 60:40 ratio of Muslim and non-Muslim students. This was not by design but due to the large number of courses like Arabic, Urdu and Farsi for which only Muslim students applied.

Seniority often dominated in the selections, paving the way to the run-down of the university. Once Dr Bannerji, reader in economics, was superseded in the name of merit. A high court judgment was quoted in public: 'Seniority is as sure as motherhood, while Merit is as uncertain as the father.'[22]

Professor Tariq Mansoor superannuated. It was perhaps the first instance when the vice-chancellor of AMU did not have to abandon the university. During his term, Prime Minister Narendra Modi delivered the convocation address online only. His efforts to keep the right-wing BJP and the RSS leaders paid rich dividends as soon after his retirement, he was nominated as the BJP member of the Uttar Pradesh Legislative Council and soon after as the Vice President of the national unit of the BJP.

AMU operated without a full-time VC for such a long period barring one instance: between October 1989 and October 1990. The acting VC Mohammed Gulrez (he was the PVC at the time of relinquishment of the post of VC by Dr Tariq Mansoor), chaired the meeting of the executive council on 30 October 2023 and also voted for his wife Naima Khatoon, principal of AMU's Women's College, for the panel of five names to be forwarded to the AMU court for the selection of VC. Objections were raised in public on the issue of conflict of interest.

On 7 November 2023, the court forwarded a panel of three names, Prof. M.U. Rabbani, Prof. Faizan Mustafa and Prof. Naima Khatoon Gulrez, to the visitor, President Droupadi Murmu, as potential picks for the varsity's next vice-chancellor. The names of Prof. Furqan Qamar and Prof. Qayyum Husain in the panel of five forwarded by the Executive Council were eliminated.

On 22 April 2024, when the country was bracing for the general elections, Mrs Naima Khatoon was appointed as the new VC of the university. She is the first woman to hold the prestigious seat in over a century old existence of the university. Antara Baruah writes in The Print, a news and views portal,

> Over four decades ago, Naima Khatoon's family gathered in a room to discuss whether she should be allowed to cross state lines. Her brother was doing his PhD at the Aligarh Muslim University, but it was entirely unheard of for a young, college-going woman to make the trek from Odisha to Uttar Pradesh. Her uncle dug his heels in—insisting she couldn't go. But her mother persevered.
>
> AMU was a massive culture shock. Odia Muslims speak Urdu differently, and she was mocked mercilessly for her accent, her pronunciation, her constant mixing up of masculine and feminine words. But like her mother, she too was determined. And like her uncle, she dug her heels in.
>
> Now, Naima Khatoon is the new Vice-Chancellor of AMU. And it hasn't been easy this time either. There were no uncles. But, today, there's the 'bearded elite' of AMU who question her capabilities, faculty who spread canards about how it isn't her but her husband who is the real VC, and those who say she is a sell-out in hushed whispers.
>
> It's taking her mind back to the first moment of rebellion against her family in Odisha.
>
> After living many lives at AMU—student, scholar, Students Union member, provost, principal—Naima Khatoon took over as Vice-Chancellor. For some, it's not a feminist victory—she's rumoured to be a symbol of Modi's outreach to Muslim women. Jamia Millia Islamia's last VC was also a woman, and so is JNU's.
>
> She took the charge of the storied institution at a time when many in India were increasingly viewing the words 'Muslim' and 'minority' with suspicion. But also when AMU itself is changing.[23]

The vice-chancellor may not be a paragon of excellence as the authorities would have us believe but apportioning all the ills of the university to one person, even if he/she is the vice-chancellor, is not likely to help find a remedy.

10

TUSSLE OVER ADMISSIONS

AMU was a reasonably small university when India became independent. With the AMU (Amendment) Act of 1951, the Government of India took on the entire responsibility for its maintenance and provided it with a largely democratic and autonomous structure. It was the beginning of a phase of expansion of the university with central government funds (afterwards routed through the UGC). The G.C. Chatterji Committee, appointed by the President of India as the visitor of the university to review the university's work in 1960, agreed that a policy of admissions where some preference was given to internal students should continue. The amendment of 1951 in Article 8 forbade the admission of students through any 'test of religious belief', and no one raised the question of reservation for Muslims.

Vice-chancellor Badruddin Tyabji (November 1962 to February 1965) had increased the reservation in admission for internal candidates from 50 to 75 per cent at the fag end of his tenure. His successor Nawab Ali Yavar Jung decided to revert to the 50 per cent reservation in 1965, leading to the students going on the warpath – though the same Academic Council and Executive Council had voted for 75 per cent a few weeks ago. Three Executive Council members dissented (Justice Basheer Sayeed, Professor Baseer Khan and Mujtaba Siddiqi). The Students Union objected to this decision.

A committee headed by UGC chairperson Ms Madhuri Shah was constituted in 1982, after the enactment of the AMU (Amendment) Act of 1981, to report on the issue of admissions, among other matters. As per the report, 79.1 per cent of the 27,738 students admitted between 1978 and 1982 were from Uttar Pradesh and that too primarily from Aligarh and its adjoining districts; 10.79 per cent from adjoining states; 6.95 per cent from distant states and 3.16 per cent from foreign countries.[1]

The Academic Council, in its meeting held on 5 April 1986, authorised the vice-chancellor to constitute a committee for implementing Section 5(2) (c) of the Act. Subsequently, a 32-member committee under the convenorship of Professor Mohammad Shafi (former pro-vice-chancellor) was appointed. Its report on the social and educational upliftment of Muslims was accepted in principle. The incumbent vice-chancellor, however, appointed another committee for an in-depth study of the same before its implementation.

Meanwhile, the University Court met in September 1987 and discussed reservations for Muslims in admissions. Three resolutions relating to the issue were independently moved by Syed Shahbuddin, Dr A.U. Sheikh and Shujatullah Khan. The Court appointed another committee chaired by former vice-chancellor Badruddin Tyabji. Professor Raees Ahmed, former director of CSIR, Professor M.S. Agwani, Justice M.M. Ismail, Justice R.A. Ansari, Syed Shahbuddin, a former member of Parliament, Dr A.U. Sheikh, and Shujatullah Khan were its other members. Professor Wasiur Rehman, pro-vice-chancellor, was appointed its convener. The committee recommended 50 per cent reservation for Muslims. It further recommended that the marks of the internal candidates be enhanced by 10 per cent and the merit lists be drawn after that. Regarding nomination by the vice-chancellor, a gradual reduction from 20 to 5 per cent over three years was recommended.[2]

The court accepted the recommendations on 20 August 1989. The report was sent to the visitor of the university (President of India) for approval in accordance with Section 29(6) of the AMU (Amendment) Act 1981. The visitor, in turn, under Section 13(6) of the Act, pointed out on 10 October the same year that the recommendations were violative of Section 8 of the Act and Article 39(2) of the Constitution of India.

After a lapse of 16 months, the University Court appointed yet another committee on 22 April 1991 to prepare a reply to the communication from the visitor. This committee comprised Justice M.M. Ismail, Justice M.R.A. Ansari, Shujatullah Khan, Badruddin Tyabji and Zafaryab Jilani. Dr A.U. Sheikh was its convener.

This committee sent its 222-page reply to the visitor on 22 November 1992. The visitor never responded.

The vice-chancellor appointed another committee to review the admission policy. Dr Mumtaz Ahmed, the then pro-vice-chancellor, was appointed its chairman. Other members were K. Rehman Khan, a Member of Parliament, Mossa Raza, a former IAS officer, Syed Shahbuddin, a former Member of Parliament. Professor (Mrs) Hamida Ahmed, director of the Centre for Distance Education of the university, was its convener.

Since the visitor's reply had not been received, the Mumtaz Ahmed Committee opined that Tayabji's report should be implemented. 'Serious thought must be given to further amendment of the AMU Act to place its status as a minority institution established under Article 30 of the Constitution on statutory foundations,' it added.

This committee also recommended that 70 per cent of the seats be filled from the first block of students hailing from Uttar Pradesh and adjacent states and the remaining 30 per cent from the second block of distant states. Regarding internal candidates, the committee recommended the enhancement of their marks by 7 per cent.

Before this report could be placed before the Academic Council, Executive Council and University Court for their approval and subsequent implementation, the university was confronted with the issue of the Common Entrance Test (CET), an idea mooted by Dr Murli Manohar Joshi, the Union minister for Human Resources and Development (HRD) in Atal Behari Vajpayee's government.

The UGC conveyed on 7 December 2001 the decision of the union government to conduct an All India Engineering Entrance Examination (AIEEE) for admissions to engineering, architecture and pharmacy courses at the undergraduate level at all the institutions in the country, including central universities. The Academic Council of AMU, in its special meeting on New Year's Day of 2002, unanimously resolved, 'The present academically sound and time-tested admission policy of the AMU about B.Tech and B.Arch and other professional courses must continue.' This resolution was conveyed to the union government. The CET became a contention between the AMU and the union government.

The UGC took slightly less than two years to convey the decision of the Vajpayee government and asked the university not to issue any notification in respect to admissions for B.Tech and B.Arch and other professional courses. The government cited (1) the judgment of the apex court delivered by an 11-member bench in the TMA Pai Foundation and others vs. State of Karnataka and others on 31 October 2002 (2) the judgment of the apex court delivered by a five-member bench on 14 August 2003 in Islamic Academy of Education and others vs. State of Karnataka and others.

The university informed the union government about the steps it had already taken, and since a retreat after notification might have resulted in litigations, it asked for the government's advice. The government did not respond. The communication was placed before the Academic Council, which noted that the imposition of the CET would amount to interference in the autonomy of the university and an attack on its minority character.

Thereupon, the university notified its schedule for admission tests for various courses. A delegation of the AMU Teachers' Association (AMUTA) met some members of parliament and apprised them of the university's stand. The issue was raised in the Lok Sabha on 22 and 23 December 2003 and in the Rajya Sabha on 23 December. Some members opined that no administrative order could override the powers conferred on an institution established through an Act of Parliament. The issue was once again raised in parliament on 4 Feb 2004.

To bring uniformity in admissions to all professional courses in the country, the HRD ministry sanctioned a 50 per cent Muslim quota to Jamia Hamdard (a 'deemed university') and offered the same to the AMU. The university rejected the offer.

The issue remained unresolved. A few months later, Vajpayee-led NDA government of Vajpayee was replaced by the UPA government headed by Dr Manmohan Singh of the Congress. AMU got an exemption from the CET on 4 October 2004.

On 4 November 2003, the Supreme Court ruled on a writ petition that 'reservation by way of institutional preference should be confined to 50 per cent of the seats.'[3] Accordingly, the union government on 3 December 2004 conveyed to the university that it should allocate 50 per cent of the seats (for admission to MS/MD/PG diploma courses in the faculty of medicine) based on the CET, to be conducted by the All India Institute of Medical Sciences (AIIMS).

Following deliberations in its meeting on 15 January 2005, the Academic Council recommended to the Executive Council that (1) 25 per cent of students may be admitted from amongst the internal candidates based on the entrance test to be conducted by the university; (2) 50 per cent may be reserved for Muslims of India based on a test conducted by the university and (3) remaining 25 per cent seats may be filled up based on the entrance test to be conducted by AIIMS.

The Executive Council also authorised the vice-chancellor to constitute a committee to formulate the admission policy of the university for different courses of study, taking into consideration the relevant statutes of the university as well as the relevant judgements of the apex court about minority institutions.

When the issue of the UGC's letter was hotly debated in the Parliament, the ministry of HRD directed the vice-chancellor of the AMU to fax its admission policy immediately, showing the quantum of reservation. Despite the clear-cut provision of Section 5(2) (c) in the AMU (Amendment) Act of 1981, the university conveniently avoided its implementation by not reserving any fixed percentage for Muslims. The Tyabji Committee report was simply shelved. The implementation of the Mumtaz Ahmed committee report too was put off. When the dust of the CET fracas settled, a new committee was appointed by the Executive Council.

Another committee, chaired by Professor Saleemuddin, chairman of the Department of Biochemistry, was constituted in January 2015. Its members were professors Ms Amina Kishore (Principal, Women's College), Akhtar Haseeb (dean of Faculty of Agriculture), M. Amanullah Khan (chairman, Department of Surgery), Shahbuddin Iraqi (Department of History) and Ahmad Shahid Khan (Department of Electronics Engineering). It was perhaps the first time that academicians exclusively formed the committee.

This committee recommended that 25 per cent of the seats be filled based on merit, another 20 per cent (or 25 per cent if there was no provision for nomination in a course) from internal candidates and the remaining 50 per cent amongst Muslim candidates. All such admissions were to be made strictly in accordance with the merit list drawn based on entrance tests conducted by the university for the various courses. The reservation in admission to internal candidates should be gradually reduced to 10 per cent over five years. Besides, of the total seats, 5 per cent were to be filled by nominations (if the provision existed) by the vice-chancellor encompassing different defined categories. Of the total seats in each category, 3 per cent were to be reserved for differently-abled candidates as per UGC guidelines.

Earlier, in September 1994, the university's proctor lodged an FIR with the police alleging that as many as 149 students had secured admissions to various courses based on illegally obtained admission cards. Out of them, 140 had been granted admission to some courses but managed to switch over to other courses through illegal admission cards. Six students had not been offered admission to any course, while three other candidates had not even submitted a form for admission. The admission committee took a lenient view and allowed them to pursue the courses in which they had initially been offered admission by the university. They were merely fined Rs 1,000 each.

Vice-chancellor Syed Hashim Ali rued:

> Admission time is an opportune time in which the destabilisation process gains momentum by spreading rumours that the number of Muslim students on the campus has drastically reduced. This is normally followed by a campaign in the press against the admission policy of the university. Reservation for Muslims was in vogue in some quarters. The students' union also demanded a 75 per cent reservation of seats for Muslims.[4]

To the student, AMU is an institution where Muslim culture and identity have an opportunity to develop. Academic incompetence, feels Ali, is behind all the troubles. The students who do not get jobs through different competitive examinations stay behind in the university and enrol as research students. It won't be challenging to assess the quality of the 'research'. He quit the university a few days later on his superannuation and never visited it again and did not participate in the meeting of the University Court, of which he was an ex-officio member.

All this goes on in the name of the 'minority character' of the university. Frankly speaking, remarked former vice-chancellor Badruddin Tyabji,

> I have been opposed to this from the very beginning. What is the minority here? What is the character? If you are aware, then spell it out and say that it is an Islamic University and has nothing other than this. But it is a composite university. How can it be called a minority university? We are trying to influence the majority to recognise our values. The teachers are bothered by how their relatives can get a job or admission.[5]

Justice Arun Tandon of the Allahabad High Court quashed the order of the university regarding 50 per cent reservation to Muslim candidates.[6] The judgment noted that the AMU had for the previous 85 years been a Muslim University in name only. It could, of course, be that minority status was discussed in the halls of the university privately. On appeal by the university, a division bench comprising Justices Ajoy Nath Ray and Ashok Bhushan upheld the decision of the single judge. The January 2006 order quashed the resolution of the AMU's Academic Council (dated 15 January 2005), the decision of the Executive Council (dated 19 February), and the Union of India's letter of approval to the decision (dated 25 February) reserving 50 per cent of seats for Muslims.[7]

The court directed the AMU to conduct a fresh entrance examination for the 50 per cent seats of the postgraduate medical courses without making any reservations based on religion.

'The Act of 1951 forbade in its article 8 the admission of students through any "test of religious belief", and anyone did not raise the question of reservation for Muslims,' pointed out Professor Irfan Habib. He added,

> Unfortunately, a sudden enhancement of the internal quota to 75 per cent in 1963 and its proposed reduction in 1965 created a violent incident in the latter year. Soon after the UPA government took office, it fell to the attraction of the supposed political mileage expected from pursuing the path pioneered by the NDA...
>
> All this has been done without any claims that the proportion of Muslims in various test-based courses is so low as to make Muslim reservation a material issue. One would have thought that the proponents of the religion-based quota should have presented statistics about the actual Muslim proportion in the university and the test-based admissions. It can no longer be said that the admissions to AMU are not communally oriented. The substantive reduction of the general quota cannot but dilute the competitive element in the admission tests and depreciate the value of the AMU's degrees in the public eye.[8]

Currently, seats in the graduation and post-graduation courses at the AMU have been broken up into three categories: 40 per cent for internal students, 40 per cent for external students, and 20 per cent for vice-chancellor's nominees. This nomination quota suits everyone, and despite several resolutions in the Academic Council and Executive Council, there is no effort to abolish it or reduce it gradually.

Nomination and reservation are twin brothers. Noted Sociologist Imtiaz Ahmad opines,

> Reservation is a mechanism to create a collaborative class from among the underprivileged groups. The dominance of the elite class of Muslims serves the same purpose. The State has a legitimate collaborative class willing enough to be on its side. If this state of affairs changes, the entire institutional structure, University Court, the EC, and other institutions would have to be revamped. Neither the reigning elite nor the State want to break the status quo.[9]

Dr Faizan Mustafa, vice-chancellor of the Chanakya National Law University, Patna, opines that the AMU still follows the pre-2005 admission policy.[10] But after a decision, in this case, it be would either a minority or a non minority institution. If it is a minority university under Article 15(5), it would be exempted from SC/ST/OBC reservation and entitled to Muslim reservation to 50 per cent under Article 30 of the Constitution. If it is not a minority institution, SC/ST/OBC reservation both in admission and jobs has to be implemented. Thus, the pre-2005 policy has to go either way.

One offshoot of the nomination system was that unscrupulous elements collected money from gullible parents claiming reliable connections with the vice-chancellor. Once, a whole gang of fraudsters was arrested in this connection.

Vice-chancellor Professor N.M. Farooqi said,

> The main argument advanced by the proponents of the nomination to continue as of today is that the university can admit more Muslim students this way. This is strictly not true. By nominations, we actually admit students of lower calibre but having the influence of some kind (corruption possibly) whereas better Muslim students are available though not admitted.[11]

Sir Syed was anxious to build up an Aligarh not on the basis of religion but sympathy for Islamic values. His idea of Aligarh was not one of whether all or the majority of students here were Muslims, but that it should harbour students interested in Islam, its history, its values, its civilising effect, how it has affected the non-Muslim communities, its contribution to various aspects of life. He felt that Muslims were as guilty of not knowing about various Indian religions as Hindus were about not knowing about Islam.

Quoting Justice Frankfurter of the United States on the issue, the Chatterji Committee had underscored: It is the business of a university to provide an atmosphere which is most conducive to speculation, experiment and creation in which prevail the four essential freedoms of a university – to determine for itself on academic grounds, who may teach, what may be taught, how shall it be taught and who may be admitted to study.

Sapru, a member of the Chatterji Committee, had once asked the chairman of the UGC, Dr C.D. Deshmukh, 'Should the university have the right to regulate its admission policy?' Dr Deshmukh replied:

> The unspoken, inarticulate assumption in this regard is that the university will want to admit students who are academically well-qualified and raise their reputation. But where the facts show that they wish to admit inferior material because they belong to a denomination, this being a secular state, the state should interfere. For them, autonomy and sovereignty have been abused. In all these discussions, when we say academic freedom, we mean it should be exercised reasonably.

The committee wholeheartedly supported this view, 'not only in its narrower application to the matter of admissions but in all aspects of university policy and administration'.

However, it disapproved of various methods, the vested interests devised at AMU to maintain its 'special character'. Providing an answer to what the AMU's unique character should be, it said,

Every university must recognise, develop and emphasise the study of what we may describe as the contribution of AMU to the complex pattern of our national culture and, in fact, to the worldwide culture of humanity. That Islam has made very substantial and notable contributions to this heritage, both historically and currently in our age, is a patent truth that no one with any pretensions to the study of the history of civilisation will dare to deny. It is this living tradition, this dynamic force, which we should like to preserve and cherish in AMU.

11

MINORITY STATUS: A MATTER OF LIFE AND DEATH

The six-decade-old issue of the 'minority status' of Aligarh Muslim University received fresh impetus when the Allahabad high court struck down the decision of the university to reserve 50 per cent seats in admission the Union HRD ministry on 25 February 2005 had permitted the university to do so. The then vice-chancellor Lt Gen. Zameer Uddin Shah prophetically said the issue was a 'matter of life and death' for the university.[1]

The high court was considering whether the AMU was entitled to the benefits of a 'minority' institution. The issue arose while the court dealt with five connected writ petitions filed by 34 petitioners who had obtained MBBS degrees and claimed a right to admission to the postgraduate medical courses.

The petitioners were all Hindu candidates deprived of their right to participate in the selection process for admission to these courses against seats reserved for Muslims. They challenged it because the reservation was without jurisdiction, as Article 30 did not apply to AMU and was violative of Article 29(2) of the Constitution, which states, that no citizen shall be denied admission to any educational institution receiving aid from state funds on grounds of religion, race, caste or language.

Justice Arun Tandon quashed 50 per cent reservation for Muslims in admission and gave relief to the petitioners on 4 October 2005. The popular perception is that the court quashed the AMU (Amendment) Act 1981. In its 48-page judgment, the court creatively interpreted and 'read down' a section of the Act. ('Reading down' in legal language means inventing for a provision – a meaning that the lawmakers perhaps did not intend but is otherwise consistent with the Act.)

The court agreed that the nucleus of AMU was MAO College, which had until then been a teaching institution under Allahabad Muslim University. The conversion of the college into a university was, however, not affected by the Muslim minority; it took place by virtue of the Act of 1920. The court reasoned that the Act of 1920 might have been passed as a result of the efforts of the Muslim minority, but that did not mean they had established the university. The court said:

> Those who were in charge of MAO College, the Muslim University Association and the Muslim University Foundation Committee were keen to bring into existence a university at Aligarh.... if they had brought into existence a university on their own, the degrees of that university were not bound to be recognised by the government ... That is why the three institutions approached the government to bring into existence a university whose degrees would be recognised by [the] government. If that is so, the Muslim minority cannot claim to administer it, for it was not brought into existence by it.[2]

Does the judgment deprive the AMU of its 'minority' character? Within the meaning of Article 30? Yes. Historian Irfan Habib, professor emeritus of history at the AMU, put it succinctly:

> It was not thought that the AMU was covered by Article 30 even after the Amendment Act of 1981 came into force. Even the Union minister of education, Sheila Kaul, who had moved the bill to amend the AMU Act in 1981, did not cite Article 30 during the debate in Parliament. The government took the position that Article 30 applied to the university only recently. By striking down the new reservation policy, the judgment has not hurt the minority character of the university.[3]

Critics of the judgment point out that the court had not struck down Section 5(2), according to which the university has the power to promote the educational and cultural advancement of the Muslims of India. The 1981 amendment also inserted this sub-section, and the judgment does not deal with it. However, the claim of the university to reserve seats in admission under this section comes into conflict with Section 8 of the Act – inserted in 1981 – which stipulates that the university shall be open to all persons (including the teachers and the taught) of either sex and irrespective of race, religion, creed, caste or class.

On an appeal by the university, a division bench of the Allahabad high court of Justices Ajoy Nath Ray and Ashok Bhushan upheld this judgment on 5 January 2006.

Justice Ray observed:

> India of 1920 is not the same as the India of 2005 or 2006. It was not an India where one community could wait for a more supportive and sympathetic political party to come into power and then gain their objective; there was no democracy. What the British said went. The degrees of a university, even if it could be set up independently then, which was in the bad books of the English government, but wholly Mohammadan and wholly green, and perhaps wholly good, was of no practical value; it would either die or go underground.
>
> Justice Ashok Bhushan held that the AMU, a body corporate, came into existence only by an Act of [the] legislature. By merely changing the definition of Section 2(1) by amending the Preamble and long title can the fact that the university came into being by an Act of [the] legislature be forgotten?[4]

Reservation in the postgraduate and doctoral courses were introduced in the university in 2005. The high court clearly stated:

> The AMU is declared to have always been and is a free institution and not a minority institution within the meaning of Article 30 of the Constitution.

> Sections 2(1) and 5(2)(c) introduced in the AMU Act of 1920 by the said 1981 amendment are invalid, and these insertions are struck out; the removal of the words 'establish and' from the preamble of the 1920 Act by the 1981 Act is invalid, and those words are restored to the preamble; the claim of 50 per cent Mohammedan quota for the post-graduate medical courses by the University is declared as unconstitutional and impermissible and, they shall make no claim of minority quota in like or another manner in future; the Union's communication dated 25 February 2005 vetting the purported minority status of AMU by permitting their claim of Muslim reservation is quashed and set aside; the admission of Muslim students made on the invalidly claimed quota of 50 per cent is maintained on account of pure practicality.
>
> The University shall undertake an exercise of recasting the results of the examinations of 2005 and will ascertain thereby which of the cross appellants would have secured admission instead of which of the Mohammadan students admitted in the 50 per cent quota; alternatively, which of the 34 cross appellants would have obtained a more preferred choice of discipline according to their priorities, and instead, which Mohammadan students were permitted to have such disciplines because and only because of the 50 per cent quota.

The court order recalled that two rival groups emerged at the AMU in its early days. One group, often called the Aligarh Party, was led by the Raja of Mahmudabad. Its chief representatives were Aftab Ahmad Khan, Ziauddin and Sheikh Abdullah (educationist). They were in favour of giving the government broad powers in the proposed university's constitution. Mohammed Ali and Abul Kalam Azad were in the other group. They were against government interference in the university's administration and asserted that it should be fully autonomous.

The Union government and AMU appealed against the Allahabad high court judgment in the Supreme Court. The minority character issue case came up for hearing in January 2016.

Unperturbed by the 'intolerance' charge, the BJP-led NDA government's attorney general Mukul Rohatgi told a bench of justices J.S. Khehar, M.Y. Eqbal and C. Nagappan that, 'It is the stand of the Union of India that the AMU is not a minority university. As the executive government at the Centre, we can't be seen as setting up a minority institution in a secular state.'[5]

The Attorney General's stand drew an immediate reaction from Justice Eqbal,[6] who asked, 'Is the change of stand because of a change in the government at the Centre?' Rohatgi said, 'The previous stand was wrong.'

Interestingly, erstwhile Jana Sangh leaders Atal Behari Vajpayee, L.K. Advani and Nananji Deshmukh supported the cause of AMU's minority character in 1977. The Jana Sangh had merged into the Janata Party in January 1977. During the 1979 mid-term Lok Sabha elections, the Janata Party issued its election manifesto justifying its stand. 'The Janata government had successfully evolved, in consultation with all concerned, a consensus on restoring the autonomy and original character of the AMU, which the previous government had gradually impaired.'

Moving the bill on 22 December 1981, the then education minister Mrs Sheila Kaul (Congress)[7] had said that the amendments to the AMU Act had been under discussion for quite some time. 'Earlier attempts of amendment, viz. in 1979, were infructuous. It was against this background that we pledged our support to a measure assuring the restoration of the historical character of the university. It is this pledge that we are redeeming today,' she said.

Participating in the debate, the then BJP Vice President and Lok Sabha member Ram Jethmalani said,

> There are very distinguished Muslim gentleman on the treasury benches; and if they have found this bill satisfactory, it is no part of my business really to raise any objection. Equally there are some distinguished Muslim gentlemen on this side (opposition). I hope they too find the bill satisfactory.[8]

Janata Party member Subramaniam Swamy said the AMU was 'not as just a university but as movement... the basic points about the AMU are its minority character and autonomy'.[9] Over a period of 18 years (1965–81) they had gone through a process of losing it. In 1965, they lost the minority character and the decision of the central government was upheld later on in a Supreme Court judgment in 1967. And in 1972, autonomy also went. It was in 1978 that the Minorities Commission, which was also a concept of the Janata Government, said that the autonomy and the minority character of the AMU should be restored.

The Chatterji Committee observed,

> The AMU with its open-door policy of admitting members of all communities and giving them opportunities to share fully in its residential and corporate life, is in a specially privileged position to foster that emotional integration which is essential for the preservation of India's cultural and political unity.... We recommend that the AMU should build up strong departments for the study of languages associated with Muslim culture, such as Arabic, Persian and Urdu. It should have a strong department of history which should pay special attention to the contributions which Islam has made not only to world history but also to the development of Indian polity, thought, and art.[10]

Quoting Mahatma Gandhi, a distinguished professor of law Dr Faizan Mustafa says that protecting its minorities is the hallmark of civilisation. He argues that the constitution's framers showed utmost sensitivity to the needs and aspirations of the minorities.

> There are fundamental issues involved in this historic case of substantial constitutional importance. Why have special minority rights been given in the Constitution in the first place? Can minorities establish universities? How can the minority character of an institution be determined? Who would determine this status? Can fundamental rights be waived? Can Parliament pass a law helping the incorporation of a minority university? If a minority institution accepts governmental supervision in order to ensure the efficiency of administration, does it lose the minority tag?[11]

Dr Mustafa argues,

> Since universal individualistic rights were considered insufficient for the protection of the interests of the minorities, special rights were given to them. Article 29 gives a right to conserve a distinct culture, script and language. This can be best done in minority educational institutions. Article 30(1) gives minorities, whether based on religion or language, the right to "establish and administer educational institutions of their choice". Most of the minority institutions in the country are institutions of linguistic minorities among the Hindus….
>
> The state under Article 30(2) cannot, in granting aid to educational institutions, discriminate against any educational institution because it is a minority institution. The Supreme Court has given highly liberal interpretations to expressions used in Article 30.[12]

When Justice Chagla was the education minister, he wanted to remove the words 'Hindu' and 'Muslim' from the names of BHU and AMU. If minorities were given the right to run their institutions, it was with the objective of promoting their distinct culture, be it the language or the religion, which was fair. But if such institutions offered general courses in science, engineering, medicine or humanities, would it be right for a disproportionate number of seats to be reserved for one community.

Hitting back at the government panel that suggested the word 'Muslim' be dropped from its name, AMU, in its formal response to the UGC, called the proposition 'preposterous' for ignoring the institution's long history and unique character. Criticising the committee for going beyond its mandate, AMU Registrar Javaid Akhter wrote to the government:

> The name of the university gives us an idea about its history, purpose and character and preserving the same is our bounden Constitutional duty. The committee incorrectly draws the conclusion that renaming AMU as Aligarh University would instil secular values. One must recall that in India, the concept of

> secularism arises more from the discourse of justice and equality than from an anti-religious position mostly practiced in the West.[13]

The BHU, the predecessor of the AMU by six years, had also faced the issue of exclusion of the word 'Hindu' from its name at the time of its inception in 1914. A secular freedom fighter, Ganesh Shankar Vidyarthi had decried such a move in the editorial of his newspaper *Pratap*.

Arshad Alam, who teaches at the University of Erfurt, Germany, writes:

> Now, AMU, a central university which has not implemented the SC/ST quota, is going all out to attach a communal tag to itself. University authorities offer two reasons in support of Muslim reservation.
>
> First, they argue, that the move will attract students from all parts of the country, as against north India alone.
>
> Second, they say that it will raise the academic standards of the university by attracting the best talent, especially from among Muslim candidates. Both the arguments are bogus. The reservation clause is selective.
>
> Fifty per cent Muslim reservation applies only to 38 select professional departments, the combined strength of which comes to 2,000 students only. It is illogical to argue that in the campus strength of about 30,000 students, a mere 2,000 will alter its regional profile and make it more representative.[14]
>
> ...
>
> Rather than looking inward and standardising the recruitment of teachers, the University conveniently shifts the blame on the students for falling academic standards. The authorities seem to have realised that the University has turned so rotten that the only way to give it the veneer of a central university is to attract good students from outside.
>
> ...
>
> Benefits of reservations will only accrue to a select section of upper class Muslims. Since the AMU is not even discussing excluding creamy-layer Muslims from the ambit of reservations,

> one suspects that the prime beneficiaries of such a move will be those Muslims who do not need it.

Do AMU and BHU have the right to reserve admissions based on religion? History does not claim anywhere that Sir Syed or Pandit Malaviya reserved majority admissions for their co-religionists. It cannot because the two institutions were not conceived in that manner. Both had received significant support from people who did not share the religion of the founders. The use of the term 'minority character' is only a subterfuge. The 'Muslim' character of AMU lies in the educational requirements there and not in the number of its Muslim students.[15]

Professor Emeritus Irfan Habib reiterates,

> No government-maintained institution can be a minority institute. Only privately managed institutes can be minority institutes ... In 1898, one Rafiuddin Ahmad clearly explained what kind of university the Muslims had in mind. And that was for a 'secular, modern university of/for Muslims, though avoiding parochialism'. It had to be universal and inclusive in its admission and recruitment policy. Thus, as much as three or four bodies came up to raise MAO College to the status of a university for Muslims – the Sir Syed Memorial Fund, the Old Boys Association, the Mohammedan Educational Conference, the Duty Society, etc. – Mohammad Ali Jauhar (1878–1931) said in no uncertain terms, 'A popular movement had generated the idea of a Muslim university. Aligarh's is the people's very own institution.' During 1910–12, a friendly competition to raise funds took place between the BHU and the AMU. The Aga Khan visited Banaras and contributed some amount to its fund. This was reciprocated by the Maharaja of Darbhanga, who visited Aligarh. The incentive that the AMU will have the authority to affiliate the (Muslim) 'minority' colleges all over the country injected enthusiasm among the rapidly emerging aspirants of modern education among Indian Muslims.
>
> Consequently, the funds started pouring in. Several landed aristocrats among Muslims contributed lakhs of rupees. The Raja of Mehmoodabad in August 1911 and Syed Aziz Mirza in August

1912 came out with the draft constitution for the AMU to be controlled by Muslims even though non-Muslims could very well get admission.

The Viceroy had proposed that he would be the chancellor and appoint visitors to all the universities to enquire into university affairs, which would advise the courses of study, academic regulations, etc. The Viceroy also clarified that the court of trustees of the proposed AMU would constitute exclusively Muslims who would elect 25 members of the executive council, each having a term of three years. This arrangement was made for the proposed AMU with the express purpose of making it, indeed, a Muslim-controlled university. Then the education member in the viceroy's council, Butler, said, '...It was now up to the Muslims to raise the money and put together an acceptable constitution for the AMU to define the composition and principles of functioning of the AMU.'

Accordingly, a Muslim University Foundation Committee was formed in 1912, with members towering nationalists like Maulana Azad, Mazhar ul Haq, and Mohammed Ali Jauhar. (Interestingly, the Aga Khan, in his autobiography, records the date of AMU being granted in 1912.)

But this proposed university was not given the mandate to affiliate with other Muslim 'minority' colleges of India, hence leading to divided opinion within the committee. Meanwhile, on 01 October 1915, the BHU bill was passed, leading to desperation among Muslims to get a similar status to the proposed AMU.

It should be remembered that many other universities were established during the period, such as Patna, Lucknow, Dacca, etc. None of them was given that special status conferred upon the AMU. Dacca University was brought to satisfy Muslim demand since the annulment of the partition of Bengal in 1911. Yet, Dacca University was not given a Muslim character/status.

The AMU's history proves that it was established by Muslims, and therefore, the Act of 1920 granted the right to administer it to Muslims.[16]

In a speech in 1883 in Lahore, informs Professor Habib, Aligarh's founder Sir Syed Ahmad Khan said proudly of MAO College (AMU predecessor): 'There is no discrimination between Hindus and Muslims.'[17] The founder and his successors did not, at any time, see any conflict in keeping its doors open to all while promoting modern education among Muslims.

With the Amendment Act 1951, says Professor Habib, the Government of India took up the entire responsibility for its maintenance and provided it with a largely democratic and autonomous structure. The Chatterji Committee appointed to review the working of the university (1960) commended the Act of 1951 and agreed that a policy of admissions, where some preference may be given to internal students, should continue. The Act of 1951 forbade in its Article 8 the admission of students through any 'test of religious belief'; no one raised the question of reservation for Muslims.

> Unfortunately, a sudden enhancement of the internal quota to 75 per cent in 1963 and its proposed reduction in 1965, created a violent incident in the latter year. The government of India took the opportunity to practically scuttle the Act of 1951, through an ordinance and in effect took over the control of the university's administration by its nominees. This action had the most disastrous consequences. As against government control, the issue of AMU's autonomy as a minority institution was raised for the first time by many critics of the government's ham-handed act. It was only after seven years that in 1972 certain amendments were made to restore some internal authority to the AMU. Still, there were yet far too many undemocratic provisions, duly pointed out by the CPI (M) in parliament.
>
> The amendment of 1972 remained the focus of controversy. Finally, in 1981, Mrs Indira Gandhi's government brought forth amendments designed to placate Muslim politicians who wished to control the university through the university court.
>
> The Act of 1981 had several features, like the mode of the VC's election, the composition of the court, etc, which the AMU's well-wishers could not support.
>
> What the university authorities and MHRD have entirely failed to recognise is the blow they have struck at the character and repute of the AMU. The letter from MHRD to allied parties quotes the

speech from Indrajit Gupta, where he rightly said that a university does not become communal if it has a majority of Muslims, which for the AMU has always been the case. But if a religious test is imposed, it can no longer be said that the admissions to the AMU are not communally oriented.

Though it is doubtful that the AMU is a 'minority' institution, the law cannot force even a minority institution to have a religion-based reservation. Many minority colleges do not have such reservations at all. This is clear from Article 30 of the constitution that its framers had in mind only educational institutions with private management when they conceived of minority institutions.

The introduction of the communal element in the AMU's admission policy thus seems to be an unmitigated tragedy. That it seems a *fait accompli* does not make it less of a tragedy,

Professor Habib concluded.[18]

Mohammad Sajjad, Professor of Modern History in AMU, says:

An objection was raised from certain quarters that such an arrangement would lead to the consumption of the cake by the creamy layer of Muslims, as the minority character does not take into account its backward castes ... Let us hope that a strong political demand for the exclusion of the creamy layer from reservations in all the minority institutions of India comes up sooner than later.[19]

Joining the issue with his professor, Dr Faizan Mustafa argued:

Few people know that Prof. Habib has himself signed a contract with the university at the time of his appointment some 50 years ago that 'he would do nothing against the Muslim character of the university'. Thus, he himself admitted the AMU to be a minority university at the time of joining. However, in the best traditions of free speech and tolerance of dissent, university always takes his statements in the right perspective.[20]

Responding to Professor Habib's argument on the funding of minority institutions out of taxpayers' money, Dr Mustafa contends,

> Article 30(2) of the Constitution makes it abundantly clear that in granting funds, the state cannot discriminate against the minority institutions. Thus, there can even be 100% government-funded minority institutions. A funded minority institution cannot be a private institution. Of course, there can be unaided private minority institutions as well, but the AMU will not be such an unaided private institution.
>
> Prof. Habib's view that the AMU is not a minority institution is far from the truth. The Allahabad high court had explicitly held that the present AMU Act, as amended in 1981, is the "declaration of minority character of the AMU." But the court quashed some of the provisions of the Act as unconstitutional.

Former vice-chancellor M.N. Farooqi says,

> The AMU had a minority character but was not a minority institution. There is quite a difference between the two statements. For instance, the AMU Act of 1981 says: 'AMU is an institution established by Muslims of India as an Institution of their choice and is hereby incorporated in this act as AMU…' The Act also enjoins the University to promote especially the cultural and educational needs of the Muslims of India.[21]

In 2006, the Union government and the university challenged the high court verdict quashing the minority status of the AMU and 50 per cent quota for Muslim students, in the Supreme Court. On 24 April 2006, a division bench of Justices K.G. Balakrishnan and D.K. Jain put a stay on the reservation policy of the AMU. The constitutionality of the policy was referred to a larger bench to decide.

A section of Aligarians claims that the stage was set for the victory of this case in 2010. But the university's advocate did not appear on 25 March 2010 when the case was called for hearing. The Union of India had filed the appeal in the Supreme Court against the order of the Allahabad high court.

There is a premium on claiming minority status since this supposedly brings some degree of protection from government meddling and academic interference. But why should only minority institutions get this freedom and not all? The 'minority' character or status can continue to excite passions only in this divided nation. The only issues that matter in running an educational institution are whether it has sufficient autonomy to do a good job and whether it has the resources and leadership to do so. A minority character or lack thereof is hardly relevant to its central purpose.

But successive governments never missed an opportunity to draw political mileage out of the issue. Therefore, when the Allahabad high court disallowed the university from offering quotas for Muslims on the ground that an act of Parliament set up the university and hence could not be deemed a minority institution, the UPA quickly filed an appeal in the Supreme Court. Not to be outdone, the NDA has reversed this position, with Attorney General Mukul Rohatgi telling two benches of the Supreme Court that the AMU was a central university.

The widespread perception in Aligarh is that there is a strong case for adding provisions to Articles 25–30, which gives minority institutions the right to administer their own educational and cultural institutions. In our country, this means that only minority institutions require this freedom. On the contrary, what is needed is to be clear that nothing in Articles 25–30 can be construed to mean that non-minority institutions cannot have the same protection from interference by the government. The NDA government may assert its ownership of the AMU, but this does not mean it should grant itself the right to mess around with the university's academic autonomy. They recall what Franklin Roosevelt said: 'No democracy can long survive which does not accept as fundamental to its very existence the recognition of the rights of minorities.'[22] Accordingly, special safeguards were guaranteed.

In the 1967 case, the Supreme Court did not rule out the possibility of a central university being a minority institution. It merely said that from the provisions of the AMU Act of 1920, it is not clear that it is a minority institution.

Parliament clarified doubts raised by the apex court through the 1981 Act by conveying that the AMU had, in fact, been established by Muslims themselves as 'an institution of their choice' and the legislature in 1920 merely incorporated it. As to the purpose of this university, Parliament again made it explicit by laying down that it is to 'especially promote educational and cultural advancement of Muslims of India'... Minority status cannot be determined by looking at the law. We need to look at the history before the enactment of the law. The best course would be to treat these provisions as mere supervision by the government. The apex court has consistently held in several cases, including the TMA Pai case, that the government cannot take over minority institutions. Even governmental aid cannot come with such conditions as are destructive of minority character. There can be no nationalisation of minority universities.

It is interesting to note what Veer Savarkar, a votary of the Hindutva, has said in this regard. 'Every minority may have separate schools to train their children in their tongue, religious or cultural institutions and can receive government help also for these, but always in proportion to the taxes they pay into the common exchequer.'[23] However, he capped his statement by adding that the same principle must, of course, hold good in the case of the majority too.

On 14 September 1920, the Aligarh Muslim University Act, 1920 (AMU Act) was passed to incorporate the MAO College and another Muslim University Association into a single university named the Aligarh Muslim University (AMU). According to Section 23 of the AMU Act, the Court of the University, the governing body of the university, must only consist of persons belonging to the Islamic faith.

In 1951, the AMU Act was amended to do away with the compulsory religious education provided to Muslim students by the university. Further, the amendment removed the provision which mandated only Muslim representation in the Court of the University. Later, the Act was amended in 1965. The Court was no longer the supreme governing body of the AMU. It became a body whose members were nominated by the visitor (the president of India). The powers were distributed among other bodies of the university, like the executive council, to democratise the management.

Petitioners in *S. Azeez Basha and Anr v Union of India* (1967) argued that the amendment violated their right to establish and administer educational institutions under Article 30 (1) of the Constitution of India. Further, they contended that the amendments violated the institution's right to carry out religious and charitable causes (Article 26[a]), the freedom of religion (Article 25), the right to conserve culture and language (Article 29), and the right to acquire property (Article 31).

On 20 October 1967, a five-judge bench, comprising Chief Justice K.N. Wanchoo and Justices R.S. Bachawat, V Ramaswami, G.K. Mitter and K.S. Hegde, held that no fundamental rights of the petitioners were violated and upheld the amendment. The bench reasoned that AMU was neither established nor administered by the Muslim minority. Pointing out that the Act was enacted through a Central Legislation, the Court stated, 'It may be that the 1920-Act was passed due to the efforts of the Muslim minority. But that does not mean that the Aligarh University, when it came into being under the 1920 Act was established by the Muslim minority.' They held that the provisions of the Act 'clearly show' that the administration of AMU was not 'vested in the Muslim minority'.

In 1981, the Act was amended to redefine 'university' as an educational institution 'established by the Muslims of India', which was initially MAO College and later became AMU. Powers of the university under Section 5 were amended to include a new clause for promoting the educational and cultural advancement of the 'Muslims of India'.

In 2005, the AMU reserved 50% of seats in postgraduate medical courses for Muslim candidates by claiming it to be a minority institution. This was challenged in *Dr. Naresh Agarwal v Union of India* (2005). The petitioners relied on S. Azeez Basha to argue that AMU is not a minority institution. The Union and the university contended that S. Azeez Basha was nullified by the 1981 amendment. Therefore, it can make provisions for the benefit of Muslim students. The Allahabad high court struck down the reservation policy and held that the AMU could not have an exclusive reservation because it was not a minority institution according to S. Azeez Basha.

In 2006, the Union government and the university challenged the high court decision in the Supreme Court. On 24 April 2006, a division bench of Justices K.G. Balakrishnan and D.K. Jain put a stay on the reservation policy of the AMU. The constitutionality of the policy was referred to a larger bench to decide.

In 2016, the National Democratic Alliance government, elected to the Union in 2014, withdrew from the appeal, contending that it does not acknowledge the minority status of the university. The university pleads its case alone.

On 12 February 2019, a three-judge bench comprising Chief Justice Ranjan Gogoi and Justices L. Nageswara Rao and Sanjiv Khanna referred the decision in *S. Azeez Basha* for reconsideration by a seven-judge bench.

On 12 October 2023, the matter was listed before the Chief Justice of India D.Y. Chandrachud, who constituted a seven-judge bench consisting of himself and Justices S.K. Kaul, Sanjiv Khanna, B.R. Gavai, Surya Kant, J.B. Pardiwala and Manoj Misra, to hear the matter.

The bench started hearing in the first month of 2024 and concluded on 01 Feb. The judgement was reserved. The Court was tasked with deciding whether AMU is eligible to be a minority institution under Article 30 of the Constitution of India. Article 30 states that religious and linguistic minorities have the right to 'establish and administer' educational institutions. On 8 November 2024, a 7-judge bench of the Supreme Court (by 4:3 majority) overruled the 1967 judgement in S. Azeez Basha vs. Union Of India, which held that an institution incorporated by a statute cannot claim to be a minority institution. The issue of whether Aligarh Muslim University is a minority institution is now left to a regular bench based on this view of the majority.

12

TRADITION TRAP FOR SECOND SEX

Sir Syed wanted Muslim boys to shun orthodoxy and acquire knowledge for career advancement. However, he expected Muslim girls, points out Gail Minault, to submit to 'family traditions and observances, obedience and authority'.[1]

David Lelyveld, the author of the much-acclaimed *Aligarh's First Generation; Muslim Solidarity in British India*, had some surprisingly little-known things to say about Sir Syed. He raised an uncomfortable question: 'Why, with all his radical ideas for reform and change and liberalism, including his admiration for European ideas and ways of life, did he (Sir Syed) oppose granting full equality to women?'[2]

The question was raised in the context of an incident mentioned by Gail Minault in her seminal work.[3] One incident described in the book is of Khan's disciple from Lahore, Sayyid Mumtaz Ali, visiting him with a manuscript of 'Huqquq-I-Niswan', a text on women's rights. Minault says that as Sir Syed went through the pages of that book, his face reddened, and his hands trembled. 'Finally, he tore up the manuscript and threw it in a waste paper basket,' Lelyveld said. Ali, however, retrieved the book and got it published after Sir Syed's death. 'The book that so upset Sir Syed called for full equality for women and refutes the standard reasons, both religious and practical, for confining them to a limited set of household roles,' he said.[4]

After his book had been published, on the advice of Sir Syed, Sayyid Mumtaz Ali, an ardent supporter of Sir Syed, started the publication of a magazine devoted to women's subject *Tehzeeb-ul-Miswan*, in 1893, which continued for the next 53 years. The book was published after the death of Sir Syed.

Deposing before the Education Commission in 1892, Sir Syed said:

> Those who hold that women should be educated and civilised before men are greatly mistaken. The present state of education among Mohammadan females is, in my opinion, enough for domestic happiness, considering the present social and economic condition of the life of Mohammadans in India.[5]

He believed that no culture of the world had betterment in the condition of women preceded that of men. Also, there was no community in the world where improvement in many men did not result in a corresponding betterment in many women.

Sir Syed was, in this matter, a firm traditionalist. He supported the most conservative opinion on the matter of *purdah*. Professor Shamas Ur Rehman, in his *Hayat e Abdullah*, writes:

> When there was a plague outbreak in the 1850s in Kanpur and people were put in quarantine by the government, people protested against quarantine on the reason women can't be secluded from homes even if it is plague. Sir Syed supported protesters on women's issues.[6]

Be that as it may, the AMU can be called an early bird, as it was one of the very first institutions in this country where women were allowed to receive higher education. Against the then-prevailing mindset, Begum Wahid Jahan and her husband, Sheikh Abdullah, founded the Women's College at AMU.[7] It was in Aligarh where Sheikh renounced the Ahamadiya faith and became a Sunni Muslim. The university had become a forum for an ideological struggle between shrill conservatism and rationalism as regards women's right to an equal education. The battle goes on. A level-headed student has put it: 'The AMU will not transform into a gender-equal campus overnight. But we can prove to be agents of change in the course of time.'

Every incidence of pressing the university to prove itself sends a slight disappointment across more than 3,000 homes. And every time it does, the university suffers more than its fair share.

Recalling the atmosphere in 1978, K.M. Devarajan writes:

> There were 23 students in one class, with six girls, and I have the faintest idea of what any of them, save one, looked like. They sat separated from the boys by a curtain strung across the middle of the spacious classroom. The exception was the girl who did not wear a burqa.[8]

The university has long been known for the segregation of the sexes. In most cases, men and women do not even study on the same campus until they are doing their post-graduation. Male and female students rarely sit together or walk around the institution together without attracting disapproving frowns from clerics, old-timers and dominating student leaders.

In the summer of 1917, the first batch of girls passed the first middle examination from the Girls' School at Aligarh. They were only a handful in strength of which a few were Muslims. This was still a reasonably unusual achievement for girls. In the prevailing atmosphere, there were not many who favoured exposure to girls (from 'respectable' families) outside the four walls of their houses. So, it was quite a revolutionary development.

Poverty has been the chief cause of the decline of female education among Muslims. It is still a custom among the well-to-do and respectable families of Mohammadans to employ tutoresses (*ustadnis or mullains*) to get their girls instructed in the *Holy Quran* and elementary theology in the Urdu language. Nasreen Ahmad opines: 'He (Sir Syed) believed that women's education would lead them to immorality.'[9]

Professor Mohammad Sajjad, when writing about Khwaja Altaf Husain Hali (1837–1914), whom he called Sir Syed's 'sidekick' said,

> On the gender issue too, Hali was a critic of the *purdah* system. His poems, *Munajat-e-Bewah*, and *Chup ki Daad* (1905), are known for exposing the subjugation of aristocratic Muslim women. He advocated modern education for women even more strongly than he opposed *purdah*. At times, like many colonial-era reformists, he seems to contradict himself, and Jazbi accuses him of not being brave enough. His cautiousness is an oblique signal to Sir Syed as well, which expresses itself in the poem *Reform Ki Had* (Limit of Reform) in particular.[10]

Modern Muslim leadership's emphasis on female education grew gradually. Sir Syed did not want to unsettle the already aggrieved clergy. During all deliberations of the All India Muslim Educational Conference (AIMEC), a purdah demarcated the male and female sections.

Eight years later, the AIMEC recommended the establishment of secular educational institutions for girls to be supervised by provincial Islamic committees. In 1896, a proposal to start a women's education wing was accepted in the annual executive session of the AIMEC, held at Aligarh. Justice Karamat Hussain was appointed its founding secretary. Nawab Mohsinul Mulk, Sahabzada Aftab Ahmad Khan, Sultan Ahmad and Haji Ismail Khan were asked to assist Justice Hussain.

In the annual session of the AIMEC at Lahore in 1898, a separate women's education section was established, and Sahabzada Aftab Ahmad Khan was elected its secretary. This attracted the wrath of conservative Muslims, but a dedicated team of prominent Muslims wrote letters and articles in *Aligarh Institute Gazette* and other reputable journals to defend the AIMEC's decision to start a women's educational movement. Justice Amir Ali presided over the annual session of the AIMEC in Calcutta in 1899, and the proposal for starting girls' schools in all the state capitals was accepted. It was also agreed that the *ulema* would be consulted for developing their curriculum, including the modern subjects of science and social science. In yet another session in Delhi in December 1902, under the leadership of Sir Agha Khan, young Sheikh Abdullah was appointed secretary to look into the women's educational project with a proactive approach.

The following year, the AIMEC introduced mathematics, history, geography and metaphysics as additional subjects for women. Sixteen years later, the AIMEC decided to promote girls' high schools in all districts of all provinces. Still, it was only in 1927 that the leadership recognised the need for Muslim female education in universities and colleges.

Sheikh Abdullah (not to be confused with Sheikh Abdullah, the legendary Kashmiri political leader), a first-generation Muslim, remained committed to spreading education among girls. Born in a village in the Poonch district of Jammu and Kashmir, his grandfather, Mehta Mast Ram, was the numbardar (a petty revenue official) of the village. Before conversion to Islam, the name of Sheikh Abdullah was Thakur Das. He embraced Islam in 1891 in Lahore, where he had gone to study. He settled in Aligarh after taking his bachelors and LLB degrees there. One of his daughters, Mumtaz Jahan (Mrs Haider), served as principal of the Women's College for over three decades.

Hayaat Fatemah (perhaps name changed), an undergraduate student at AMU, commented:

> The campaign for female education was carried out by the proponents of Aligarh movement on the ground that women with adequate and censored education, in proper *purdah*, would make better wives than uneducated women ...Abdullah convinced families to send their *sharif* daughters to the residential school where he created an atmosphere that was a mirror image of the suppressive domestic household environment prevalent then.[11]

Abdullah's leadership shaped the women's educational movement and played a vital role in the future of women's education in India.

Abdullah and his team started writing articles in different journals favouring women's education. A special issue of the *Aligarh Monthly* on women entitled *Hum aur Hamari Khawateen* was published in November 1903. It had articles about women's education and problems written by Syed Ghulam Neerang, Syed Sajjad Haider Yaldaram, Maulana Abul Kalam Azad and Maulvi Muhammad Akhtar.

To further promote the cause of women's education, in 1904, Abdullah started the journal *Khatoon* from Aligarh, which led to the foundation of the 'Female Education Association'. The journal was continuously published till 1914, and articles by Nawab Mohsinul Mulk, Maulvi Zakaullah Khan, Justice Karamat Hussain, Shaikh Abdul Qadir, Syed Ahmad Dehlavi, Maulana Aslam Jairajpuri, Muhammadi Begum, Nazar Sajjad, Nafees Dulhan (Maulana Habibur Rahman Khan Sherwani's wife), Zay Khai Sherwani (Nawab Muzammilullah Khan's daughter), Zauhara and her younger sister Atiya Fyzee[12] and Sughra Humayun Mirza regularly appeared in its pages. Atiya Fayzee attended the second session of the women's wing of the AIMEC at Aligarh in 1903.

In the annual session of the AIMEC at Aligarh in 1905, Begum Zauhara Fyzee (Murood-Janjeerah Bombay) led the women's education section, with the help of the president of the session, Khalifa Muhammad Hussain, a minister of the state of Patiala. A resolution was adopted to start a girls' school under the Islamic tradition of purdah and with modern science and sports activities.

Tracing the history of the institution, Afzal Usmani says: Sheikh Abdullah led a delegation to the Lt Governor of Uttar Pradesh and also sent a proposal for promoting women's education to Begum Sultan Jahan, ruler of Bhopal, who accepted the proposal and allocated a grant of Rs 100 per month as a grant. Abdullah faced solid and stiff resistance from the community, but his commitment paid dividends. Finally, he started a girl's school with six students and one teacher at a rented facility at Mohalla Tantanpara Balai Qila in Aligarh town on 19 October 1906. His wife, Begum Waheed Wahid Jahan, alias 'Aala Bi', provided him with the most vital support. After three years, the school received more support and popularity and moved to a more extensive rented facility in the Bani Israila area.

In 1908, Sheikh Abdullah bought 14 bighas of land at Nanak Rai Bag. The Uttar Pradesh state government allocated Rs 17,000 for the school building and a regular grant of Rs 250 per annum. On 7 November 1911, the foundation stone for the school building was laid down by H.H. Lady Porter, wife of Lt Governor of Uttar Pradesh. Waheedia Hostel (later renamed Waheed Jahan hostel and divided into two hostels: Old and New) was also constructed. The school and the hostel were inaugurated on 14 February 1914 by H.H. Begum Sultan Jahan.

Begum Khurshid Mirza, another daughter of Sheikh Abdullah, founder of the Women's College Aligarh, wrote about her sister Khatoon Jahan, who later served as the principal of the college:

> In 1914, the Waheedia Hostel was ready. Classes were held in one half of the building, and the other half was used as a boarding house. When Khatoon was eight, she came to Aligarh and was among the first seven boarders. She and her sister, Rashid Jahan, were admitted to the fourth class. Three girls occupied a room, where an older girl was in charge of the younger girls. Khatoon was serious and sober, unlike her sister Rashid Jahan, so Papa marked her out for service in the school and gave her many responsibilities.... She was the first girl who matriculated with one other student in 1921, a year earlier than Rashid Jahan. Aligarh had no Intermediate classes for girls, but with Waheed Jahan alias Aala bi's persuasion, Khatoon was allowed to go to Lucknow and study at Isabella Thoburn College. Other sisters and cousins followed her. Another supportive gesture from Aala bi was that she discarded purdah at the University for her lectures. Her Hindu colleagues did not hide behind blinds and were left alone, but remarks were passed against her, such was the prejudice against Muslim girls. Papa recalled 'that there were some wicked persons who hired youngsters to hide, then pounce upon the palanquins as they reached the school, pull the curtains apart and run away clapping and shouting'. Sheikh Abdulla hid in

ambush and sprang upon the boys with a whip in hand and gave them such a beating that they dared not show up again.

In 1916, the foundation stone of another hostel, named Sultania Hostel, was laid again by Begum Sultan Jahan. In her address, Begum Bhopal remarked about tightening the hostel doors and considered it a continuing obstacle in girls' education. Farha Nizami, an alumnus, writes,

> When Begum Sahiba tried to enter the hostel, she did unlock the door but could not open it, which was newly fitted. After many efforts, Begum Abdul Majeed Khwaja succeeded in opening it, but she hurt herself. Begum Zanjeera said, 'Ladies, see, these are the doors to women's education, and we are successful in opening them, though it took meticulous efforts and hardship.'[13]

In 1917, the girls of this school appeared in the middle school examinations, and one of the students, Hanifa Begum, secured the first position with a scholarship. In 1919, the first batch of this school appeared in the matriculation examinations of the U.P. Board, and all of them were successful. Begum Sultan Jahan, the founding chancellor of the newly-formed AMU, was the chief guest at the annual function of 1922. She emphasised the need for women's education and requested the AMU authorities to adopt this school as the role model for women's education.

In 1929, the school became an intermediate college; the following year, the women's college was affiliated with the AMU. In 1932, Begum Khatoon Jahan, daughter of Sheikh Abdullah, who had just returned from the UK after obtaining a post-graduation degree in education from Ladies University, was appointed principal of Women's College. In 1935, a graduation course in the Arts faculty was introduced. The Uttar Pradesh government later helped establish new hostels and science laboratories. In 1937, Sheikh Abdullah's other daughter, Mumtaz Jahan, was appointed principal and served the Women's College for over 30 years.

Maulana Abul Kalam Azad visited Aligarh in 1949 to address the annual convocation of the university. He paid a visit to the Women's College and was impressed by its progress and announced an annual grant of Rs 900,000 and assured a regular share to the Women's College from the grants received by the AMU occasionally.

Reliving the old days in his distinct style, noted Urdu writer Professor Rashid Ahmad Siddiqui said:

> When the solar system of the Mughal empire was disturbed, the satellites and planets associated with it also changed their orbit. Men-at-arms began to escape from Delhi's grip. That had become evident since the reign of Aurangzeb. The end had to be faced by Bahadur Shah 'Zafar'. Our people created havoc, but the British achieved victory.[14]

Hyderabad, Oudh, Rampur, Murshidabad, Dhaka and other big and small states were established far and near. And then those goblets overflowed with the heady wine as if every corner of the chessboard was the crown of *saqi*!

As the political power of Delhi weakened, its texture strengthened, and the cultural scene brightened up, so much so that when the political supremacy of Delhi diminished, the cultural glory was at its zenith. The rise of civilisation is sometimes the precursor to the fall of political power. Along with the learning and greatness of Delhi, clutching the charm and magnanimity of that glorious city and with firmness of purpose, came Sir Syed and his companions to Aligarh. They carried on their shoulders the splendour of the throne of Delhi and the sanctity of Jama Masjid. Then was born the seat of learning and intellect.

Sir Syed's energy for improving life was directed towards Muslim boys. His views on women's education fitted well with the system prevalent in the homes of Muslim noblemen in Delhi. Maybe he was apprehensive that, when there was such a storm of opposition against the new education system for boys, any move for girls' education would blow away the whole scheme. Not wanting to open multiple battlefronts, he concentrated on boys' education.

At this difficult stage, the young Sheikh Abdullah, fortified by Sir Syed's training, received the message of midnight travails. He had seen the miserable condition of all classes of women. Moved by their plight, he ignored stiff opposition and its consequences and started his movement for girls' education.

Begum Abdullah bestowed her love and care on the girls of the institution founded by her husband. It was the sincerity and dignity of her personality that prompted parents of noble families to send their girls away from the protection and care of their homes and into the affectionate care of that great woman.

Within the limits of decency befitting Muslim culture, Abdullah's tireless campaign for women's education transformed their lives. Among other achievements, Muslim women become aware of the sane and sensible elements of classical and modern education.

The girls still refer to Aala Bi with the same reverence that the boys of the university hold for Sir Syed. The sapling planted by Sheikh Abdullah in 1906 has now grown into a mighty banyan tree. Affiliated to the AMU, the college has many sections, which are grouped under the faculties of science, life science, social science and arts, besides a career-planning centre.

It has mostly been an evolutionary process than a revolutionary one for girls to defy the norms of the university, come out of their shells and assert their idea of a learning space that is more inclusive. Instead of simply letting their lives at the campus be defined simply by the limits set for them, they have shaped what they are becoming and what their student life at the campus needs to be.

In 1933, Muslims of India were shocked, and a majority agitated against *Angarey*, a collection of short stories in Urdu with a progressive outlook on sexuality and private lives of Indian Muslims. The four contributing authors were Sajjad Zaheer, Ahmed Ali, Mahmud Zafar and Rashid Jahan. Since Rashid Jahan was the daughter of Begum Wahid and Sheikh Abdullah (founders of Women's College in Aligarh), critics also attacked the institution. In Aligarh, a local cleric, Shahid Ahrarwi, was leading the charge against Women's College. He wrote articles and published cartoons asking for the closure of the college. The college was called a brothel, which should be brought down for good. Ismat Chughtai was a student of the college at the time. She read the stories and articles of Ahrarwi. Ismat responded to Ahrarwi with an article published in the Aligarh Gazette, calling male students of Aligarh to save the college. In response, male students beat up Ahrarwi. Ismat Chughtai recalled the incident:

> After reading *Angarey*, I read Ahrarwi's rag. I felt deeply offended and wrote an article in which I said, 'Muslim girls are backward and deprived of many opportunities. On top of it, Mulla Ahrarwi has become their mortal enemy. Let the college be closed, but only our corpses would go from here. Who will come to close the college? We will deal with him appropriately. We have six thousand brothers in the university; will they see our corpses being defiled and remain quiet? Whenever Mulla Ahrarwi comes to our mind, we remember our six thousand brothers in the university and the venerable professors and teachers, and we feel emboldened. As long as they are there, no son of a mother can do any harm to us. The queen of Jhansi sent a rakhi to Emperor Humayun. All the college girls are sending their best wishes and rakhis of esteem and affection to thousands of our brothers. We are sure they will take some steps for our protection.'

I read out the long and rather emotional article to the girls. There was great commotion. Papa Mian got to know of it and came to see me. When he heard the contents, he sealed the letter in an envelope and sent it to the Aligarh Gazette. It was published the following day. The boys read the article and, on the same night, gave Mulla Ahrarwi a thrashing and vandalised his office. No one dared to support him. We conveyed our gratitude to the boys through the girls who were related to them. After that, Mulla Ahrarwi disappeared from the scene.

Dr Rahat Abrar recalls how Chughtai had challenged Mullah Ahrari.[15] She even went to the local court and filed a defamation case against him and the newspaper he edited. She won the legal battle too.

In her paper 'Reform and Identity: Purdah in Muslim Women's Education in Aligarh in the Early Twentieth Century', Ms Shadab Bano, a former teacher of the Women's College, describes the influence of Wahid Jahan's daughter Rashid Jahan (1905–52) on Ismat Chughtai.[16] Rashid Jahan was a member of the Communist Party of India and the Progressive Writer's Association and is best known for her one-act play *Parde ke Peechhe* (In the Women's Quarters), published in a literary collection in Urdu titled *Angarey* edited by Sajjad Zaheer.

Recalling an incident, Bano says that when the 'Keats of Urdu Poetry', Asrar-ul Haq Majaz Lakhnawai, made fun of the restrictions under which women lived and asked Ismat Chughtai, 'How do you stay under such rules?' She retorted in her usual style that rules existed for women because of men like him, who were liberal but did nothing to encourage equality for women. Chughtai once protested against the screen that blocked the physical interaction of girls, even with the founder of the college, Sheikh Abdullah. The screen was later removed from the college.

She wrote:

> Clearly, the observance of *purdah* remained crucial to the entire project of women's education at Aligarh. Abdullah Hall was laid out with high enclosing walls, and the hostel/school building placed within were separate enclosures again with high obscuring walls. Some sort of double protection from outside gaze was provided. Special arrangements for *purdah* were made even though it was enclosed from all sides. Particular care for *purdah* was taken in all its details to appear perfectly safe from criticism. Whatever the requirements of *purdah* at that stage, it had a deep impact on the founding of the institution and fixing its nature and rendering it more 'respectable'.
>
> The *purdah* had been so strong that even letters for the girls would be first scanned by Wahid Jahan and then passed on to girls. When Abdullah addressed the students, there was a screen between him and the students. Students who were not blood relatives could not go out to meet him. So while the confinement of women in the smaller settings of household spaces was regarded as excessive,

> confinement of girls in the larger enclosure of the boarding school with only conditional guarded movement was considered perfectly legitimate.[17]

With lush green lawns, beautiful gardens and tree-lined avenues, the campus of the Women's College provides an environment congenial to the mental and physical growth of young girls. Within the campus, there are women's institutions such as the Girls' High School, Senior Secondary School, Papa Mian Union School, Kasturba Creche and a health centre.

The Women's College produced many women of substance who made sure to shine above and beyond *purdah,* some figuratively and others literally. These ladies excelled in various fields, from teaching to medicine to writing.

Rashid Jahan, Wahid Jahan's daughter, became a successful physician, a radical writer and a staunch communist. Her short stories in *Angare* (1932) became the opening salvo of the Urdu Progressive Writers Movement (1936). Rakhshanda Jalil, in her biographical work on Rashid, *A Rebel and Her Cause: The Life and Work of Rashid Jahan*, writes that *Angare* was a 'document of disquiet'; a self-conscious attempt 'to shock people out of their inertia, to show how hypocrisy and sexual oppression had so crept in everyday life'. Rashid inspired a generation of women writers such as Ismat Chughtai, Attia Hosain, Sadia Begum Sohravi, and Razia Sajjad Zaheer, among others.[18]

Like all other reform movements of that time period, the Aligarh movement had its limitations too. For a start, it did prioritise men's education over women's for various reasons, but by the early 20th century, things were changing. The Aligarh movement not only took up the cause of women's education actively, but it also let women (Like Wahid Jahan) be a part of the process.

There is a long list of prominent women who graduated from Women's College. Begum Khatoon Jahan, Mrs Mumtaz Jahan Haider, Khursheed Jahan and Birjis Jahan (daughters of Shaikh Abdullah, Papa Mian) were among the early alumnae of this college.

Later, literary giants such as Ismat Chughtai and Dr Salma Siddiqi (a prolific fiction writer, biographer and daughter of Professor Rasheed Ahmad Siddiqi), famous painter Zarina Hashmi, a well-known actress of Pakistan Nayyar Sultana and Hindi and Sanskrit writer Mrs Kusum Ansal joined their ranks. Begum Abida Ahmad (wife of a former President of India, Fakhruddin Ali Ahmad), Mrs Salma Ansari (wife of a former vice-president of India, Hamid Ansari), Dr Qudsia Tahseen (the first female student of the AMU to become a fellow of the Indian Academy of Sciences, Bangalore) are also proud alumnae of Women's College. Ms Batool Kazim (a psychiatrist at the Harvard Medical School faculty) is nostalgically recalled as the great-granddaughter of the remarkable couple Papa Mian and Aala Bi. (Kazim's grandmother was their daughter Khurshid Jahan. Known as Begum Khurshid Mirza, she was the only one of their children who migrated to Pakistan in 1947.)

The Women's Polytechnic runs several diploma-level courses in electronics and computer engineering, information technology, costume designing, secretarial practices, etc. These courses are part of vocationalisation scheme. The university has a grievance redressal cell for matters exclusively relating to women, apart from the general grievance cell for looking into the complaints of the staff and male students. Women's College provides undergraduate teaching to women students in the faculty of arts, social science, science, life science and commerce. It has a postgraduate course in home science too. It has a coaching and guidance centre for training and grooming students, especially for the weaker sections of society, and for preparing them for various all-India services.

Students of Women's College, an institution of international standards of undergraduate teaching, are always frontrunners. Every year several girls are selected for MBA, MCA, MIBM, MBBS and B.Tech courses, and other competitive exams of the AMU and other institutes of India.

The Women's College campus includes an academic complex of classrooms and seminar rooms, an auditorium, a well-equipped library, administrative buildings and several residential hostels for about 1,500 students. A career-planning centre for women has been established on the college premises with the UGC's assistance. A wide range of opportunities is available to students for co-curricular and extracurricular activities. The students run several clubs and societies. There are facilities for cultural events, National Cadet Corps (NCC), yoga, taekwondo, volleyball, table tennis and basketball. At present, around 2,700 students are enrolled in Women's College. There are around 100 faculty members. The subjects taught include English, Urdu, Hindi, Sanskrit, Arabic, linguistics, fine arts (faculty of arts), history, economics, education, political science, Islamic studies, sociology (faculty of social sciences), botany, zoology, biochemistry (faculty of life sciences), chemistry, physics, mathematics, statistics, geology, geography (faculty of science), home science (faculty of agriculture), theology (faculty of theology) and physical education.

From the very beginning, Women's College students are on par with male AMU students in all fields. The residential life in Women's College hostels and their activities are still remembered by their alumnae, who often share nostalgic moments and events in their gatherings. Similar stories abound about the traditional 'introductions' of the freshers on campus and in hostels as those of their male counterparts. They are not far behind in allocating honorary titles and nicknames to fellow students and teachers. Teasing visiting male students is one of the favourite games on the Women's College campus. A male student, who prefers to remain anonymous, recalls,

> While we were participating in the annual literary and cultural activities of Abdullah Hall on the Women's College campus, fellow Women's College alumni punctured our bicycles, and we were forced to walk on our way back. They did not spare even their male teachers. I came to know from my elders, who had served as faculty in the Women's College, had to walk to their residence quite often.

The AMU may evoke strong affection and emotions among its alumni. For many former students, the varsity remains a second home, and the time they spent here forms the narrative for stories of the golden times they spent at the institution. However, more often than not, the men recount fond memories of their Aligarh days. Most female students had to deal with conservative principals, nosy hostel wardens and strict rules to protect them from going 'astray'.

A woman student laments:

> Women are professors, principals, librarians, part of the non-teaching staff. They are always at the forefront of organising events for the University's Cultural Education Centre, the arts and literary activities. However, when evening sets in, they are supposed to retreat to their hostel rooms or homes or wherever they live.
>
> And yes, the general perception is that they should be at places meant for them. Mingling with the opposite sex is frowned upon; something which they say is not expected of an Aligarian girl.

In 2012, the Supreme Court of India bifurcated the AMUSU, giving Women's College its separate union.[19] Women's College is an institute of the university that incorporates undergraduate students of BA, BSc, BCom and BSW courses. Women's College Students' Union has become a university-wide representative body for students of Women's College. It has pioneered a sense of leadership among female students and channelled their talents and strengths towards their representation.

The same year, residents of Begum Sultan Jahan Hall called for a protest against the provost of the Hall and her entire team for discrepancy in dining funds. They were told there was a deficit in the funds for many months and they had to pay extra to function the dining hall. It evoked a strong protest, and the then provost and her entire team had to quit their offices.

In 2014, The Allahabad high court held the AMU ban on entry of Women's College students into the Maulana Azad Library illegal. It said Women's College was a constituent of the AMU, and no discrimination based on caste, gender and religion could be allowed per Articles 14 and 15 of the Constitution of India.

The AMU vice-chancellor Lt Gen. (retd) Zameeruddin Shah, had to retract his remark that there would be a rush of boys in the library if girls were allowed into it. Following reports in the media, the vice-chancellor tried to justify his ban on the grounds of paucity of space. He also regretted his controversial remarks later.

The vice-chancellor had said he would not allow female students to enter the main library, as 'it would attract boys'. Following the uproar over his remarks, the Union HRD ministry wrote to the vice-chancellor saying that keeping out women from the library amounted to a 'human rights violation'.

The similar rules, the vice-chancellor later qualified in his memoirs about the entry of undergraduate girls, apply to Delhi and Mumbai universities. He added that, anyway, the AMU had permitted the girls and arranged for them to be ferried by buses on holidays. On the first Sunday, eight girls availed the offer; on the second Sunday and subsequent Sundays, none bothered. It was much ado about nothing, he claimed.

However, a girl student complained that Women's College was established in 1906 while the Maulana Azad Library was set up decades later. Still, students of Women's College were never given membership in the library. Women students were angry and upset. 'Aren't we part of the AMU? At least let us borrow books if we can't sit inside,' said another student. Still, another one said, 'We have not even looked inside the library. Don't we deserve this facility? We only wanted library cards.' Commented one more student: 'No library in India has enough space for all the students of the concerned college or university. Yet, they never think of such crazy excuses.' She added, 'Many universities or colleges have congested library buildings and not sufficient space/seating to accommodate even 10% of the students eligible to use them.[20]

With such an absurd move, AMU not only set the clock back to the dark ages but it also gave out some rather dangerous messages to the student community and anyone who bothered to follow the university's politics. It lent a sense of legitimacy to the idea of woman as object, one that distracts and takes the focus off academics. Also, when the university vice-chancellor declares that men would throng the library to ogle at women, it places the responsibility for the phenomenon on the women. It doesn't question the men whose intentions of using the library are suspect. It suggests that women will be the reason these men will be compelled to misuse the library. Second, it infers that the only kind of relationship possible between grown-up men and women is sexual. While it is true that under normal circumstances, men and women in colleges and universities engage in relationships, flirtations, etc., suggesting that this is the only way men and women can or will engage with one another is preposterous.

Third, even if sexual relations were to take place (and we all know they do), it is essential to remember that the students involved are consenting adults, so there is no need for the university to police them. The diktat not only questions the priorities of its students, it also doubts their intelligence by suggesting that women in a university would only engage in activities that would harm them. Finally, it falls back on the old, pathetic antidote against sexual violence and harassment: confine women within the 'safe' four walls of the home.

The AMU's diktat also raises questions about women's safety within an educational institution. If the authorities are worried about untoward incidents within a library, it also means they have not taken ample measures to ensure the safety and security of students.

Female leadership plays an integral role at AMU; female students have actively joined all protest movements on the campus and never remained mute spectators. They do not just attend public meetings that address social and political issues but also speak their mind. The university authorities have been in trouble before over a controversial diktat asking women to wear 'proper and decent looking dresses' and own not more than one mobile. Regarding the dress code, a student screamed, '*Shariya* law in our backyard! That's alarming!' Her friend quipped, 'Not in our backyard, my friend. Right in front of us!'

In 2016, the residents of Indira Gandhi Hall (a residential hall for postgraduate students) organised a protest against their provost for slut shaming, mental harassment and character assassination. The provost was sent on an extended leave and never returned to the office.

When the university authorities postponed examinations, thereby disrupting the academic calendar in 2018, students from Women's College blocked Bab-e-Syed (the university main gate), demanding that either the postponement be taken back or the girls who had booked tickets to return to their homes be compensated. It was the first time the Women's College Students' Union (WCSU) broke an age-old tradition and took a bold initiative independently. It was now clear to everybody that the WCSU was no longer a mere shadow of the male-dominated AMUSU.

The same year, residents of Abdullah Hall and Indira Gandhi Hall – both Girls' hostels – wanted to join the ongoing protest called by AMUSU against the targeting of the AMU by right-wing goons. They were denied permission and locked inside their halls; they broke open the locks and joined the protest to defend the university, smashing all prejudices against the weaker sex.

The following year, when the AMU rose against hate mongering via an audio-visual medium by some right-wing fanatics, women students all by themselves locked the registrar's office and demanded immediate action against the authorities who had turned a blind eye to the issue.

However, the stronghold of patriarchy is hard to break. Hayaat Fatemah laments in a post on a news portal:

> In recent months, an undergraduate student at AMU's Abdullah Hall has witnessed deliberate restrictions on free movement, an unacceptable invasion of privacy, unduly character assassination, misuse of power by post holders, slander and curtailment of basic freedom … Any outing requires a long process which includes acquiring a written consent from a parent and the permission of the warden, who is free to decline as per her will. Incidentally, other girls' residential halls in Aligarh Muslim University—wherein the undergraduate students of engineering, medicine and law reside—do not observe such absurd rules.

On 24 September 2019, a new provost, Ghazala Naheed, was appointed to Abdullah Hall. Within a week of her appointment, she issued a diktat cancelling the provision of special outings (what is so special about stepping out on a Monday?) since there are already three normal outings in a week, imposing a curfew hour at 5.30 pm, forbidding one to one interactions with Zomato and Swiggy delivery executives after 6 pm, planting surveillance cameras everywhere and discouraging girls from participating in competitions and workshops held outside the girls' campus.[21]

The girl lamented,

even after a hundred years, the Abdullah Hall [Girls Hostel] is still struggling with issues that should have long been done away with. The outside world can scarcely imagine what goes on inside the campus. With seven hostels accommodating undergraduate and high school girls, a small library, a gymnasium, a canteen, two small shops, a tailor, a shady beauty parlour, a playground and an auditorium, Abdullah Hall is a small village with utilities placed in the vicinity…

She added,

The campus has witnessed rebellion several times recently; girls have broken locks to protest only to face severe ramifications and character assassination. In 2013, a manual made it compulsory for women to be dressed in decent '*salwar kameez*' with a '*dupatta*' and imposed a fine of Rs 500 if the regulations weren't followed….

Such cases are countless: four girls in a two-seated room were caught smoking cigarettes in September 2019. Smoking inside the premises of residential halls is an unstated offence that does not apply to men employed in the hall, the gatekeepers and the workers. The canteen behind the Maulana Azad Library offers a spectacle where boys can be seen smoking cigarettes along with their professors.

Thus, smoking, indeed hazardous, is an offence inside the campus for girls because it is directly associated with the character of the girl caught smoking. Does an offence of this magnitude give

> the head girl and the wardens the liberty to snatch a girl's phone and scroll through her personal pictures? Five wardens with the then provost, interrogated the girls for four hours, used abusive language for them, '*yeh tawaif hain* (these girls are harlots)', and instead of punishing them, used it as an excuse to call a girl's parent and say, '*Apki beti ke nudes hain, dekhenge aap? Bhejoon aapko? Puchiye kya karti hai*' (Should I send your daughter's nudes to you? Ask her about her activities). The girl's father suffered a heart stroke. Her phone was unlocked and kept in the warden's custody for three days.
>
> ...The idea of a university is challenged every day by the administration, the soul of this institution is asleep, and it needs to be reawakened... '*Aligarh ki shehzadiyan*' sit with a suspended internet connection and no outing.[22]

Shadab Bano writes:

> Ironically and unfortunately, the revolt of students faces three layers of resistance – the administration, women who are radical anti-feminists and a section of male students in the university, the *sherwani* posh who claim to be the protectors of Aligarh *tehzeeb* (tradition). Newman once wrote: 'university training is the excellent ordinary means to a great but ordinary end; it aims at raising the intellectual tone of society. It is the education which gives a man a clear conscious view of his own opinions and judgments, a truth in developing them, an eloquence in expressing them and a force in urging them.'[23]

Begum Khurshid Mirza, the daughter of Sheikh Abdullah and Wahid Jahan Begum, the founders of Aligarh Women's College, has written extensively on Aligarh.[24] Her daughter Lubna Kazim has edited memoirs of her mother. It spans the years 1857 to 1963. It provides an insight into the social conditions of Indian Muslims, the state of Muslim women's education, and the transition to Pakistan while illuminating Khurshid Mirza's rich and varied life as an actor, activist, radio and TV artiste, writer, and devoted daughter, wife and mother.

Khurshid Mirza's vitality and dynamism, her pioneering spirit and unconventionality led her to leave the cloistered world of Aligarh after an early marriage to a police officer and then pursue a career in films in Bombay. She rapidly climbed the ladder to stardom as Renuka Devi and worked alongside well-known actors and directors of the time. Unfortunately, Partition cut short her film career and she left for the new country.

Noted NASA scientist Dr Hashima Hasan, the Program Scientist for NuSTAR, expressed thanks to the AMU for helping her materialise her dream. She reminisces:

> The student life at AMU from 1968 to 1973 and the academic credentials gained there helped me attain a prestigious scholarship to further pursue higher studies in Nuclear Science at the University of Oxford … I worked hard and gave this land all I had. This great nation paid me back in spades, but it all started at AMU. I was a little girl back then. Still, the spectacular satellite launch made me eager to follow every success and failure in the newspaper. I clearly remember the day man landed on the moon … The work at NASA is dynamic, challenging and energising. My journey to becoming a space scientist began after a post-graduate degree in Nuclear Physics at the Aligarh Muslim University.[25]

Another illustrious alumnus, Professor Dr Rashida Ertufaq Ali, who, at age 85, used to visit the University of Karachi with her driver, had been giving her students MPhil and PhD degrees for several years without pay. She taught at the department of applied chemistry, University of Karachi. Then she convinced the then vice-chancellor Dr Syed Masoom Ali Tirmizi to establish the department of food science and technology, which has so far given hundreds of experts in this field.

Dr Rashida's husband, Dr Syed Ertifaq Ali, was also the vice-chancellor of the University of Karachi and a botany professor. She is from the city of Kanpur in India. Her father sent her to Aligarh for higher education, where she stayed in the hostel and did her Master's in Organic Chemistry in 1953. Ertefaq Ali was dear to her;

he went to India from Pakistan, married his wife, and brought her to Pakistan.

When asked why the idea of establishing a department of food science came up, she said... 'We used to see a huge department of food science in every major university in the world, which was very supportive of the industry – here people thought that this department would probably mean teaching cooking!'

Within a few years, of its establishment, the department gained so much importance that now it gets admission on the highest merit after pharmacy.

When asked why does she come and teach in the university even at this age when she has been retired for several years!

'Do teachers ever retire?'[26]

13

A VC FACES TANTRUMS FROM SIX MASTERS

In 2017, the UGC recommended that the selection process for the appointment of the AMU vice-chancellor be tweaked to match the procedure followed by other central universities. Currently, AMU has a more significant say in the appointment process. The university's Executive Council shortlists a panel of five candidates. It forwards it to the AMU court, which, in turn, prunes the list to three names and forwards the same to the HRD ministry, which in turn passes it to the president of India, the ex-officio visitor of the university for the final decision.

The university defends its process, saying that it is in line with top-class world universities who have all the freedom and autonomy to choose their VCs.

> The criticism of the vice-chancellor's election is also misplaced. The V-C's election process is in accordance with the procedure laid down by Parliament in the AMU's statute 2(1). Moreover, the AMU's procedure is quite democratic and transparent as all stakeholders, including past and present students, employees, parliamentarians etc, participate in selecting a V-C, though the final say remains with the President of India.[1]

Professor Faizan Mustafa, an Aligarian, argues that the UGC should have recommended this unique process of AMU to other central universities too. He admitted that India's leading universities are not where they ought to have been both in terms of international rankings as well as the promotion of free thinking and dissent. Of course, the vice-chancellor cannot be entirely blamed for this, but how we select people to lead universities does have a bearing.

In many cases, the vice-chancellors, who head universities, are appointed not because they are reputable scholars or distinguished administrators but because they have the right political connections in the HRD ministry in the case of central universities or the appropriate political or caste affiliations in state universities. There are also whispers regarding money exchange in filling the post in state universities. Not surprisingly, expediency, and not merit, often prompts the choice. This mess has resulted in several appointments being quashed by the judiciary on the grounds of ineligibility, absence of consultation between the governor and the state government, problems in the composition of the search committee and so on.

The AMU's method is in line with the AMU Act of 1920. A similar process was outlined for BHU by a 1915 Act. Unfortunately, the BHU Act has been suspended for decades, and a government-nominated Executive Council runs the university.

The vice-chancellor remains the fulcrum of resilience of a university system and the keeper of its university's conscience. It is to facilitate this expected role that the universities need people with high moral values, leadership qualities and integrity, academic excellence and administrative experience. The government continues to play a crucial role in the appointment of vice-chancellors. The autonomy of universities is much talked about but seldom regarded. There are different levels of governmental intervention: Vice-chancellors of central universities are appointed by the president of India, who is an ex-officio visitor of all central universities, and s/he generally acts on the advice of the central government; in state universities, appointments are made by the governor on their own or in consultation with the state government, and seldom in consultation with the university.

Each university has its distinctive identity and its peculiar problems, so ideally, universities should be free to elect their vice-chancellors who they think are best suited to lead them at a particular point in time.

In the Western world, universities can choose their vice-chancellors. The AMU follows the Western model. While advertisements for the post of a vice-chancellor look like a step in the direction of transparency, the exercise has not proven to be the most robust in the selection of the most appropriate candidate. This is perhaps why the UGC Regulations, 2010, have not made advertisements mandatory. The position of a vice-chancellor is so high and important that it is perhaps better to offer it to someone after inviting nominations from the present and former vice-chancellors and other eminent people. People who lobby for the post or enthusiastically apply alone would not be considered.

However, any individual or institution can take an unreasonable position on any issue. Historian M. Rajivlochan points out, 'For once, it is the HRD ministry that accuses a VC of AMU of appointing a non-academic to administer the university.'[2] Usually, it is the other way around.

So far as the appointment of a vice-chancellor is concerned, it seems all formulations have failed. It is usually believed that the academic credentials of a university head are more important than anything else. Sometimes, however, academics have proved to be bad administrators, and non-academics have become more suitable for academic administration. No generalisation is possible.

However, the UGC has formulated rules that a person being considered for vice-chancellor's office should have at least 10 years of experience as a professor. Perhaps this is meant to curb the official propensity to appoint bureaucrats, police or army officers to this august position. M. Rajivlochan opines,

> It is another matter that the Indian university system is such that anyone appointed Vice-Chancellor is liable to come under

> intense attack from students and faculty should he not be able to manipulate both these groups. Managing the politicians is an important 'ability'.
>
> Academic leadership is the least of the bothers before a VC. The university body – students and faculty – today does not seek the approval of the VC, nor do they look up to him for any leadership. Rather, it is the VC who falls the onus of seeking the approval of the students and faculty. Any lapses on his part attract serious criticism from whomsoever had not been cultivated. 'Draconian', 'incompetent', 'undemocratic', 'fascist' and 'stooge of the government' are often heard in this context.
>
> In contrast is the case of the numerous private universities that have sprung up all over India. VCs in such universities are mostly not academics of any particular standing. Puppets in the hands of the owners certainly are. The owners wield absolute control over everything. Yet, by all reports, those universities are not doing badly. Many leading academics have joined such universities without ever making public mention of how these universities are managed and the academic consequences of such governance ... Rather than providing academic leadership, the current generation of academics in Indian universities manages the conflicting aspirations within and outside the campuses. In some cases, this could mean the VC needs to be a good manager of people and politics. In other cases, the VC may need to be a good fundraiser. An academic of great standing he need not be.[3]

Protests can be organised against any vice-chancellor, however well-meaning his/her administration might be. Former union minister Salman Khurshid cites the case of Saiyid Hamid, who had gone to Aligarh determined to put things in order, and he proceeded to do just that by ensuring that university teachers did not quickly get paid leave to take up lucrative assignments in the Middle East; that examination schedules were adhered to meticulously; that admissions were restricted to deserving applicants and the system of nominations at the behest of student leaders was completely eradicated.[4] Saiyid Hamid failed just as all educated liberal Muslims will if they continue to look over their shoulders. Left alone, Saiyid

Hamid would have achieved wonders for educational standards and discipline at Aligarh.

Former vice-chancellor Saiyid Hamid admits: An atmosphere of general discontent prevails on the AMU campus, and agitation mongers can easily exploit this. Neglecting ground realities, we often blame the head of the institution, ignoring the root causes, while the press tends to confine itself to reasons that meet the eye.[5]

A vice-chancellor brought into such a situation finds himself on the horns of a dilemma; he has to attempt to streamline the institution, which would include a gradual slimming operation or adopt the line of least resistance and let things continue. But the latter alternative will go against the grain with any conscientious person who intends to work for the betterment of the university. Some vice-chancellors take the populist line, garnering kudos for maintaining peace on the campus, passing their time, and leaving the university at the end of their tenure a few shades worse than when they took it over.

The university administration consists predominantly of teachers who provide the element of continuity. If they are interested in the plans for the university's development, deviations and agitations can be avoided or minimised. Students' agitation is generally believed not to occur if teachers didn't inspire or support them.

Legacy also plays a vital role on the campus. A vice-chancellor, howsoever competent, may be stymied by his legacy. If his predecessor has been weak, succumbed to pressures, or adopted a populist stance, the successor will have to suffer the consequences.

AMU witnessed conditions of chaos before Mahmood-ur Rahman took over as the vice-chancellor. His predecessor, Professor M.N. Faruqui, had descended to a level wherein he sought shelter from lumpen elements and ran the university under their protection. Any effort to divest those elements of the power they had been habituated to would result in an explosion.

Saiyid Hamid often and conveniently held his predecessor, Professor A.M. Khusro, responsible for laxity, which led to frequent crises during the former regime. His successor Syed Hashim Ali, too, had to face problems during his tenure. Does that mean that Syed Hashim Ali, too, would have been justified in blaming it on the legacy he had inherited from Saiyid Hamid?

Syed Hashim Ali admitted that before his arrival, a large contingent of police had been sanctioned on the campus and said: 'Twenty teachers had been beaten up by the rusticated students and their hirelings within the short period of 11 days intervening the departure of my predecessor Saiyid Hamid, and my arrival as VC.'[6]

Community leaders form opinions about the functioning of the AMU on the briefings of disgruntled students and the staff. Needless to say such motivated reports are often different from the actual situation on the campus.

The position of the AMU vice-chancellor is quite challenging. Former vice-chancellor Badruddin Tyabji says that letters from all classes of Muslims from all over India poured into his office every day.[7] Some commended them, some criticised his performance, while many sought his views, guidance and help in various matters affecting them personally or the community as a whole. Before going to Aligarh, he had no idea of the unique position that the AMU vice-chancellor holds in the eyes of Indian Muslims. Quite a revelation! He only realised it after he had lived in Aligarh for some time.

Another former vice-chancellor, Col B.H. Zaidi, said a vice-chancellor is like 'a woman with six husbands – the state government, the central government, the *millat*, the teachers, the students and the court'.[8] He has to meet everybody's expectations. The real problem arises when expectations of diverse groups are diametrically opposed, he added.

A vice-chancellor's achievement is also judged by the size of grants he can obtain from the government and donations from non-government sources. He is measured even by the number of dignitaries who visit the university to deliver convocation addresses or receive honorary degrees and what he can do to secure jobs for students and find opportunities to satisfy the ambitions of his junior colleagues, besides maintaining law and order on the campus.

Former AMU law professor Tahir Mahmood records:

> You are a Central university. UGC regulations apply to you as they are mandatory. If every other Central university follows the regulation, why can't you? Why to appoint a former army officer? This rather intriguing question was put the other day to the authorities of Aligarh Muslim University (AMU) by a Supreme Court bench, while hearing a case against its sitting vice-chancellor (VC). The norm set for the purpose by the University Grants Commission for appointment of VCs, which the bench referred to, is 10 years experience as a university professor or in an equivalent position at a research or academic institution.[9]

Former vice-chancellor of Punjabi University in Patiala, Professor Amrik Singh, described the unenvious position of a vice-chancellor,

> Any VC would be better than none. Any vice chancellor! Who will answer the prerequisites that are being enumerated? Where is the human being who will not be too soft, too rigid, too flamboyant? Who will be a proud practising Muslim but not an obscurantist? Armed with impeccable secular credentials, but showing proper respect to traditionalists? Who will exude love and understanding for the students? Communicate with them? Display tact and vision in relation with the teaching staff? Listen to the politicians without either antagonising them or succumbing to their pressure? Cope with the administration and with the requirements of the government? Elicit commitment when and where there is none? Squaring a circle would be easier.[10]

The glamour attached to the post of the AMU vice-chancellor's post makes it one of the most sought-after posts in the Muslim community. A look at some races for this post in 1995 offers exciting insights.

In the second half of February 1995, all ears were tuned to New Delhi to find out who had been chosen to steer the ship of AMU (following the exit of Professor M.N. Faruqui) as a panel of three names was pending with the union government for consideration.[11]

The panel comprised three bureaucrats, two of whom had experience tackling terrorism in the strife-torn Kashmir valley while the third was a police officer of the West Bengal cadre. Two of these officers were in service while the third had recently retired. They were additional chief secretary to the Jammu and Kashmir government, Mahmood-ur-Rahman; inspector general of police, West Bengal, S.A. Safawi; and former advisor to the governor of Jammu and Kashmir, S.M. Murshed.

The Executive Council of the university had first selected a panel of five names at its meeting on 11 February. The other two names were Ishrat Aziz of the Indian Foreign Service and Professor Shamim Jairajpuri from the university itself. At the meeting of the university court the next day, these two names were eliminated in the voting process. Rahman secured the highest number of votes in the university court. Murshed came third.

The Executive Council had recommended another panel of five names at its meeting on 31 December. Professor Shamim Jairajpuri had secured the highest number of votes there. Others on the panel were Professor Abul Hasan Siddiqui (former pro-vice-chancellor of the university), Hasan Iqbal (financial advisor to the Ministry of Railways), Mahmood-ur-Rahman (IAS of Jammu and Kashmir Cadre) and Moosa Raza (former chief secretary to the Jammu and Kashmir government). Just before the meeting of the court, Moosa Raza decided to withdraw. He was reportedly upset over the virulent campaign unleashed against him by a section within the university. It was alleged that Raza was a Shia, his wife a Hindu, and he was related to the late M.C. Chagla, who, as union minister for education, had superseded the AMU Act in 1965.

Later, Moosa Raza confided to a visitor from Aligarh that the main reason for his withdrawal was something else. He recounted how a community leader approached him as soon as his name was put up in the Executive Council's panel and asked Raza what the latter would do in exchange for support in the court for his candidature. Appalled at such a brazen attempt at bribery, Raza decided to opt out.

The court returned the list, directing the Executive Council to send a complete one. When Professor M.N. Faruqui had been elected, the court referred back to the panel on the grounds of withdrawal by one among the panel. The union HRD ministry considered the matter, and it was held that the court had no power to refer the panel back. This precedent cast a shadow on the present panel.

Another doubt about the panel was cast by sheer carelessness on the part of the Executive Council and the court while electing S.A. Safawi (his correct name was Haider Aziz Safawi), an alumnus of the university. Interestingly enough, two of the candidates, acting vice-chancellor Shamim Ahmad and Professor Shamim Jairajpuri, were also members of the Executive Council. Both of them had voted themselves.

Then, some people began a smear campaign against S.M. Murshed. Wall posters accused him of love for Bacchus and his Rushdian ways. Photostat copies of his article 'Bibulous Rites of a Full Mussalman'[12]) made the rounds on campus. In retaliation, the Marxist supporters of Murshed, a retired IAS officer from the West Bengal cadre, came out with photostat copies of another article, 'The Muslim Factor' by him in the same newspaper (16 February 1993), lamenting the destruction of the Babri Masjid at Ayodhya even though he had not minced words to express his utter lack of faith in Marxist principles.

The appointment of the new incumbent had a crucial significance because almost one-third of the university's faculty was to retire in the next few years, creating a sort of vacuum. The university was also opposed to playing a vital role in helping the Muslim psyche realistically face the challenge of the post-Babri scenario. The most critical task before an incoming vice-chancellor was not merely to maintain law and order but to provide the intellectual input which neither a bureaucrat nor a simple academic could do.

The selection of the successor of M. Rahman as the AMU vice-chancellor was the usual murky story of manipulation and underhand tactics. The university witnessed some very high-voltage drama, with battle lines sharply drawn between Rahman's supporters and his detractors, splitting the university into two warring camps. The outgoing vice-chancellor's vigorous attempts to get another term was seen as part of a hidden agenda of the BJP. The visitor, President K.R. Narayanan, succumbed to the pressure of the anti-Rahman lobby. The Marxist inclinations of the visitor also went against the anti-Marxist M. Rahman.

It was perhaps the first time that the visitor sought to be influenced in such a manner. Rahman's detractors accused him of drumming up support for himself first in the Executive Council and then the court. They also alleged that he had sent busloads of his supporters to exert pressure on the visitor. For weeks, AMU remained paralysed while rival groups indulged in a slugfest. His backers used backdoor tactics to garner support for Rahman. At the same time, his detractors went around proclaiming that, instead of filling up the 40-odd vacancies, Rahman had conveniently transferred or removed all those 'inconvenient' ex-officio members of the court and replaced them with nine new members and also inducted four others in the Executive Council.

During the meeting of the Executive Council, M. Rahman bagged 20 votes, the highest. Of 28 members, 24 attended the crucial meeting. Wajahat Habibullah, another IAS officer of the Jammu and Kashmir cadre, Professor A.H. Siddiqui, a former pro-vice-chancellor, Mohammad Hamid Ansari, a former career diplomat, and Professor Faratullah Khan were the other panellists whose names were forwarded to the court for consideration. H.A.S. Jafri, pro-vice-chancellor, M.Y. Qadri, vice-chancellor of Kashmir University, Mohammad Zahoor, Manzoor Ahmad, vice-chancellor of Dr B.R. Ambedkar University (Agra) and Syed Tahir Mahmood, a former Chairman of the Minorities Commission were voted out. The names of three other IAS officers – S.A.T. Rizvi of the Uttar Pradesh cadre and S.Y. Qureshi and Naseem Ahmad of the Haryana cadre too cropped up during the discussions in the Executive Council. In the court, M. Rahman again secured the highest number of votes (74), while Mohammad Hamid Ansari and Professor Faratullah Khan bagged 70 each.

The lobbies worked overtime attacking the opponents. The AMU's dirty linen was washed in full public view. Anonymous letters to newspapers were part of the game. The AMUTA passed a unanimous resolution on 29 April saying Rahman was 'morally obliged and constitutionally bound' to hand over charge of his office as per rules. Rahman's term expired on 30 April. However, the HRD ministry had asked him to continue till the decision of the visitor who finally announced the name of Mohammad Hamid Ansari, an Aligarian and a retired career diplomat, as the new vice-chancellor on 24 May.

Recording the developments, the then HRD secretary to the government of India M.K. Kaw wrote,

> In the case of the AMU, both Joshi [the minister Dr Murli Manohar Joshi] and I agreed that the current incumbent Mehmud-ur-Rahman had had a very peaceful stint and deserved a second tenure.
>
> One other name that the search committee had shortlisted was that of Hamid Ansari. As he had just one year and four months of service left, I dismissed him in one sentence that it would not be wise to appoint a lame-duck vice chancellor just for a short period. I had also commented that he had merely diplomatic experience and had no pretensions to academic administration.
>
> To my surprise, we got the file back with a strong note in Ansari's favour penned by the great man [K.R. Narayanan, president of India] himself. He had taken the trouble to counter my points with a one-page note signed by himself.[13]

Man proposes, God disposes. M. Rahman, a seasoned bureaucrat serving as the vice-chancellor of AMU, had the upper hand in preparing the panel for his successor. He wanted a second term. When he explained that it was impossible, he viewed the advisor as a sworn enemy. The panel sent to the visitor (president of India) via the HRD ministry included three names. Of course, M. Rahman topped the list, followed by Ansari and Professor Khan. Rahman calculated that Ansari, who had only 22 months left in his term, would be eliminated in the process, and Rahman's ascension to the coveted post for the second term would be a smooth affair. HRD minister Murli Manohar Joshi favoured Rehman. The clever Ansari outwitted him. Rahman failed to note that the president of India, K.R. Narayanan was a former Indian Foreign Service (IFS) man. His secretary, Gopalkrishan Gandhi, was also a serving IFS man. It was a coincidence that Gandhi was on leave when the concerned file reached the president's house. Senior IAS officer Shumsher K. Sheriff, 1977 batch (AGMUT), was the joint secretary to the president of India. The president of India overruled the recommendation of the HRD ministry and appointed Ansari as the vice-chancellor for the shortest-ever term of 22 months.

Later, when Ansari became the vice-president of India, Sheriff joined him as his secretary and was later elevated to secretary-general of the Rajya Sabha in 2012 with the rank and status of Cabinet secretary, on deputation for a period of little more than one year till superannuation and after that on a contractual basis for a period of two years.

Rahman was scheduled to hand over the charge to the incumbent on 29 May but abruptly left his residence the previous day. When he left, disgruntled students barged into the vice-chancellor lodge. They were demanding readmission for the rusticated students. A few days before Rahman's departure, some hostel inmates had observed *yom-e-chiragh* (day of lighting candles) to protest the 'atrocities' unleashed on the students by Rahman during his tenure. They had even manhandled Rahman and his wife during a farewell function at the university library. Rahman denies any such ugly incident.

Ansari served for about 22 months. A career diplomat, he ran the university, his alma mater like a foreign mission, depending on a group of faithful employees to keep a watch on their colleagues and inform the vice-chancellor. He did not lag in placating the ego of historian Professor Irfan Habib, and this action paid him a rich dividend as the left lobby succeeded in getting a term of vice-president of India to him. He was lucky to get the second term too.

He was succeeded by Naseem Ahmed, a Haryana cadre serving IAS whose term can be described as a disaster for the university. Like most vice-chancellors, he could not complete his term and resigned in the wake of student unrest. He fell into the trap of regional groups in the university. He was succeeded by Professor P.K. Abdul Aziz, who hailed from Kerala. After a long stint, a vice-chancellor came from a southern state. His term too was a lacklustre one. He was succeeded by a non-academician and Army veteran Lt Gen. Zameer Uddin Shah in 2012.

Days after it sought to assert that AMU was not a minority institution but a central university in August 2016, the HRD ministry decided not to support the UGC in holding that AMU was bound by its regulations like other central universities.

An affidavit filed by the ministry in the Supreme Court countered the submission by the UGC on whether AMU was obligated under law to abide by the UGC Regulations 2010, which prescribed minimum qualifications for the appointment of the academic staff.

The UGC had told the court that its regulations, once notified in the gazette, had the force of law and were 'statutorily mandatory' for all central universities, irrespective of whether state governments or universities had formally adopted them.

But the HRD ministry stated that state governments and central universities were required to adopt the regulations formally and that there could not be an automatic amendment because the UGC had created new rules. The differences between the ministry and UGC came to the fore as they responded to a petition that sought a direction to quash the appointment of AMU vice-chancellor Lt Gen. Zameer Uddin Shah in May 2012.

AMU alumnus Syed Abrar Ahmed had challenged the appointment because Shah did not fulfil the UGC requirements. He had not worked for at least 10 years as a professor in a university or an equivalent post in an academic research institute. After the

Allahabad high court ruled in favour of the appointment, Ahmed appealed in the top court.

The UGC had filed its affidavit in March, stating that its regulations had the force of law and were not dependent upon adoption by a state government since, after the notification, they were legally binding on all central universities. This argument jeopardised Shah's appointment as vice-chancellor since the UGC meant that any appointment violating its 2010 Regulations was legally wrong, especially when AMU had approved, adopted and implemented these regulations. The HRD ministry stated that after a Supreme Court ruling in 2015, it had written to all central universities to adopt the regulations and carry out amendments to their statutes. Regarding the appointment of vice-chancellor for AMU, the ministry pointed out that the clause regarding the vice-chancellor's appointment had been kept in abeyance by AMU when it went ahead with the appointment in 2012.

The university had sent a panel of three names to the HRD ministry. The ministry did not take a rigid stand when forwarding the panel to the visitor in May 2012, as the post of the vice-chancellor was vacant and required to be filled up without delay. The ministry said that it was the visitor who appointed Shah.

Lt Gen. Zameer Uddin Shah recollects that in 2006, he had received a call from a former Rajya Sabha member imploring him to attest his willingness to be considered as the vice-chancellor of AMU. He had been told that bouts of indiscipline had crippled the university. He was willing, but former vice-chancellor Hamid Ansari cautioned me 'about what I was in for and said that the benefactor, who was pushing my candidature, would definitely ask for his "pound of flesh" and he indeed did so'.[14]

He claims that in April 2014, the HRD minister Kapil Sibal wanted him to rush to Aligarh as AMU was headless. The minister suggested a way out to which he did not agree. On his showing reluctance, a retired IAS officer, Noor Mohammad, was appointed. He assumed charge that night. A few AMU professors in the Allahabad high court successfully challenged the 'backdoor' entry.

Shah recalls,

> The election to draw out the panel for VC attracts a lot of canvassing and character assassination. It was widely advertised that I was an alcoholic who would be too drunk in the evenings to attend any university business. Also bandied around were the old allegations that I had a clandestine affair with a woman in Ahmedabad while dousing the communal flames.[15]

He fell out with the former Rajya Sabha member. Despite his written reservation against the nomination of the former Rajya Sabha member to the Executive Council, his detractor was re-nominated. It proved a significant impediment to any progressive measures to be undertaken by him. Shah said,

> The self-appointed guardian invariably levelled allegations of corruption and spared no effort to keep the university in the last century. I could only 'hamstring' him once it was discovered that he had preferred a travel claim for a journey he had not undertaken. An enquiry found him culpable. The former Rajya Sabha MP managed to stay afloat and was often in the corridors of power in Delhi, hurling wild allegations against me.[16]

The tenure of Shah came to an end on 16 May 2017. He claims,

> Unlike in the past, where some VCs had thrown in the towel and quit prematurely or had moved out after finishing their tenures, leaving the institution headless for long periods, I was determined to ensure that the procedure of selection of my reliever was undertaken well in time. And I handed over the charge.[17]

A farewell was planned for his departure on 17 May. He indicated 9 a.m. as his departure time. Still, in a well-planned and surprising move, he visited the grave of the AMU founder Sir Syed at 5 a.m. that morning, offered a silent prayer and then his son drove him out, in his private car, through the portals of AMU, without fanfare.

Professor Mansoor secured 94 votes, Dr Shariff secured 90 votes and Dr Jameel secured 86 votes. In contrast, Professor Javaid Akhter, AMU Registrar, secured 84 votes, and Professor Mazahir Kidwai, vice-chancellor of IIMT University, Meerut, secured 36 votes. AMU court members polled a total of 130 votes. The AMU court recommended the names of Professor Tariq Mansoor, principal and CMS, Jawaharlal Nehru Medical College and Hospital; Dr Abusaleh Shariff, executive director and chief scholar, US-India Policy Institute, Washington, and Dr Shahid Jameel, CEO, Welcome Trust and DBT India Alliance, to the visitor for the post of the next vice-chancellor.

Murkey games on the selection of Aligarh Muslim University vice chancellor remain unabated. On the superannuation of Dr Tariq Mansoor (he later became a member of the legislative council of the ruling BJP. He was also nominated as one of the 12 Vice Presidents of the All India body of the BJP). A few months before his term ended, he had appointed Professor Gulrez Ansari as the Pro-Vice Chancellor. A controversy has erupted over the process for the selection of the next vice-chancellor of the Aligarh Muslim University (AMU). A panel headed by AMU's acting vice-chancellor Mohammad Gulrez has picked his wife, Naima Khatoon Gulrez, among five candidates shortlisted for the VC's post, raising questions of conflict of interest.

AMU's Executive Council had on 30 October 2024 shortlisted five names, including Professor Faizan Mustafa (vice-chancellor, Chanakya Law University, Patna, and former vice chancellor, NALSAR, Hyderabad), Professor MU Rabbani (former dean, faculty of medicine, AMU); Professor Naima Khatoon (principal, Women's College, AMU); Professor Furqan Qamar (former vice-chancellor, University of Rajasthan and first vice-chancellor, Central University of Himachal Pradesh) and Professor Qayyum Husain (vice-chancellor, Cluster university, Srinagar, J&K).

The five names were sent to the AMU court, which, in its meeting after a few days, finalised three probables for the prestigious post. They are Professor Muzaffar Uruj Rabbani, former dean, faculty of medicine, AMU, Professor Faizan Mustafa, and Professor Naima

> Khatoon. Prior to this, 20 names were nominated, of which five were shortlisted by the EC to be sent to the AMU court. Professor Mujahid Baig, one of the candidates amongst 20 names who did not make it to the list of five, has written a letter to the President of India (who is also a Visitor to the university), alleging violation of norms in the Executive Council meeting held on Monday.
>
> He objected to AMU's officiating VC Professor Mohd Gulrez chairing the EC meeting during which the name of the latter's wife and principal of Women College of AMU, Professor Naima Khatoon Gulrez found a place in the panel of five names forwarded to the AMU court.
>
> 'The AMU Act, Statutes and Executive Ordinance and the UGC Regulations 2018 should have been complied with. Acting VC of AMU not only presided over the meeting but also cast the decisive vote in favour of his wife, paving the way for her inclusion in the panel in blatant violation of norms,' alleged Baig.[18]

Hasan Saroor, an Aligarian, asks,

> Why is AMU so vulnerable to controversy? Almost every VC has faced or triggered frayed tempers, and invariably the 'fight' has been over extra-academic issues. At the heart of the problem is the tussle between competing Muslim groups to control this minority university, which gives the 'controlling' group immense political clout. Few VCs, even though they may have started as independent-minded men, have remained independent of the various lobbies backed by influential Muslim leaders.[19]

Former AMU vice-chancellor Saiyid Hamid refers to the present procedure of appointing the vice-chancellor as a significant defect in the AMU (Amendment) Act of 1981. The general procedure prevalent in other universities is that the Executive Council selects two eminent persons for a three-member committee to look for a vice-chancellor. The visitor nominates the third person who chairs the committee. A panel of three names is submitted to the visitor, who selects and appoints one of them. Under this system, the names of the persons being considered by the selection committee remain a closely guarded secret. There is no room for lobbying by different groups. The selected person comes to know that he was under consideration only after the offer is made to him.

Contrary to this general practice, the AMU Act contains a clumsy provision. The Executive Council meets to consider many names, from which a panel of five is selected after a detailed and often heated discussion, sometimes punctuated by voting.

Some of the candidates, in furtherance of their cases, start canvassing and overt as well as covert lobbying. This continues till the court meets. Again, a detailed discussion ensues. The court drops two names or sends all five to the visitor who makes the final selection and appointment. It means a person is commissioned to design a system for the selection of the vice-chancellor in a manner calculated to erode his authority and create opposition to him from the outset.

The results are apparent. The groups supporting the successful candidate expect favours from him as a quid pro quo for their support. The groups whose candidates fail nurse a grudge against the successful candidate. These groups are slow to bury the hatchet. This creates a twofold difficulty for the vice-chancellor.

Nowhere in the country does a vice-chancellor enjoy so much power, particularly emergency power, under Section 19(C) of the AMU Act. No vice-chancellor wants to dispense with this power, though hardly anyone has criticised such vast power after relinquishing the coveted post.

Former vice-chancellor Lt Gen. Zameer Uddin Shah claims that during his reign, AMU became the leading university in (a) Recycling wastewater without energy costs, and its scientists were deeply involved in projects to restore our sacred rivers to their pristine glory (b) Harnessing solar energy for automotive purposes; (c) Production of Nano fertilisers, which do not pollute the environment; and (d) Production of Nano filters for the desalination of seawater. This would resolve water scarcity in our coastal cities and be a boon to regions with brackish water. About academic performance, he reeled out the ranking of the university in several newspapers and magazines, to which the HRD minister Smriti Irani, who did not hide her displeasure with him, quipped, 'I know how these rankings are obtained,' disclosed the vice-chancellor to Rana Sidiqqui Zaman in an interview.[20]

In a separate note submitted before the Chatterji Committee of Enquiry, Justice P.N. Sapru (retd) stated that vice-chancellors should resist the tendency to use emergency powers except in specific cases. The law should be amended to substitute some objective tests to prevent its possible misuse. Alternatively, he suggested, the Executive Council may be given the power to delegate authority to the vice-chancellor within strictly defined limits to act on its behalf in cases that cannot wait for a decision until it meets. M.A. Shahmiri, another member of the Chatterji Committee, agreed with Sapru.

As many as 52 cases where 'emergency powers need not have been involved' were cited before the Committee. The Rahimtoola enquiry committee had also stated in 1927 that 'emergency powers of the VC have been strained and broken'.

Ibn Khaldun Bharati writes:

> My contention is that AMU, though it runs on the money paid by the Indian State for the advancement of the Indian Muslims, is controlled by a small social group of a subregion who exploit it for their vested interests. I also said that every VC has been most extravagant in using his emergency powers to benefit the group that has installed him in the position. That group, which controls the governing bodies of AMU like the court, the EC and the AC, are incestuous clubs where everyone is everyone's someone. If I am wrong, how come, every VC has either been an Ashrāf from UP or his cousin from the nobility of Nizam? How come it has never agitated you that AMU hasn't ever had a Bihari or a Nari (woman) or an Ansari as VC? Ever thought why not a Hindu has been the VC of AMU if it is not a Succession State of the Mughal empire?[21]

Strechey Hall

Strechey Hall and University Mosque

Minto Circle

Sir Syed House Gate

Victoria Gate

Sir Syed House

University Mosque

A.K. Tibbiya College

14

FEUDING FEUDAL OF AMU

The man who dreamt of AMU and took the first concrete step to realise the dream had conceived of the institution as a training ground for leadership of the Muslim community in the best values of Western traditions. In post-Independence India, three significant changes occurred: (i) The institution was converted into a national centre for educational excellence, and thus, its aims were limited. (ii) The proliferation of educational institutions throughout the country reduced the catchment area for AMU. Most students and teachers came from northern states, particularly Uttar Pradesh and Bihar, reducing the institution to a regional rather than a national centre. (iii) The university came to be perceived by the Muslims as a symbol of traditional Islamic values. Little wonder that an endemic conflict ensued between the perception of the university as an educational and as a cultural institution.

The two perceptions involve a fundamental contradiction. As a centre of educational excellence, the university is expected to subscribe to secularism, rationality and modernisation. However, as a repository of traditions, it must view Westernisation and modernisation as challenges. Specific structural features of AMU strengthen the ideological contradiction.

Large-scale migration of teaching and non-teaching staff to Pakistan in the wake of Partition led to a vacuum. In this vacuum, certain extended families and their minions, followers and hangers-on mushroomed. The Chatterji Committee in 1961 reported 61 appointments of family members. At one time, as many as 93 members of one particular family were employed in different capacities on the campus.

The tsars of AMU form cliques to preserve and perpetuate their hegemony. (According to Roman mythology, God Janus could look ahead and behind simultaneously.) Some members of one clique project themselves as secular, progressive and keepers of modern values, while others comfortably practise fundamentalism on the campus simultaneously. The constituents of axes typically put up separate shows but unite in expediency. After Independence, these 'pincers' have always managed to keep the campus under their grip. To a secular government, this group presents a secular facade complete with solid condemnation of Muslim conservatism. To the orthodox leadership, the fundamentalist elements of the clique present themselves as protectors of tradition.

The clique operates uniquely. Whenever its authority is threatened, the two faces of the clique join hands in squeezing out the moderates or liberals on the campus who remain unorganised and individualistic in their approach. Many violent incidents can be traced to the clique's quest for power. When Professor A.M. Khusro was the vice-chancellor, power slipped out of the hands of this clique. But it managed to hit back, exploiting a trivial incident.

Students of one faction raided a hostel at night, beating up their rivals. The clique played up the incident to launch an attack on the vice-chancellor for alleged 'incompetence'. Allegations that Professor Khusro was encouraging communal and criminal elements on campus flew thick and fast. Memoranda were presented to the visitor and the union education minister with demands for an enquiry into the incident. Heated debates took place at the Executive Council, and demonstrations were organised in Delhi. Riots broke out in Aligarh following the beating up of some students by commuters at Dadri. The clique alleged that the subsequent police firing took place because of the sheer ineptitude of the university administration.

Khusro ran the institution openly and transparently, except that an uncontrollable situation at the far end of his tenure forced him to close it down for a while. That gave birth to the remark: 'Khusro pulled the whole elephant out of the bottle, but its tail got stuck.'[1] He resigned in November 1979, handing over the charge of the university to the pro-vice chancellor Professor Mohd Shafi of the Geography department. M.Z.R. Khan remarked: 'You can run a university either with the help of police or goons.'[2] People like Khusro were meant to lead a gentlemen's society to cultural and economic prosperity.

Khusro was proud of the training in student union politics he had received during his Oxford days. From a few years of stay in England as a student at that time, perhaps mellowed also with his family's Sufi tradition, he was a tolerant incarnate. When his first wife reportedly grew a dislike for him in Delhi, she divorced him to marry the young man of her liking and vacated his house to their benefit. Then a little after he took over as AMU vice-chancellor, his second wife Tayeba was so charming to begin with, that while taking her with him to the music evenings in Kennedy Hall, Khusro had to protect her from mobbing students, spreading both his hands with all his physical force. In a while, she started disliking his excessive devotion to official duties, interpreting his friendly relations with some teachers as womanising. It was during this period that he married her grown-up daughter from the first husband as he would his own. Tayeba ran a crèche in the vice-chancellor's lodge as a pastime and reportedly published a booklet against Khusro at this juncture. Their distance continued increasing till after Khusro left Aligarh to complete his tenure. They divorced, and Khusro's first wife returned to his bosom for the rest of his life. In light of his background, it should not be difficult to understand how Khusro handled students, teachers and other employees of the university, appeasing them and not taking decisive action on any occasion. At a tense moment during the students' union election counting time, he pacified irritated students by showing them his cycling tricks. A little after the new union's installation, he was presiding over an unfriendly meeting of the Academic Council, two rival student processions came from opposite sides shouting hostile slogans. That unnerved some professors, and they recalled the scenario when the unruly union had been violent to the vice-chancellor Ali Yaavar Jang and others at a University Court meeting a decade ago. But Khusro dashed out of the meeting hall, right up to face the processionists, addressed them individually, and forced them back by the power of his shear oratory. 'Did you see how I deflated them,' he claimed on his triumphed return to the meeting, and the very disgruntled professors passed for him a resolution of praise.[3] Losing wits against Khusro tactics, a group of students resorted to hunger strike under a tent flung at his door inside the premises of the vice-chancellor lodge, not so protected then as now. After a few days, past midnight, one student leader woke up from slumber to find a stranger lying by his side, fully dressed in *shervani* and cap! And lo and behold, he was none other than Professor Ali Mohammad Khusro, the vice-chancellor. Badly startled, the student leader gets up and asks him 'what are you doing here, Sir, like this; you are the Head of the Institution!' 'I am enjoying' was the simple reply; the tent was uprooted the very morning.[4]

When Professor Shafi assumed charge of the university as caretaker vice-chancellor hoping to be regularised, discipline had slacked considerably further due to lack of corrective action since the time of Professor Abdul Aleem. Friends advised Shafi to reverse the trend of irresponsibility and announce a new beginning, but he could not choose that course. Everyone could see him working in the office all day as Khusro used to do, and he wished to satisfy the visitors with his brief and polite replies. But that won't impress the determined activists, who would continue to argue and raise their voice. Shafi would then get rid of them only by appeasing them. Often admitted a good-for-nothing student who would not follow teaching, joining miscreants to ruin the university discipline at every level, and pressurise teachers to promote him despite his dismal performance. Shafi endured this torture for half a year, hoping his continued popularity would bring permanent appointment. Still, it eluded him, reportedly, in addition to other factors, because of his distant and close friends' counter intrigues. Meanwhile, one of his young lieutenants advised him to avoid his office from time to time taking refuge in the Proctor Office for a while to relax. One day one of the selected goons of the area, nesting in the backyard of that office, put his revolver on his chest and forced the admission of his boy. This broke down the nerves of Shafi, forcing him to get hospitalised for about a week in Delhi and he resigned from the vice-chancellor office. Following this event, the first professor in seniority officiated as vice-chancellor, to be followed by the next in seniority as per rules. Qamar Farooqi of the commerce faculty was the last one from whom Saiyid Hamid took charge as the next permanent head of the institution.[5]

When Saiyid Hamid was the vice-chancellor, he fell prey to the machinations of the clique. After a student was killed in police firing, the vice-chancellor came under tremendous pressure. Ultimately, he succumbed to the arm-twisting of the clique, both prongs of which rallied to his support for a price. The deal was that he would save their skins in the bargain. This clique, made and unmade professors, succeeded in getting employment for its friends and relatives as officers and ministerial berths for its minions while strengthening its hold in the process. His successor, Hashim Ali, somehow succeeded in balancing both groups.

Quoting Professor Harold Laski, the Chatterji Committee recorded, 'The quality of a university is always in direct proportion to the quality of its teachers. And the success in choosing the right teaching staff, particularly professors, is probably more important than any other single factor in the success of a university.'

Vice-chancellor Saiyid Hamid observed:

> The quality of teachers has unfortunately declined rather steeply. There are a few oases in what I consider a desert. In selection committees, attempts are made to influence experts. It is not something peculiar to Aligarh, rather more intense here. It so often happens that there is reciprocity among heads of departments in respect to selection committees. This is a pernicious practice which

> ought to go. The VC finds it very difficult to break this system of patronage superseding merit.

His successor, Syed Hashim Ali, adds that the academic control of deans and chairmen is not practical in many cases. The system of rotation, in a way, makes them timid, as they are afraid of retaliation by the future chairman after they relinquish office. Academics are not used to exercising power and when they get that power towards the end of their career, they use it with retrospective effect. Power used properly is a great responsibility, but unfortunately for most people the absolute pleasure of power lies in its misuse. Academics are no exception.

Recollecting a case, former vice-chancellor Badruddin Tyabji recorded that a post had been created in the university for looking after students' welfare.[6] Obviously, such a person would require a good personality, be interested in students and combine scholastic qualifications with proficiency in sports and an ability to maintain a rapport with students. As usual, not only did a large number of persons (who had absolutely no qualifications for the post) applied, but several of them also attached letters of recommendations from influential persons. One such letter came from Prime Minister Jawaharlal Nehru himself. The person recommended, Jamal Khwaja, was the son of an old friend of Nehru from Cambridge days. He had served as a Congress member in (second) Parliament. He was now a lecturer at AMU. He was a pleasant young man and a promising academician, but Tyabji did not find him qualified for the post of the dean of students' welfare.

However, Tayabji's self-righteous claim can be taken with a grain of salt as Dr Ram Gopal, later vice-chancellor of Maharishi Dayanand University, Rohtak, and a renowned Sanskrit scholar, recalled that when he was to appear before the selection committee for the job of reader in the Sanskrit department of AMU, Tyabji took him into confidence not to press the claim as there was someone else who had been selected for the post and the meeting of the selection committee was an eyewash.[7]

Academician Amrik Singh recalls while paying tribute to Saiyid Hamid,

> When Hamid Saheb took over, the circumstances were not very satisfactory. Some kind of palpable chaos pervaded the working of AMU. For example, professors from different faculties, who had been on long leave and were serving in the Middle East, had not shown up even after the expiry of their sanctioned leave. Obviously, they took the university and the whole system taken for granted. Despite his respect for the teachers and professors, Saiyid Hamid decided to take action by sending notices to such delinquent professors. He asked them to resume their duties immediately or else resign. Such an action could not but have a disturbing impact on almost everybody.[8]

Professor M.N. Farooqi, yet another former vice-chancellor, narrates another interesting anecdote. Professor Nafees Ahmad of the Institute of Ophthalmology, who possessed a doctorate in biochemistry but did not have an MBBS degree, had been appointed the director of the Institute of Ophthalmology. There was a representation from other teachers and students that his appointment was illegal, as a non-clinical person could not hold the position of chairperson of a clinical department. The Academic Council upheld his appointment, but the case was referred to the Medical Council of India.

People with talented images often behave like strict bosses when dealing with students. Professor Nafees Ahmad refused to listen to students (about 40 out of 50) who found themselves inexplicably short of attendance. The students approached the vice-chancellor and complained that a student, who had died more than two years earlier, had over 80 per cent attendance. Similar was the case with another student who had left AMU three years earlier. The vice-chancellor described the case as not only unique but also tragic. There was a department whose chairperson had not bothered to check the list when 80 per cent of students were losing six precious months of their careers on account of shortage of attendance.

'No self-respecting teacher', Professor Faruqui said, 'with a conscience can allow such development. I consider this the biggest sin a teacher can commit against his students. Professor Nafees Ahmad had a maximum of four lectures to deliver in an academic year.'

When the Medical Council of India recommended Ahmad's removal from the post, he became a diehard critic of Professor Faruqui so much so that he complained to the police that the vice-chancellor had a hand in the abduction of his wife in mid-August 1992. When she returned under mysterious circumstances a few days later, she did not complain against anyone. The police accused Professor Nafees Ahmad of concocting the incident to malign senior university officers to settle scores with them.

On 9 November 1994, Professor Mohammad Shabbir, a member of a committee examining cases of the use of unfair means in university examinations, was abducted from his residence on the periphery of the university campus just before a crucial meeting. On his return the following day, he told the university authorities he had been assaulted, blindfolded and taken to a village. The kidnappers had threatened him with dire consequences if he did not soften his tough stand on a particular case of using unfair means in the examinations. This is not the lone case of its kind.

The Aligarh Muslim University Teachers Association (AMUTA) had begun as a club for teachers and their families. Traditionally, the senior-most teacher used to be its president, but the agitation against the amendment of 1972 changed its character. Rahman Ali Khan, a reader in the Law faculty, was elected its president. A social body was turned into a political one. The AMUTA, since 1981, has become a nucleus for opposing successive vice-chancellors. It has earned the dubious distinction of swinging into 'action' whenever a vice-chancellor reaches the second half of his term. Though neither ambivalent nor innocuous, the demand for an enquiry into the university affairs and removal of the vice-chancellor seems more like a mid-term ritual, repeated with monotonous but effective regularity that is disturbing and destabilising. Such a demand is usually given a concern for ethical, academic and law and order situations on the campus. Beneath that facade are the sordid machinations of one or other cliques operating on organised lines according to a well-thought-out scheme for grabbing or retaining power.

Coercive careerists frequently use the AMUTA. In the process, vociferousness is mistaken for valour, and deliberate cultivation of anti-establishment attitudes provides the needed glamour. However, the fact remains that AMUTA is nothing but a paper tiger. Professor V.S. Rekhi, unanimously elected to head the AMUTA during the Emergency days, recalls, 'A senior don advised me not to delude myself that by becoming the AMUTA president, I had acquired a large mass following.'[9] Hardly a couple of hundred of the 1200-odd teachers would attend any meeting, however influential the agenda. Therefore, the AMUTA could never become a teacher-welfare-oriented body.

The teachers were often accused of exploiting them by research scholars, numbering about 1,100. The AMU Research Scholars Association (AMURSA) alleged in 1995 that Imran Khan enrolled in the Department of Botany for research under Professor S.K. Saxena in 1984 but could not complete his PhD even after 11 years. Similarly, in the department of biochemistry, Rizwan Ahmad joined MPhil in January 1993, but his guide, Professor Zafar Beg, refused to check his dissertation. He had to change his guide.

It's a virtual tightrope walk for a vice-chancellor who must spend most of his time balancing warring cliques. Alternatively, he joins hands with one or the other, momentarily serving his purpose. In such a situation, a vital element of clannish domination comes to the fore to subvert the academic atmosphere. A similar situation exists in every university in the country. Still, in Aligarh, the internecine struggle among the faculty is particularly poignant because a particular group has successfully cornered power for many years. Its influence is apparent in the appointments and promotions across the board. When a vice-chancellor tries to steer clear of clique politics, he receives the worst of both worlds.

Out of the 80-odd departments in the university, the UGC has awarded eight Special Assistance Programmes (SAP), and one has been recognised as the Centre for Advanced Studies in Medieval History. The positions of SAP and the Centre for Advanced Studies (CAS) coordinators cause much heartburning among the senior dons. Manipulations to retain these prestigious positions are common.

The history of the CAS in the Department of History bears testimony to such machinations by unscrupulous elements to retain hegemony by hook or crook. In 1968, the UGC recognised the Department of History as a CAS. The Executive Council of the university in August of the same year decided that only the head (now chairman) of the department is authorised as ex-officio director to sanction and incur expenditure. The UGC endorsed the decision. The department retained the commitment for two decades. But, with the expiry of Professor Irfan Habib's term as chairman in May 1988, the centre and the department were bifurcated. Though the chairman kept changing, Professor Irfan Habib continued as coordinator through an administrative order of 3 May 1988.

By another order on similar lines, on 24 August of the same year, the funds were divided. All this was in contravention of Section 2(e) of the AMU Act, which said that any administrative order, which brings about a change in the position and functions of a department by carving a centre out of it, could not be imposed without an Ordinance.

Professor Irfan Habib continued as coordinator on the plea that the incumbent chairman, Professor R.C. Gaur, was not from the thrust area (medieval India) of the Centre. The Executive Council, at its meeting in June 1988, endorsed the decision by stating that If the head of the department is a professor from the thrust area, then he should necessarily be designated as the coordinator of the CAS.

On this basis, after taking over the charge as the chairman of the Department of History, Professor Z.U. Siddiqui (who was from the thrust area) claimed the post of coordinator, but Professor Irfan Habib continued. The revised guidelines of the UGC, vide letter dated 24 November 1989 – which also recognised the chairman of the department, if from the thrust area, as coordinator of the

CAS – were not implemented. Interestingly, the UGC sent another letter on 8 December, contradicting its earlier stand, enabling Professor Irfan Habib to continue as coordinator. In subsequent correspondence on this subject, the UGC only referred to its revised guidelines and never referred to its order dated 8 December, based on which Professor Habib continued to function.

When Professor Habib retired on 11 August 1991, he was re-employed for three years by the university. An administrative order, issued after two days of re-employment, saw that Professor Irfan Habib continued as coordinator. This order was in violation of Statute 29(9)(b), which reads: 'Provided further that during the period of re-employment, a teacher shall not be given any administrative responsibility.'

Even after the expiry of his three-year term of re-employment, another administrative order dated 1 September 1994 allowed Professor Habib to continue as CAS coordinator till further orders. In the meantime, bypassing all the norms and rules, he was given the professor emeritus status. In a signed memorandum to the vice-chancellor on 26 August 1994, four elected members of the Academic Council alleged gross irregularities in granting Professor Irfan Habib the status. It was only on 13 May 1996 that Professor Habib was dethroned as the CAS coordinator.

He remained in that capacity for 12 years, and his removal plunged him and his coterie into a frenzy of ire and despair. They unleashed a virulent campaign against the vice-chancellor Mahmud-ur-Rahman, who had mustered the courage to combat Professor Habib's hegemony over the Department of History and its CAS. Professor Irfan Habib accused the vice-chancellor of hobnobbing with the Bharatiya Janata Party (BJP). Even Professor I.H. Siddiqui, the then chairman of the department and ex-officio coordinator of the CAS, with an annual budget of Rs 47 lakh was not spared. His successor, Professor Shireen Moosavi, accused him of being a member of the 'RSS-sponsored History Congress'. Herself a member of the Habib coterie, she doubted the professed commitment of Professor Siddiqui to secular, progressive and scientific history.

His credentials had not been doubted until a few weeks earlier when he used to toe Professor Habib's line in the department.

All-out war raged in the department with the combatants trading allegations and counter-allegations. Not content with restricting the fight to the university campus, they carried the 'struggle' to the media.

Meanwhile, Professor Habib floated a new organisation named the Association for the Study of History and Archaeology (ASHA). Its second conference was held at Aligarh from 15 to 17 June. The university did not accede to the request for holding the conference on campus as an essential admission test (for Class XI) was to be held on 16 June. This became another bone of contention. By the end of April, the pre-election opinion polls had begun to predict a massive BJP win. Weeks later, the BJP staked its claim to form a government at the Centre. Habib suspected that under the new dispensation, ASHA would be a liability for those who wished to curry favour with the new government. Sure enough, some of Professor Habib's erstwhile Marxist comrades became his bitter critics.

In the pages of a Marxist journal *Udbhavna*, former colleague and one-time comrade, Kanwar Pal Singh (Hindi) targeted sarcasm at 'a certain friend with a Marxist image'. Singh's long association with Habib broke when Ms Shireen Moosavi once referred to the former as a 'Hindu comrade'.[10] The article by Singh, without naming Habib, punched holes in the *kuleenta* (elitism) of Habib's origins and lifestyle. And, as if to add insult to injury, a review of Habib's latest book *Akbar and His Time,* by a former comrade, Sanjay Subrahmanyam, accused him of using the book as a platform for lauding his friends while attempting to settle scores with detractors.

A former vice-chancellor, Lt Gen. Zameer Uddin Shah, recorded in his memoirs:

> The teaching profession is the only one where under the cloak of 'academic freedom' there is very little accountability. Once a teacher attains the rank of a professor, he or she needs to do very little work

> because there is no accountability or even a confidential report. A teacher can become a professor within 20 years of service. Teachers set an example for their students. Therefore, their discipline has to be exemplary. This, unfortunately, needs improvement. It is difficult to initiate disciplinary proceedings against a teacher. There was no sense of punctuality. I had to ban teachers from taking refreshments in class when they were on invigilation duty. It did not seem right to be gobbling 'samosas' in sight of students taking examinations.[11]

However, Shah suggested raising the age of retirement of teachers from 65 to 70 in the wake of acute deficiency of teachers in institutions. On the other hand, he recommended that there should be a total ban on teachers' unions or associations, as the sole aim of these bodies is to protect recalcitrant teachers. The heads of the institutions need special training in administration and finances because that is generally their 'Achilles heel'.

He came down heavy on a 'clique of teacher-politicians' who found a safe platform in the AMUTA.

> The avowed charter of this organisation was to protect the interests of teachers but their sole aim was to ensure that teachers drew a fat salary but did the least amount of work. I found that that the major occupation of the office-bearers of the AMUTA was to keep bombarding the social media with irrelevant posts. They had very little time for teaching. Anyway, I treated them with the contempt they deserved and never gave importance to their shenanigans. We go down to the task of cleaning the Augean stables. The 'parasites' who had pillaged the university for years, were sidelined and ignored. Teachers were instructed to abide by the university's working hours, dress properly and come shaven, if they did not sport beards. There were howls of protest and accusations of 'Military Raj'.[12]

Strange is the functioning of AMU. Vice-chancellor Lt Gen. Zameer Uddin Shah succeeded in calling on Prime Minister Narendra Modi on 5 March 2016 and claimed to discuss the AMU affairs with the prime minister and a patient and sympathetic hearing. The Press Information Bureau of the Union government in a press release mentioned, 'The AMU delegation discussed issues related to research and education, skill development and Ganga rejuvenation.' A member of the delegation disclosed that vice-chancellor Shah did not utter a single word about AMU.

Similar was the treatment another former vice-chancellor M. Rahman gave to the faculty members. He used to grant audience to the teachers after sitting on their requests for a couple of days and the appointment invariable used to be for a few seconds in which he would to point out mistakes in the submission, made by the visitors. Another former vice-chancellor Badruddin Tayabji had already successfully used this formula for belittling the teachers.

There was no place for a historian like S.A.A. Rizvi (Saiyid Ather Abbas Rizvi) in the AMU. Even the university librarian had once embarked upon such audacity that he slapped Professor Rizvi across his cheek. He had to migrate to Australia. Syed Ali Nadeem Rezavi recalls:

> When I started work on Fatehpur Sikri, one of my first papers to be presented was in the presence of S.A.A. Rizvi in the audience. He was an old man and Irfan Habib had told me that if Ather Sahib does not tear it down and maul you for writing it (it was very critical to some of his views) then you carry on with the topic, else forget it. When I made the presentation, he shuffled up from his seat, resting himself on the stick, cleared his voice and said, 'I wish a day comes when you are an old man, and a young man tears you down!' My face went pale; there was a pin drop silence but he did not harbor any rancour against me.[13]

Once a scholar reading a manuscript detailing Babur's conquest read a statement in Persian '*baafwaj iI qahira humla namud!*' And exclaimed 'Oh Babur came to India with the contingents from Cairo!' Professor Rizvi intervened to explain that '*afwaj i qahira*' only meant ferocious army.

Till the 1970s, deans used to be decisive in cases of admissions. In one such case, Neelakanta Ramakrishna (N.R.) Madhava Menon was accommodated as a student by Professor Hafizur Rehman. Menon could not get admission to the University of Delhi. His Marxist friends referred him to AMU, where he got a seat for a master's degree in law program (LLM). Later he obtained a PhD on the topic 'White white-collar crime'. He was the first PhD student in the faculty of law at AMU. He was appointed as a lecturer and also became the first non-Muslim to be appointed warden of a hostel in S.S. Hall at AMU. Later, he shifted to Delhi and, in his later life, emerged as the father of modern law education in the country by establishing the National Law School, Bangalore, offering five-year integrated course in law.

Mahmood Ur Rahman, as vice-chancellor, had mooted the idea of making teachers' jobs in central universities transferrable. Still, in the want of support from the HRD, the suggestion died in infancy in the wake of stiff opposition from the AMU dons. No wonder Ale Ahmad Suroor, an Urdu critic, had suggested in the columns of the *Young Indian Weekly* that in most degree colleges and universities the teachers got full-time pay for part-time jobs. The situation continued to deteriorate while the pay packets soared disproportionally.

Perhaps Dr Zakir Hussain was the last vice-chancellor who performed his academic duties as per the demand of the post. Otherwise, his successors performed in fields other than academics. Professor M.N. Farooqi was the sole exception who tried to computerise the university. M. Rahman consolidated the university properties; M. Hamid Ansari in his brief period of 18 months ran the university like an office of the consulate; Naseem Ahmed, in a Tughlaqi *farman*, issued the order banning the use of motorcycles by the hostellers; Lt Gen. Zameer Uddin Shah loved to highlight the retrieval of silver trophies, lying unnoticed in the office of the Sports Committee for decades, as one of the achievements. At the same time, Professor P.K. Azis was more interested in installing CCTV cameras. There was hardly any mention of any academic achievement.

Another former vice-chancellor M.N. Farooqi records:

> One could imagine the distressing situation when seven posts of Senior Technical Assistants lapsed in the Medical College because the college did not advertise the posts for filling up. Maybe the positions were at such a level that no relation of any staff or faculty member was available to fill them.[14]

Naved Masood, a senior bureaucrat, recalls the sordid tale of Dr Aziz-ur Rahman (1928–73), an Indian chemist who left the country on account of career-related frustrations at AMU. He found the name, fame and meteoric rise in all the places in Argentina, becoming a vice-chancellor and one of the founding fathers of research in chemistry in that country.[15] It is also a tale of life's strange quirks in a particular family.

Even a tiny biographical note on this maverick scientist cannot start without a minimal reference to his extraordinary family history. In 1856, the then ruler of Bhopal, Nawab Sikandar Jahan Begum, undertook a voyage for Haj with an entourage that included her principal Adviser (Vizier) Munshi Jamaluddin (of Phulat near Meerut), who was a disciple of Syed Ahmad 'Shaheed' in his Jihad against 'infidel Sikhs' in what is now the border of Pakistan with Afghanistan. Like his old mentor, Jamaluddin was an adherent of Ahli Hadees sect, which his son-in-law 'Nawab' Siddiq Hasan Khan (later to be the second husband of Sikandar Jahan) did much to expand in India. Jamaluddin appears to have induced his employer to terminate the sea voyage at the Yemeni port of Al Hodeidah (then recently established by the Ottoman government) instead of the more convenient Jeddah with a purpose. Hodeidah was a centre of learning Hadis under its Qazi Shaikh Mohammed, a prominent pupil of the great Yemeni Scholar Allama Mohammed Al Shawkani (1759–1834). Jamaluddin is believed to have persuaded the Qazi to send a member of his family with the 'Bhopal party' for Haj and back to Bhopal to propagate knowledge and teaching of Hadis.

The Qazi agreed to let one of his younger brothers Zainul Abidin accompany the pilgrims to Hejaz and then to Bhopal, where he was designated the Qazi of the State. Zainul Abidin was later joined by another elder brother, Shaikh Hussain, who started teaching Hadis in an institution run by Bhopal State. The brothers kept travelling back and forth to Yemen till they permanently settled down in Bhopal with their families in 1879.

Dr Aziz-ur Rahman's father, Habibur Rahman, was the grandson of Shaikh Husain. Dr Rahman was born in Bhopal on 29 March 1928, a few months after his father, a qualified civil engineer working as a building contractor, was found mysteriously murdered at Raisen in Bhopal State, apparently by a business associate whose corrupt practices he had exposed. Dr Rahman's mother, Memooda Begum, went back to her parents in Lucknow along with her two children. Young Aziz had his entire education in Lucknow, completing high school and intermediate courses from the Christian College with first division in 1941 and 1943 with a good grounding in physics, chemistry and mathematics along with Persian language and literature. He did his BSc and MSc in chemistry from Lucknow University in 1947. At that stage, Dr Omar Farooq, professor of chemistry at AMU, took him under his wings as a research scholar. Professor Farooq was much more than a research guide – he was in loco parentis to the young man barely out of his teens who had seen no father. Until his departure for Germany, Dr Aziz continued to stay at Dr Farooq's place. The large-scale migration of teachers in the wake of Partition of the country led to his appointment as a lecturer in chemistry at AMU in 1947. He became a prolific researcher publishing his works co-authored with his mentor. He obtained a PhD from AMU in 1953. He proceeded to the University of Tubingen for research in biochemistry under Professor Alfred Butenandt (1903–1995), recipient of the Nobel Prize in chemistry in 1939 and equally well known as among the few top-notch scientists who had formally become Nazis by joining the National Socialist German Workers' Party. He obtained the Doctor of Natural Sciences (Dr.rer.nat) from that university in 1955.

While in Germany, he married Hilde Garcia, with whom and a young daughter he returned to Aligarh apparently to carry out and guide research of international standards.

He started doing research in earnest in Aligarh despite the financial constraints of a family with a European spouse at the measly salary of a Lecturer in an Indian university, which led him to supplement his income reportedly by doing some work for some industry in the city. While coping thus, he underwent the trauma of being denied promotion to the post of a reader when a senior colleague with no research degree was preferred over him. The trauma appears to have been aggravated as its ostensible source was someone who was a father figure to him. Speculations aside, he was determined to make a break with the institution which, according to his lights, he had served well and which had let him down for no good reason. Around that time, he attended a conference in the US where he met Dr Lelong, a Franco-Argentinean who had just joined as the director of the newly established Department of Chemistry at the National University of Bahia Blanca. Dr Lelong seeing a disgruntled, experienced teacher and researcher, made him the outlandish offer of a research professorship at the nascent university, apparently promising him all the infrastructural support. Argentina then was a major magnet for professionals wishing to leave parts of Europe that had not yet fully recovered from the after-effects of World War II – in the words of his son, it was the 'emerging US of Latin America' – in short, a land of hope and opportunity where the disappointed young scientist from Aligarh dreamed of building a career as a teacher and researcher. The migratory genes that brought his great-grandfather from Yemen to India made him take the plunge in the terra incognita of Argentina.

Aziz-ur Rahman joined the University of Bahia Blanca on 1 February 1959 as a professor with no knowledge of Spanish, the medium of instruction. According to his student Professor Julio Podesta, during the first year, he would deliver his lectures in German or English with someone doing simultaneous translation in Spanish! By the second year, he picked up enough Spanish to manage independently. He started his research earnestly, and within a year, the university emerged as a significant centre of chemistry research in Argentina. He ensured that two of his research students at Aligarh, Ausat Ali Khan and Mohammed Sami Khan, were given fellowships to continue their research under him at Bahia Blanca. These two young Indians thus became pioneers of chemistry research in Bahia Blanca! The Department of Chemistry at the university soon became the epicentre of quality research in Argentina. The young Professor enthused with his success, decided to throw his lot with the country that had provided him with all that was denied to him in his 'home country' and obtained the nationality of Argentina.

The maverick Indian did not go unnoticed either. President Arturo Frondizi (1905–1995), himself from an Italian migrant family, appointed the Indian migrant as the rector (vice-chancellor) of the university, a post that he held with distinction till 1967, though with a tumultuous termination. By all accounts, the young rector rose to the occasion, and soon his university claimed a position of excellence in teaching and research in several disciplines. In 1964, he was also appointed the president of the Inter University Council of National Universities, i.e., Central Universities of the country. This position gave him a role in evolving higher education policies and maintaining standards of tertiary education in his adopted country. The position of leadership did not dampen his penchant for research; during his tenure as the rector, he contributed as many as 15 papers as the first author for international journals and continued to guide research, making the chemistry department of the National University at Bahia Blanca the preferred destination for serious students of chemistry in that country. A recent historical review of education and research on the subject in Argentina identifies Professor Aziz-ur Rahman as one of the chief benefactors of chemistry education in that country.

Argentina, like much of Latin America, saw acute turmoil in the 1960s. Quite apart from the radical Leftist movement in the wake of the Cuban revolution and the exertions of the charismatic Ernesto

'Che' Guevara (1928–1967) throughout the region, the country bore the additional burden of that confused 'hybrid ideology', Peronism and a politically ambitious military; the country became a cauldron of strife. Professor Aziz being a rank outsider had occupied a necessarily ambivalent perch: While his lack of political affiliation was an asset, it was also the Achilles heel with his imperfect understanding of local history and culture. With universities in the 1960s becoming the crucible of all political movements – after all, students in the 1960s of the last century were the stormtroopers of political uprisings all over the world – the rector, born and brought up in the genteel Muslim middle class of India, was increasingly at sea. He tried to face a situation alien to the chemist-cum-academic administrator. He tried in vain to stand his ground with the radical leftist students. It all resulted in his losing the position of head of the university sometime in 1967. He attempted to retrieve the lost ground by trying to buy peace with the then president, the dictator Juan Carlos Ongania (1914–1995), to no avail. As his son Professor Shahid Rahman puts it: 'The Peronists saw him as an enemy; the radicals did not like that he had an interview with the dictator; the dictator mistrusted him; and the left-wing students (who had supported him) felt betrayed.'

His last few years in Bahia Blanca were an anti-climax – a reversal of the first eight years. The family became increasingly isolated, and his colleagues minimised their contacts for fear of falling foul of the establishment. A few years later, he accepted an offer of a visiting professorship – 'Invited Professor' – at a private university in Guadalajara (Mexico) to be away from a violence-ridden Argentina where the family was feeling insecure on account of threats from various quarters. The unpredictable man that he was, Dr Aziz also enrolled himself as a medical student! The family has the impression that he had, in the meantime, secured a professorship in Munich. He succumbed to a heart stroke on 9 July 1973, where his mortal remains were interred.

The family had to return to Argentina, and his elder son (three siblings, a daughter and two sons) had to work as a cleaner in the university library, where his father was the rector, with the family supplementing his meagre earnings by letting out a part of their house.

Reflecting on the pervasive culture of seminars among educators across various faculties and departments, Mehar Alam Khan recounted an insightful observation during the valedictory session of an international conference on Unani medicine held in New Delhi in February 1987. The event was graced by the then Union HRD and health minister Shri P.V. Narasimha Rao, who astutely summarised the typical format of academic seminars and conferences in India in four Persian words – *nashistan* (sitting), *guftan* (talking), *khurdan* (eating) and *barkhastan* (rising). He expressed a wistful regret, hoping that his summary was an exaggeration yet lamenting that the depiction often still rang true even then.

Professor Gurbux Singh, an eminent chemist and educationist, regarded the exit of Dr Aziz from Aligarh as symptomatic of the ills of AMU.

Professor Hisamuddin Faruqi, former professor of zoology at AMU shared many snippets about Dr Aziz, including the juicy bit that his students affectionately referred to him as 'Aziz Bitya' (on account of his loveable nature and relatively short physical stature).

In a requiem for Professor Ahsan Jan Qaisar (1929–2011), a great scholar of medieval Indian history and one of the iconic historians (to have been produced by the Aligarh Muslim University's famous Department of History, the Centre of Advanced Study), Professor Mohammad Sajjad rues,

> The Department of History, in terms of the number of teachers, research scholars, and other students, has quite a considerable strength. Then, why the small participation in his burial, even though the Muslim University claims to be a gehwaarah (cradle) of a particular culture (tehzeeb, tamaddun? Was it because Professor Qaisar was a reclusive and a bit eccentric man? Was it because he was not a power-wielding academician who could manipulate recruitments, promotions, ghost authorships, and awards of lucrative research projects regardless of the merit…? Was it because

> Professor Qaisar was not among those who run or follow lobbies of the unscrupulous power politics within the kingdom of AMU? If that is so, then we must admit that in the industry of knowledge, power-play has assumed strange and draculous and shameful forms.
>
> In AMU, teacher and student politics operate with considerable regional saliency. On these primordial bases, the regional satraps expect/ demand favours, privileges, votes, and administrative assignments. However, Professor Qaiser, a prominent historian, was free from all such narrowness, chauvinism and bigotry. While teaching us, as an aside, he had shared with us, "I am a votary of a specific kind of Sufism whereby I have cocktailed it with a happy dose of Marxism".
>
> He shared a lot about the regressive factional politicking within the Department. He warned us that in the 'bad' world of academics, self-respect is an impediment in the way of one's rise, yet one must take care of one's self-respect. It is too valuable.[16]

Professor Mohammad Sajjad continues,

> The 'majoritarian homogeneity' is seen in the list of its VCs in the last 103 years. 'UP-Hyderabad-Urdu' exercises all monopoly, with a solitary exception of a VC from Kerala. Even the Muslims of the undivided Punjab and Sindh have not been its VC. Other linguistic states of India continue to suffer from exclusion. This exclusion is not even being confessed; forget about contemplating to rectify and compensate for it! Also, watch the regional composition of the AMU–EC and AMU–Court, the two bodies that empanel the VCs. Even those who happily become VCs of other universities through Search cum Selection Committees would vehemently deny a Search cum Selection Committee for AMU–VC.[17]

Noted journalist M.J. Akbar quipped in a webinar (December 2020) that the Taj is a grave while the AMU is a living institution.[18] However, the need of the hour is to get out of this morass of faction-based outrageous favours and victimisations. The stories of the machinations indulged in by the other feudal families of AMU are worse.

In the *Friday Times* (24 July 2024), Syed Amir recalled his days at AMU's chemistry department in the 1950s, which was very different from today's. The facilities were primitive, and we spent most of our time in the analytical laboratory, analysing salt mixtures that had no utility in later years. We had a few dedicated teachers with PhD degrees. Dr Akhlaq Ur Rehman Kidwai, a young man who recently returned from the US, taught us biochemistry using modern techniques. He later became chairman of the Union Public Service Commission and the governor of Bihar.

Dr Waheed Uddin Mallick, the other revered teacher, taught us inorganic and physical chemistry. He had a phenomenal memory and could remember the most complex and illogical formulas of inorganic compounds. Dr Mallick was a kind teacher. He suffered from chronic acidity, for which he drank anti-acid mixtures during his class. Later, Kidwai sahib became the chairman of CSIR, the most prestigious science body in the country, and Mallick sahib became the vice-chancellor of the University of Roorkee, a premier technological institution in the country.

The most colourful personality on the faculty was the chairman, Dr Omar Farooq, a short but intimidating figure. An eccentric man, he was known to stop students randomly and admonish them for not greeting him appropriately in Lucknow style. He had done no serious teaching in years and had forgotten introductory organic chemistry. Yet, he took a one-hour-long MSc final class in a seminar room with no blackboard, spending the hour talking about non-chemistry-related subjects. At the time, the culture in academic institutions was such that no one dared to raise a voice in protest.

In their final year, MSc students were required to work on a research project and assigned to a senior faculty member for guidance. To my dismay, Professor Farooq chose me to work with him. However, I never saw him in my laboratory, and he never came to discuss my project. My final results were unsurprisingly not as good as I would have liked.

15

ARE FAMILIES HOLDING AMU TO RANSOM?

In response to the UGC's criticism that AMU promotes a culture of 'inbreeding' in which a majority of faculty appointments are of its former students, the university cited statistics that 388 of its teachers had experience of working outside AMU and 237 had worked abroad, including in reputed institutions like the universities of Harvard, Michigan and Washington.

Responding to the Chatterji Committee's suggestion that there a five-year gap after the award of a master's/PhD from AMU for taking up teaching assignments in the university, AMU authorities argued that meritorious students could not be denied appointment merely by being its alumni.

However, the fact remains that the blind inbreeding of teachers resulted in the stagnation of this institution. In 1961, the Chatterji Committee received several complaints alleging that as many as 61 posts had been filled by persons related to five senior teachers of the university, including the then vice-chancellor Col Zaidi. Others were Dr A. Aleem (later elevated as vice-chancellor for a term), Professor Mohammad Hosain, Dr A.A. Suroor and Dr A.R. Kidwai (who later became the Governor of Bihar and West Bengal). The complaints said that as many as 19 relatives of Col Zaidi, 20 of Dr A. Aleem, 9 of Professor Mohammad Hosain, 5 of Professor A.A. Suroor and 8 of Dr A. R. Kidwai were employed in the university in various capacities.

Sounding a note of caution, the committee observed that barring a few allegations of relationship, most were true. Public institutions make regulations to ensure that employees do not obtain their positions only because they are related to persons in authority. A large number of inter-related employees in the university may be prejudicial to the maintenance of discipline or implementation of policies. The warning went unheeded.

Nothing surprises or shocks people in AMU as far as 'in-laws' among the staff members. They have become more or less an accepted norm of the university's life. Lobbies have flourished under successive vice-chancellors who find it reasonable to side with the ruling 'junta'.

Some of the relatives of one or other teachers in the university might have been appointed on merit. Former vice-chancellor Professor M.N. Farooqi saw nothing wrong in such 'dynasties'. According to him, marriage between two staff members could not be described as an act of nepotism.

Professor A.M. Khusro, another former vice-chancellor said that one thing that interferes with the university's proper functioning is that many teachers are related to one another and come from families settled for years within the university.

Naseem Ahmed, another vice-chancellor, justified the practice of inbreeding and said that it was more or less similar in other universities in the country. He added that what was the harm in giving preference to your own product.[1]

Professor Farooqi said AMU has about 1,400 teachers distributed over 10 faculties. They do not include the 400-odd schoolteachers who are also employees of the university. The scene has changed notably over the past few decades. The sense of dedication among teachers is now missing. Notwithstanding the slogans raised by everybody, AMU is just another workplace for these teachers. There are three reasons for the lack of dedication.

First is the academic inbreeding (not restricted to Aligarh alone). Over the years, many people became related and developed exclusive mutual interests in one another. The second reason is the place itself. People have found Aligarh a safe and friendly place to build and make a home. Easy access to education for children plays a vital role in settling down in Aligarh. Third, possibly the most important reason, is that the physical sciences and social sciences have made rapid progress recently, but Aligarh dons have not kept pace with them. The easy-going lifestyle of Aligarh is most suitable if one does not have to bother about the rapid advancements occurring outside the world.

The first by-product of inbreeding is the faculty's resistance to any changes proposed in the syllabi and the curricula of programmes offered by the university. Products of inbreeding do not feel comfortable with fresh ideas. Any modernisation programme leaves them cold and confused. Despite rapid changes sweeping across all academic fields, the AMU faculty continues to teach the same old material that it has taught for decades.

A student leader disclosed that there was a teacher in the department of economics for whom the exchange value of one US dollar to the Rupee fluctuated between Rs 8 and Rs 8.50 (in 1984), which must have been the exchange value when the teacher was a student, but he is still stuck to the same exchange rate!

Most of the teachers of AMU, adds Professor Farooqi, are still feudal in their attitudes.[2] They show great interest in taking up extracurricular assignments like the job of a provost or a warden or a member-in-charge of some other activity. It surprises me immensely that a person of a modest background assumes the airs of an overlord when he occupies a position of importance. He wants daily wage earners as servants, a vehicle, sofa and furniture and a telephone to symbolise recognition as some big shot in the university. Very polished and polite externally, such position-seekers are artificial in their behaviour. They desire and try to please their bosses at all costs.

The practice is to fill the temporarily vacant teacher position on leave for more than 45 days. Professor Farooqi reveals that deans typically fill such temporary vacancies through a local selection committee (LSC). The chairman of the LSC is the dean of the faculty concerned. The dean can also appoint, on an ad hoc basis, a qualified person as a lecturer for 30 days if a vacancy exists in the concerned department. All these are done with the formal permission of the vice-chancellor.

Such temporary appointments through the LSC are open to misuse for favouritism, and much heartburning ensues. Only those who manage to please the dean or chairperson can hope to get an appointment for temporary vacancies. Once a person gets into the system, they can continue to hang on one pretext or the other. If the General Selection Committee (GSC) rejects the candidate as unsuitable for long-term appointment, the department begins to plead that throwing them out would be too cruel after they have served for so many years. Backdoor appointments, backed by the feudal families, are frequent.

The re-employment of teachers after superannuation at the age of 65 too has become a racket. Though the rules restrict re-employment to a maximum period of three years in deserving cases, many senior teachers have been re-employed for decades.[3]

AMU has earned another dubious distinction by introducing an ingenious method for playing favourites. The 'novel' concept of 'global vacancies' was pursued with great zeal during the tenure of Professor Farooqi himself. Under this system, all posts in the university were considered common property, and the vice-chancellor acquired the discretionary authority to decide which department needed more teachers and which needed fewer. This once enabled AMU bosses to get away with three appointments in the faculty of law where vacancies for only two existed. A teacher could not be appointed in the Sanskrit department as the post had been 'globalised' and usurped by some other department. Not surprisingly, some departments got overstaffed while others remained understaffed.

In another unprecedented decision by the university administration, an office memo dated 25 June 1994 stated: 'This memo may be deemed to have been issued on 10 May 1994.' It concerned the appointment of Dr Asif Ali and Dr Mashiatullah Siddiqui in the Department of Biochemistry at the JN Medical

College of the university. Dr Asif Ali was appointed on probation for one year against a vacancy in the Department of Biophysics. At the same time, Dr Mashiatullah Siddiqui was placed on probation as and when a lien-free post of reader was made available in the department. The order added that the appointment of Dr Siddiqui 'will be the first charge on the Ninth Plan for the faculty of medicine'.

In 1995, noted sociologist André Beteille, in an article headlined 'Universities as Institutions', had observed, 'Every living institution has to accommodate some corruption and some injustice as a part of its ordinary existence. The real challenge is to remain loyal to the ideals of science and scholarship in a world that offers other and more immediate attractions.'

Most professors in most of the universities of India aspire to get their students into their departments as lecturers, not because they are bright, but because it increases their hold in the department. The universities in Western countries are opposed to this system. In overseas universities, particularly in the US and many European countries, faculty recruitment is quite open. The candidates are prompted to leave the parent university and obtain their first job at a university other than the one from where they have obtained their degrees.

There is no ethnographic account, narrative study or even a write-up as to how things function and work, in general, in the various departments and centres of the university.

What is amazing, and at the same time troubling, is that there is complete silence from academics that have been denied legitimate positions in academics. This reveals the kind of terror the lords of the university have spread on campus. The various kinds of fixing that happen in the academic realm of AMU will put a cricketer to shame in terms of the sheer ingenuity and cussedness employed in an institution of learning. The dons have maintained a tight lid on how misuse, manipulation and corruption prevail in this 'noble' profession.

In the very first decade of the university's birth, a committee headed by Sir Ibrahim Rahimtoola was appointed by the chancellor in October 1927 to enquire into and report on the academic, administrative and financial affairs of the university.

The findings were shocking. The Rahimtoola Committee report stated,

> Care should be taken to have the advice of competent external experts for making appointments to professorship and readerships, the incumbents of which should possess the high qualifications corresponding to the salaries attached to such posts by the university ... In the past, the university has not always selected suitable members of the Committee of Appointment. In one case, for a professorship of economics, the relevant committee consisted of the VC, the pro-VC, a professor of Botany and a reader in Persian. In another case, a reader has been appointed a member of a Committee of Appointment for a professorship in the same department. (He himself was a candidate for the post.)
>
> There are irregular promotions from a permanent post to another permanent post of a higher grade. We feel equal objection to promotions from a temporary post to a permanent post of the same grade without advertisement the operation of a selection committee or the consideration of other candidates whose qualifications may be far superior to those of a teacher chosen as a stopgap. If a temporary teacher has done well, he will have an advantage and a deserved advantage over other candidates. But it must not be assumed that he is the best man available to teach the students.

Regarding the functioning of the 'new' departments, the committee noted:

> In 1924, the pro-Vice-Chancellor stated that 'the courses of Islamic Studies have now been drafted, and teaching will commence during the next academic year.' But we have ascertained that though a reader was appointed in 1924, only three students were in that department in 1925. It is of interest that this teacher of

> the university has been appointed in succession to the posts of lecturer, honorary reader and reader without an appointment committee having been instituted at the time of each promotion and that his emoluments have advanced from Rs 175 in 1921 to Rs 480 in 1926.

In 1926, according to the committee, the pro-vice-chancellor stated, 'We have added the department of geography.' This department has had a chequered history. In 1924, the department was opened, and the principal of the intermediate college was appointed (without an appointment committee) to the post of reader in geography, while his successor at the intermediate college was also appointed without an appointment committee by the emergency powers of the vice-chancellor. The same gentleman was transferred from the Department of Geography to the Department of English because the former department is now left in charge of a student.

Indian universities have suffered immensely due to the combined impact of rotating headships and near-automatic promotion for all. Almost everybody gets promoted regardless of merit, and heads of departments (HODs) are appointed by rotation, so all get to be HOD without being qualified or suitable. It is no coincidence that the Indian university system has suffered immensely since the 1980s when these twin measures took effect. Academic merit has been severely neglected as a consequence. Many faculty members, who would ordinarily have retired at lower positions, are now assured of being appointed full-time professors and becoming HOD in time.

Notwithstanding the warnings by successive inquiry commissions and a long story headlined 'AMU – "in-laws" and "outlaws"' which appeared in the *National Herald* in September 1978, no attempts worth the name were ever made to contain the malaise. To some extent, it was halted by another virus, in the form of 'in-breeding', afflicting other universities in equal measure.

AMU seems to have surpassed all other universities in India and worldwide, in another dubious respect – that is, the matrimonial alliances between the domestic helps working in the bungalows of faculty members. A maidservant working in the house of a professor, searching for a match for her son or daughter, looks for one only in the family of another maidservant, engaged in domestic chores in the house of another professor. The inbreeding is supplemented by status. Former vice-chancellor Naseem Ahmad described such allegations as a figment of imagination. In March 1994, a news story headlined 'In-laws and outlaws make laws in the AMU' was published prominently in the *Hindustan Times*.

16
SHAGIRDS

Ustad to ustad they Subhan Allah Shagird kahan kam rahe Masha Allah
Is daur mein ustad kya shagird kahan Lahaul vila Quwwat-e-Ila Billah
(The teachers then were real teachers, God's chosen ones
The students too were no less, by the grace of God!
Who are the teachers now, whither the students?
It is all an unholy mess!)
(With apologies to Haider Dehalvi)

Kathpullay say bahar ki duniya nahin dekhi hai (They have not seen the world beyond Kathpulla). Kathpulla is a wooden railway overhead bridge for pedestrians, connecting Aligarh town to Civil Lines and the university. This oft-repeated comment aptly summarised the mindset of Aligarians. But no longer. In the wake of globalisation, Aligarians are aware like their counterparts in the metros. However, they still carry the legacy of the small-town mentality.

At a meeting several decades ago, the vice-chancellor of a university in Gujarat told the then AMU vice-chancellor Syed Hashim Ali, that the personality of the former's son had undergone a metamorphosis since he had joined the AMU for a professional course. The elation of the AMU vice-chancellor, however, turned into chagrin as his counterpart hastened to add, 'My son has turned into a Hindu fundamentalist.'[1] Hindu students at AMU suffer from a persecution complex. However, the fact is that the AMU campus has been almost free of the communal bug that rents the fabric of our society so frequently. Though Aligarh town enjoys the dubious distinction of witnessing communal riots, on several occasions, the virus has failed to enter the portals of the university.

Curiously, however, a majority of the Muslim League leaders who had insisted on partition were products of AMU. Therefore, a hangover of the pre-partition rivalry between the two communities still casts its shadow on any event on the campus.

These varying images of Aligarh students persist. A majority of students in Aligarh come from lower-middle or middle-class families. Despite a proliferation of educational institutions and universities in the country, Muslim students continue to throng Aligarh where they feel at home. Another attraction is that internal candidates get some preference in admission to various prestigious professional courses.

In this residential university, strong ties develop and flourish among the residents because they stay together in the halls for seven to eight years, on an average. Students enter here as young boys and pass out from here as men. They are sufficiently homogeneous from the class point of view. In addition, their economic motivations are fairly obvious.

Noted Urdu poet and Bollywood screenplay, dialogue and storywriter Akhtar ul Iman (1916–96) records an anecdote.[2] His daughter, Shahla, had stood first in a graduation course at AMU, and Akhtar ul Iman hoped she would get a medal. To his dismay, he learned that the then vice-chancellor Abdul Aleem, who was a communist and was known for his integrity, was going to award the medal to a boy who hadn't even taken the examination. On getting Shahla's frantic call, Iman rushed to Aligarh, and took Alay Ahmad Suroor along to meet the vice-chancellor, who said, 'I didn't know Shahla is your daughter.' Even more disgusted, Akhtar ul Iman said, 'It is not a question of knowing the parentage of a student; rather it is a question of wrong and right, of *dayanat-daari* and *bad-dayanati*.' When the vice-chancellor didn't budge, Iman threatened to go to the court of law. Shahla was awarded the medal at a low-key and lacklustre ceremony. Back in Bombay, she married Amjad Khan, who performed the role of Gabbar in the movie *Sholay* (1975).

Jawaharlal Nehru said of MAO College: 'A feudal spirit reigned over it, and the goal of the average student was government service.'[3] The feudal spirit may now have withered away with the decline of feudalism and the emergence of a *nouveau riche* class among Muslims after independence. Aligarh, nevertheless, has frequently been the focus of efforts to formulate a Muslim political consciousness, varying in its contents and colours from time to time. Students are often caught in a dilemma. A vice-chancellor wants to prove his credentials by facilitating the selection of many students for administrative jobs; political leaders wish to recruit cadres from student supporters. For the students living in an isolated atmosphere and socially segregated compartments, the university becomes a *biradari*, a brotherhood, to make 'the *qaum* a *qaum*', as Sir Syed himself had desired.

University educators and teachers have made a few attempts to try a healthy inter-mix of students belonging to different communities. Dr Matin Zuberi recollects that Professor Nurul Hasan, as the provost of Aftab Hall in the mid-50s, sent three Hindu students for accommodation in the hostel under the former's charge.[4] Dr Zuberi, who was the warden, took a calculated risk. Instead of putting all three in a three-seater room, he wanted to lodge them in three different rooms with Muslim roommates. Senior residents raised objections on two grounds: (a) the Hindu residents may be vegetarian, (b) the presence of Hindus would prove a hindrance to their Muslim roommates in offering *namaz* (prayers). While even the Hindu boys preferred to stay in one room, Dr Zuberi was adamant. They were accommodated in three separate rooms with Muslim roommates. The experiment worked well, though in this matter the warden had not even taken the provost into confidence.

Another problem in Indian universities, more pronounced in Aligarh, is that the nouveau riche families desire their wards to get higher education but the wards themselves may not be keen to have it. A majority of them are not career conscious. On top of that, their home environment does not help them in making career choices and going seriously after them. A student of ordinary merit cannot be expected to do well in studies. Having secured admission in some subject (without an idea of its utility) at AMU, the students manage to coast along. Inadequate facilities in hostels do not matter to them because they pay the lowest possible fees and rents. The rooms are crowded but there is bonhomie and a sense of community living inside the halls that sustains student residents. A majority of students suffer from the handicap of poor knowledge of English. In spite of the founder Sir Syed's insistence on English, the standard of teaching of that language in Aligarh remains poor. Students brought up almost exclusively in Urdu-speaking households, with perhaps a smattering of Persian and Arabic, find it extremely difficult to speak or write English fluently and correctly.

In a population consisting of about 26,000 students (including schoolboys), the notorious ones are few, but they are well entrenched in the university. They may not have left their homes for studies at AMU. These are the locals, the wards and the relatives of the employees who create the maximum problems. Since the university has a quota of 20 per cent of the total admissions, barring medical courses, for admission for the offspring of employees, they get admitted to various courses, particularly professional ones, with a lower performance level. Once admitted, they are in no hurry to leave. They often enjoy the powerful backing of one extended family or the other. The employees feel their wards must be admitted to the university as a matter of right.

Notwithstanding the recommendations of various inquiry committees to reduce 20 per cent and abolish this discretionary quota in the due course, no vice-chancellor has cared to take any corrective measure. The discretionary quota continues unabated like Section 19 (C) of the AMU Act empowering a vice-chancellor to take adhoc decisions, later to be confirmed by the Executive Councils invariably. Little wonder, maximum decisions of a VC are taken using (or misusing) this provision, which nobody wants to dispense with. Dr Faizan Mustafa justifies this provision saying that almost all the universities has this provisions. In the absence of such provision in the Act and statute of the university, no VC could work efficiently.

The disparity between internal and external students in admissions to non-competitive courses is rather large and sometimes alarming. Internal students with as low as 55 per cent marks in qualifying examinations are admitted to science courses while external ones may be refused admission even when they have 76 per cent marks.

The declining standards and its reputation as a centre of nepotism are leading to a feeling of paranoia at AMU. The students often grumble '*Hame kaun lega?*' (Who will take us?). Loss of self-confidence is a natural corollary. Muslim students of AMU are particularly paranoid of venturing outside their sadly shrunken world and working in an unfamiliar environment and with persons unknown to them. Speaking at a seminar at AMU on 5 September 1997, similar sentiments were expressed by Parvaiz Alam, an Aligarian and a newsreader with the BBC, as he exhorted the fellow Aligarians to shun their inhibitions and come out of the ghetto mentality to find their place in the world where all avenues were open for them. He discounted the apprehension of discrimination in the job market on the basis of religion.

Political parties in India, said Professor Farooqi, have been playing a game of numbers with the Muslim community.[5] They pay only lip service in order to corner the Muslim votes. Paradoxically, the leaders of the hapless community derive maximum benefits, doing hardly anything for the well-being of the masses. The success of some of these leaders depends upon creating a divide between Hindus and Muslims.

Muslims of Uttar Pradesh and Bihar who spearheaded the movement for the creation of Pakistan suffered the most, chasing a chimera of Islamic brotherhood that exists either on paper or in the speeches of the *mullahs*. Cultural, linguistic and regional pulls have always been much stronger than the lure of religion. The fundamentalists do not see the great dichotomy. Today, almost all the Islamic countries are fighting one another in the name of Islam.

An ordinary Muslim in a small town or village of Uttar Pradesh is not clever enough to recognise false symbols. It so is often carried away by the rhetoric of fanatics. Generations of Muslims in India have paid the price, and generations more will continue to do so for the follies of the leadership in the 1940s and 1950s.

The blinkers put on by the Muslim intellectuals on AMU campus have created an artificial feeling of a haven. The outside world is often portrayed as harmful. This prejudice wore off only too slowly.

In his autobiography *Is Aabaada Kharaabe Mein*, the esteemed poet Akhtarul Iman reflects on a memorable dialogue with Rasheed Ahmed Siddiqui. Siddiqui had a habit of inquiring whether a bright young man had studied in Aligarh; if not, he would lament, 'What a pity!'

During his tenure at Aligarh Muslim University, Iman fondly remembers his initial encounters with Rasheed Sahib. By then, Iman's poetry collection *Girdaab* had been published, eliciting a piquant critique from Firaq Gorakhpuri in the AIR magazine *Awaz*: 'It seems as if the poet has swallowed a cactus.'

The Urdu department boasted notable scholars such as Ale Ahmed Suroor and Abul Lais Siddiqui, alongside Rasheed Sahib, renowned for his biting wit and teaching criticism. One day, Iman inquired about the essence of genuine criticism, to which Rasheed Sahib whimsically responded, 'Young sir, what is two plus two?' Upon hearing 'four', he advised, 'If someone says five, then you should say that you are nearly correct.'

Iman, eager to learn, also sought guidance on the primary considerations while reviewing literary works. Rasheed Sahib's immediate reply was 'civility'. He emphasised the importance of respectful discourse, a value often overlooked in the heat of criticism.

While Suroor sahib's lectures were enthralling, Zaheer sahib was perceived as less intellectually vigorous. There was an unconfirmed rumour about Zaheer sahib's doctoral thesis being consumed by a goat. This led to a humorous classroom exchange where a student mimicked a goat's sound, cheekily suggesting it was the same goat that ate his thesis.

Iman's relationship with Abul Lais Siddiqui was notably strained. Once, Siddiqui questioned whether Iman's poetry could be deemed classical. Iman retorted by asking for a clear definition of classical poetry, to which Siddiqui could only offer examples like *Faust* and *The Divine Comedy* before resorting to ambiguous gestures such as making a half circle in the air with two index fingers and then making a full circle in the air. Frustrated by the lack of clarity, Iman challenged him further, leading Siddiqui to leave the classroom abruptly.

When Rasheed sahib heard his conversation, he advised Iman to avoid attending Siddiqui's lectures and instead study independently, assuring him that his attendance would be accounted for. Rasheed even hinted at offering Iman a lecturer position after finishing his studies, though Iman was beginning to feel that the university environment, while conducive for research, stifled creative expressions.

AMU students are often misused by various political leaders for advancing the latter's narrow and vested interests. Although the AMUSU (Siddons' Debating Club) originally started for a noble purpose, it has degenerated under the stewardship of student leaders with narrow political ambitions. The union has succumbed to populism, which benefits neither the institution nor the student community. Sometimes, particular student groups are taken into confidence by a vice-chancellor, as a result of which the other groups turn hostile. The student groups, on whose support a vice-chancellor depends heavily on for his survival, then demand their pound of flesh for services rendered. Vice-chancellor Lt Gen. Zameer Uddin Shah laments,

> A few student leaders (*netas*) are ever ready to make a quick buck from contractors doing building projects. Some students' union leaders thought they were a law unto themselves till I had to rusticate and expel the president of the students' union for misuse and misappropriation of funds.[6]

How Sir Syed chose the AMU uniform: 'In the court of the Turkish sovereign all nobles and attendants also wear shoes and the red fez, and this is the dress we have chosen for you.'

In January 1935, the famous Turkish writer and political activist Khalida Adeeb Khanum (Halide Edib Adıvar) came to India on a lecture tour at the invitation of Dr Mukhtar Ahmad Ansari, the leader of the Indian National Congress. During her two-month stay, she visited various cities and met many people. She compiled her impression in a memoir, *Inside India*, which showcases her remarkable insight into people and events. She also visited AMU during her tour and was welcomed at the Union. She was delighted by the sight of students in Turkish coats, white trousers and red Turkish caps, the official uniform at the time. An even greater surprise awaited her; she wrote, 'When I stood up to speak, I was drowned in a deluge of flowers. I could neither open my mouth nor my eyes. This display of affection for an aged Turkish woman was overwhelming and moved me greatly.'

Postscript: Professor Saad Tayyab of the interdisciplinary biotechnology unit at the AMU wrote in 1998 in *current science*: 'If there is a thesis on the purification and properties of a compound, someone is duplicating the whole study by simply carrying out the same procedure in another species.'

But why on earth does one do such research? Tayyab writes: 'The answer is simple. First, this is very simple to do. Second, teachers are least concerned with this kind of research because by simply following the methodology of one thesis, they can collect the data from another species.'[7] The reason, Tayyab feels, and rightly so, is that the type of interaction needs to change immediately. Since then, enough water has flown beneath the mighty rivers of India, but the situation is turning bad to worse as far as the academic life at the university is concerned.

17

WHEN JACKALS RULED THE ROOST

Barring the pre-partition days when the Muslim League had almost captured the university, students' organisations have only a symbolic presence among the students at the university. They are merely paper tigers but can disturb the much-needed tranquillity on campus. In September 2000, two AMU students, Syed Mobin and Maroof Ahmad, were arrested by the police. While Maroof was arrested in Agra, Mobin was caught in what the police call a 'sting' operation. Mobin, a student at Unani College, was crossing Anoopshahr Road outside his hostel, Habib Hall when he was dragged into a Tata Sumo vehicle and taken away. Police said he was carrying half a kilo of RDX. The students vehemently disputed this.

News magazine *India Today* reported that the two had been accused in the Agra bomb blasts before the US president Bill Clinton's visit.[1] 'We thought Mobin had been kidnapped. We even registered an FIR. For 24 hours, there was no news as we tried desperately to find out who had picked him up,' says Atif Rafi, a final year MBA student. Phone calls were made to Bulandshahr, Etah and Agra, but there was no news of Mobin. The vice-chancellor Mohammad Hamid Ansari then spoke to Home Minister L.K. Advani. A day later, the vice-chancellor got a call from Agra police saying that the Special Task Force had picked up Mobin and was in judicial custody in Agra.

Local dailies flashed provocative headlines like 'ISI racket busted in AMU', 'Terrorists nabbed on AMU camps' and 'AMU is becoming the hub of terrorist activities'.

According to the Inspector-General of Police, Kanpur zone, A.K. Mitra, Mobin was supplied explosives and given training by Gulzar, a Kashmiri student of AMU who had links with the Lashkar-e-Taiba. Gulzar's father had been detained by the police in Kashmir and a search was on for Gulzar.

The story did not end with the arrest of Mobin and Maroof. A couple of days later, an Intelligence Bureau officer Rajan Sharma entered Habib Hall and settled into a room reading a newspaper. He was on a mission to gather details on Gulzar's whereabouts. Some students spotted him and asked who he was. When he evaded a straight answer, he was roughed up. Police said the students kept Sharma in a room for five hours, broke his jaws and hit him with a hard object on his back. The students, whose numbers had swelled by then, also extracted a written confession from Sharma saying that Mobin was innocent and the police had planted the RDX. As the crowd grew at Habib Hall, the teachers tried to persuade the students to release Sharma. Eventually, they agreed to release him at a press conference on campus.

The following day, the local media was full of wild stories. Some even said the students had drilled '*Allah-o Akbar*' on Sharma's back. Other reports said Sharma's back had been branded with the word 'Allah'. The district police and administration denied the news reports. The officer was admitted to the local Malkhan Singh Hospital. Within hours, about 10 people, claiming to be Sangh Parivar activists, tried in vain to put up a tent outside the hospital to pray for the 'brave Hindu' who had single-handedly faced 4000 'Muslims'.

After a few days, around 10,000 students took out a silent procession. They were carrying placards. Some hand-made posters at the rally read, 'Neither fascist nor communal but only secular', 'We are Indians', and 'We are not ISI Agents'.

The government wanted the university to close sine die but the vice-chancellor refused. The then district magistrate Deo Datta said that the university administration had handed over the intelligence officer only when warned of repercussions.[2] Then, the injured officer was taken to the residence of the district magistrate, where he was given preliminary care before transferring him to the hospital for further medical treatment. The district magistrate said the university educators were complicit in extracting a 'confession' from the officer under duress.

Besides being in league with political leaders for mutual help and support, student groups have also started mustering the support of criminals in and around Aligarh who are also willing to get involved. Thus starts a chain of events in which the university becomes a breeding ground for anti-social activities, with a large number of undesirable persons occupying hostel rooms – armed with country-made pistols and other weapons – terrorising students and other members of the university community in a manner that makes the administration of the university extremely difficult for any vice-chancellor. Sometimes some rooms in the university halls become safe havens for criminals.

In July 2000, two youths, including an engineering student, were arrested from room no. 7 of Ross Masood Hall. A cache of small arms, including a .22 bore rifle, a .12 bore rifle, 13 cartridges, three .315 bore country-made pistols, and one .32 bore pistol, was recovered. Earlier, a school student was abducted from M.M. Hall, and a ransom of Rs two lakh was demanded from his parents. The victim, with his hands and legs tied, was taken to S.S. Hall where he was locked in a room. The police raided the hostel to rescue him.

Three days after this incident, two students, Mohammad Mustaqeem and Meraj, were kidnapped from Sir Ziauddin Hall for ransom. The culprits later released the victims as they failed to realise the ransom.

A news report alleged that the different lobbies of teachers were patronising criminal elements.[3] Reported by Ehtashamuddin Khan, the report said: Hostel rooms were indiscriminately occupied by anti-socials whereas recently admitted students, who had been officially allotted the rooms, were running from pillar to post. About one hundred rooms were illegally occupied in R.M. Hall alone. Similar was the case with room no. 13 of S.S. Hall (South), room no. 154 of S.S. Hall (North) and warden houses of both halls. These warden houses were furnished. Similar conditions were prevailing in almost all the hostels. The annexe of S.S. Hall (South), reportedly used by the drug mafia, was sealed by the intimidated provost. The facility was finally reopened for the crooks.

In December 1999, towards the fag end of the tenure of vice-chancellor Mehmood Ur Rahman, the students had put the area around the university to ransom. Anoopshahr Road had been blocked. The vice-chancellor went to the police station to lodge an FIR against some unwanted elements among the students. The students were on a warpath. The state government asked Deo Datta to take over as the district magistrate of Aligarh. On 6 December evening, two injured students were admitted to the university hospital. The new district magistrate persuaded the vice-chancellor to transfer them to Delhi to avoid further violence. On the advice of the district administration, the university was closed sine die. In the deadpan of the night, the district administration cleared the blockade on the road. The Uttar Pradesh State Road Transport Corporation was asked to make a provision of 250 buses to ferry students to their hometowns. Additional coaches were added to the trains passing from Aligarh. The situation was brought under control.

During the reign of Professor Farooqi as the vice-chancellor, at least 75 cases were reported to the authorities, including incidents in which Professor S.M. Yahya, the pro-vice-chancellor and several teachers were beaten up or threatened by students and unwanted elements. During this period, according to a white paper released by the AMUTA, half a dozen students were murdered. Iqbal Hasan Khan 'Barula', a senior teacher, was killed in broad daylight. Deposing before the Aligarh Enquiry Commission, 1993, Dilip Kumar Kotia and Arun Kumar Gupta, the then district magistrate and police chief of Aligarh, respectively, gave a list of 36 incidents of violence in and around the AMU campus between February 1992 and September 1993 in which students were involved. They added that several more complaints had been lodged with the Civil Lines police station, while some cases were not reported. They held the then vice-chancellor Professor Farooqi and his administration responsible for increased violence on the campus.

In a letter to the Uttar Pradesh chief minister, written on 6 June 1994, the vice-chancellor requested a CBI probe into the murder of Barula. The same day, in a separate letter, he demanded the posting of the CRPF personnel on campus besides providing personal security to Khalid Masood, the then president of the students' union. He also demanded the posting of a superintendent of police rank officer inside the campus to maintain law and order.

During the reign of Saiyid Hamid as vice-chancellor, the then security advisor to the university, A.M. Shah, had recommended that AMU raise its security force to tackle problems of law and order within the campus per the recommendations of the National Police Commission. Shah, a former assistant inspector general of Uttar Pradesh Police, had also suggested a purge to cleanse the proctorial department, which was said to be dominated by corrupt and inefficient elements. The blueprint also suggested bifurcation of the department into a proctor's force and a security force.

A 32-member high-powered committee, appointed by the chancellor in 1994 to look into the university's affairs stated:

> It is evident that discipline on the campus is at its lowest ebb, and violence has increased considerably. There have been several cases of gang warfare, and undesirable elements are freely using unlicensed arms. Teachers who tried to prevent some students from using unfair means in examinations and admissions have been threatened or assaulted.[4]

The toughs at AMU had suddenly become a force to reckon with since the incident of May 1992 at the Staff Club, where some hooligans, allegedly favoured by the top wing of the administration, converted a tea party into a brawl and compromised the dignity of some teachers. Since then, these *dadas* (hooligans) came to have an upper hand in getting their base motives forcibly accepted by the administration, which lost considerable ground. These toughs, who work individually and in gangs, pressurised the administration in diverse ways.

There have been indiscriminate ad-hocism and mercurial changes in decision-making, the inquiry committee noted, often in utter disregard to the existing rules and regulations and sometimes bypassing the relevant university bodies and authorities. This often results in pressure tactics by vested interests, and factional conflicts and ego problems worsen the situation.

Dadas have always been in evidence in the institution, as in most others. Still, the administration has always felt that they could be identified, brought to book and punished. In recent times, however, this situation has changed, and hooligans with criminal tendencies have come out to be on top. Teachers, deans, chairmen of departments, the proctor, the vice-chancellor and the other wings of the university administration have been feeling powerless. Reversing the situation is no mean task and requires a will and concentrated attention by all the functionaries on the campus, including students, teachers, non-teaching staff and administration.

> There are thick green cables of 72 CCTV cameras everywhere in the University, snaking up the outer walls of the Maulana Azad Library, hanging nearly unnoticed at the corner of the Department of Museology building, prominent at the entrance to every residential hall. The cables do their job – busily transmitting data packets on everything that happens at the University. This is a campus that watches itself, day in and day out.
>
> The University claims the cameras are there for security reasons. 'The initiative to upgrade security came from the union home ministry after students burned down the VC lodge on the night of September 2007', claims the University. The AMUTA had opposed the move.
>
> The Godrej-installed CCTV cameras, costing Rs 10 crore, are inferred-enabled and fitted with backup power. Many of them have 360-degree vision, and the one outside the Vice-Chancellor's lodge has a visibility radius of 800 metres.[5]

The cameras are just one part of the university's surveillance mechanism. The Watch and Ward staff of 300 men in khaki is known as 'Bulls'. There is the Local Intelligence Unit (LIU) of UP Police. Then there is another organised chain of proctors and deputy proctors at the top and proctorial monitors and deputy proctorial monitors among the students who act as paid informers. The surveillance became more organised during the short term of IFS Officer M. Hamid Ansari, who ran the administration like a foreign office.

The campus has a violent record. A student was murdered on campus in 2007, and another outside in 2009. The murders rocked the university, and the hostels had to be shut down for several weeks. After the 2007 murder, the vice-chancellor's lodge was attacked and burnt down. In 2006, the students' union was dissolved, ostensibly to contain violence.

In April 2016, the AMUTA demanded a CBI probe into the campus violence that led to the death of two youths in a cross-firing between rival gangs. The AMUTA passed a resolution alleging that unauthorised occupants in different university hostels acted with impunity only because they were getting 'patronage from some sections of the University administration'.[6]

Whereas a vice-chancellor described the violence as 'a case of sudden, abrupt vandalism', the AMUTA asserted that it was a fallout of the accumulated mishandling caused by 'gross violation of norms and procedures' by the university administration.

> The condemnable incident of firing that resulted in the total loss of vision (with over a hundred pellets in the brain) of a brilliant MTech student, Kaleem Ahmad, who had successfully competed in the Railway Engineering Services in north India and was about to join, is beyond horror.
>
> The second incident of the attempted abduction of a university student (reportedly a case of mistaken identity) by police within the campus also shows the extremely sorry state of relations between the civil administration and the University.
>
> ...

> The broad daylight murder in September 2015 of another student, Alamgir, for which we all demanded a CBI enquiry, remains unsolved.[7]

The AMU administration said the police would get a free hand to take action against the erring students and punish them by cancelling their passports and other official documents. 'We are identifying the students, and strict action will be taken against them. There will be no mercy, and they will be disqualified. We do not want the campus life to be disturbed,' the vice-chancellor announced.

'We have lodged an FIR against four students and several outsiders. Random checking is also going on in the hostels. We have requested the local administration to assist us in weeding out such elements,' the proctor of the university said. Even the shops and eating joints near the campus had been asked to down their shutters by 10 pm.

Various constituents of the Sangh Parivar find the sordid developments on campus congenial for advancing their pernicious agenda. The local BJP Member of Parliament Satish Gautam asked the vice-chancellor not to allow 'anti-government' and 'anti-national' programmes on the campus, such as hanging a portrait of Jinnah. A few days earlier, Shakunatala Bharti, the mayor of Aligarh, also from the BJP, accused the university of selling beef in a canteen on the campus, a claim that AMU vehemently denied. The canteen attached to the Jawaharlal Nehru Medical College at AMU was closed when Bharti made the allegation.

18

FAKE MORALITY FINDS A SCAPEGOAT

Dr Shrinivas Ramchandra Siras, the head of the Department of Modern Indian Languages at AMU, was found dead under mysterious circumstances at his rented home on 7 April 2010. Blood was visible around his mouth. Was it murder or suicide? He was under suspension for having consensual sex with a male partner. About two months before his death, a TV crew had barged into his house at night and filmed him. Some reports suggest that some of his 'students' had entered his house earlier to set up secret video cameras. The video clip was then given to the university authorities, who promptly suspended the professor for 'gross misconduct'. The AMU authorities were either ignorant of the law of the land, or they had the 'impunity' to behave per their whims and prejudices.

In collaboration with the university authority, the Aligarh police invoked section 377 of the IPC, which the colonialists had introduced way back in 1861 to criminalise sexual activities against the 'order of nature'. The Delhi high court and the Supreme Court of India later decriminalised the so-called 'offence'.

Economic and Political Weekly commented:

> The ease with which homosexuality was equated with 'gross misconduct' by the AMU underlined the continued existence of a large 'homophobic' common sense, which can be put to political use for a variety of unrelated issues, regardless of the well-publicised judgment on Section 377. Despite Siras's reluctance to challenge

his suspension, there have been many voices raised against the gross illegality and misconduct of the entire affair.[1]

The suspension of Dr Siras, which came less than a year after the historic judgment of the Delhi high court decriminalising consensual sex between same-sex adults, as well as the intrusion and filming of Dr Siras in the privacy of his home, prompted nationwide outrage. A fact-finding mission of a consortium of NGOs visited Aligarh on 3 March 2010.

The main findings of the mission pointed the finger at the complicity of the university authorities in various illegal actions against Dr Siras. The team's conversation with the journalist responsible made it evident that he would never have dared to conduct a 'sting' operation on the university premises without a go-ahead from the authorities. Then, in an apparent but unbelievable coincidence, the officers 'landed up' at Dr Siras's house on the night that he was filmed. The authority also failed to explain why they did not report the intruding journalists to the police and why they rushed to the press through a statement about Dr Siras's 'offence' and the 'moral action' taken by them. The AMU authorities were obviously involved in drumming up support for their actions and silencing and shaming Dr Siras.

The fact-finding mission exposed two possible explanations for the inexplicable and vindictive actions of the university. First, the immediate provocation for the entire incident may have been the fact that the vice-chancellor P.K. Abdul Azis was under enormous pressure, due to the inquiry ordered by the visitor following the unearthing of financial bungling and mismanagement in the university. 'Operation Siras' may have been an effort to turn the spotlight away, and Dr Siras served as a convenient scapegoat. Second, by deliberately raking up and taking a strident position against homosexuality, the university was seeking to bolster its own 'credentials' as upholder of a certain conservative morality even at the cost of the constitutional rights of its faculty.

The team also had a meeting with the 'homophobic' public relations officer of AMU, Rahat Abrar, who stated, 'Homosexuality even in the privacy of the home is immoral. This is a 133-year-old institution, and it has its moral values that must be upheld.' Apparently, the recent judgment of the Delhi high court that read down Sec 377 of the IPC ('We declare that Section 377 IPC, insofar it criminalises consensual sexual acts of adults in private, is violative of Articles 21, 14 and 15 of the Constitution') had no meaning for the authorities of AMU. They believed their moral indignation was sufficient explanation for their actions. But in fact, the historic judgment goes on to say 'Moral indignation, however strong, is not a valid basis for overriding an individual's fundamental right to dignity and privacy'.

Contrary to what AMU authorities had hoped for, Dr Siras refused to fade into the background or be shamed into silence. Despite his extreme sorrow and pain, he felt strengthened by the support and solidarity he received from many people. Consequently, he challenged the actions of AMU in the Allahabad high court as being violative of his civil liberties. He was vindicated with a stay order granted on his suspension and unlawful removal from his campus accommodation on 1 April 2010. A day after the judgment, he sounded pleased and was determined to pursue his FIR against AMU officials and media persons who had filmed him. Following his tragic death, on court orders, an FIR was lodged by the police under sections 347 (wrongful confinement), 355 (assault with intent to dishonour a person), 452 (house trespass), 506 (criminal intimidation), and 120B (criminal conspiracy) against some university officials and journalists.

The 'mysterious' circumstances under which Dr Siras died led to an uproar. For many weeks, the newspapers were full of headlines like 'Death of AMU's gay Prof, FIR against 6 people' (NDTV), 'In letter to AMU, Siras called sting a plot' (*Indian Express*), 'Judicial probe demanded into gay AMU teacher's death' (*Times of India*), 'AMU Professor case: Two journalists arrested' (Sify), 'AMU VC had ordered sting operation on Dr Siras' (*India Today*) and 'Shadow of AMU's spy wing on Siras sting' (*Indian Express*).

In the activist circle, Dr Siras's death caused dismay and anger. On 12 April 2010, many concerned individuals, women's groups, student unions, teachers' associations, as well as members of the lesbian, gay, bisexual and transgender (LGBT) community and other progressive movements got together. They held a protest in Delhi demanding justice for Dr Siras. Candles were lit, and one minute's silence was observed, along with a vow to fight for justice.

A few weeks later, Irfan, the man who was filmed having sex with Dr Siras, tried to immolate himself – a desperate act that exposed the constant harassment he had been facing from the police over several months. Irfan told the media that the police would pick him up and keep him in the police station for days on end and interrogate him about Dr Siras, and consequently, he was too weak to earn his livelihood. The Aligarh police obviously was on a mission to target Irfan and prove him and Dr Siras guilty, justifying the actions of AMU against Siras.

In 2015, five years after the incident, Hansal Mehta directed a two-hour movie on the tragic episode. Written by Apurva Asrani, with acclaimed actor Manoj Bajpai playing the role of victim Siras, the film was screened at several international festivals and welcomed by critics all over the Western world.

Siras's companion, Irfan, told a journalist that he wanted to meet the people in power and tell them his story.

> Police grilled me and people spat on me. Some days after Siras committed suicide I set myself ablaze but survived. My wife saved me. She told me I have to live to take care of my children. I was not gay, but over time, we became intimate. I was his saathi (friend).
>
> We had come back from a fair and suddenly three boys, who claimed to be from the media, came inside our room. They had filmed us. They kept asking, '*Aap sharminda hain*?' (Are you ashamed?) And Siras replied, '*Haan, main sharminda hoon. Ab mujhe jaane dijiye* (Yes, I am ashamed. Now, please leave me alone).' Of course, no one left them alone.

> 'Why is homosexuality a crime in India?' he asked. Had it not been for the fear of persecution, Siras would have fought. The case should not have been closed. Siras wanted to go to America after his retirement. I think he would have taken me with him.[2]

Irfan asked when told of the historic Supreme Court verdict decriminalising consensual gay sex. Irfan could scarcely make ends meet, and he survived, earning about Rs 8,000 a month by pulling a rickshaw in downtown Aligarh.

Living the life of a recluse, the rickshaw-puller hardly interacts with anyone now. His wife is a homemaker. Father of five grown-up daughters, his son died last year.

Siras had been associated with AMU since 1988 as a lecturer of Marathi in the Department of Modern Indian Languages. He was promoted to reader in 2003 under the Career Advancement Scheme.

Journalist Adil Murtaza, whose sting operation led to Siras's suicide, remains unapologetic. The tragic event underscored widespread homophobia on a largely conservative campus.

Even in the 1970s, AMU could swing to the extreme regard to its etiquette of a bygone era, like the regal 'procession' that used to accompany a resident Prince Wasif Ali Mirza alias Prince Nayyar Qadar Ali Shah in the long corridors of SS Hall. He was the great-grandson of the last ruler of Oudh (Lucknow), Nawab Wajid Ali Shah and Begum Hazrat Mahal. Nayyar Qadar was a celebrity among the residents then and held court every evening in his room.

Champions of conservative morality, who would force a gay professor to commit suicide, never had any compunction in abusing, threatening and harassing the women students if they dared to venture out near the library canteen in the evenings. Most of the victims never complained for fear of 'physical repercussions'.

In February 2006, Farah Aziz Khanum, a plucky 21-year-old student of mass communication, was verbally threatened for wearing a T-shirt and jeans.[3] She complained to the vice-chancellor after two youths snatched her shawl and sped away on their bike.

As per the directive of the Supreme Court, AMU had constituted a women's grievance cell in 2001. Its task is to register complaints of sexual harassment against women and take action. Still, AMU authorities had not taken any concrete action on any of the 11 complaints registered till 2006. Farah Aziz Khanum complained to the National Women's Commission (NCW) that AMU women's grievance cell was running only on paper. On her complaint, the NCW issued a notice to the AMU vice-chancellor who reconstituted the cell, but the harassment continues unabated.

Asma Javed, a postgraduate student from the Department of Hindi, dared to stand up and protest against the alleged lecherous advances of Dr Mohammad Sharif, a reader in the Sanskrit department, before AMU women's grievances redressal cell in March 2006.[4] The teacher was placed under suspension till investigations were over. Asma remained under immense pressure from faculty members and an influential lobby to withdraw the charges. The girl, who was also allegedly shot at immediately after she voiced her complaint in the proctor's office, sounded highly worked up about the systematic attempt at character assassination directed at her and alleged that the university authorities had been trying to shield the perpetrator.

The case drew a clear wedge between the teachers and students at AMU. The girls were, by and large, sympathetic to Asma. The president of AMU Women's College Students Union, Tabinda Iqbal, said that she had already demanded that a retired high court judge be made head of the probe panel. The AMUTA, on the other hand, seemed to have risen in support of the accused. The teachers' association expressed concern about the complete absence of any guidelines for the women's cell. Incidentally, the cell later came under attack for being soft on another accused, Mohammad Shabbir, a professor at the law department. Shabbir faced the charge of harassing a visiting US student in 2013.

There were attempts to push the matter under the carpet as the professor was well connected. Claiming that such cases were on the rise, a senior faculty member said a good number of research scholars were known to have abandoned their research projects in the recent past due to sexual advances made by teachers.

Asma also cited the name of Afsar Mustafa Khan, a professor of zoology: 'Whose objectionable behaviour with a research student had led to a big controversy at AMU, but the matter was hushed up.' The university dismissed the allegations of bias and wilful delay. Another senior official of AMU said Asma's case was weak as nothing physical was done to her, and whatever happened was verbal.[5]

Asma Javed sat on a hunger strike outside the vice-chancellor lodge. She said, 'I have been punished for daring to complain against a professor. I have been threatened time and again. They want me to withdraw my complaint ... The professor used to invite me over to his place and offer money.'

'This isn't the first complaint against Sharif. I am being victimised for speaking up,' Asma further said. She also alleged she was being denied admission to a PhD course.[6]

In May 2015, Asma Javed, 28, the first woman AMU Students' Union leader, was found murdered in her apartment. She had apprehended danger to her life at the hands of Malik Mohammad Akram, the son of a restaurant owner in the city. Before her death, she had alleged she was under pressure to withdraw the case against the accused.

She had done her PhD on the portrayal of the middle class in Hindi writer Premchand's novels, and ten years ago, she had accused a university professor of undue aggression. She sat on a *dharna* (protest). The AMU had never before witnessed such a protest by a woman.

In 2006, as many as nine girls tried to lodge complaints with the women's cell, but only three were accepted. Meanwhile, over six members had resigned (for different reasons) from the women's cell, which had always been mired in controversy. The AMU authorities confessed that the services of one teacher in the AMU Blind School had to be terminated. At the same time, another professor was suspended (but was later exonerated by the court) on complaints of female students.

In September of the same year, two teachers were suspended for sexual harassment. A female student quit because she could not take it anymore. Another had her clothes pulled for dressing in an 'un-Islamic' fashion. An angry student sat on a hunger strike. Worse, many of AMU's female students – they number 5,000 of the 22,000 AMU students – were being told that they were bringing a 'bad name' to the university by protesting. The girl students said enough was enough. They alleged that the authorities did not even allow them to leave the campus. They had to get permission if they even went out for coaching classes. There were no such curbs on male students.

In 2012, a law student got into trouble after writing about issues at the university. The student, now at Harvard Law School, was disowned and forced to quit.

> In 2022, Aligarh's additional district judge Rajesh Bhardwaj quashed the acquittal by a trial court of Bilal Mustafa, a professor in the management department of Aligarh Muslim University (AMU), and sentenced him to one year's rigorous imprisonment with penalty for making sexual remarks, unwelcome physical contact and advances towards an Iranian girl research scholar studying under him…
>
> A case was registered under section 354A(i)(iv) (offence of making sexual remarks, unwelcome physical contact and advances) of the Indian Penal Code at the Civil Lines police station of Aligarh in 2014 on a complaint by the Iranian girl research scholar against Mustafa.
>
> The scholar, who had joined research work in 2013 under Mustafa, had first complained to the AMU administration and later to the Aligarh police.
>
> The police, after a probe, registered a case under relevant sections of the IPC and Information Technology Act at the Civil Lines police station in 2014.[7]

In 2017, the victim revealed to a newsperson how Bilal Mustafa would summon her to his office for no substantial reason and tried to make 'unwelcome advances and explicit sexual overtures'.[8] He also allegedly stalked her on social media sites. She explained how

Bilal Mustafa was exonerated by the varsity's in-house committee even as the vice-chancellor Lt Gen. Zameer Uddin Shah had directed the accused to tender a written apology to her. However, the professor never submitted an apology nor informed the scholar.

Professor Mohammad Shabbir, chairman of the law department, who had been suspended on charges of sexual harassment, skilfully abused the processes of law to avoid jail and managed the AMU administration to get himself reinstated on the day of his retirement on 31 May 2014, sparking outrage among teachers as well as students.[9] Over two dozen faculty members had questioned how the internal inquiry had been conducted.

In January 2007, Tanzeem Fatima, the only female faculty in the Department of Law, felt uncomfortable about sharing the staff room with 11 male members and went to the then vice-chancellor, Naseem Ahmad, with the plea that she be allotted a separate chamber. She alleged that her male colleagues 'passed comments and made fun' of her. There was no washroom for women, she added.[10]

Soon, the chairman of the law department who also held the charge of the university proctor and the dean, who also held the post of registrar, allegedly turned against her. Tanzeem was suspended, and the services of the guest faculty who assaulted her was terminated. The guest faculty was soon back on the campus; Tanzeem remained suspended.

At the Malappram (Kerala) centre of the university, in December 2015, girls protested against an all-male panel to probe the harassment of a girl by a male faculty member. Pending the inquiry, faculty member M.H. Faridi was removed from the post of proctor. 'There should be at least one woman in the committee. It is better to discuss such things with a woman teacher. It is also prescribed by the Supreme Court. The charges are of a serious nature. The faculty member is still on the campus,' a girl student told *The Indian Express*.[11]

In a similar incident reported at AMU's Kishanganj centre in Bihar, a female member was included in the inquiry committee.

At the main campus (in Aligarh), a committee headed by a woman is already functional. Why were AMU centres going against the norms, asked another student.

Over 100 students, about half of them girls, alleged that Faridi, despite having no official authority, used to visit the girls' hostel often without intimation. He also made girls sit in his chamber for long hours. He called some girls at odd hours and asked for information about others. He had even called up the parents of some girls and given them false information about their 'questionable' activities. One girl had already left the campus due to his alleged high-handedness, the protesting girls claimed. The university said that since harassment of girls was not the main issue, no woman was included in the committee.

Justice Sudhir Agarwal of Allahabad high court upheld the decision of AMU authorities to dismiss Mr Mohammad Hasan, a teacher at the Ahmadi School for the Blind who had committed acts of sexual harassment against a blind student, Miss Azra Firdaus, amounting to gross misconduct unbecoming of a teacher. The case happened in 2002. The appeal was filed in 2004 and judgement was delivered on 30 January 2019.[12]

In another similar case, a division bench of the Allahabad high court, comprising Justices B. Chauhan and A. Tandon dismissed the writ petition of Dr Bishambhar Dayal Gupta, who was employed as a reader at the Department of Psychology, AMU, in 1986 and whose services were terminated by the university authorities in 1989 for making attempts to harass three girl students sexually. The judgment was pronounced on 16 August 2005.

Hailing it as the most significant step, the then vice-chancellor Zameer Uddin Shah mentions in his memoirs,

> His Holiness the Syedna Mufaddal Saifuddin, spiritual head of the Dawoodi Bohra community, was elected the Chancellor of AMU against stiff opposition from some persons who wished to occupy this exalted position for personal aggrandisement. We also wanted to demolish the myth of the so-called Sunni-Shia divide. We wanted a Chancellor whose voice would be heard by the government

and who would not 'milk' the University for various favours. In his Holiness, we found a generous benefactor who financed the restoration of the leading school run by the University, named after his grandfather.[13]

Interestingly, the vice-chancellor added,

The Chancellor's benediction and blessings added splendour to the university Convocation when hundreds of the Bohra community from all over the world visited AMU. During this ceremony, the Chancellor gifted the university with 1000 top-of-the-line computers to enable IT education to start from class! Was the convocation converted into a public show? Moreover, no one dared to ask Syedna about his views on female genital mutilation and the bodily autonomy of women. It seems human rights have no value whatsoever while installing people at the helm of affairs.14

Outspoken historian Irfan Habib did not mince words when he said in an interview with the news portal Scroll.in that during pre-partition days, the dominating Muslim League was not orthodox. Its members were communal, but not religious. Jinnah himself was not religious. In fact, among the Muslims supporting the Congress, there were a large number of theologians who began to influence government policy.

Talking about the increasing influence of orthodox elements on the campus, which has such a pull on Muslims, Professor Habib said,

When I was studying there, one-third of students were non-Muslim, as also one-fourth of teachers. Today, 90 per cent are Muslims. There are very few non-Muslim teachers left now. They are simply weeded out in the recruitment process. There are a few Hindu students living in hostels. The change in AMU's composition has changed its mentality. In my student days, Diwali and Guru Nanak's birthday were celebrated. Truckloads of *laddoos* would come from the city gurudwara to the AMU. The atmosphere

> was different. Hindus and Muslims would really live together then. Today, that isn't there.[15]

Noted sociologist Imtiaz Ahmad says:

> Revisiting the AMU after a gap of 25 years, the first thing that struck me, at the Faculty of Arts and elsewhere on the campus, was that in every classroom, there were students wearing burqas and skullcaps. In the late-1980s, when I studied there, no girl would be seen wearing a burqa or a boy donning a skullcap. The sociological shift indicates that at some point, from the 1990s onwards, religiosity became overtly significant to the lives of the university students. This is part of the trends among the Muslims in India and abroad.16

Clothes are not, sometimes, just clothes. They are ideas which have their own autonomous trajectories. At the Maulana Azad Library, one of the largest libraries in Asia, which is open till 2 a.m., students started offering prayers in the corridors some years ago, forcing the university officials to designate a separate room for prayers within the library informally. Later, the AMU administration designated two separate reading rooms at the library for female students, though these students are also allowed to sit anywhere in the library, alongside male students, and some of them do so.

Aftab Alam, a professor at the political science department, opined, 'Earlier too, girls would sit separately from boys and they wouldn't talk. Now, there is growing mixing between boys and girls. Burqa-wearing girls can be seen talking to boys freely.'[17]

However, Alam notes that the AMU campus has its own *mizaaj* (character), which reflects a mix of tradition and modernity. 'This campus will live with this challenge', he added. Whatever he might have meant by that, if the founder Sir Syed Ahmad Khan's objective was to provide modern education and inculcate a liberal temperament among Muslims, the overt religiosity on its campus is indeed posing a serious severe challenge to the university's intellectual environment.

Professor Irfan Habib recalls that when he was at Oxford University in the 1950s, frock-wearing girls from Pakistan would mock Indian girls for being orthodox. Religiosity has grown everywhere, not just in India and Pakistan. Religiosity is also growing among Hindus. In the life of societies, ideas, whether good or bad, are essentially important, whether or not we want them.[18]

Attempting to analyse recent trends at AMU, Abdul Waheed, a professor of sociology at the university, cites historical studies that show that during the Khilafat Movement for the restoration of the Turkey-led Islamic caliphate in the 1920s, Indian society witnessed the rise of beards and caps but adds that these disappeared after Partition.[19]

In Waheed's words, 'beards and caps disappeared after Partition haunted me, as I am left wondering if the rise of burqas and skullcaps on AMU campus will disappear after another Partition, which need not be territorial in nature'.

19

THE LUXURY OF ENQUIRIES

In a democratic polity, no institution enjoys immunity from 'inquiries'. However, the AMU and its predecessor MAO College have enjoyed the dubious distinction of facing an unprecedented number of probes into their murky affairs.

P.K. Abdul Azis, the vice-chancellor from 2007 to 2012, faced two enquiries for alleged 'embezzlement' of about Rs 5 lakh. The two probe panels ran up a bill of Rs 82 lakh and without any conclusive findings. The government referred the case to the CBI, which recommended that the amount be recovered from Aziz but did not file any criminal case against him. In its preliminary report, the CBI had indicted the vice-chancellor of having 'committed financial impropriety and claimed TA on first joining and also home town concession to which he was not entitled'.[1]

Professor Azis had submitted bills worth Rs 81,654 for travelling with family from Cochin to New Delhi and Rs 93,053 for travel from New Delhi to Thiruvananthapuram. He was allegedly not entitled to the claim of Rs 93,053. It was also found that the vice-chancellor had drawn Rs 82,356 for paying personal income tax and sanctioned Rs 44,315 to Registrar V.K. Abdul Jaleel for the same purpose.

The CBI had probed allegations related to travel concession for family, income tax payment from university funds and purchase of luxury cars. There were as many as 35 charges of financial irregularities, including one of drawing travel allowances from the university before joining it. In September 2009, the HRD ministry set up a probe panel of Justice Fakhruddin, former judge of the Madhya Pradesh high court and retired bureaucrat A.H. Jung, a former secretary of the Union Ministry of Civil Aviation, to investigate the matter. However, the team could not work as the two could not agree on whether the vice-chancellor should be represented by the university lawyer in the inquiry proceedings. Jung believed that since the allegations were explicitly against the vice-chancellor, the university lawyer should not represent him. Justice Fakhruddin believed that under the AMU Act, the vice-chancellor was entitled to be represented. Jung withdrew from the committee. Later, Justice Fakhruddin also quit. Even intervention by Kapil Sibal, the Union HRD minister, could not resolve the issue. By then, Rs 2 lakh had been spent on the committee's expenses.

In February 2010, the ministry set up another judicial probe panel of Justices B.A. Khan and A.N. Divecha.[2] After one year, the committee handed in an interim report that touched on only four charges and sought an extension to look into the remaining 31. By then, Rs 80 lakh had been spent on the committee, whose members were entitled to the same pay as a sitting high court judge. Besides, each was entitled to an air-conditioned car and air travel for the conduct of hearings. In their interim report, the two judges gave different findings. Justice Khan said that Aziz alone could not be blamed for the scandal, whereas Justice Divecha held the vice-chancellor guilty. In the absence of a conclusive finding, the ministry could not act. It sought the permission of the visitor to refer the matter to the CBI.

Even when MAO College was in its infancy, Sir Syed discovered in 1896 that his English language clerk, Shyam Behari Lal (Mathur), had embezzled Rs 1,05,409 from the college fund. Hailing from a distinguished family in Aligarh, Lal had been recruited by Sir Syed in June 1883. He remained in the same office till July 1895, when he suffered a paralytic stroke.

A large sum of the college fund had been deposited in the Agra branch of the Bank of Bengal. The money could be withdrawn by cheque. Promissory notes of Rs 49,000, deposited in the same bank, formed the capital fund. They carried an interest of Rs 2,000 per annum. Sir Syed used to keep the chequebook locked in a box, with the key in his possession. Whenever the need arose, Lal would ask for the key, fill out a cheque for the required amount and obtain Sir Syed's signature. Hali, one of the teachers at MAO College and biographer of Sir Syed, writes, 'Since Sir Syed did not know English and had confidence in his clerk, he never hesitated to give his signature whenever requested. Sometimes, Lal even forged Sir Syed's signature.'[3]

In his statement before the court, Sir Syed said:

> I can neither read nor write in English but can only understand simple English sentences if spoken slowly in easy words and can sign my name in English... For this reason, all official work required to be done in English was entrusted to the English head clerk of my office.[4]

It is difficult to imagine that Sir Syed, who spent his entire life in the British Indian judicial service, accompanied his son to Britain for a year, and was influenced by the Western style of learning, was so ignorant of rudimentary English that he could not read figures in the cheques signed by him.

Sir Syed had a personal rapport with several Englishmen, and using a translator during private meetings and exchanging ideas was not always feasible. Broken Hindustani and English probably formed the means of communication between them. When he stayed in England for a year and a half, he benefited greatly from English books there. Also, while getting his books (particularly *Khutbat-i Ahmadiyya*) translated into English, his ability to read, understand and speak English improved considerably. There are explicit references to show that Sir Syed could speak English well. In his letter to Mohsin ul-Mulk from England on 20 August 1869, he wrote: 'I met the Secretary for India once, Hamid and Mahmood, and twice met him alone. I replied to all his points in English, grasped everything, and made all replies correctly (though) in quite Bedouin-like, bad English.'[5]

Moreover, poetry, dance and music were an integral part of the atmosphere Sir Syed was brought up in, where easy virtues punctuated the affairs during the reign of the last Mughal ruler.

Sir Syed's mother's brother, Dabiruddaulah Khwaja Zain ul-Abideen Khan, was a connoisseur of dance and music; his love for music had become a craze. He had acquired particular expertise in playing the *been* (a kind of wind instrument). He did not display any other interest in those days except these hobbies. Several renowned Dhrupad and Khayal singers were on his payroll. *Beens* were explicitly prepared for him. Meer Nasir Ahmad, one of the grandsons of prominent players Himmat Khan and Rag Ras Khan, came to play for him and display their expertise in this field.[6]

This went on until the capital deposited with the bank was exhausted. Then Shyam Behari Lal took another step to break the capital fund comprising promissory notes. Since the promissory notes could not be encashed, the clerk allegedly forged a power of attorney in his name, authorising the bank to issue a loan with interest to the college on the security of the promissory notes. The clerk forged the signatures of seven trustees and took a loan of Rs 42,750. He had already withdrawn Rs 62,659 from the main account. The total amount embezzled was Rs 1,07,198, but including the interest that had to be paid to the bank on various advances, the total loss came to rupees 1,17,353 paisa two and pie 9.

In the meantime, Lal suffered a paralytic stroke, incapacitating him. Letters were sent to the college by the bank. In his absence, another clerk opened the letters and uncovered the scandal. A thorough examination of the chequebook and recapitulation of the entries in the account revealed that a large sum of money was missing. A statement from the bank confirmed this suspicion. Sir Syed immediately informed the government and launched criminal proceedings against Lal. The magistrate remanded the clerk.

Mirza Abid Ali Bey, a trustee of the college committee, and Syed Vilayat Husain, the second master in the school, spent about three months patiently examining the accounts of the college. Their report stated that no money was embezzled in the honorary secretary's office but was withdrawn using forged cheques.

However, Hali observes that the fact that a thief was able to draw forged cheques for such a long period without detection was undoubtedly a case of gross negligence. It is not fair to argue that he (Sir Syed) should have hesitated to put his signature to the documents in the English language that his clerk had drawn up. Subordinates are trusted to this extent in all branches of administration, as without a certain measure of confidence in one's employees, nothing could possibly be accomplished. Moreover, the clerk did not seek Sir Syed's signature on all the cheques but instead forged his signature on most of them. Sir Syed cannot be accused of negligence in the matter regarding the loan obtained from the bank based on the promissory notes, for he was confident, as indeed he had the right to be, that the bank would not allow anyone to touch even a single penny in the capital fund. No one could have guessed that the clerk would send a counterfeit power of attorney, bearing the forged signature of Sir Syed and other trustees, to the bank.

While the criminal proceedings against the clerk were going on, Sir Syed wrote to Hali:

> I have recently become seriously indisposed. The strain of giving evidence in court is far too much for me. But no one can fight with destiny ... Some believe that Lal stole the money because I am very old and drawing closer to death's door daily. I should soon perish, and the action of Shyam Behari Lal would have been overlooked in the confusion. But I thank God his deceit and betrayal were discovered before I died. Otherwise, people might have accused me of having a hand in the crime. I am grateful, therefore, that I have lived to see the matter brought to light. Some people stupidly believe that the money was under my care and control. This assumption is wrong. Following the stipulations in the Trustee Bill, the money was put into the bank. It was withdrawn using forged cheques which no one could possibly have stopped until the fraud was discovered. I, nevertheless, regard it as the mercy of the

> Almighty that the crime was detected during my lifetime, though it has caused me grief and pain.[7]

After listening to Sir Syed's report, the trustees voted confidently in the honorary secretary. In a resolution adopted at the meeting, they declared that neither had Sir Syed been negligent nor had he trusted his clerk more than usual in English offices. However, one person later suggested that the trustees had no alternative but to pass the vote of confidence, as they were also guilty of the charge from which they, too, wished to absolve their secretary.

Hali adds:

> It must, of course, be admitted that the trustees would have found it challenging to give a convincing answer to the objection that Maulvi Samiullah raised in a letter to the secretary on 25 January 1896. Had the trustees taken a little more care and considered it as part of their duty to examine the accounts of the college every year or so, the fraud, which robbed Muslims of thousands of rupees, would never have occurred.

It seems that Hali, who was a close friend of Sir Syed's from the latter's Delhi days, was caught in a predicament on this issue, as he also mentions in his book:

> It is indeed unreasonable to expect the secretary to concern himself with every minute detail of the administration. Among the people of our poverty-stricken nation, where shall we find a man who will devote himself day and night to the affairs of the college, who will go in search of money when it is needed, who will combine the qualities of a speaker, writer and treasurer, and who, like an experienced clerk, will always be aware of the tricks of his cunning subordinates?

It was a severe shock to Sir Syed.[8] Opponents began to gossip, and new doubts were invented. Supporters had to keep low. All kinds of malicious propaganda were being circulated. Moreover, by an unfortunate twist of fate, Shyam Behari Lal, arrested after an FIR was filed, died in custody. Some people thought that, while in jail, he had committed suicide out of shame. Syed Mahmood and Karamat Husain believed a court case might still be instituted despite his death and all his property forfeited. It is another matter that even if his entire property had been appropriated, its total value would not exceed ten thousand rupees, while the case needed to be pursued for years together. This was perhaps why the case was put in cold storage after Shyam Behari Lal died.

This embezzlement affected Sir Syed's health so severely that he could never fully recover. This was possibly why (with the advancing age) his health gradually deteriorated, and the end came in March 1898. This embezzlement impacted all the work in the college; the construction of college buildings suffered in particular. There were delays in constructing the debenture boarding house (Morrison Court of today) and all other facilities. According to Sir Syed, only the mosque's construction was continued with meagre monthly contributions from a few close friends. These amounted to only about two hundred and fifty rupees a month.

In the aftermath of that scandal, Theodore Beck, the second principal of MAO College, was able to add the role of bursar to his administrative domain. Lal's death in prison saved Sir Syed from further embarrassment.

Just seven years after the establishment of the university, in October 1927, the governor general of India, known as Lord Rector, advised the chancellor to appoint an enquiry committee to examine the working of the AMU. He had taken a serious view of the complaints in a pamphlet issued by Sahebzada Aftab Ahmad Khan, the second vice-chancellor of the AMU.

A year earlier, the vice-chancellor had proceeded on leave on health grounds. Sahebzada had appointed an enquiry committee of four members of the teaching staff under the chairmanship of Sheikh Abdullah, the treasurer of the university, to inquire into discipline, teaching and other matters connected with the university. The committee submitted its report in September. Sahebzada recommended action. When the University Court ignored his advice to take action against pro-vice-chancellor Dr Ziauddin, he quit the office and released a pamphlet.

Consequently, a committee consisting of Sir Ibrahim Rahimtoola (chairman), Sir Philip Joseph Hartog, Sir George Anderson (members) and A.F. Rehman (secretary) was appointed by the chancellor to enquire into and report about the academic, administrative and financial affairs of the university.[9] The committee pointed out shortcomings and irregularities. It quoted from the Sheikh Abdullah Committee, which had remarked a year earlier: There has been general laxity in observing rules, and that the administration, the staff and even the students, all are responsible for this laxity, no one dares to deny. Nor can anyone deny that this laxity is the basis of all our troubles. It is no use apportioning blame, for everyone shares it according to his measure; there exists no justification for it now, even on the score of expediency. Let principle replace expediency in the future, and let rules and regulations be strictly enforced. Every activity and every aspect of university life was tainted by strife, with the unhappy result that ideals were blunted and what was intended to be good had been subverted into evil.

The committee noted that there might have been some justification for making a giant number of admissions during the early years of the university. Still, even in recent years, there has been little attempt to regulate the pace of expansion by the limits of the teaching power and residential accommodation. As a result, teaching efficiency has suffered, the hostels are seriously overcrowded, and the number of students has outstripped the provision of playgrounds. The committee emphasised that the expansion should follow adequate provision for competent teachers and residential accommodation to maintain the high standard of the past.

Care should be taken to have the advice of competent external experts for making appointments to professorship and readership, the incumbents of which should possess high qualifications corresponding to the salaries attached to such posts by the university.

In the past, the university has not always made a suitable selection of the members of the Committee of Appointment.

Members of the staff have been irregular in the performance of their duties. With irregularities in the attendance of the staff, it is but natural that they should be reflected among the students. Although the ordinances require an attendance of 75 per cent of the prescribed lectures, little or no effort has been made to enforce this salutary provision. The students have become indifferent to punctual and regular habits and sustained study. One of the senior professors has summed up the present position with the concise statement that 'students are under the impression that rules are not meant to be obeyed'. A single example of the procedure recently brought to our notice may explain this impression more clearly. Hitherto, class promotion has been claimed by students as a matter of right. In 1927, after two staff meetings, the Academic Council approved the proposal that terminal examinations should be held. These examinations took place last summer, and while only a tiny percentage of the students appeared for the examination, all (or nearly all) obtained class promotion.

About the conduct of examinations, the committee stated:

> Complaints have been made to us that an unduly large number of candidates have written their examinations while admitted to the hospital. From the experience of other universities, we think that such cases ought to be rare. A candidate sufficiently ill to be a patient in a hospital is not often sufficiently well to take an examination. We do not wish the practice to be forbidden. Still, it should be carefully scrutinised, and every precaution taken should ensure that the invigilation is no less strict in the hospital than in the ordinary examination room.

On private candidates for intermediate examinations of the university, the committee observed:

> The fact that in 1926, there were 402 private candidates as against 332 regular candidates and that in 1927 the numbers were 420

> and 391, respectively, indicate that the concession of admitting private candidates has been very liberally interspersed. (In 1925, there were only 237 private candidates.) The private candidates thus admitted are in two categories: those who are enrolled in a recognised school and those who have ceased to be so enrolled for seven months. In one instance, a boy who failed in his eighth-class examination at the Muslim University School was re-examined later and again failed. He left the school but appeared only seven months later in the high school examination as a private candidate and was successful. There is no report by the headmaster about either his class record or his character. In other words, not only was the boy's failure in his class examination condoned, but he appeared for and passed the examination two years earlier than would have been admissible had he remained at school!

The committee recommended that the university teachers not be permitted to stand for election to a legislature. It regretted that Aligarh appeared to be in danger of being used by some staff members as a stepping-stone to political advancement. It noted:

> In 1921, the institution was passing through an abrupt and challenging period of transition from the status of a college to that of a university and arduous difficulties were experienced in placing the new institution on a definite and well-marked line of progress. Such a task necessarily required the whole time and attention of the university authorities, and yet, in 1923, Dr Ziauddin, pro-VC, and Dr Hyder, professor of economics, decided to enter politics and stand for election, the former to the U.P. legislative council and the latter to the legislative assembly.

Concluding its report, the committee said:

> The university's lifeblood is being sapped by faction and intrigue. The Act and its provisions, instead of proving themselves a safeguard and a bulwark against irregularity, have become a tool and a plaything in the hands of factions. The way lies clear for

> drastic action. If Aligarh is to expand and prosper, the spirit of factionalism must be banished; and a new spirit must pervade all its activities.

The audit report of the accountant general of Uttar Pradesh in March 1953 had alleged embezzlement, defalcation, misappropriation and loss of, or tampering with the records of the AMU. It was, inter alia, mentioned in the report that the university had sustained heavy losses in certain financial transactions at the hands of its employees, some of whom had migrated to Pakistan. The audit report suggested a departmental enquiry regarding the irregularities it had brought out. A three-member committee was appointed by Dr Zakir Husain, the then vice-chancellor. However the committee failed to submit a report.

To look into the criticism regarding accounts of the building activities in the College of Engineering, the university appointed an expert technical committee headed by P.C. Aggarwal, a retired chief engineer. It also could not work because the information required could not be supplied by the university since the supervising engineer had left the university and the relevant papers and accounts were not traceable.

The union government concluded that a thorough and detailed enquiry was necessary to examine the financial affairs of the university and how it dealt with the audit objections. The government had also received several complaints of irregular appointments by the university and the absence of a uniform standard for admission to the various courses. It, therefore, felt that the proposed enquiry could also cover these matters. Under these circumstances, the Union Ministry of Education requested the visitor to order such an enquiry.

However, the AMU vice-chancellor Col B.H. Zaidi urged that the Executive Council of the university be allowed to appoint a committee for enquiry. The visitor disagreed. However, the Executive Council announced the formation of the enquiry committee with Professor G.C. Chatterji (former vice-chancellor of Rajasthan University) as chairman.[10] The committee submitted a comprehensive report in 1961.

Successive enquiries have suggested remedial measures to improve law and order and the deteriorating academic standard in the university. Still, educators have not paid much heed to them. The chancellor of the university appointed a 32-member high-powered committee in April 1994. Its members included the Governor of Madhya Pradesh, Mohammad Shafi Qureshi; a member of Lok Sabha, Mani Shankar Aiyar; retired Professors K.A. Nizami, Aal-e-Ahmed Suroor and Masoodul Hasan; the AMU old boys, representatives of the students' union, non-teaching staff, staff association and some serving professors. Its terms of reference included: (i) to discuss current problems faced by the university; (ii) to analyse the causality of these problems by bringing together the various elements in the functioning of the university; (iii) to effect a conciliation amongst these elements and safeguard their honour and self-respect; (iv) to lay down approaches and set up the mechanism of the value system; (v) to determine the spheres of activity of different interests such as the teachers; and (vi) in general, to install a system of peaceful functioning of the university. The committee submitted its report in May.

The report stated:

> The University Court had noted in successive meetings that the working and living conditions of the university are charged with tension and fear. There have been numerous and frequent episodes of strikes, *gheraos*, use of country-made pistols; pressuring the VC and other functionaries into making wrong decisions, including those in admission and appointments; compromising the dignity of the university authorities, teachers and various office-bearers; and hooliganism to the point of bodily harm or threat of bodily harm. Examinations have been changed under mob pressure or physical threat, copying has been resorted to by many, and vacation dates and holidays have been unilaterally declared by student bullies who force the students not to attend classes. Non-student rowdies have

> taken residence in halls of residence and have made common cause with some university members to foul up the atmosphere.

The committee noted with grave concern that the number of students in the university had increased beyond 20,000 and, by some reckoning, beyond 22,000 – impossible numbers to handle on a single campus of approximately 3 sq. km. The responsibilities of the administration had been stretched far beyond its competence. An oversized unitary educational institution was itself the cause of many unsavoury happenings. In a consequence of overcrowding, dining rooms in the halls of residence had been converted into living rooms, and students were denied the collegial and healthy atmosphere of social interaction. Living rooms in the hostels were congested, with six or seven students clustering in a space meant for two or three. In such an atmosphere, norms of decent living were being violated, the peace and quiet required for studies and students wishing to concentrate on their work were suffering at the hands of three officials – the vice-chancellor, the pro-vice-chancellor and the controller of admissions and examinations.

The frequent bypassing of bodies, authorities and relevant committees such as the Executive Council, the Academic Council and the Discipline Committee, the excessive and non-judicious use by the vice-chancellors of emergency power under Section 19-3(c) for relatively trivial purposes, the encouragement, cultivation and patronage of rowdies, giving in to their pressures in nominations, admissions and appointments, and the changing of decisions abruptly under duress were some illustrations of arbitrariness and concentration of power. The cultivation of hooligans to protect themselves against other hooligans had not paid off as these very protectors had started bullying and pressurising the administration into wrongdoing.

Significantly, the committee felt that during the frequent agitation on issues and non-issues, many zealous agitators shouted from rooftops about justice and fair play, lamented the decline of standards and criticised the administration and the academic bodies for populism. And then, at the very next moment, these elements came to plead for the admission or appointment of their kith and kin, their supporters and friends, and pressurised and threatened the vice-chancellor and the other wings of the administration with dire consequences in the event of resistance.

Describing them as enemies of the university and its potential destroyers, the committee suggested that a mechanism be developed to fight these destructive elements and resist pressures so that admissions could be made in predetermined numbers, according to the university's rules and recommendations of the relevant bodies.

The committee saw the failure of law and order as a critical problem in itself, which needed to be tackled firmly and immediately, and also as a cause of many other problems such as the strengthening of hooliganism, the occupation of halls of residence by outside goons and young relatives and friends, corrupt practices in university admissions, malpractice in examinations and severe irregularities in appointments. According to the committee, these problems, of course, existed on their own but were magnified manifold in a deteriorating law and order situation. As the law and order situation had become much worse than ever, these and many other problems had become more extensive and problematic than ever before.

The committee also recorded that it is difficult to say who can be exempted from the responsibility of worsening the law-and-order situation in the university in recent times. Criticisms have been made of every category of elements in the university – the administration, the student community, the teaching community, the non-teaching staff and many outsiders who live on the campus and meddle with it.

Carrying on with the endless process of inquiries, vice-chancellor M. Rahman instituted an inquiry into the alleged irregularities during the tenure of his predecessor N.M. Farooqi. The inquiry was headed by Justice John K. Mathew (retd) of the Kerala high court. He submitted his report in 1999, but it was placed before the university Executive Council in 2007, after a lapse of about a decade.

In the same meeting, the Executive Council decided to institute a broad-based inquiry into the matters (excluding the criminal acts of murder of two students), with the following terms of reference: (i) To enquire into the state of affairs which prevailed the university right from the commencement of the academic session 2006–07 and ascertain the reasons that could have resulted in the sudden resignation of the then vice chancellor Naseem Ahmad on 7 July 2007; (ii) To identify and enquire into the various events following the resignation of the then vice-chancellor and the elements behind those incidents; (iii) To enquire into the lapses on the part of the university administration that led to the escalation of the atmosphere of distrust; (iv) the university and its failure to take appropriate and timely action into those matters; (v) to give its recommendations for the prevention of such events in future and the general upliftment of the academic and residential atmosphere in the university.

Earlier, Justice S.R. Mishra (retd.) of the Calcutta high court headed the enquiry commission into the violent incidents in 1998, in which the house of the then registrar H.A.S. Jafri was burnt by miscreants. Its report, too, has not been placed before the Executive Council.

M. Hamid Ansari, M. Rahman's successor, instituted another inquiry into the construction of a beautiful garden adjoining the university's Sir Ziauddin Ahmed Dental College. The inquiry officer found no irregularity.

In July 2010, the AMU administration silently moved against 97 employees alleged to have furnished fake documents to get their jobs. The action had to be taken on an order from the Allahabad high court. As many as 27 non-teaching employees were dismissed, and 38 others, including two professors, were suspended with immediate effect. The pension benefits of 32 staffers, found to have worked till retirement with fake papers, were frozen.

The ball had been set rolling by a former employee, Naseem Ali Khan, who filed a comprehensive writ petition listing the names of 125 persons, including professors, non-teaching and class IV staff, who were allegedly employed with fake certificates. Moving swiftly on the petition, the court asked the university to furnish relevant documents. After finding corroborative evidence, Justice A. Tandon set a deadline for the university to take action and asked it to report to the court.

In September 2014, the vice-chancellor accepted the resignation of the Registrar Shahrukh Shamshad, who two hours later tried to retract it, claiming that he had been 'forced to resign under duress'. The resignation had come weeks after the office of the vice president of India had asked the union HRD ministry to look into the complaints of alleged manipulations in Shahrukh Shamshad's appointment as registrar.

Using special powers, the vice-chancellor appointed Shahrukh Shamshad as Registrar on an ad-hoc basis on 17 May 2012. The post was advertised a month later. Also, instead of the 45 days given to respond to the advertisement, the time was extended to two months for Shamshad, who did not meet the mandatory criteria of having a Master's degree and was waiting for his 'fake' degree to arrive.

Right to Information (RTI) replies further revealed that Shahrukh Shamshad had received his Master's degree from the controversial Eastern Institute for Integrated Learning in Management (EIILM), Sikkim, on 27 August 2012, i.e., after he was appointed Registrar. A few months earlier, the vice-chancellor and registrar of the EIILM had been arrested for issuing fake degrees, and the UGC asked it to discontinue all distance courses. It was also alleged that Shahrukh Shamshad had done his MBA between January 2010 and December 2011 from EILLM, even when he was with the Indian Air Force between 2005 and 2011.

20

FADING WIT, HUMOUR AND GRACIOUSNESS

Rashid Ahmad Siddiqi, professor of Urdu at AMU, was a mild-mannered man who rarely raised his voice, even in anger. Once, when the boisterous antics of his children kept disturbing him in his work, he called out to his wife, saying, 'Look here, *begum*, your children won't let me work!' The *begum sahiba* replied archly, 'What do you mean by my children? I didn't bring them in my *dahej* (dowry)'. Not to be outwitted, the professor said, 'I never brought them with my *baraat* (marriage procession) either.'[1]

On another occasion, an admirer asked him. 'Professor *sahib*, you are always making fun of other people and laughing at them. Do you ever tell jokes about yourself?' Professor Siddiqi narrated one when he had to read a paper at a seminar and asked a learned member of the audience what he thought of it. The other excused himself, saying, 'I am a *jaahil* (illiterate); my opinions don't matter'. Siddiqi insisted that 'often illiterate people express profound opinions'. 'Exactly', retorted the other 'just as you did in your paper'.[2]

Tales abound about the Aligarians, famous for their pranks, culture, adab and lehaz, and *tahzib*. 'What's in a name?' said the bard. He was right, of course, but his statement involved some poetic licence like all great poets. Aligarh did not exist at that time. Otherwise, the poet would have known Aligarh had a rich tradition of bestowing *nomen specificum*. One could be named informally by others after fruits, vegetables, animals, style of working, dress, fondness for a particular eatable, etc. The passion for nicknames is in the blood of Aligarians. They have nurtured this art since the establishment of MAO College. Sometimes, the bestowed surnames have a lot of relevance to knowing their forefathers' identity, history, and profession.

In Aligarh, one can find about 50 persons known by their *nom de convenience* than by their proper names or surnames. These names carry clues to the personalities of these persons, and over the years, such names have turned into labels of identity.

Perhaps it is easier to remember a person's nickname than his real name – either because nicknames are rarely complimentary since they hinge on a person's weakness, eccentricity or some characteristic feature. Or, nicknames could arise because the original names are not self-explanatory. Also, a person is generally better known by his nickname, the reason for which is perhaps that we human beings find it easier to remember a man's deficiency rather than his merits or maybe because nicknames tend to sit so well on the tongue. Those nicknamed may try hard to shake off their pejorative, but the harder they try, the more tenaciously they cling to them. Nicknames often give a truthful and accurate description of the person so 'nicked in the name'. And truth and reality are hard to get rid of. The man himself may shut his eyes to it. But others will always see.

A senior don and renowned wit to boast was called *anda* (egg). Some hold that he got this name because he never took a firm stand on any issue. The same title had also been shared by a student leader who had made the stay of Dr Zakir Husain, the then-vice chancellor, miserable.

One student leader, who later became a member of the Rajya Sabha for a brief period, was popularly known by his *nomen specificum: bhindi* (okra or ladies' finger, with the long-ridged seed pods), either because of his penchant for clinging on or on account of his grinning incessantly like a Cheshire cat at the drop of a hat, at which, his mouth resembled a ripped piece of ladies' finger. Another clinger with more or less the same characteristic had been named a *cheenta* (ant). In stature, political or physical, perhaps, he wasn't equal enough to share the more august nickname awarded to our leader.

These hypocoristic forms have crossed the boundaries of intimate circles and travelled beyond familiar or friendly situations. So much so that these names better know some persons. In the 1930s, there was a witty Maulavi *Matka* (a round earthen pot), perhaps so named for his potbelly. About 40 years later, a young man approached a teacher and introduced himself as the son of Maulavi *Matka*. The host immediately recalled the Maulavi.

Another worthy who cherished and tried to fulfil the rather unworthy ambition of nibbling on the maximum number of meat bones at parties was fondly called *haddi* (bone). One unlucky soul, unfortunate enough to have been cursed with bowlegs, was called *bhisti* (water carrier) because his gait resembled a splay-legged *bhisti* struggling to retain his centre of gravity under the weight of an invisible leather water sack. Then there were two gentlemen, both were popularly known as, and maybe also answered to the appellation of, *ghoda* (horse). One, because of his excessive height and the habit of galloping about the campus. The other is due to his horse mania and the university riding club.

A teacher was named Gama, the legendary wrestler. Maybe this title was bestowed on him because his physique resembled a rectangle. A dear departed used to be known as *barula* for his weakness for potato rolls. Another person was known as *memna* (lamb) because he was shy and reticent. A person was known as *moonch* (moustache) because he sported a handlebar moustache. Similarly, another worthy was labelled as *tidda* (grasshopper) because his mannerisms closely resembled that of a grasshopper – flitting about from place to place and chirping constantly.

A man was going by the name of *bhangi* (scavenger). Another, who was always found haunting the campus crossroads for reasons best known only to himself, was called *chauraha* (a road crossing). A teacher was called *shabzi* (vegetables) because he pronounced 's' as 'sh'. A leader of the non-teaching staff, who had recently retired, was called *tuiyan* because he is short-statured. Another person was called *pistol* because he never got tired of playing his favourite game of fiddling with a *la Hindi* cinema villains, with a key ring shaped like a pistol. Then there is every cause, like a rat deserting a sinking ship. A former pro-vice-chancellor was referred to by the students as *qavval* (singer) because when he donned a cap on his head, his flowing locks hung about his shoulders like those of a *qavval.* A senior teacher who could retain the confidence of any vice-chancellor during the initial months of the incumbent's tenure was known by the nickname *bakra* (goat). He sported a goat-like beard and looked like a venerable Billy goat when he talked. A student leader was nicknamed 'Barula'. Another was named 'polio' as he had taken keen interest in the polio eradication drive. A Deputy proctor was called 'Gatta Baseer'. The list is not a comprehensive one. However, the tradition persists.

Remarking on this propensity, Professor M. Habib once recalled an incident during his days in the MAO College. Recalling it, Dr Rahat Abrar said:

> The Honorary Secretary, Nawab Mushtaq Husain Sahib, *Viqar-ui-Mulk*, was a respected figure. He lived a simple life and practised abstinence in a house in the Tarwala Bungala compound. Neither had he a drawing room nor a conveyance. A man of average build with a tonsured head and face adorned by a flowing white beard, he came regularly to the Juma congregation with his son Mushtaq Ahmad (to quote Maulana Shaukat Ali's appropriate simile) 'looking like the map of India with Ceylon'.[3]

He recollected another incident:

> We did not like the British professors but respected them. Going for a walk one evening, Principal J H Towle asked a student, 'Why did you not salute me?' 'I do not salute every Englishman I meet in the street', came the curt reply. 'But won't you salute your own Principal?' Towle asked. 'In that case, Good Morning, Sir, and please forgive me, sir,' the student said cheekily.

He recalled another prank, narrated by Professor M. Habib said:

> Maulana Sulaiman Ashraf Sahib used to deliver a *waaz* (post-prayer sermon) every Friday. After the prayer, the *muezzin* used to announce *waaz hoga sahib*. The *waaz* used to be well attended, but opinions as to its efficacy differed. I remember one student remarking, 'His tongue moves well', to which another rejoined, 'Yes, remarkably well, considering that his brain is immobile.' Once Sulaiman Ashraf *Sahib* did not deliver a *waaz* for several Fridays, he was rumoured to deliver it next Friday as the Honorary Secretary was coming. Therefore, my cousin Khaliquazzaman (of Muslim League fame) quietly arranged for the following:
>
> Among the noted students of SS Hall was a tall, hefty Punjabi, Ishaq, popularly known as *Ladhauray Khan*, a philosophy student who talked about religion. The muezzin made the usual announcement: *waaz hoga sahib*. It happened that Ladhauray Khan had come to the mosque too late, and my cousin convinced him that 'his' *waaz* had been announced and that all his friends would feel let down if he did not go and begin his *waaz* immediately.
>
> Even as Sulaiman Ashraf *Sahib* was proceeding to the pulpit leisurely from one end of the mosque, from the other end got up Ladhauray Khan. Head bent and gaze glued to the ground, he reached the pulpit with rapid strides and began his *waaz*. Sulaiman Ashraf Sahib, surprised at the unexpected competition, sat down. The audience did not know what was happening, but Ladhauray Khan gave it the substance of Fraser's Introduction to Berkeley. Since one is expected to keep quiet in a mosque and one doesn't need to understand all that is said, Ladhauray Khan flowed uninterrupted. After he had finished, Sulaiman Ashraf went up the pulpit. In a few chosen words, he welcomed Ladhauray Khan as a wa'iz (one who delivers sermons) if he would only take the trouble of getting properly qualified. While Maulana *Sahib* enjoyed the joke, a shamefaced Ladhauray Khan remained angry for a long time.[4]

According to Professor M. Habib, Aligarh traditions – even at the school stage – allowed decent jokes:

> Mustoo, a fair-complexioned student whose physique closely resembled the headmaster's, once came attired in a sola hat and trench coat, like the headmaster. Being in the know, the class would whisper 'headmaster Sahib', rise and salute loudly. We all arose and saluted when Mustoo entered, the class teacher bowing more respectfully than any student. Mustoo raised his hand to acknowledge the class teacher's respectful salutation and quietly sat. 'I am sorry for being late, Sir,' he said. The class teacher chagrined at the joke played on him, rushed up to Mustoo's desk and gave him two slaps: Mustoo, as had been decided, bore the slaps patiently. His successful prank became the talk of the whole school circuit.[5]

Aligarh traditions (*Rivayat-i-Aligarh*) owe their genesis to the 'Aligarh spirit'. The term sounds like an Anglo-Indian coinage, but it is a meaningful expression. Aligarh's spirit embodies the spirit of service towards all mankind, participation in the happiness and sorrow of people, and being of use in times of need, compassion and philanthropy. This aligns with the basic tenets of Islam. However, Aligarh spirit and sportsman spirit are sometimes used interchangeably. Aligarh spirit means 'rising to the occasion', in the words of Dr Ziuauddin Ahmad. The real meaning of it is the establishment of educational institutions and the proliferation of knowledge. Wherever the lamp of wisdom is lit, it is always day, and the sun never sets. Therefore, it qualifies to be called the 'Sir Syed spirit'.

> *Yeh jante the ki ham hain chirage akhri shab;*
> *hamare bad andhera nahin ujala hai.*
> (We know that we are not enough to light up the last hour of the night; however, even after we are exhausted, there will be light, not darkness.)

Several traditions were institutionalised in Sir Syed's time and under his direct supervision, as some incidents reveal. Often, Sir Syed would bring home sick students to be well-looked after. Once, a couple of convalescents staying with him ate up all the pomegranates in his orchard. They told the bewildered attendant that the squirrels had eaten them. The poor attendant gave the same excuse to Sir Syed, who smilingly said that iron traps had been made for squirrels. Predictably, the 'squirrels' became warier and wiser.[6]

> Once, some students sat in a light rain shower. Those were summer days. They were eating melons. After having their fill, they tossed out the basketful of skin and seeds through the rear window. As luck would have it, Sir Syed was passing by in his phaeton. The skins and seeds fell into his lap. The students were thunderstruck but pretended to do their work as if nothing had happened. A little later, there was the sound of horses' hooves. Sir Syed's phaeton stopped in front of their hostel room. Carrying the basket, Sir Syed alighted. The warden was summoned. And he summoned the boarders in turn. Sir Syed spoke, 'I understood right away that it is the doing of these *Rampuris* (residents of Rampur state). They get so engrossed while eating that they forget all etiquette.' The beginning of the charge sheet made students shiver. Then he addressed the warden, 'Is this what you teach them?' The shamefaced warden spoke, 'Sir, I have given them stringent instructions to check for some gentleman passing by before throwing out the garbage'. 'Then they are not to be blamed because they could hardly hope to find such a gentleman like me in Aligarh', so saying he left. There was no censure, but the way he spoke had a lasting impact.
>
> One evening, some students played cricket in the ground behind the mosque. They got so engrossed they failed to return to their hostel, though it was time for evening prayers. Suddenly, they observed Sir Syed proceeding towards the mosque for evening prayers. All were unnerved. With a significant presence of mind, the captain quickly said, 'Fall in line for offering prayers so that we may escape this danger'. When all of them bowed down, instead of saying '*Allah-o-Akbar* (God is Great)', they chanted aloud, 'Has the old man gone?' As they rose, they found the old man a part of their own congregation. Such was his magnanimity that he forgave them.[7]

An Aligarian recalls that just as flowers of all colours fill a garden with beauty and splendour during spring, the young men in hostel rooms, compound and lawns present a similar picture at the beginning of an academic term. 'The whole university looks beautiful. It is like a spring festival. And when they speak, it sounds like birds at dawn.'[8]

He says the tradition of elections for the students' union has changed. Defeat and success no longer result in pallbearers or elegy singers. However, the black *shervani* sets the students of AMU apart and differentiates them from other colleges and universities.

'We are neither *Barelvis* nor *Wahhabis* [two schools of thought among Muslims in India]. We believe in the Aligana Sect, which encompasses all other sects,' added the Aligarian.

Jo darsgah-e-muhabbat main ek bar aya;
vah sue dair-o-haram umr bhar nahi jata.
(He who enters the university of love never does proceed towards a temple or a mosque.)

Pranks (*ahwala shararat*) are another distinction of Aligarh. Once in 1915, it rained incessantly for days. Students living in the Kuchcha Barrack were in a pitiable condition; roofs leaked, and they had hardly any dry spots remaining in their rooms. Once, they came out in heavy rains in the dead of night and began 'mud-wrestling'. Hearing the commotion, Principal J.H. Towle apprehended some untoward incident and rushed there on horseback, soaked in the rain. Reaching there, he asked the students what the commotion was all about. One of the students mustered courage and replied, 'Sir, nothing – only combating the storm'. Towle smiled and said, 'Congratulations' and cantered away. Then there is the classification of pranks in circulation among the university public.

Mud Bath: It occurred once a year in each hostel when the college used to be closed on rainy days. Students and professors vied to besmear each other with mud.

Fish Pond: It was another interesting annual function when titles were awarded, indicating the characteristics of each student by a carefully selected word or phrase. However, bubbling wit and puckish humour began to give way to vulgarity, and the institution gradually faded away. But before that, the students frequently indulged in innocent jokes and made life charming.

Fakhta Urana (*Dove Flight*): It used to be of two kinds, 'hot' or 'cold'. Hot meant a piece of thread would be kept close to a fast-sleeping boy. The string would be lit with a matchstick. The perpetrators then hid themselves. The boy would wake up with a start and look distracted. In the 'cold *fakhta*', pieces of ice were kept on a sleeping boy. Sometimes, the bed on which a student slept was taken to a lonely, distant place.

Of Funeral: In 1905, mathematics, hitherto a compulsory subject at the intermediate level, was made optional. Elated, the students collected a few old mathematics books, loaded them on an upside-down cot, covered it with a white shroud and decorated it with leaves and flowers. About five hundred students marched to the Cricket lawn with the bier behind a funeral band playing at full volume. Funeral orations were delivered, and the 'remains' of the books were consigned to the grave with a Fatiha recitation and shouts of *Hisab murda shud – Khub shud* (Mathematics is dead, very good).

Another viral joke at the university is that Sir Syed died and went to heaven, which he richly deserved. A few years later, he yearned to see his beloved Aligarh. One day, his spirit came down to look at Aligarh. Everywhere he looked, he got a shock. So much had changed that he doubted whether it was Aligarh. The campus, the teachers, the students, and the atmosphere – all had changed. Then he went to the mess of a hall. And there, on the dining tables, were the *Dunlop rotis* (a huge *roti* or bread prepared from flour and yeast), and then he knew that this indeed was Aligarh. Satisfied, he nipped back to heaven. (*Dunlop roti* is a tradition peculiar to AMU.)

Tact and wit were not the privileges of students; teachers also practised them on students. An incident is related to how a law professor made a fool of his student. Even after several decades, the incident is recollected and enjoyed with impunity in the university circles. The professor lived in Jaiganj – a far-off locality in Aligarh- and used to come in his horse carriage to deliver lectures at the institute building. The student lived in Russel Ganj, which lay en route. He hovered around the carriage, indirectly expressing a desire to be given a lift. The professor agreed. But the carriage did not stop at Russel Ganj and moved on for another two miles. The student protested. The professor wryly replied, 'My horse has a queer habit – it stops only at my residence, sorry'. The student never dared come near the carriage again, much less ask for a lift.

Tahir Mahmood, former chairman of the Minorities Commission, once wrote to vice-chancellor M. Rahman, assuring the latter of all sincerity in coming to the aid of AMU whenever necessary. In his letter, Mahmood said that his heart, soul and body were all dedicated to the service of AMU. The vice-chancellor, who visibly puffed up while extolling Mahmood's nobility of sentiment before a group of educators, was rudely brought to the ground when one of them quipped, 'You are right, sir; we are facing a shortage of bodies in our dissection section. Mehmood *Saheb*'s body would be a welcome addition.'[9]

In 1920, the college magazine published a pamphlet that became famous as the character of a creed called *Jhapalism*. It brought out certain evil features of the college society and prescribed remedies. It suggested punishments such as punching the offender's nose. Vanity of one's birth or race, or relationship or influence with persons of importance and subservience to such persons were considered crimes, for which graded scales of punishment were suggested.

These were the days when the unmistakable *khilandra* (sports loving) had the leaven in a student. He would move about the place like a monarch. He surveyed in carefree, effortless style dressed in spotlessly clean clothes, wearing *saleemshahi* (named after the Mughal prince Saleem) slippers, cracking a joke here, putting up a fight there, and exchanging railleries elsewhere. This must have been 1893. The college recently introduced the monitorial system, and Muhammed Ali was elected food monitor. As luck would have it, a *chooranwala* (a vendor selling appetising powder) entered the college premises, singing praise of his wares in a thunderous and attractive voice. No sooner did Muhammed Ali hear the cry, than he rushed up to the *chooranwala* and, with folded hands, demanded if he wanted his head on a charger. The poor *chooranwala* was surprised out of his wits but was promptly told that the boys had such a keen appetite that he was having the time of his life to satisfy them. If his excellent appetiser got added to their digestive system, he would have very short shrift. The *chooranwala* caught the joke and was rarely seen again.

Mohammed Zakir Ali Khan, an engineer who was instrumental in establishing the Sir Syed University of Engineering and Technology in Karachi (Pakistan), has written a delightful book, *Riwayat e Aligarh*, in a lighter vein about life in Aligarh before independence.

The Aligarians had a canny presence of mind. The university administration was perplexed when it got a request from the mother of General Pervez Musharraf, the president of Pakistan, to accompany her son during the latter's visit to India to participate in the famous Agra Summit between Prime Minister Vajpayee and President Musharraf. She had expressed her desire to visit the hostel room where her husband used to stay during his university days in the 1930s. The Government of India sent AMU authorities a message. It was a herculean task to identify the said room. The university administration was only aware that Pervez's father used to live in one of the hostels under the aegis of the Aftab Hall but was clueless about the actual room. Searching and finding the same in the more than six-decade-old hall was a tedious job. A quick-witted, ingenious resident of the Aftab Hall came to the rescue of the university administration by claiming that he was now staying in the same room in which the father of Pervez Musharraf used to stay.

No one had the time to verify the claim put forward by the student. The university administration undertook the renovation and whitewashing of the room. But at least that room was whitewashed, and petty repairs were undertaken before that. Mrs Musharraf visited the room where her husband was supposed to have lived during his student days.[10]

Mercurial, jubilant and slightly portly, Sardar Ali was a notable figure in student politics at AMU for several years. His energetic and lively demeanour made him a prominent and beloved figure on campus. After his vibrant days at AMU, Sardar Ali transitioned into a successful legal career in Delhi, eventually ascending to the prestigious position of the chairman of the Monopoly and Restrictive Trade Practices Commission (MRTPC).

I once asked him about his perpetually cheerful demeanour, which reminded many of the Laughing Buddha. He explained candidly that his days in student politics required him to constantly interact with many students, greeting them with a smile regardless of the circumstances. This habit became so ingrained in him that he half-jokingly feared that even at a funeral, he might inadvertently maintain a smiling expression.

Sardar Ali was allotted government accommodation in the coveted Pandara Park area in central Delhi, which placed him near many influential figures. One morning, he walked across the park to visit the bungalow of BJP leader L.K. Advani. Given his status as a neighbour – or '*hamsaya*' – he was quickly granted an audience. During their meeting, Sardar Ali expressed his respect for Advani as a senior politician but delivered a poignant critique. He told Advani that in the aftermath of the Babri Masjid demolition, his name became a symbol of fear among Muslims. He shared an anecdote illustrating this: 'Janab Advani sahib, I respect you, but the situation has reached such a pass that even wailing children in our community stop crying when they are told that Advani sahib is coming.' This encounter between Sardar Ali and L.K. Advani encapsulates a complex moment in Indian politics, reflecting the broader communal tensions and the personal integrity and courage it took for individuals like Sardar Ali to speak truth to power.

Famous painter and calligrapher Sadequain visited AMU in 1981–82. They did a calligraphic work depicting the university logo at Maulana Azad Library and a huge abstract mural in metal at the entrance of the Department of Geography. Besides the usual interactions and seminars, Sadequain was also accorded a traditional welcome by the AMU Students Union at the Union Hall during his stay. Students presented him with the black uniform Shervanii, which had the university monogram with AMU written on it stitched on the collar. Sadequain was so enamoured with this *shervani* that when he completed his work in Aligarh and moved to Delhi for his next assignment, he would wear it to parties there. Once at a social party, he met the famous journalist and author Uma Vasudev. After talking to Sadequain for a few minutes, Uma could not contain her curiosity and asked him if he was an alumnus of AMU. When he replied in the negative, she became even more intrigued and exclaimed 'then why are you wearing this shervani with AMU written on the collar'?!

Sadequain replied, '*Wo isleye, kyoki jab bhi mein Ainey dekhta hoon to* AMU *ke jagah mujhe* UMA *dikhta hai aur mein khush ho jaata hoon ke* Uma *mere gardan se liptey huwe hai*' (It is because whenever I look in the mirror, because of the mirror image, instead of AMU looks, I see UMA to me, and I become happy that Uma is wrapped around my neck).[11]

Once, the member-in-charge of games submitted a list of selected players for a game but could not accommodate the sons of two prominent members of the university Executive Council, including the son of Zafaryab Jilani of Babri Masjid Action Committee fame. While submitting the list to the vice-chancellor M. Rahman, the member-in-charge said diplomatically, 'I am carrying a "*bojh*" (burden) in my heart by taking the risk of displeasing powerful men.' The vice-chancellor assured the professor not to worry as the prominent personalities were themselves '*bojh*' on the community.[12]

Then there is a sort of local informal lexicon, which is in vogue.

Aligarh Dictionary

1. *Bahut Bada Wala Hai*	Very stupid
2. *Bhasad*	To disturb the calm environment
3. *Chettah*	Subordinate in dealing
4. *Chhotu*	Any and every boy working in a tea stall

5. Dealer	Politically active student
6. *Dhurrah*	Fresher student from the countryside
7. *Jugad*	Source of technique to tackle anything
8. *Matri*	A particular baked item of Aligarh
9. Mirinda fry	A special kind of egg dish
10. *Kharra*	Cheating paper in the examinations
11. *Purana Chawal*	Most senior
12. Pipe	Chatterbox
13. Tempo *High Hai*	Moral on zenith
14. *Terri*	Forerunner of e-rickshaw
15. *Numaish*	A temporary romance accompanied by unusual twists and happenings
16. Abdullah Hall	A tourist destination open only on Sundays
17. Union	A committee that first tries to create a problem and then makes promises to resolve
18. *Dahba*	A place for a lively discussion about nothing, anything or everything
19. *Amir Nisha*	A beautiful place for window shopping

Perhaps most of these pranks and antics were hatched at two places – Café de Phoos and Cafe de Laila, presumably used to come alive in the evening when students such as Ali Sardar Jafri and Majaz Lakhnavi (who later emerged as a renowned poet) would regale those present with their *shairi*. Similarly, outdoor canteen where the boys would collect for *namakparas*, buttered buns and tea and, thus nourished, would engage in verbal fencing with foils of exquisite wit.

Mehar Alam Khan vividly recalled the enjoyable dinner and the poignant tribute paid to the founder of their alma mater. He evoked the eloquence of Dagh Dehlvi's verse to capture the essence of the experience:

lutf-e-mai tujh se kyā kahūñ zāhid
haa.e kam-bakht tū ne pī hī nahīñ
O ascetic, what can I tell you of the pleasures of wine
You, unfortunate one, have never tasted it

This couplet underscored the disconnect between experiencing and merely discussing, much like the difference between genuinely engaging with a conference's substance and attending its formalities.

21

Aligarh's Historic Cafes

The oft-repeated phrase *Aligarh key bachcho ki ragho main khoon nahi chai daudati hai* (Not blood, but tea circulates in the veins of AMU students) is attributed to Naseeruddin Shah, a veteran film and theatre actor who is also an Aligarian. Chai in Aligarh is not just a beverage but deeply ingrained in local culture.

Aligarh town is famous for a lot of things. But ask anyone who has ever been to or lived in this quaint place, and one will immediately tell you that the first love of every Aligarian is a magical brew, a cup of chai, at one of the many *dhabas* (wayside eateries) in the city. These *dhabas* or cafés have played an important role in the social, cultural and intellectual atmosphere of the AMU.

Students gather in groups at their favourite tea stalls and keep sipping chai from their glasses. Chai is always accompanied by lengthy discussions about Muslim issues. The chai and gossip never seem to end. Many students spend as much as a quarter of the day at the chai stalls.

Dhaba or café culture is famous in every university in the world. However, how the Aligarh community has nurtured it, has taken it to another level. There are roadside *dhabas* in and around the university campus where kettles are always boiling, and endless rounds of tea are poured out.

Café de Laila, one of the many *dhabas* at the AMU, is named after a woman. That's a bit of an irony because women are apparently not welcome there. Old timers nostalgically recall that entering Café de Laila through its mausoleum-like door was like travelling back in time. The arched door with an iron gate led into a small compound with a lazy, earthy ambience, twenty-odd rusting chairs and an open teapot brewing continuously on a gas burner. It was the second oldest *dhaba*. Noted Urdu poet Majaz is credited with having coined the name of this oldest tea joint in Aligarh when he was a student at the university. The legend goes that when it was first established in 1933, he had named it Alif Laila, after the famous characters from *One Thousand and One Nights*, also known as Arabian Nights, a collection of Middle Eastern folk tales compiled in Arabic during the Islamic Golden Age. A British professor at the university then rechristened it Café de Laila.

The owner of the establishment, Farat Hussain, recounts that he bought the café in 1991 from Abdul Hafeez, whose son '*chai ka karobaar samajhte the, zayeka nahin*' (understood the business of tea, but not its taste); and he disposed of the historic café. Now, Hussain runs a separate establishment in Shamshad Market, as the Cafe was later dismantled to construct a swimming pool.

But Café de Phoos (Café of Straw) still exists. Scores of university public, including teachers, students, peons, clerks and *ulema*, all love to sit on its antiquated chairs. A dimly lit place for students to enjoy tea within the precincts of the university, this ancient café is now owned by Majib Ahmed. He recollects that the café was started by his *nana* (maternal grandfather), Zuberi Sahab, in 1932. After partition Zuberi Saheb moved to Pakistan, handing over the keys of the café to his *dada* (paternal grandfather). Ahmed's father took on the place after his death. In 1955, the mantle was passed to Ahmed himself.

How the place got its intriguing name is a fascinating story, he says. 'Dada named it, as when it was first started, it was only a small room with a thatched roof [*phoos*]. The place soon began to be called Café de Phoos by students and elders alike.' Right now, the place is run by Faisal Mujtaba at the same Aftab Hall where it was started.

Sipping many cups of tea while discussing various issues concerning the university, community and country, Aligarians often address fellow students whom they don't know by name partners. These 'partners' share their views, called 'dealing' in AMU dialect, for debates are not confined to friends but involve all present. These students are 'chain drinkers' of tea. A dispute can be resolved, or a favour sought over a cup of tea.

The arrival of British teachers at MAO College carried a push for 'modern' Western education brought along with the British culture education brought to the British culture, and tea happened to be its integral part. They pushed tea as an alternative to local hot drinks. Coffee was not available regularly due to the strategic hold on its supply by Middle Eastern kingdoms.

However, from an aristocratic symbol of class, the culture of tea drinking soon became integral to the life of common people. The brew underwent a drastic transformation and acquired a milky and sugary avatar far removed from the mild liquor favoured by aristocrats. Since this version of tea was more affordable, compared to anything else available at the tea shacks, it became the favourite of varsity students whiling away time in each other's company as only the carefree young can do. The varsity students began to have it whenever they wanted to relax in the company of one another. Many love stories and elections to the students' unions revolve around this drink.

In the hustle and bustle of the city of Aligarh, one cannot go a couple of metres before one spots a *dhaba* where a kettle is boiling over with strong, sizzling tea, and scores of people mill about, young and old. The city's people share their sorrows, opinions and camaraderie over cups of tea (they can't stop at just one cup).

Old-timers nostalgically refer to the times spent at the cafés and *dhabas* liberally scattered across the city, particularly in Shamshad Market and Zakariya. Here, young and old enjoy conversations and cups of tea. Purani Chungi, a few hundred yards from the famous Maulana Azad Library, is another epicentre of special tea. Different types of chai, at different rates, are available here. One can find students here having tea even in the scorching heat.

Anubhav Sinha, a well-known name in the film industry, earned his bachelor's degree in mechanical engineering from Aligarh Muslim University. Even after two decades, he recalled 'mathri omelette in Aligarh, mostly around AMU Campus'.

The status of tea has grown so much that there are 'official guidelines' issued for students in Aligarh so as to understand the nuances of enjoying not just the drink but the culture as well. The history and tradition are kept alive by several relatively new *dhaba* owners. Hasan Ahmad, who has been running Hasan ka Dhaba near Shamshad Market since 1994, says the entire road across the market is full of students almost all day and a good half of the night. Their conversation skips from topic to topic, their friends and family, their dreams and hopes, their successes and failures, politics and religion.

Most *dhaba* owners are willing to host female students, but girls seldom sit there, as they will most likely attract stares from their male counterparts.

Professor Mohammad Sajjad writes,

> On Sunday, 25 October 2009, at around 10 p.m. a student of B.Sc. Final Year Chemistry was reported to have been killed at an eatery near the Aligarh railway station; quite painful, bitter and highly unfortunate. The AMU administration could be faulted on neglecting the canteen-infrastructure and one may demand that the AMU administration should take steps towards establishing some (not one) well provisioned canteens, like the ones on the JNU campus. This particular 'demand' has been raised by many including Professor Mushirul Hasan in his column in the *Indian Express* after the September 2007 upsurge.[1]

The tea culture at AMU, once a unique and charming art form, is now in decline. The university dining halls, the canteens and the cafes and eateries around Shamshad Market were once known for their distinct flair in serving tea. Enthusiasts could craft their perfect cup as tea was served in three separate components: a pot of boiled water infused with Green Label tea leaves, a second pot with just milk and a third containing sugar. This method allowed for a personalised tea experience, with individuals able to adjust the milk and sugar proportions to their liking, a unique charm that is now fading.

This traditional practice, a unique charm of the university, was not only a staple in well-known spots such as Cafe D Phoos, Cafe D Laila and the hostels but also in smaller cafes throughout the university precinct. Establishments such as Tea House and Gay Lords in Shamshad Market were renowned for upholding these traditions of serving tea. However, this quality and uniqueness have faded, replaced universally by premixed, ready-served tea. The rich tea-making ritual has vanished, giving way to convenience but at the cost of individual preference and the once cherished quality.

Furthermore, Shamshad Market has recently transformed significantly after the smart city campaign. What was once a local marketplace with its unique charm has started to mirror urban commercialism by opening various franchises from famous Delhi eateries. This shift reflects the changing landscape of retail and dining in the area. It marks a move away from the quaint and personalised service that has defined the market and the university's dining culture for decades, a change that is making those who value tradition and local identity circumspect.

22

NASCENT FASCISM TARGETS AMU

The AMU has always been in the news for reasons right and wrong. Though declining standards, corruption and maladministration are common to all Indian universities, since the AMU is credited with traversing an extra mile to promote the idea of two nations, practise obnoxious discrimination and religious orthodoxy, it has also been a target of unfair criticism.

On a Republic Day, a student leader insisted that he would take out a *tiranga* (national flag) rally on the campus, though the University had organised its own Republic Day function. Within a week, the local BJP Member of Parliament, Satish Gautam, demanded that the word Muslim be removed from the University's name. Asked if BHU should also drop the word 'Hindu' from its name, he replied, 'India is a Hindu *Rashtra* and there is no point in removing "Hindu" from the BHU'. Frequently, issues are raised with specific motives. 'There are 5,000–6,000 Hindu students in the university. Why does only a group of five or six always have problems?' asked Nishant Bhardwaj, a leader of the students' union. Mohammad Sajjad, Professor of Modern History, sees the 'vilification of the university' as a reflection of majoritarian politics across the country. 'Elections or no elections, it will continue to happen ... [because] once you pit two communities against each other, all other significant demands are pushed aside.'[1]

There is no dearth of bigots in journalism and politics. A woman TV correspondent once described AMU as a 'university of terrorists', but she could never substantiate her charge. Another time it was rumoured that Hyderabad Member of Parliament, Asaduddin Owaisi was to attend a meeting of the country's critical Muslim leaders called by some student leaders of AMU. Days before the 'scheduled meeting', Nishit Sharma, a former student of the University and now a BJP leader in Aligarh, wrote to Union HRD minister Prakash Javadekar: 'These students are trying to hurt the sentiments of the Hindus by inviting Owaisi.' And further 'Though we will not allow him to enter Aligarh, if he comes he will not be able to go back.'[2]

On the morning of the 'meeting', a group of students led by Ajay Singh, a former presidential candidate, entered the union hall. There was no sign of Owaisi. But Singh and his supporters were determined to create a scene. They went to the Vice-Chancellor's office. Meanwhile, the other side too lodged its protest. The issues snowballed.

By the evening, the police filed a case of 'sedition' against 14 students of the University based on an FIR filed by a BJP youth wing leader, Mukesh Lodhi. 'But the police chose not to turn the students' complaint into an FIR', alleged Sharjeel Usmani, a student of the University.

The BJP leader's FIR mentioned that he saw a few AMU students assaulting the TV journalist and Hindu students from the University and heard shouts '*Hindustan Murdabad, Pakistan Zindabad*' (Death to India; Long live Pakistan). Lodhi also alleged that he was fired at. The police later dropped the sedition charges.

Jinnah's picture in the student union hall has been on display since 1938, in the company of the portraits of Mahatma Gandhi, Baba Sahib Ambedkar and Maulana Azad.

> The AMU again emerged as an arena where the centre and the state took different stands. The issue in 1965 was the portrait of M.A. Jinnah in the Maulana Azad Library of AMU, which had drawn the attention of the central government. Two controversies merged: First, having a portrait of a leader of an enemy nation in an Indian institution of repute. Second, the suspicion was that those who hung the portrait were sympathizers of Pakistan.

The Home Ministry of UP's view was that 'it may be reasonable to presume that these persons (who were responsible for the installation of the portrait) had a pro-Pakistan attitude'. The persons responsible should be blacklisted in lists 'A', 'B' and 'C' of the Intelligence Bureau. These lists of persons with 'pro-Pakistan attitudes' cannot be found now, but there is no doubt the bureau maintained such lists.

In 1968, Vice Chancellor Nawab Ali Yavar Jung wrote to N. Vittal, Under-Secretary in the Ministry of Education, summarising the issue, "I am told that the picture dates back to the pre-partition days. It should have been removed after Partition, as I do not like its continuing in the Union Hall, but as I said, the removal would better come from the members themselves... actually, it should have been raised by the nationalist Muslim students, but they have not gathered strength and the Union is dominated by students controlled by communal organisations."

Jung's admission that 'national Muslim students' were a tiny and weak force reveals that in campus politics, at least, Muslims did not just 'adjust and meekly accommodate' to the situation in UP.[3]

In May 2018, however, BJP Member of Parliament Satish Gautam objected to the picture of Jinnah when Hamid Ansari, the former Vice President of India and a former Vice-Chancellor of the University visited the campus. He was scheduled to be given a lifetime membership of the students' union, but after the protests, he returned without being honoured.[4]

Gautam, who seldom lost an opportunity to play the divisive card, instigated a group of right-wing students to remove Jinnah's portrait forcibly. The matter could have been amicably settled had Gautam, a member of the AMU Court, raised the issue with the University authorities. Arm-twisting methods only hardened the positions on both sides. The police played a partisan role in escorting out right-wing offenders who attempted forced entry into the AMU while the hapless students of the University agitating against the gate-crashing were *lathi*-charged (attacked with sticks or *lathis*).

Obviously intended to demonise a particular community and interfere in educational institutions that support free speech and liberal values, the ugly incidents created much tension, said a student.

Among the banners held by students during protests against the 2 May assault on the campus was one that said, '*Jinnah itihas hai, aastha nahi*'. (Jinnah is history, not an article of faith.) 'Jinnah is irrelevant to Indian Muslims today', said another.

By then, the media, especially some TV news channels, had gone berserk and portrayed AMU in a very negative light. A few students alleged that it was as if they had been waiting for something like this to happen so they could issue certificates of 'patriotism' and 'treachery' as per their blinkered right-wing sensibilities. Some TV channels aired videos of students protesting near Bab-e-Syed, alleging they demanded Azadi from Bharat. But as the fact-checking news website *AltNews* pointed out, the slogan was *Bharat mein lenge Azadi* and not *Bharat se lenge Azadi* – that is, the students demanded freedom in India, not freedom from India.

TV channels ran numerous programmes on 'Jinnah, the Villain' even as the students were putting up posters declaring that they were protesting against the attack on the campus and not over Jinnah's portrait. Moreover, as Mashkoor Ahmad Usmani, the president of the AMUSU pointed out, students at the University 'come from India, their grandparents chose India over Pakistan' and opposed Jinnah. Two of the rioters – Amit Goswami and Yogesh Varshney, former city president of Hindu Yuva Vahini – were arrested and sent to jail.[5]

A portrait of Sir Syed Ahmad Khan, hanging alongside the pictures of Mahatma Gandhi, Babasaheb Ambedkar and Lal Bahadur Shastri in a Public Works Department guesthouse at Khair in Aligarh district, was removed a few days prior to this incident and replaced by a portrait of Narendra Modi.[6] Why could the prime minister's picture not be put up, if it had to be, without taking down Sir Syed's?

The students' union leaders said they would remove Jinnah's portrait if the government ordered them to do so in writing.

Interestingly, Abdul Hai Kureshi, the Chief Justice of Sind High Court in Karachi, in an order dated 24 October 1984 said:[7]

> Whatever had been left by Quaid-e-Azam as a legacy for the AMU should be spent for no other purpose, except the education of the Muslims of this country. The Administrators (of the will of Jinnah) have submitted a statement that the amount of the legacy will be in the neighbourhood of Rs. Seven million. It should be utilised for the grant of scholarship in the name of "Qaid-e-Azam Aligarh fellowship" to university students for graduate and post-graduate studies in Pakistan and abroad. I accept the proposal.

In the five-page-long order, the Court said:

> Quaid-e-Azam left 1/3 of property in favour of the AMU. It is common knowledge that the AMU was a pioneer Muslim institution that had played a very great role in the renaissance of Muslims of India. One would even say, almost without fear of contradiction, that a vast majority of Muslim educated persons of Pakistan had obtained their college education and, in some cases, even school education at Aligarh. This institution has been so inextricably woven with the interest of Muslims of the sub-continent that to imagine the AMU to be anything else but a Muslim institution primarily catering to the needs of the Muslims of the subcontinent would be palpably absurd. What I am told now is that even the word 'Muslim' from the name of the University has been omitted. That being so, the complexion of the legatee had undergone a drastic and fundamental change.

In a miscellaneous application in 1983, Trustees/Administrators of the Jinnah's Estate had mentioned:

Quaid-i-Azam Mohammad Ali Jinnah created a Waqf in writing for charitable purposes as well as for the benefit of his family comprising of his sisters, brothers and daughter. Payments under the Waqf created by the Will, inter alia, were for the following charitable purposes:

a) Rs. 25,000 to Anjuman Islam School, Bombay
b) Rs. 50,000 to the University of Bombay
c) Rs. 25,000 to Arabic College Delhi
d) Residuary estate including corpus to be divided into three equal parts, one part each to (i) Aligarh University (ii) Islamia College, Peshawar and (iii) Sind Madrasa, Karachi

The above Waqf had been created by Quaid-i-Azam Mohammad Ali Jinnah in Bombay on 30 May 1939.

23

'SECULAR CONTROVERSY' OVER 'MARXIST RAJA' IN 'MUSLIM UNIVERSITY'

In the last quarter of 2014, the BJP found another pretext to hound AMU. It was the birth anniversary of Raja Mahendra Pratap on 1 December. The BJP leaders raced to honour the 'donor' the Muslims had allegedly forgotten. 'A Marxist king who gave away land for a Muslim university was sought to be feted by right-wing BJP,' screamed a headline from the *Times of India*.[1]

'The BJP has got both its history and politics wrong,' wrote Mohammed Asim, with regard to celebrating freedom fighter Raja Mahendra Pratap's 128th birth anniversary at the AMU.

> While Sir Syed's primary objective behind establishing MAO College was to spread modern scientific education among Muslims, he always emphasised that the doors of his college would always be wide open to all who need education ... My humble advice to overzealous BJP leaders is to just read up a bit on the man they have suddenly remembered to celebrate.[2]

According to a *Times of India* report, some Samajwadi Party politicians and some 'Left-leaning elements of the teachers' association of the university' had protested against the BJP's proposal to celebrate Mahendra Pratap's anniversary on the AMU campus on 1 December. Consequently, the vice-chancellor

Lt Gen. Zameer Uddin Shah denied permission, apprehending law and order issues.[3]

Raja Mahendra Pratap (1886–1979) was a freedom fighter who belonged to a Jat principality of Mursan in Mathura district (now in Hathras). He was an alumnus of MAO College. His grandfather, Raja Teekam Singh, and father Raja Ghanshyam Singh of Mursan were close to Sir Syed. His great grandfather had donated Rs 800 for the construction of the Scientific Society building in Aligarh. His father had donated a sum of Rs 1,500 for the construction of a room of the boarding house. This room still exists with a plaque on the premises of Sir Syed Hall, the oldest residential hall. Admitted to MAO College in 1895 and given two rooms in a bungalow (in front of Zahoor ward), he lived there practically all by himself, surrounded by 10 servants. He quit MAO College without completing his BA in 1907. As the oldest surviving alumnus of MAO College, he was honoured as chief guest at the centenary celebrations in 1977. His portrait hangs in the main hall of the university's Maulana Azad Library.

He was attracted to the Independence movement and joined the Berlin Committee of Indian revolutionaries. With the outbreak of World War I, he travelled to Afghanistan and in 1915 formed a government-in-exile of Free Hindustan (called *Hakumat-i-Moktar-i-Hind*) – much before the Indian National Congress adopted the goal of total independence for India in its 1929 session – with himself as president, Maulavi Barkatullah as prime minister and Maulavi Obeidullah Sindhi as home minister.

Barkatullah had procured a *fatwa* from the *Sheikh-Ul-Islam*, who governed the religious affairs of Muslims in the Ottoman empire, asking the Muslims of India to unite with the Hindus against the British. While at the outset, the whole movement appeared essentially secular, there were definite tensions underneath the surface.

Mahendra Pratap had conceded that if Germany were to hand over India to Turkey – 'the chief independent Muslim state' (and the seat of the Ottoman Empire) – then 'the position of two hundred and twenty million Hindus would have been far worse than at present'.[4] But it was the German-Turk alliance that had brought him to Afghanistan. Captain Kazim Beg was deputed by the Turkish government to accompany him.[5]

Maulvi Barkatullah was a Muslim revivalist and emphasised the 'special character of Muslim majority provinces'. Despite frictions, Mahendra Pratap and Maulvi Barkatullah shared an intense friendship. Even after Barkatullah's pan-Islamic worldview received a severe jolt with Mustafa Kemal Pasha abolishing the Turkish Caliphate, Barkatullah continued working for India's freedom. So, in 1927, when he arrived at the United States, he found crowds of Indians welcoming him with chants of '*Vande Mataram*'.[6]

Raja Mahendra Pratap had met Lenin and before him, Kaiser Wilhelm of Germany. He had no ideological affinities as such. His mission was the independence of India and for that he was ready to take the support of any force that would fight against the British colonialists. In 1919, he also met Trotsky. But when in the 1920s, under British pressure, the Amir of Afghanistan closed down the Provincial Indian government in exile, he moved to Japan and not the Soviet Union. There he joined hands with Rash Behari Bose, who had created the Indian Independence League, which would later be handed over as Azad Hind Fauj to Subhash Chandra Bose. Rash Behari was also the president of the Hindu Mahasabha in Japan.

If any ideology was close to Mahendra Pratap's heart, it was pan-Asianism. Though repelled by the creation of puppet states by the Japanese in other Asian regions, he retained the ideals of pan-Asian cooperation. He even initiated a volunteer corps of World Federation for the Province of Pan-Asia. Its objective was 'fighting for the freedom of Asia'. He also visualised 'eight corners of the world under one roof'. He travelled extensively in Japan and addressed the public on the pan-Asiatic theme.[7]

A fierce social reformer, Mahendra Pratap battled casteism and untouchability throughout his life. He established Prem Mahavidyala in Mathura. He was a maverick who once gave a call to men from his community to raid Delhi and they marched towards Delhi, the national capital, on foot, in thousands, wielding *lathis* (wooden canes).

In 1971, *The Illustrated Weekly of India* ran a series on the lesser-known non-Gandhian freedom fighters of India by Ms Qurratulain Hyder headlined 'The Terrorists'. Khushwant Singh was then editor of the magazine. To correct certain factual errors, Raja Mahendra Pratap wrote a letter to the editor, which was published in the magazine's issue dated 25 July 1971. Here, he remembered Maulvi Barkatullah's contribution to his movement and also – significantly – added:

> I am still a friend of Russia and China, but I think the Russians and Chinese ought to get liberated from the thoughts of Karl Marx. I did not succeed in bringing about the revolution in India. The defeated Russian Army found in Lenin the needed hero. Maulvi Barkatullah and Captain Kasim Beg also came to Russia. Barkatullah later had the good pull in the Soviet Foreign Office. He did not die in Germany. In 1927, he called me from Moscow. I got for him 2000 marks from the German Foreign Office.[89] In the letter, Mahendra Pratap movingly recounted that when Barkatullah died and was buried in a foreign land, he declared that it would be a temporary burial and that Barkatullah's body would be brought to India when India became independent. Beyond their separate religions, a burning desire for Indian independence united these two men.

In his autobiography, Jawaharlal Nehru described Raja Mahendra Pratap as Don Quixote.[10] He may have tilted at windmills in advocating a cause that was unacceptable to the spirit of the time, in talking of a cooperative world federation with equitable and just distribution of resources and of a religion based on love. But some of his ideals of equity came to be incorporated in the charter of the United Nations.

In 1957, he fought the elections against the Congress and Jan Sangh from Mathura Lok Sabha constituency and defeated them.

The Jan Sangh candidate, who lost even the security deposit, was Atal Behari Vajpayee.

Joining issue with Aravindan Neelkandan, who had come out with an article on Raja Mahendra Pratap fracas in the *Swarajya* weekly,[11] an anonymous commentator said,

> The primary responsibility of a University is not to celebrate the birth anniversary of the hero the institution is named after, or anyone else. BJP Government has made a good decision recently to not celebrate any icon's birth or death anniversaries except M.K. Gandhi, at the cost of government money. Individuals or private groups can celebrate using their money. If you welcome that decision, you should welcome if a University refuses to celebrate any hero, including a philanthropist or a heavy-weight politician, however much he or she had contributed to the growth of the University or the nation. Even if a University decides positively, let them do so freely: why should outsiders interfere with the freedom? If the University forgets to celebrate certain relevant people, the argument that outsiders should remind it of the responsibility is nonsensical. The VC of the AMU should be congratulated for his timely act.

The issue of Mahendra Pratap's anniversary celebrations in 2014 was resolved after talks between the AMU vice-chancellor and local BJP leaders. The vice-chancellor records in his memoirs:

> An article appeared in the press that the local Lok Sabha member had demanded that AMU must honour Raja Mahendra Pratap Singh by celebrating his birthday in the same way as they did of the founder because the Raja had donated thousands of acres of land to the university. There was an agitation in a neighbouring college and my effigy was burnt for not honouring a Hindu alumnus. Communal tempers flared up. I spoke to the MP and asked him why, as a member of the AMU court, he had not discussed the matter with me before going public. He replied that he had written a letter, which I had not yet received. I learnt later that this was his usual ploy. I also clarified that Raja had never donated any land but

> had leased out three acres for which the university was paying an annual rent. It became a communal issue. As a face-saving device, I agreed that the AMU would hold a seminar on the Raja, which we did. That defused the matter.[12]

As far as the donation of the raja was concerned, MAO College had been established much before his birth. His grandfather had leased 3.04-acre land in 1928 for 90 years to the university, which is spread over 480 acre.

The descendants of the raja served legal notice on the university in 2018, after the expiry of the 90-year lease. The Executive Council of the university authorised vice-chancellor Tariq Mansoor in September 2020 to form a committee to negotiate with the family members.

The matter was amicably resolved, and the university handed back the land of the Tikona Park, measuring about 12,000 square meters, to the descendants of the raja. As per the agreement, AMU's city school was renamed in May 2022 as Raja Mahendra Pratap Singh Aligarh Muslim University City School.[13]

It must be remembered that many non-Muslims too had contributed to the AMU. G.D. Birla had donated Rs 70,000 in 1925, which at current gold value amounts to more than Rs 5,000 crore.

24

THE CONFLICT OVER AMU SATELLITE CENTRES

The then chief minister of Madhya Pradesh, Mr Digvijay Singh, who had visited AMU as the chief guest at its annual Sir Syed's Day function in 2002, proposed to establish off-campus centres of the university. He offered 100 acres of land for this purpose to an NGO named Gharib Nawaz Foundation (GNF). The secretary of GNF met with the vice-chancellor in this connection in 2003. Later, the GNF submitted its proposal for a second campus of AMU to Arjun Singh, the then union HRD minister. Professor Anwar Khursheed writes,

> The UGC on 28 Jan 2005 wrote a letter to the GNF informing that it had asked the AMU to submit a proposal. Within two months, the GNF complained to Arjun Singh about the delay in opening the AMU off campus and requested him to promulgate an ordinance in order to expedite the process as a first step in this direction.[1]

The copy of this communication was endorsed to the vice-chancellor. The under-secretary of HRD wrote a letter to the UGC on 21 April 2005 on the same line, and then on 28 August 2006, the deputy secretary of HRD wrote to the vice-chancellor, complaining about the delay and suggested establishing the said Study Centre u/s 12(2) of the AMU Act.

In 2007, another NGO named the Belgachia Education Trust (BET), through the then chief minister of West Bengal, requested the centre to establish an AMU centre in West Bengal at Murshidabad. The HRD minister then wrote to AMU to establish a centre u/s 12(2) of the AMU Act and also reprimanded AMU later for sitting over the proposal.

The initial concept of the centres in minority-dominated areas of the country was a catchy idea, since it was a step towards fulfilment of Sir Syed's dream of furthering education among Muslims. However, when the details came to light, a surge of queries, doubts, apprehensions and uneasiness besieged people's minds. Most obnoxious was the obtainance of private trusts to get an ordinance promulgated and the ruling politicians' eagerness to oblige them.

The university was later sandwiched between the conflicting wills of different governments. First, it was pressed to establish centres and now the same HRD ministry under a different political dispensation was bent upon to close them or create a situation leading to their slow death.[2] The initial financial proposal was of Rs 1400 crore for Malappuram (Kerala) and Murshidabad (West Bengal) centres. Still, the Congress government had sanctioned only Rs 349.55 crore in the XII Five Year Plan and released only Rs 130 crore.

Sec 5(9A) of the AMU (Amendment) Act, 1972, provides that the 'University shall have the power to establish within a radius of twenty-five kilometres of the University Mosque such special Centres, specialised Laboratories or other units for research and instruction as are, in the opinion of the University, necessary for the furtherance of its objects'; whereas Sec 12(2) of the AMU (Amendment) Act, 1951, confirms that the

> University may also, with the sanction of the Visitor and subject to the Statutes and Ordinances, establish and maintain such Special Centres, Specialised Laboratories or such other institutions for research or instruction as are necessary for the furtherance of its objects either on its own or in cooperation or collaboration with any other institution.

It must be noted that section 12(2) was not struck down when 5(9A) was incorporated in 1972. Nevertheless, no such centres could be legalised without framing necessary statutes and ordinances via statutes 23(2), 28(6), and 29(1), which the university did in the meantime.

The preamble of the AMU Act of 1920 provides 'an Act to incorporate a Teaching and Residential Muslim University at Aligarh'. The debate on the residential character of the institution as per the preamble of the Act can only be decided by studying the important questions of whether the preamble is a part of the Constitution of India or not. The preamble to the Constitution of India sets out the guiding purpose and principles of the document. For some time, it was assumed that, like the preamble of a statute, the preamble is not an integral part of the Indian constitution; however, Kesavanada Bharati Case created history, and for the first time, Supreme Court has recognised that the preamble to the Constitution of India is a part of the Constitution. The preamble is neither a source of power nor a source of limitations. It has a significant role to play in the interpretation of statues, also in the interpretation of provisions of the Constitution. The inference drawn is that residential character is a part of the Act but not absolute, and there is certainly no ambiguity in the establishment of campuses/centres; this is perhaps the reason that hostel is not compulsory for students since its inception and therefore the provision of non-resident students does exist.

The president of India as the visitor of the university accorded approval for establishing these centres under Section 12(2) of the AMU Act. The Allahabad high court bench comprising the then Chief Justice F.I. Rebello and Justice A.P. Sahi dismissed a writ petition challenging the decision to establish two new centres of AMU at Malappuram and Murshidabad, since the same had been duly approved by the president of India as the visitor of the university.[3] The Kerala high court bench comprising Chief Justice J. Chelameswar and Justice P.N. Ravindran had earlier rejected the prayer for interim relief against establishing an AMU centre in Kerala.

MAO College, at the time of its establishment in 1877, possessed only 78 acres of land, which has now expanded to more than a thousand acres; almost another thousand acres of land has been further gifted by the states of Kerala, Bihar and West Bengal, which is a giant leap. Still the full benefits of such centres to the community may be far from reality in the absence of restoration of minority status of AMU pending before the Supreme Court.

Though a majority of the Indian Muslims, wrote Mushtaq Ahmad Alig in the *Milli Gazette*,[4] including a majority of the Aligarians spread across the world are in favour of the four extended centres of AMU in Kerala, West Bengal, Maharashtra and Bihar, which had been approved by the central government, a section of old boys is opposing something that has already happened. The AMU centres at Malappuram and Murshidabad are functioning since 2011.

The vice-chancellor Dr Tariq Mansoor said that the university did not have any plan to open the centres in Maharashtra in near future as the Centre had not released the full amount sanctioned for centres functioning at Malappuram (Kerala), Murshidabad (West Bengal) and Kishanganj (Bihar). In October 2011, an AMU team headed by the then vice-chancellor Professor P.K. Abdul Aziz, had visited Khuldabad and Malegaon to choose the plot and preferred Khuldabad near Aurangabad and identified a 100-acre plot for the proposed centre.

When vice-chancellor Lt Gen. (retd) Zameer Uddin Shah met HRD minister Smriti Irani to discuss the Centre's attempt to withdraw the institution's minority status and 'inadequate funding' for its three off-campus centres, fully geared and briefed minister asked the vice-chancellor how one of AMU's three off-campus centres was currently offering a B.Ed. course without the approval of the National Council for Teacher Education (NCTE). The vice-chancellor meekly replied that the university had recently applied for approval.

In the meeting, Shah expressed concern over the ministry allegedly withholding funds, to which Irani pointed out that almost Rs 90 crore was lying unused with the university. The AMU was allocated Rs 546 crore under the 12th Five Year Plan (2012–17), of which the government had released Rs 302 crore.

However, about Smriti Irani, Shah writes,

> In the first VC meet, she introduced herself as an 'actress by profession' and adding that 'histrionics were part of her nature.' I gave full marks for her articulation – both in English and Hindu. She was confident and did her homework. When she wanted to target a VC, she would read up all facts about the university and put searching question to the hapless victim. The VC under fire would generally fumble and be humiliated in front of other contemporaries.

Later, a delegation of Kerala ministers and members of parliament led by the Kerala chief minister Mr Oommen Chandy met HRD minister Smriti Irani in her office seeking her support for the AMU centre at Malappuram, which was not progressing as planned. She told them bluntly, 'This centre and other AMU centres were established without any legal sanction, hence they all will be closed down.' She added, 'How do you start a centre like this? What authority the VC has to take such an action. We are not going to give money.' She went on to say, 'There was no need for the AMU centres. I am going to close them down. We will not give any grant for this purpose.' The Kerala chief minister told her that the state had allocated 345 acres of precious land in Perinthalmanna taluk of Malappuram for this purpose on the understanding that a full-fledged AMU centre would function there. 'Take it back!' the HRD minister retorted.[5]

While this unpleasant discussion was on between the HRD minister and the Kerala delegation, the AMU vice-chancellor, Lt Gen. (retd) Zameeruddin Shah, entered the room. The vice-chancellor records in his memoirs,

> I was requested by the CM of Kerala to accompany the delegation. I reached the minister's office, well in time, on the appointed day. There I was informed that the venue had been shifted to the

> minister's residence. I could reach there after the meeting started. The CM had left a guide to usher me in. As soon as I entered, the HRD minister glared at me and asked, 'Yes, who are you?' I replied, 'Madam, you know me, I am Lt Gen Shah, VC of the AMU.' She shot back, 'Who invited you in?' I replied, 'The chief minister had requested me to be part of his delegation.' She huffed, 'Who pays your salary? The central government or the Government of Kerala?' To my regret, the CM kept silent. I beat a retreat and left the room. After the meeting, the CM apologised profusely. I am certain that the venue had been changed with the express purpose of humiliating me. In the office, I could not have been asked to leave so unceremoniously.[6]

Shah later communicated the treatment meted out to him by the HRD minister to the prime minister.

AMU had decided in 2010 to open five off-campus centres, one each at Murshidabad, Malappuram, Kishanganj, Bhopal and Pune, which all were to be fully functional by 2020. The projected growth for the Malappuram centre for the year 2015 was 13,000 students and 13 faculties but even now it is offering only three courses, *viz.*, MBA, BEd and LLB, which are attended by only 400 students at present. The Murshidabad centre too is offering only these three courses, while the Kishanganj centre is offering only BEd course. Two centers in Murshidabad (West Bengal) and Mallapuram (Kerala) are functioning well due to active assistance from the state governments, but the Kishanganj center in Bihar has failed to click as the state government is not willing to help it. The campus stretches from the land adjacent to a seasonal river, often causing damage to the building during monsoon. The Union government run by the BJP remains hostile to these centers.

The university during the reign of Lt Gen. Zameer Uddin Shah also planned to open Sir Syed National Schools through the Sir Syed Education Foundation, established under the aegis of the university, taking advantage of a clause in the AMU Amendment Act, 1982, which made AMU responsible for the 'education and cultural advancement of Muslims of India'. The ambitious scheme stipulated the serving vice-chancellor as president of the Sir Syed Education Foundation. The scheme was to build a modern secular school in every district, starting with Uttar Pradesh, where there is a sizeable Muslim population, mostly illiterate and impoverished. The schools were initially to be from nursery to Class 3 and thereafter one class was to be added each year till the schools reach class 12. The schools were to be self-sustaining with moderate tuition fees. The students from impoverished families were to be given free education. The union ministry of minority affairs assured Rs 10 crore per annum to establish 10 such schools every year under the aegis of the Centre for Promotion of Education and Cultural Advancement of Muslims of India, AMU.

However, after Shah demitted the office, the university disassociated itself from the scheme citing that it was hamstrung by a clause in the AMU Act that prohibits establishment of schools beyond (15 miles) 25 km from the university mosque.

The school, established in 2016 during the reign of Shah as the vice-chancellor of AMU, is in operation in village Jaula in Muzaffarnagar. It is adding one class every year. On the occasion of the AMU centenary in 2020, Sir Syed Education Foundation laid the foundation stone for its fifth school at Rataul in Baghpat district. The branches of Sir Syed National School at Sardhana and Saharanpur have completed their four academic sessions.

All India Management Association's Centre for Management Education, a private organisation, has been conducting a PhD programme in business administration in collaboration with Aligarh Muslim University since 2000. The programme is divided into two phases: the foundation phase, which AIMA conducts, and the research phase, which AMU conducts.

As per AIMA guidelines, the eligibility norms included a master's degree in management or allied subjects from commerce, humanities, science, engineering and law, etc. or a PGDM/PGDITM approved by AICTE with not less than 55 per cent marks or equivalent grade or chartered accountancy, cost accountancy or any other professional qualification that are considered equivalent to a master's degree with at least 55 per cent marks or equivalent grade. In addition, the candidate should have a minimum of 50 per cent marks in graduation. Besides, a minimum of 5 years of work experience in industry at the managerial level or a minimum of 5 years of teaching experience as a full-time faculty in a management Institute approved by AICTE or affiliated with a university is required.

AIMA specifies that the programme is designed for working managers inclined towards academics, B-school teaching faculty, and senior management professionals to upgrade their skills and competencies and gain deeper insights into industry-specific problems.

AMU awards the candidates the doctorate degree.

25

Unlearning Harmony

Aligarh, whose perimeters resemble the outline of a jet fighter plane has always earned the dubious distinction of being one of the major trouble spots for communal disharmony leading to violence and riots in Uttar Pradesh. The town experienced several major communal clashes in 1961, 1971, 1978 and 1990–91.

On 29 March 1946, the city witnessed disturbances over an altercation between Krishan Behari Lal, a cloth seller, and two Muslim students of the university at Mahavirganj. Later, the students returned with 50 others. The enquiry committee, instituted by the state government, found that a mob of 1,000–1,500 students was kept at bay at the railway over-bridge by the police and proctorial staff of AMU.

However, since 1991, there has been no significant communal violence in Aligarh (except for a relatively minor clash in 2006). Sajad Ahmad Dar, a young research scholar at AMU, alleged that the minorities in the BJP era had been muted, perhaps coercively.[1]

He asks that in 2017, a Hindu murdered two Muslims in broad daylight, though the perpetrator of the crime and the victims all were of questionable integrity:

> But even in the pre-BJP era, there have been instances of such silence, and the supporters of leaders of the minorities did not raise the issue. For instance, the Muslim leadership did not ask for justice in the Aligarh riots of 1990-91, when a 'Muslim friendly regime' headed by Mulayam Singh Yadav was in power ... Even in the 2013 Muzaffarnagar riots, the wilful failures of the Akhilesh

> Yadav regime in preventing and controlling the riots, rehabilitating the victims and in bringing the perpetrators to justice have been mainly ignored by Muslim politicians and the intelligentsia as well as the liberal left…
>
> Unlike the 2002 Gujarat riots, the perpetrators and collaborating police officers of Muzaffarnagar have not been chased by civil society groups up to the higher judiciary … Usually, some of the vocal Muslims are co-opted by the 'friendly regimes' and their silence on acts of injustice is in a sense, purchased. In the era of BJP's dominance and hegemony, the only difference this time is that they have been muted without any favour being offered to individual elites of the community.
>
> 'Even the intelligentsia has become palpably partisan. They shout against the omissions and commissions of saffron establishments, but they choose to become less shrill and less strident when they are needed to speak against the non-saffron forces. The liberals, for instance, did not speak out against Akhilesh Yadav's regime whose police in Dadri (*September 2015*), in Muzaffarnagar (*2013*), and elsewhere in UP failed to uphold Constitutional values' Prof. Mohammad Sajjad has argued.[2]

This also raises questions about the political and intellectual efficacy of Aligarh Muslim University. The AMUTA, AMUSU, and informal student groups like the Aligarh Activist's Society and the students of AMU chose to keep quiet along with the Urdu dailies on repression unleashed during the successive Samajwadi regimes.

It is interesting to know how Nehru reacted to violent protests in 1956 demanding the withdrawal of a book about religious leaders. The prime minister kept all options open except banning the book, which he considered 'doubtful legality'. In her seminal work, Scholar Devika Sethi has discussed this specific incident in detail.[3]

In September 1956, the reprinting by the Bhartiya Vidya Bhawan of the 1942 title *Living Biographies of Religious Leaders,* written by Henry and Dana Lee Thomas, and initially published in the US had led to communal violence in Aligarh, Madhya Pradesh (then Vindhya Pradesh) and West Bengal. The book carried short biographies of Moses, Luke, Joseph, Buddha, Prophet Muhammad and Gandhi. It was noticed only when reprinted in India.

The protesters were alleging that the Foreword by K.M. Munshi, then the Governor of Uttar Pradesh had made 'insulting' references to the Prophet. The other side floated a calculated rumour that the former side had torn and burnt the Hindu holy book Gita in Aligarh. Riots erupted, killing 15 to 22 people. Hundreds were arrested, and a curfew was imposed in Aligarh. Over 5,000 people demonstrated against K.M. Munshi, who was forced to cancel his scheduled visit to Bhopal in early September. The publisher announced under duress that the 'controversial' passages would be removed and the book would not be put on sale till then.

Actively and most visibly involved in the agitation were students of AMU. The then vice-chancellor Dr Zakir Husain (later served as India's first Muslim president) had regretted the involvement of the students of his university; he reminded them that 'your action should have caused pain to the soul of the Prophet'.[4]

Siyasat Jadid, an Urdu newspaper from Kanpur, edited, printed and published by K.G. Zaidi (also known as Ishaq Ilmi, father-in-law of politician Arif Mohammad Khan), blew the issue out of proportion.

Although the 16-page chapter contained many complimentary references to the Prophet and to Islam, the book had also printed his portrait and repeated many of the charges of promiscuity and violence that were standard tropes in biographies of the Prophet written by Westerners in the 20th century. The *Time* magazine, reporting the riots, commented: 'This story jibes essentially with the earliest and standard account of Mohammed's life (by Ibn Ishaq in the 8th century), but the tone of the book's 16-page biography might well give offence to devout Moslems.'[5]

The then prime minister J.L. Nehru himself said,

> not of a very high standard. It is a very ordinary book, neither well written nor good, a mere journalistic hotchpotch. There is no doubt that some wrong facts and often absurd things have been

> written in the chapter on Hazrat Muhammad. It was wrong, there was no doubt about it.
>
> Anyhow, that does not mean that just because someone has written a useless book or said some wrong things, we should fight among ourselves. Let us take whatever action we can regarding the book and try to have it banned or change the text or something. This is the sensible way of going about things instead of creating uproar.[6]

By the time he made these comments, Nehru had already taken action against the book and conducted damage control on several fronts: he had written to K.M. Munshi, more or less ordering him to withdraw the book, as it was 'second-rate', was causing him (Nehru) to be inundated with telegrams asking that the book be banned, and because it had raised a big issue not only in India but also in Pakistan. Nehru's reprimand was unequivocal: 'I think you should withdraw this book immediately and announce this fact. Presumably, you had not read the book, although you are a General Editor of the series.'[7]

He also instructed Munshi to issue a press communiqué as he felt that a public statement was necessary. Nehru then communicated to the chief minister of Bombay, Morarji Desai, Maulana Azad's suggestion that the publisher hand over the remaining copies to the Bombay government. Seven thousand copies had been printed of which 3,000 had already been sold. Even prior to this communication, Bhartiya Vidya Bhawan had already announced that they were stopping the sale of the book, and this announcement was released by the director of information of the Uttar Pradesh government, thereby reaching a larger audience. This did not, however, stop riots in Aligarh and elsewhere in mid-September.

Eventually, Bihar and West Bengal governments banned the book but the Uttar Pradesh government refused to ban it – the chief minister Dr Sampurnanand being unsure of the legality of such an action.

He also publicly expressed the opinion that 'penal action will have to be decided by law, not by the desire of any individual'.

In his opinion, legal action could be based on proof of 'malicious intent' alone, and this would be difficult to prove. He did not contest that religious feelings had been hurt, but since the book had been withdrawn, he thought legal action impossible.[8]

Nehru responded to a letter by the Uttar Pradesh chief minister about the issue by agreeing that although the agitation over the book had begun some 'dangerous trends', slogan shouting per se could not be penalised as it was challenging to identify the culprit in a crowd. Nehru asked the chief minister to ensure that the impression was not created that the government was partial (to Hindus) in communal matters.

He also did not consider the demand for banning a bona fide one. Nehru repeatedly emphasised (in public meetings as well as in letters to chief ministers) that vested interests had manufactured the agitation:

> I can understand people objecting to some passages in that book and drawing attention to them. But there was something much deeper, and it was obvious that mischief was afoot and had been deliberately organised. The offending passages were broadcast in cyclostyled papers by the very persons who objected to them.

Nehru's faith in the freedom of the press was shaken after this episode. Although he conceded the right of people to take offence, he found it worrying that during demonstrations against the book, some Muslims had raised slogans (such as '*Pakistan Zindabad*' [Long Live Pakistan]) that were 'not only anti-national but also treasonable'.

In the post-Independence period, the Hindu–Muslim conflict crystallised over the issue of the affiliation of the predominantly Hindu colleges of the town. Issues related to AMU often sparked off communal riots in the town, such as in 1961 when the crushing defeat of all the Hindu candidates in the AMUSU elections led to violence in the city. Similarly, in 1978, the campaign to restore the 'minority character' of the institution contributed to tensions, which culminated in widespread rioting.

The 1946 Aligarh riots Committee had reported,

> We refer to the position of the university and its students and measures taken to deal with offenders. It has in the past been the custom to act as far as possible through the University Proctorial Staff, both to uphold their disciplinary powers and because in a large proportion of cases the proctor was able to identify and punish students whom local complainants were unable to identify and who would otherwise have escaped punishment altogether. We suggest it would be wise to review the position and to consider how far and in what manner students should cease to receive any differential treatment and in what way any changes in the present custom can be applied in practice, in view of the great difficulty of recognising individual students.

The report was tabled on the floor of the Uttar Pradesh Legislative Council on 22 February 1947. No action was taken in this regard.

26

MAJAZ: MERA CHAMAN AMU

'*Ye mera chaman hai mera chaman, main apne chaman ka bulbul hun.*' This is a magical line that connects millions of Aligarians all over the world. Their head and feet move at the same pitch, tempo and rhythm with *Tarana-e-Aligarh.* Little wonder, listeners of this song get goose bumps on hearing this repeatedly. Writer Rana Safvi claims in a Tweet, 'Majaz composed the AMU *Tarana* in one night because Nehruji had come on a visit (and) commented that AMU did not have an anthem.'[1]

Asrar-ul-Haq Majaz was a student of AMU from 1930 to 1936.[2] It was during his last academic year when the 24-year-old student penned his famous poem 'Nazr-e-Aligarh', an ode to his alma mater and recited it in 1936 in the Union Hall, in the presence of the pro-vice-chancellor A.B. Abul Haleem, who intervened Majaz decisively when he reached the lines '*Yahaan hamne kamanden daalii hain, Yahan humne shabkhoon (night raids) maaray hain; Yahan hum nay qabaayen nochii hain, yahan hum nay taaj utaarey hain*' (We have scaled buildings here and ambushed here; we have torn garments here and removed crowns here). The massive gathering of students urged him to continue, but Majaz walked out. He had to relent later and completed the *nazm* in the Union Hall's lawns (between Morrison Court and the Union Hall building).

A year earlier, the Union Hall of AMU was brimming with students, and the atmosphere was electric. As his turn came, a young man in *shervani* (long coat) stood up. Running his right hand through his long locks, he recited his poem 'Inquilab' in his inimitable style:

Kohsaaron ki taraf se surkh aandhi aayegi
Ja-baja aabaadiyon mein aag si lag jaayegi
Aur is rang-e-shafaq mein ba-hazaraan aab-o taab
Jagmagaaega watan ki hurriyat ka aaftaab

[A red storm is approaching from over the mountains
Sparking a fire in the settlements
And on this horizon, amidst a thousand tumults
Shall shine the sun of our land's freedom] [3]

The hall reverberated with thunderous applause. Majaz was destined for greatness! Even after Majaz left the campus, his poetry left an indelible impression on the students. Ishtiaque Ahmad Khan, a student of BEd (1954–55) was also among his admirers. An address by the vice-chancellor Dr Zakir Husain to the final year students inspired Khan to do something long-lasting for the university. He thought of putting Majaz's *Nazr-e-Aligarh* to tune and was confident of it becoming the university *tarana* (song). Khan composed the *tarana* in the last week of September 1954 and requested the president of the students' union, Ahmad Saeed, for his permission to present it to the university. The student leader refused because Majaz was considered a progressive writer. But the vice-chancellor not only lauded the poem but also acknowledged that it was one of the Majaz's best works.

About two decades after this *nazm* was penned, on 17 October, when Ishtiaque Ahmad Khan walked to the dais at the Strachey Hall along with his troupe (Saleh Naiyyar, Ghulam Haider Ejaz and Fasih), Izzat Yaar Khan, the secretary of SS Hall Music Club, started the tune on the harmonium, and soon, the hall reverberated with the sound of *Ye mera chaman.* The vice-chancellor was impressed. Even the student leader who had reservations earlier appreciated the poem and apologised to Ishtiaque Ahmed Khan about his earlier stand. Ishtiaque Ahmed Khan was an incredible actor who also played the role of the nawab, father of Farooq Sheikh, in the movie *Umrao Jaan* by Muzaffar Ali.

And the Aligarh *Tarana* came into being. Majaz died less than 14 months later. Poetic justice, indeed!

The *nazm* of Majaz titled *Nazr-e-Aligarh* has been abridged and adopted as the lyrics of AMU *tarana*. The complete *nazm* is:

ye mera chaman hai mera chaman, main apne chaman ka bulbul hun
sarshaar-e-nigaah-e-nargis hun, paa-bastaa-e-gesu-e-sumbul hun
[*chaman*: garden; *bulbul*: nightingale; *sarshaar*: overflowing, soaked; *nigaah*: sight; *nargis*: flower, narcissus; *paa-bastaa*: embedded; *gesuu*: tresses; *sumbul*: a plant of sweet odour]

har aan yahan sehbaa-e-kuhan ek saaghar-e-nau men dhalti hai
kalion se husn tapaktaa hai, phoolon se javaani ubalti hai
[*sehbaa-e-kuhan*: old wine; *saaghar-e-nau*: new goblet]

jo taaq-e-haram men roshan hai, vo shamaa yahaan bhi jalti hai
is dasht ke goshe-goshe se, ek joo-e-hayaat ubalti hai
[*taaq-e-haram*: vault in the sacred territory of mecca; *roshan*: glowing; *shamaa*: flame; *dasht*: wilderness, desert; *goshaa*: corner; *juu-e-hayaat*: stream of life]

islam ke is but-khaane men asnaam bhi hain aur aazaar bhi
tahzib ke is mai-khaane men shamshir bhi hai aur saaghar bhi
[*but-khaanaa*: temple; *asnaam:* idols; *aazaar:* Abraham's father, an idol-worshipper; *tahziib*: culture; *shamshir:* sword; *saaghar:* wine goblet]

yaan husn ki barq chamakti hai, yaan noor ki baarish hoti hai
har aah yahaan ek naghmaa hai, har ashk yahaan ek moti hai
[*barq:* lightening; *nuur*: light]

har shaam hai shaam-e-misr yahaan, har shab hai shab-e-sheeraz yahaan
hai saare jahaan ka soz yahaan aur saare jahaan kaa saaz yahaan
[*shaam-e-Misr:* evenings of Egypt; *shab-e-Sheeraz:* nights of Sheeraz, a famous city of Iran; *soz*: pain]

Ye dasht-e-junun deevanon kaa, ye bazm-e-vafa parvaanon ki
ye shahr-e-tarab roomaanon kaa, ye khuld-e-bareen armanon ki

[*dasht:* desert, wilderness; *junuun:* frenzy; *bazm:* gathering; *vafaa:* faithfulness; *shahr-e-tarab:* city of mirth; *khuld-e-bareen:* sublime paradise; *armaan:* hope]

fitrat ne sikhaee hai ham ko, uftaad yahaan parvaaz yahaan
gaaye hain vafaa ke geet yahaan, chheraa hai junun kaa saaz yahaan

[*fitrat*: nature; *uftaad*: beginning of life; *parvaaz*: flight; *saaz*: song on an instrument]

is farsh se hamne ud ud kar aflaak ke taare tode hain
naheed se ki hai sargoshi, parveen se rishte jore hain

[*farsh*: base; *aflaak*: heavens; *naheed*: Venus; *parveen*: Pleiades]

is bazm men teghen khencheen hain, is bazm men saghar tode hain
is bazm men aankh bichaa'ee hai, is bazm men dil tak jore hain

[*tegh*: swords; *saghar:* goblet]

is bazm men neze khenche hain, is bazm men khanjar choome hain
is bazm men gir-gir tadpe hain, is bazm men pee kar jhoome hain

[*neze:* spears; *khanjar*: dagger; *bazm*: gathering]

Aa aa kar hazaaron baar yahaan khud aag bhi hamne lagaayee hai
phir saare jahaan ne dekhaa hai ye aag hameen ne bujha'ee
haiyaan ham ne kamanden
daali hain, yaan hamne shab-khoon maare hain
yaan ham ne qabaayen nochee hain, yaan hamne taaj utaare hain

[*kamand*: a noose; *shab-khoon*: night raids; *qabaayen*: dress]

har aah hai khud taaseer yahaan, har khvaab hai khud taabeer yahaan
tadbeer ke paa-e-sangin per jhuk jaati hai taqdeer yahaan

[*aah*: sigh; *taaeer*: effect; *taabeer*: interpretation; *tadbeer*: forethought; *paa-e-sangin*: firm footing; *taqdeer*: destiny]

zarraat kaa bosaa lene ko, sau baar jhukaa aakaash yahaan
khud aankh se ham ne dekhi hai, baatil ki shikast-e-faash yahaan

[*zarraat*: dust; *bosaa*: kiss; *baatil*: evil; *shikast-e-faash*: clear defeat]

is gul-kadah paarinaa men phir aag bharakne vaali hai
phir abr garajne vaale hain, phir barq karakne vaali hai

[*gul-kadah*: garden; *paarinaa*: ancient; *abr*: cloud; *barq*: lightening]

jo abr yahaan se uththega, vo saare jahaan par barsegaa
har juu-e-ravaan par barsegaa, har koh-e-garaan par barsegaa

[*abr*: cloud; *juu-e-ravaan*: flowing streams; *koh-e-garaan*: big mountains]
har sard-o-saman par barsegaa, har dasht-o-daman par barsegaa
khud apne chaman par barsegaa, ghairon ke chaman par barsegaa
[*sard-o-saman*: open and shelter; *dasht-o-daman*: wild and subdued; *qasr-e-tarab*: citadel of joy]
har shahr-e-tarab par garjegaa, har qasr-e-tarab par kadkegaa
ye abr hameshaa barsaa hai, ye abr hameshaa barsegaa
[*shahr-e-tarab*: city of joy; *qasr-e-tarab*: citadel of joy]

After truncating the original nazm, its present form is:

Ye mera Chaman hai mera chaman, mein apne chaman ka bulbul hoo(n)
Sirshaare nigaahe nargis hoo(n), paabasta-e-gesoo-e Sumbul hoo(n)
Ye mera chaman, ye mera chaman, ye mera chaman hai mera chaman,
mein apne chaman ka bulbul hoo(n)!
Jo taaq-e-haram mein roshan hai who shama yehan bhi jalti hai,
Iss dasht ke goshey goshey se ik jooy-e-hayat ubalti hai
Ye dasht-e-junoo(n) deewano(n) ka, ye bazm-e-wafaa parwano(n) ki
Ye shehr-e-tarab roomano(n) ka, ye khald-e-baree(n) armaano(n) ki
Fitrat ne sikhayee hai humko eftaad yehan parwaaz yehan Gaaye hain wafaa ke geet yehan,
chheda hai junoo(n) ka saaz yehan
Ye mera chaman hai mera chaman, mein apne chaman ka bulbul hoo(n)!
Iss bazm mein teghi(n) khichi hain, is bazm mein saagar todey hain
Iss bazm mein aankh bichhaayee hai, iss bazm mein dil tak jodey hain
Har shaarri hai shaam-e-misr yehan, har shab hai shab-e Shiraz yehan
Hai saarey jahan ka soz yehan aur saarey jahan ka saaz yehan
Zarraat ka boasa lene ko sau baar jhuka aakaash yehan Khud aankh se hamne dekhi hai baatil ki shikast faash yehan
Ye mera chaman, ye mera chaman, ye mera chaman hai mera chaman,
mein apne chaman ka bulbul hoo(n)!
Jo abr yehan se utthega, wo sarey jahan par barsega

Har jooy-e-rawaa(n) par barsega, har koh-e-geraa(n) par barsega
Har sarb-o-saman par barsega, har dasht-o-daman par barsega
Khud apne chaman par barsega, gairo(n) ke chaman par barsega
Har shahr-e-tarab par garjega, har qisr-e-tarab par kadkega
Ye abr hamesha barsa hai, ye abr hamesha barsega
Ye abr hamesha bara hai, ye abr hamesha barsega Ye abr hamesha barsa hai, ye abr hamesha barsega Barsega, barsega, barsega!4
—Asrar-ui-Haq Majaz Lakhnavi

The English translation is by Shantiveer Kaul:

This is my garden
Mine own garden
And I am its 'bulbul'. (1)
Drunk am I on the look
This is my garden, my own garden
And I am its 'bulbul'.
Drunk am I on the look
Of the narcissus Bound by the tresses of the 'sumbul'. (2)
This is my garden
My own garden
Indeed, my very own garden
And I am its 'bulbul'. The light on the arch
Of the sanctum
It is lit here as well.
In every corner of the desert
The spring of life wells up
This is the wilderness of passion, The area of faith of the covenanted the city of serenades by romantics, The area of faith of the covenanted, city of serenades by romantics, the Sublime heaven of desires.
Nature has taught us flight and descent Here.
We have sung the songs of the faith and struck the lute of passion Here.
This is my garden. Mine is my own garden, And I am its 'bulbul'.
We have drawn the swords here
Smashed the goblets Laid out our waiting Effected union of hearts
Every evening is 'Sham-I-Misr' (3) Here

Every night 'Shab-I-Shiraz' (4) The music of the whole world is here. As is its entire musicality.
A hundred times has the sky.
Bowed down to kiss the ground here. With our own eyes, we have witnessed the defeat and unmasking of falsehood here.
This is my garden. Mine is my own garden, And I am its 'bulbul'.
This is my garden Mine is my own garden
Indeed, my very own garden
And I am its 'bulbul'
The cloud rising from here
It will rain down on the whole world
It will rain on every rivulet and stream
And on every mountain heavyset
It will rain down on every cypress
And jasmine
And on every wilderness
It will rain down on its own garden
And on the garden of others
It will strike its own note
Of thunder, on every city of musical notes.
It will write its own script
Of lightning, on every deficient score.
This cloud has always rained down. This cloud will always rain down. This cloud has always rained down. This cloud will always rain down. This cloud has always rained down. This cloud will always rain down. Rain down, rain down, rain down.
(1) Nightingale (2) Spikenard, hyacinth (3) The evening of Egypt, figuratively, the most beautiful evening (4) The night of Shiraz, figuratively, the most beautiful night.

But the story of Majaz, Keats of Indian poetry, cannot be completed without mentioning his popularity among the female students. His romantic poetry made him the beloved poet of the young generation, particularly the girls. Noted writer Ismat Chughtai once remarked that there was a time when the female inmates in the hostel of the Women's College of AMU threw lots with Majaz's name on their chits. His poems were under their pillows, and they used to present his poetry collection as gifts. They often swore that they would name their sons 'Majaz' if nothing worked out.

She wrote how she and her hostel mates in Women's College Aligarh were introduced to his poetry by reading his book Ahang during summer vacations and fell in love with his writings:

> *Majaz se kuch rishtadari si mahsuus hone lagi, jaise ek hi qabile (tribe) ke ho, balke kuch ek hi Khaandaan (family) ke. Par na jaane kiski nazar lagi ke dori (string) kuchh dheelii padni shuru hui. Suna majaz radio mai naukar ho gaye aur Aligarh bhar ki ladkiyo ko samet samet kar taqriiren (speeches) karwaane le jaaya karte hain. Aur phir suna, nikaal diye gaye, radio station se! Phir suna kuchh nahi karte phir suna kuchh bhii nahi karte aur phir suna, aji kuchh bhi to nahi karte!!! Nikhattuu! Jo kahin naukarna ho yaani mahiine ke aakhir mai muqarrara (fixed) raqam (money) bataur tankhwaah (as salary) na laata ho, use urf-e-aam (commonly called) mai nikhattu kehte hain. Ji haan! aap hi dekhiye hain na nikhattuu.*

Actress Nargis was also a fan of Majaz and his poetry. During a visit to Lucknow, she met Majaz to get his autograph.

However, he failed to mention famous Indian cities, in particular 'Sham-e-Oudh', and preferred to recall the city in the Middle East from where Islam came to India.

Har shaam hai shaam-e-misr yahaan, har shab hai shab-e-sheeraz yahaan.

[*shaam-e-Misr*: evenings of Egypt; *shab-e-Sheeraz*: nights of Sheeraz, a famous city of Iran; *soz*: pain]

27

BRIDGE COURSE

Vice-chancellor Lt Gen. Zameer Uddin Shah initiated a bridge course – a one-year course in which students from madrasas were enrolled to study English and social sciences. Rashid Shaz, a former member of the now-banned radical group Students Islamic Movement of India (SIMI), ran the course, where guest lecturers were also invited. Giving details of his ambitious project, Zameer Uddin Shah claimed,

> We selected 75 boys and 25 girls, who were madrasa passouts, for a short one-year course aptly named the 'Bridge Course'. We taught English, computers and Social Sciences. We have run the course for four years and achieved 100% results. These ex-madrasa students have obtained admissions in several universities where admission is through competitive examinations, some even for law and English Honours. These Bridge Course graduates are now returning to visit their madrasas and are the agents of change for modernising the syllabi.[1]

There were also courses on inter-faith and intra-faith subjects, such as doctrinal differences between Muslim sects, but these courses were taught only by Rashid Shaz, whose radical books in Urdu are well known. 'This course has brought a change in my thinking,' says Israr Ali, formerly a student of Jamia Arafia Madrasa at Ser Sarawan near Allahabad. After completing the bridge course, Ali earned a bachelor's degree in social work. Coming from a madrasa background, this is a significant experience in his outlook, but he is young. Talking about backwardness among Muslims, he says: 'Muslims should have a political platform.'[2]

On being asked what would happen if Hindus, Christians and other religions too started having their own political platform or a political party, Israr Ali responds: '*Sir, hum siyasi platform ki baat naheen karte, lekin Hindustan mein Musalmanon ka jo istahsal ho raha hai, aisi halat mein hum kya karein* (Sir, I wouldn't talk of a political platform. But in the face of the discrimination Muslims have been facing in India, what can we do?'[3]

Noted sociologist Imtiaz Ahmad forewarned that the bridge course, though a good initiative on paper for integrating madrasa students into the educational mainstream, was diluting the character of AMU.[4] Concerning the role of the bridge course, Irfan Habib, professor emeritus at the history department, says, 'The AMU is divesting itself of its modern character.'[5]

There was a concern that after completing the one-year bridge course, madrasa students would become eligible as 'internal students', cornering preference in admissions to further courses at AMU. 'If you take 20 percent Muslims from madrasas, then AMU was still pushing 20 percent Muslims (who could potentially enrol here) to go elsewhere,' Habib said, arguing against the belief that the bridge course was helping Indian Muslims.[6]

There were concerns over the course because these madrasa students had not studied non-Islamic subjects such as geography, mathematics, social and physical sciences, and therefore, in the coming decade, the course could transform the character of AMU on a religious path.

This process contradicted another process that was introduced in AMU soon after Independence. Habib reminds that the government of the newly independent India ordered AMU that it could no longer deny admissions to female students into postgraduate courses. Until then, the female students studied at the university's separate women's college till graduation and were not allowed into postgraduate courses on the main AMU campus. Shireen Moosvi, a retired professor of history at AMU, noted that the bridge course was also degrading the academic standards of AMU.[7]

Aftab Alam, a professor at the political science department, told Professor Imtiaz Ahmad that the AMU campus has its own *mizaj* (temperament), which reflects a mix of tradition and modernity. 'This campus will live with this challenge,' he says.[8] If AMU founder Sir Syed Ahmad Khan's objective was to provide modern education and inculcate liberal temperament among Muslims, the overt religiosity on its campus is indeed posing a severe challenge to the university's intellectual environment.

The successor of Shah as vice-chancellor closed down the course.

28

'WE HAVE A RICH PAST WHICH NEEDS TO BE PRESERVED'

AMU has *planned* an ambitious project to dig up the 143-year-old time capsule embedded under the campus and burying a new one containing details of the institution's achievements and an account of contemporary history and current affairs.[1] The officials of AMU thought of digging out the time capsule as no one was aware of its exact contents, but it was likely to reveal records of the rich history of the college at the time of its inception in 19th century.

The move coincided with the centenary celebrations.

The older time capsule was buried on 8 January 1877, the foundation day of the Muhammadan Anglo-Oriental (MAO) College, which later became Aligarh Muslim University in 1920 through an Act of Parliament. According to the *Aligarh Institute Gazette*, published on 12 January 1877, the old capsule was placed under the Strachey Hall on the campus in the presence of Sir Syed, the then king of Varanasi Shambhu Narayan and the then Viceroy of India Edward Robert Lytton. Kunwar Lutuf Khan, a member of MAO Funds Committee, presented a bottle carrying the scroll enlisting the details of how Madrasatul Uloom Musalmanan-e-Hind (the precursor to MAO College) came into being, along with gold, silver and copper coins to Viceroy (Lord Lytton), who put it inside a cavity of the foundation stone specially created for it.

The capsule contained the records of the donors (towards the establishment of the college) and the struggles of Sir Syed Ahmed

Khan, the founder of the college – pictures of the occasion are available in the university archives. The *Aligarh Institute Gazette*, launched in 1866, was associated with the Scientific Society, instituted by Sir Syed in 1863 to promote a scientific temper among students.

On Republic Day in 2021, Aligarh Muslim University buried a time capsule containing documents that carried the history of the institution's 100-year journey. During an online function on the 72nd Republic Day, AMU vice-chancellor Professor Tariq Mansoor said this was a historic occasion because preserving historical documents is critical for the benefit of future generations. Professor Mansoor quoted the noted Spanish philosopher George Santayana: 'Those who cannot remember the past are condemned to repeat it.'

The 1.5-tonne steel capsule was buried about 9 meters in depth in front of the iconic Victoria Gate. It contained the entire gamut of historical documents and chronicles covering the institution's history over the past 100 years. The documents include a brief of all convocations, the original AMU Act of 1920 and the book *Sir Syed Album* by noted historian Professor Khaliq Ahmed Nizami.

The university also proposed to adorn the inner wall of Victoria Gate with the institution's history since the late 19th century in Arabic, which has now been transcribed into English and will soon be put up on a plaque. A decision was also taken to 'excavate the original time capsule which had been buried at the time of the establishment of the MAO College in 1877'. A committee of experts has been formed to oversee the excavation process. A wag remarked, 'Each and every book or document can be easily saved on Google till eternity. Burying a time capsule is Stone Age act.'

29

EPILOGUE

Ms Scheherazade Alim, great-great-grand-daughter of Sir Syed, staked claim to a part of the appertaining land to the sprawling bungalow in which Sir Syed lived. The bungalow is known as Sir Syed House inside the AMU campus. Following prolonged litigation, in 1999, the then vice-chancellor M. Rahman agreed to part with about 1800 sq. metres of the land to Ms Alim. She had earlier obtained the title from a court. The evacuee property had been purchased by the university from the Government of India during the tenure of Col B.H. Zaidi as the vice-chancellor. The university Executive Committee approved the decision.

Scheherazade Alim, who now lives in Aligarh, later sold the land to a builder.

GLOSSARY

Achkan: Long coat
Adab: Courtesy; concession; regards
Ahl-i-Hadees: The partisans of Prophetic tradition
Ahl-e-Hunud: Adherents of Hindu religion
Ahl-e-Islam: Adherents of Islam
A jam: Countries beyond Arabia
Aalim: The singular of *ulama* or *ulema,* meaning one who possesses the quality of *ilm*, knowledge, learning, science in the widest sense, though normally used to denote a Muslim priest
Allama: Great scholar; superlative form of action
Anjuman: An association; *mehfil*
Anjuman-i-Khuddam-i-Kaba: The Society of the Servants of the Holy Place in Saudi Arabia
Aqiqah: Tonsure ceremony of infants
Ashraf: Elites
Auqaf: Plural of *waqf* (endowment)
Azaan: Call to prayer
Azdaham: Massive gathering
Bahr-ui-Uium: 'Sea of Sciences', one of the madrasas of the Firangi Mahal, the famous Dar ul-Ulum in Lucknow
Bhakti Movement: A Hindu religious movement
Bid'at: A reprehensible innovation in religion
Bismillah: In the name of God
Bohra: Trader; merchant; name of a small group of Shia Muslim community in Western India
Brahmo Samaj: A Hindu reformist movement
Chishtiya: A Sufi school of thought

Chehlum: Fortieth day after death
Dar-ul-Harb: The abode of war, a territory in which the *Shariat* is not observed and which, according to classical Muslim jurisprudence, should be made so, if necessary, by force
Dar-ul-Islam: 'The abode of Islam', a territory in which the *Shariat* is observed
Dar-ul-Ulum: 'The Abode of Sciences', a Muslim higher theological seminary such as one in Deoband
Dar-us-Sadar: A judicial official during the British period
Dars-i-Nizami: Traditional curriculum, emphasising Arabic, philosophy and jurisprudence, used in Muslim *madrassas* and *dar-ul-ulums* in India
Din-i-Ilahi: A religion, founded by the Mughal Emperor Akbar
Fatwah: A formal opinion, given by a *mufti* or an *aalim* of standing, on a point of Islamic law
Firangis: British
Gandhiji ki Jai: 'Hail Gandhi'
Ghadr: Perfidy, ingratitude, mutiny, rebellion; used in Urdu speeches and writings for the Mutiny of 1857
Ghlba-Islam: Islamic supremacy
Hadees: The traditions, the record of the sayings and doings of the Prophet Mohammad
Haj: The annual pilgrimage to Mecca
Hanafi: Belonging to the school of Islamic jurisprudence named after its eponymous founder, Abu Hanifa al-Numan
Haram: Forbidden by the *Shariat*
Harun-al-Rashid: Legendary caliph of Baghdad; a descendant of the Prophet
Hijrat: Act of migration by Muslims to Dar-ul-Islam after the territory in which they are living has been declared Dar-ul-Harb; migration of the Prophet from Mecca to Medina
Id: Muslim festival, especially Id-ul-fitr, the breaking of the fast of Ramazan, and Id-ul-zuha, the sacrificial festival on 10 Zu-al-hijja
lddat: Waiting period of four months and 10 days, observed by widows and female divorcees

Ihrar: Independents
Ijma: Consensus of religious opinion
Ijtihad: Exerting oneself to the utmost degree to attain an object, i.e., the utmost effort to understand points of Islamic law
Imam: A person exercising supreme leadership of the Muslim community after the death of the Prophet, used specifically (but not exclusively) for Shia claimants; also honorifically for the founders of the four Sunni schools of jurisprudence; title of a prayer-leader in the mosque
Ismaili: A member of the Shia sect which believes that the descendants of Ismail ibn Jafar al-Sadiq, the seventh in line of Shia imams should lead the community and communicate both the exoteric and the esoteric truths of divine revelation to mankind
Istifta: A questionnaire circulated to *ulama* for their opinion on a point of Islamic law; it forms the prelude to the issue of a *fatwah*
Jehad: Holy war, the religiously obligatory duty, violent if necessary, which may be performed to establish the sway of Islam over the world, or to defend the Dar-ui-Islam
Kaaba: The shrine of the sacred stone at Mecca situated in the centre of the great mosque
Kafir: One who is ungrateful to God, hence an unbeliever
Kalma: Declaration of faith (God is one and Mohammad is his prophet)
Karbala: The place in Iraq where Hazrat Hussain, Grandson of Hazrat Muhammad was martyred
Kayasth: Clerical caste among Hindus
Khadim-ui-Khuddam: 'Servant of the Servants', the title born by the head of the Anjuman-i-Khuddam-i-Kaaba
Khaksar: A sociopolitical movement in British India
Khalifa: Caliph, the successor of the Prophet Muhammad as head of the Muslim community, and in recent times, i.e., up to 1924, the Sultan of Turkey
Khidmat-e-Khalq: Social service
Khilafat: Caliphate, the office the Khalifa filled
Khilafat Andolan: Caliphate movement

Khoja: A Muslim of the Shia Ismaili sect

Khutba: A bidding prayer or sermon delivered before the congregation in a mosque on Fridays in which God's blessings on the reigning prince are invoked, thus constituting a symbolic acknowledgement of sovereignty; any address

Lingam: Phallus, worshipped by the Hindus

Lehaz: Consideration

Madrassa: A secondary school or college for Muslims; a collegiate mosque; a seminary

Madrisa-I-Madina: Name of a seminary

Maghrib: West

Majlis: Gathering, assembly

Majlis-I-shura: Consultative assembly

Maktab: A school for teaching children the elements of reading, writing and *Quranic* recitation

Maulana: Title usually applied to an *aalim*

Maulavi: A title equal to *Maulana*

Millat: Religion, religious community; sometimes used in the modern Muslim world as a synonym for 'nation'

Mir Munshi: Head clerk

Mofussil: The country stations and districts as opposed to the principal town

Moharram: Month in the Hijri calendar in which Hazrat Hussain was martyred

Mohurrir: A clerk

Muezzin: One who gives call to the faithful for prayers

Mufti: One qualified to give a *fatwah*

Mujahid (plural *Mujahidin*): one who is engaged in *jehad*

Mujtahid: A religious preceptor or instructor; usually applied to the Shia *ulama*

Mulla: Term often used for a Muslim schoolmaster

Munsif: The lowest grade of judge

Nadwat-ui-Ulama: 'The Congress of Muslim Theologians', and also the name given to the seminary established at Lucknow in the 1890s

Naib: Deputy
Namaz: Prayers
Naqshbandia: A sufi school of thought
Nawab: plural of *naib,* a style assumed by governors of provinces in later Mughal times and coming under the British to have the general meaning of prince
Nizam: Governor, ruler, prince
Nifaq: Schism
Papa: Father
Patwari: Village, or *zamindari*, record keeper and accountant; the lowest rank in the British revenue administration
Pesh-Imam: Prayer-leader
Peshkar: A subordinate court official
Pir: A religious guide; a sufi teacher or director
Pirzada: Son of a *pir*
Qaum: tribe, kinship group, religious community, nation according to period and context
Qazi: A judge trained in Islamic law, though often the title was inherited as a name by men with no such training
Quaid: Leader
Rais: An Indian of respectable position
Rama and Mahadev: Hindu deities
Sadr-amin: Subordinate magistrate under East India Company rule
Salana: Annual observance after a death
Sati: A virtuous wife; the faithful wife who burns herself with her husband's corpse, a custom banned by the British Indian administration
Satyagrah: Truth-force, Soul-force; Gandhian passive resistance
Saywam: Third day after a death
Shaikh-ul-Islam: The title applied to the mufti of Constantinople, the supreme lawgiver of the Ottoman Empire
Shams-ul-ulama: An honorific title, literally meaning 'sun among the *ulama*, bestowed by the British on leading *ulama*
Shash Mahi: Six-monthly observance after a death

Shariat: The path to be followed; the divinely revealed law of Islam; code of conduct

Sheristadar: The head Indian clerk in a collector's office or court of justice

Sherwani: A long coat, the official dress for the university community in Aligarh

Shia: The followers of Ali, the fourth caliph, who formed a heterodox sect in Islam

Shuddhi: 'Purification', the reconversion to Hinduism of those who have embraced other faiths

Stibdadi: Reactionaries

Subhanallah: By God's grace

Sufi: A Muslim mystic, so called after the early ascetics in Islam who wore garments of coarse wool (*suf*)

Sulahkul: Amity amongst all

Sunnat: The Prophet's precedence

Sunni: 'One who follows the trodden path'; an orthodox Muslim

Swadeshi: Produced in one' own country

Swaraj: Self-rule

Tafsir: Commentary on Islamic texts

Takflr: To declare one a *kafir*

Tehzib: Manners; civilization; civility

Takhullus: A poet's pen name

Taluqdar: In Uttar Pradesh, a superior *zamindar* who engaged with the state to collect the revenue from his own and other *zamindart* estates; after 1858, *taluqdars* in Oudh were given proprietary rights over the whole area from which they had previously collected revenue

Taluqdari: The rights of a *taluqdar*, collectively

Tanzim: Consolidation, Muslim efforts to resist the *Shuddhi* movement

Tehrik: Movement

Ulema or Ulama: Plural of *aalim*

Ulum: Plural of *ilam*

Vakil: An authorised pleader in a court of justice, though, more generally, it could mean any advocate or representative

Waaz: Sermon
Wa'iz: One who gives sermon
Wahabi: A follower of Abdul Wahab, an 18th-century Arab. With the emergence of Wahibism, the liberal and reformist trends in Islam were forcibly eliminated. Wahibism was puritanical and vigorous. Its message was straightforward: return to classical Islam. The followers of Islam believe that Hazrat Mohammad is the last Prophet and the Holy Quran is the last revelation of God.
Walima: Marriage feast
Waqf: An irrevocable settlement to safeguard the usufruct of property for charitable purposes; endowment
Zakat: The alms tax, one of the principal obligations of Islam, reckoned, usually, as a proportion of the Muslim's annual income
Zamindar: Under the British, the holder of a right of property in land, who individually or jointly engaged to pay rent to the government and had the right to collect rent and to regulate the occupancy of all other tenures on his estate
Zamindari: The rights of a *zamindar* collectively

NOTES

Chapter 1: Introduction

1 Lok Sabha Debates, Vol. XV, p. 147.

2 Rajya Sabha Debates, Vol. LXXX, no. 20.

3 Khurshid Ahmad Khan Yusufi, *Statements and Messages of the Quaid-e-Azam*, Vol. II, Lahore: Bazm-i-Iqbal, p. 1350.

4 Iftikhar Alam Khan, *Sir Syed: A Private Life* (unpublished English translation of Urdu book), p. 30.

5 Fatma Khanem (ed.), *Spirit of the Time: A Journal of Islamic, Indian and International Culture and Politics*, Aligarh: Muslim University Press, Vol. 1, 1938–1939.

6 M. Mujeeb, *Dr Zakir Husain: A Biography*, New Delhi: NBT, 1992, pp. 156–57.

7 Rahmani Begum Mohammad Ruknuddin Hassaan, *Sir Syed Ahmed Khan: The Politics of Educational Reforms*, Lahore: Vanguard, 1985, p. 191.

8 https://www.siasat.com/amu-produced-most-successful-muslim-personalities-in-india-2244164/ (accessed 28 August 2023)

9 Rahmani Begum Mohammad Ruknuddin Hassaan, *Sir Syed Ahmed Khan: The Politics of Educational Reforms*, Lahore: Vanguard, 1985, p. 10.

10 *The Times*, London, 6 April 1898.

11 Iftikhar Alam Khan, *Sir Syed: A Private Life* (unpublished English translation of Urdu book), p. 12.

12 *Hindustan Standard*, Calcutta (now Kolkata), 9 March 1970.

13 https://www.epw.in/journal/2010/09/editorials/gross-misconduct-aligarh-muslim-university.html (accessed 25 October 2022).

14 https://www.hindustantimes.com/lok-sabha-elections/ideological-conflict-takes-centre-stage-at-aligarh-muslim-university/

story-70hVdVW1HwOATL8YibHV4N.html (accessed 25 October 2022).

15 https://www.outlookindia.com/newsscroll/muslims-must-be-part-of-indias-growth-frank-islam/1476095 (accessed 22 August 2023).

16 https://www.newsclick.in/What-Aligarh-Muslim-University-Means-Muslims-India (accessed 22 August 2023).

17 https://theprint.in/opinion/amu-can-be-indian-national-university-not-remain-allah-miyans-university-in-ashraaf-hands/1421030/ (accessed 23 January 2023).

Chapter 2: Aligarh Town

1 https://www.livehistoryindia.com/amazing-india/2019/02/24/aligarhs-french-connection?fbclid=IwAR0W-UJH1zp9Wh0Ljik48qz2-m1SWKqQrmHbsCNnxcRpowTcf72Hv5oKzBw (accessed 4 April 2021).

2 Pratinav Anil, *Another India*, London: Hurst & Company, 2023, p. 12.

3 Irfan Ahmad, *Islamism and Democracy in India: The Transformation of Jamaat-e-Islami*, Princeton: Princeton University Press, 2009, p. 278.

4 Laurent Gayer & Christophe Jaffrelot (editors), *Muslims in Indian Cities: Trajectories of Marginalisation*, New Delhi: HarperCollins, 2012, p. 178.

5 http://timesofindia.indiatimes.com/articleshow/86340807.cms?utm_source=contentofinterest&utm_medium=text&utm_campaign=cppst (accessed 31 Jan 2024)

6 E.A. Mann, *Boundaries and Identities: Muslims, Work and Status in Aligarh*, New Delhi: Sage, 1992, p. 98.

7 Jamal M. Siddiqui, *Aligarh District: A Historical Survey from Ancient Times to 1803 AD, Aligarh: Department of History, 2018, p. 12.*

8 Edward Atkinson, *Descriptive and Historical Account of the Aligarh District* (1875), Reprint, Aligarh: Palala Press, 2015, p. 21.

Chapter 3: Sir Syed Walks the Razor's Edge

1 Eric Hobsbawm, *The Age of Revolution: Europe 1789–1848*, New Delhi: Viking, 1995, p. 139.

2 Quoted in Sir Syed Ahmad Khan's *Writings on 1857 Revolt: A Documentary Record*, edited by Rahat Abrar, New Delhi: Manak Publications, 2022, p. 20.

3 https://www.newageislam.com/books-and-documents/masood-alam-falahi-tr-new-age-islam/caste-and-caste-based-discrimination-among-indian-muslims--part-12-modern-indian-ulema-on-the-caste-question/d/3678 (accessed 23 April 2023).

4 Quoted by Hafeez Malik, *Sir Syed Ahmad Khan and Modern Modernization in India and Pakistan*, Karachi: Royal Book Company, 1988, pp. 175–176.

5 https://www.dawn.com/news/1277341/the-forgotten-future-sir-syed-and-the-birth-of-muslim-nationalism-in-south-asia (accessed 23 April 2021).

6 W.W. Hunter, *The Indian Muslamans*, Reprint, New Delhi: Rupa, 2002, p. 59.

7 Syed Ahmed Khan, *The Causes of the Indian Revolt,* translated by Francis Robinson, Pakistan: OUP, 2001, p 56

8 Syed Ahmad Khan, *Risala Khair Khwahan-e Musalmanan-e-Hind (An Account of the Loyal Mohammedans of India)*, Meerut, 1860, p. 20.

9 file:///C:/Users/Admin/Downloads/Surendranath%20Banerjee%20-%20a%20Nation%20in%20the%20Making%20(6).pdf (accessed 20 January 2024).

10 http://www.medbeats.com/amu/introductionofamu.htm (accessed 20 April 2021).

11 B.R. Nanda, *Road to Pakistan: The Life and Times of Mohammad Ali Jinnah*, New Delhi: Routledge, 2013, p. 154.

12 Nadeem F. Paracha, *The Forgotten Future: Sir Syed and the Birth of Muslim Nationalism in South Asia*, 15 August 2016, https://www.dawn.com/news/1277341 (accessed 15 June 2022).

13 Ayesha Jalal, *The Sole Spokesman: Jinnah, the Muslim League and the Demand for Pakistan*, Reprint, Cambridge University Press, 2007, p. 107.

14 http://www.columbia.edu/itc/mealac/pritchett/00islamlinks/txt_muhammadali_1930.html (accessed 10 October 2023).

15 Tufail Ahmad Manglori, *Towards A Common Destiny: A Nationist Manifesto*, translated by Ali Ashraf, New Delhi: People's Publishing House, 1994, p. 194.

16 *Institute Gazette*, journal from Aligarh, printed, published and edited by Sir Syed Ahmad Khan, 12 December 1887.

17 Ishwari Prasad, Hindu–Muslim Problems, https://aptribes.ap.gov.in/pdfViewer.jsp?pdf=3178&id=digital (accessed 15 April 2022).

18 Shan Mohammad, *Sir Syed Ahmad Khan: A Political Approach*, Meerut: Meenakshi, 1969, p. 82.
19 Kulliyat-i-Iqbal, *Lahore: Iqbal Academy Pakistan*, 1990, p. 533. English translation by A.J. Arberry, London, 1966, p. 54.
20 https://www.asianstudies.org/publications/eaa/archives/akhtar-hameed-khan-a-legendary-social-scientist/ (accessed 10 March 2021).
21 https://www.newageislam.com/letter-editor/arif-mohammad-khan/demeaning-sir-syed-glorify-clergy-indian-ulema-still-afraid-sir-syed-arif-mohammad-khan-writes-sultan-shahin/d/1963 (accessed 28 August 2023).
22 http://nuktacheen.blogspot.com/2019/04/syed-ahmad-khans-asar-us-sanadid-review.html?m=1 (accessed 21 March 2021).
23 Dr Ather Farauqui, General Secretary, Anjuman-i-Taraqqi-Hin, Personal Interview, 20 August 2023.
24 https://www.dawn.com/news/558122/a-passage-to-london (accessed 21 March 2021).
25 https://www.rekhta.org/couplets/sidhaaren-shaikh-kaaba-ko-ham-inglistaan-dekhenge-akbar-allahabadi-couplets?lang=hi (accessed 2 February 2024).
26 Ibid.
27 This was published in the monthly journal *Tahzibul Akhlaq*, established by Sir Syed Ahmad Khan as an organ of his educational, ethical and social reforms in December 1870. This is from the issue dated January 1988.
28 Rahat Abrar (ed.), *Sir Syed Ahmad Khan's Writings on 1857 Revolt: A Documentary Record*, New Delhi: Manak Publications, 2022, pp. 30–31.
29 Altaf Husain Hali, *Hyat-i-Javed (A Biography of Sir Syed)*, translated by David D Mathews, New Delhi: Rupa & Co, 1994, p. 311.
30 https://inc.in/brief-history-of-congress/1915-1925 (assessed 4 April 2021).
31 Tufail Ahmad Manglori, *Towards A Common Destiny: A Nationalist Manifesto*, translated by Ali Ashraf, New Delhi: People's Publishing House, 1994, p. 160.
32 Arif Mohammad Khan, *Text and Context*, New Delhi: Rupa, 2010, p. 203.

33 https://timesofindia.indiatimes.com/india/how-the-clergy-wanted-sir-syed-beheaded/articleshow/5137469.cms (accessed 10 May 2019).

34 Altaf Husain Hali, *Hayat-i-Javed (A Biography of Sir Syed)*, translated by David J Mathews, New Delhi: Rupa, 1994, p. 252.

35 Graham's work, even in the second edition, virtually stops at 1885, and though it ostensibly deals with the whole of Sir Syed's life, it concentrates in effect on the years 1869–85. Much space is devoted to long verbatim extracts from Sir Syed's letters and speeches, so *The Life and Work of Syed Ahmad Khan* becomes a sourcebook rather than an assessment. G.F.I. Graham, *The Life and Work of Syed Ahmad Khan*, Idarah-iAdabiyat-i-Delhi, 1974.

36 https://www.rediff.com/news/column/caught-between-worship-and-blame/20171028.htm#:~:text=So%20much%20so%20that%20when,dead%20things%20of%20the%20past (accessed 2 February 2024).

37 https://franpritchett.com/00islamlinks/txt_sir_sayyid_meerut_1888.html (accessed 2 February 2024).

38 Sir Sayyid Ahmad Khan, *Mukammal Majmu'ah Lekchers Wa Spiches*, Lahore 1891 p 353

39 Quoted by M. Mujeeb in *Dr Zakir Husain: A Biography*; New Delhi: NBT, 1992, p. 154.

40 Sayyid Tufayl Ahmed Mangalori, *Musalmanon Ka Raushan Mustaqbil* (The Bright Future of Muslim), New Delhi: Rekhta, 2022, p. 105.

41 Tufail Ahmad Manglori, *Towards A Common Destiny: A Nationalist Manifesto*, translated from Urdu to English by Ali Ashraf, New Delhi: People's Publishing House, 1994, p. 182.

42 https://unacademy.com/content/mppsc/study-material/history/indian-councils-act-1892/ (accessed 2 February 2024).

43 https://www.hudson.org/terrorism/sayyid-ahmad-khans-search-modern-muslim (accessed 10 March 2022).

44 Sayyad Iqbal Ali, *Sir Syed Ahmad Khan ka Safar nama-e-Punjab*, Aligarh: Sir Syed Academy, Aligarh Muslim University, 2009, p. 39.

45 Sayyid Tufayl Ahmed Mangalori, *Musalmanon Ka Raushan Mustaqbil.*

46 Mukhtar Masood, *Ḥarf-i shauq*, Karachi: Al Ata Publications, 2017, p. 45.

47 Iftikhar Alam Khan, *Sir Syed: A Private Life* (Unpublished English translation), 2021, p. 21.

48 https://www.hudson.org/terrorism/sayyid-ahmad-khans-search-modern-muslim (accessed 10 March 2022).
49 https://www.youthkiawaaz.com/2021/10/sir-syed-ahmad-khan-the-man-who-gave-a-new-life-to-the-muslims/ (accessed 2 February 2024).
50 https://rezavisblastfromthepast.co.in/2018/04/20/founding-a-college-or-a-university-ag-nooranis-analysis/ (accessed 20 August 2021).
51 Perwez Nazir, 'Religious. Social and Political Trends in Tahzib-ul-Akhlaq', MPhil dissertation, Aligarh Muslim University, 1995. https://core.ac.uk/download/pdf/144516237.pdf (accessed 2 Feb 2024).
52 Prof. Rasheed Ahmad Siddiqi, *Sir Syed's Concept of Western Education and Its Implementation in Aligarh*, Aligarh: The Aligarh Heritage Publications, 1978, pp. 6–7.
53 Sir Syed Memorial Lecture, 2006, Aligarh: Sir Syed Academy, 2007, p. 25.
54 Tufail Ahmsad Manglori, *Raushan Mustaqbil* (The Bright Future), New Delhi: Peoples Publishing House, 1994 p. 321.
55 Maulana Hussain Ahmed Madani, Reprint, Manohar, 2007, p. 149.
56 Mannan Ahmed Asid, *The Loss of Hindustan: The Invention of India*, 2020, Harvard University Press, 2021, p. 213.

Chapter 4: Web of History

1 Ramachandra Guha, *A Corner of a Foreign Field: The Indian History of a British Sport*, New Delhi: Penguin, 2014, p. 42.
2 Ibid., pp. 43–44.
3 http://www.littlemag.com/ghosts/davidlelyveld.html (accessed 15 August 2022).
4 Mir Wilayat Husain, *Aap Biti*, edited by Syed Mohammad of Tonk, Aligarh: Syed Hadi Hasan Zaidi, Habibullah Manzil, Lal Diggi Road, 1970, p. 126.
5 https://beyondheadlines.in/2020/12/humanism-of-an-ultraconservative-nawab-viqar-ul-mulk-and-his-english-daughter-in-law/ (accessed 10 August 2022).
6 *Khutoot-i-Viqar-ul-Mulk*, compiled by Mushtaq Ahmed, Aligarh Muslim University, Aligarh, pp. 44–46.

7 Quoted by Francis Robinson in *Separatism among Indian Muslims*, Oxford, 1993, pp. 399–400.
8 Shaikh Mohammad Abdullah, *Mushahidat-o-Tassurat*, Aligarh: Female Education Associations, 1969, p. 115.
9 Ibid., p. 117
10 Altaf Husain Hali, *Hayat-i-Javed (A Biography of Sir Syed)*, translated from Urdu by David J. Mathews, New Delhi: Rupa & Co., 1994, p. 34.
11 ekhta.org/qita/hamaarii-baaten-hii-baaten-hain-sayyad-kaam-kartaa-hai-akbar-allahabadi-qita?lang=hi
12 Tufail Ahmad Manglori, *Towards a Common Destiny: A Nationalist Manifesto*, translated by Ali Ashraf, New Delhi: People's Publishing House, 1994, p. 192.
13 Tufail Ahmad Manglori, *Towards a Common Destiny: A Nationalist Manifesto*, translated by Ali Ashraf, New Delhi: People's Publishing House, 1994, p. 215.
14 Khutoot-i-Viqar-ul-Mulk, compiled by Mushtaq Ahmed, *Aligarh Muslim University*, Aligarh, pp. 93
15 https://nation.com.pk/19-Jul-2021/the-missing-page (accessed 22 March 2022).
16 https://www.newindianexpress.com/opinions/2017/Oct/28/dont-deny-bhus-hindu-character-1685218.html#:~:text=Thus%20it%20is%20absurd%20to,impinge%20on%20our%20secular%20character (accessed 10 July 2024).
17 Khutoot-i-Viqar-ul-Mulk, compiled by Mushtaq Ahmed, *Aligarh Muslim University*, Aligarh, 2015 pp. 125.
18 Iftikhar Alam Khan, *Sir Syed: A Private Life* (unpublished English translation), p. 201.

Chapter 5: Sir Syed's Posthumous Baby Faces Pangs of Birth

1 http://aligarhmovement.com/karwaan_e_aligarh/sir_ziauddin (accessed 24 Jan 2022).
2 Aale Ahmad Suroor, *Khwab Baqi Hain*, Aligarh: Educational Book House, 1991, p. 231.
3 Andre Weil, *The Apprenticeship of a Mathematician*, translated by Jennifer Gag, Birkhäuser, 1992, p. 135.
4 Ibid., p. 137.

5 Juhi Gupta and Abdur Raheem Kidwai (editors), *Oxford of the East: Aligarh Muslim University 1920–2020*, Centenary Commemorative Volume, New Delhi: Viva Books, 2021, p. 123.
6 H.N. Mitra (editor), *The Indian Annual Register*, Vol. 1, 1920, p. 121.
7 Ibid.

Chapter 6: Clouds of Separation Hover over the AMU

1 https://asianstudies.github.io/area-studies/SouthAsia/Ideas/lika/iframe.html (accessed 15 April 2021).
2 https://timesofindia.indiatimes.com/blogs/beyond-the-burqa/sir-syed-and-scientific-awakening/ (accessed 23 March 2022).
3 Ṭufail Aḥmad Manglaurī, *Towards a Common Destiny: A Nationalist Manifesto* (English translation of *Musalmanon ka Roshan Mustaqbil*), New Delhi: People's Publishing House, 1994, p. 102.
4 https://www.greaterkashmir.com/todays-paper/aba-haleem-a-forgotten-muslim-political-scientist (accessed 15 April 2023).
5 W.C. Smith, *Modern Islam in India*, Read Books, 2006, p. 115.
6 Amber Heather Abbas, Narratives of Belonging: Aligarh Muslim University and the Partitioning of South Asia, unpublished dissertation, University of Texas at Austen, 2012, pp. 152–53. https://repositories.lib.utexas.edu/server/api/core/bitstreams/d2bc40e3-2593-4798-b7d5-952ad71fc19b/content (accessed 5 February 2024).
7 A.B.A. Haleem to Maulavi Mohd. Ashiq Saheb Warsi: Report of the P.V.C. to the University Court, 25 October 1938, FMA, F 1094/340–343.
8 https://journals.sagepub.com/doi/10.1177/001946468502200101 (accessed 15 September 2021).
9 Habib Manzer, *Proceedings of the Indian History Congress*, Vol. 69, Indian History Congress, 2008, pp. 563–573.
10 https://theprint.in/opinion/jinnah-once-famously-called-amu-the-arsenal-of-muslim-india/57174/ (accessed 5 February 2024).
11 Ibid.
12 Dharam Veera, *Reminiscences: Memoirs of a Civil Servant*, New Delhi: Vikas, 1975, pp. 29–31
13 https://www.paulbrass.com/the_production_of_hindu_muslim_violence_in_contemporary_india_16681.htm (accessed 21 March 2021).

14 https://www.outlookindia.com/national/secularism-under-siege-several-parts-of-indian-subcontinent-witness-demise-of-pluralism-magazine-236057 (accessed 20 April 2022).
15 Kalim Siddiqui, *Conflict, Crisis, and War in Pakistan*, MacMillan Press, 1972, p. 52.
16 Ibid., p. 53.
17 Mukhtar Zaman, Students' Role in the Pakistan Movement, unpublished doctorate desertion, Karachi, 1978, p. 35.
18 https://archive.org/stream/SomeRecentSpeechesAndWritingsOfMr.Jinnah-JamiluddinAhmad/118546877-Some-Recent-Speeches-and-Writings-of-Mr-Jinnah-1942_djvu.txt (accessed 21 March 2021).
19 Transfer of Power, Vol. 6, Document no. 219, p. 509.
20 https://www.indiatoday.in/magazine/cover-story/story/20100329-is-india-forgetting-its-own-narrative-of-openness-742394-2010-03-17 (accessed 28 August 2023).

Chapter 7: A New Beginning

1 Shamim Akhtar, 'Aligarh Muslim University: A Study of the Critical Period of Transition', *Social Scientist*, Vol. 44, No. 7/8 (July–August 2016), p. 80.
2 Durga Das (editor), *Sardar Patel: Selective Correspondence*, Ahmedabad: Navjivan Trust, 2011, Vol. 3, pp. 424–427.
3 Personal Interview, New Delhi, 25 October 1997.
4 https://timesofindia.indiatimes.com/india/partition-recalled-couldnt-live-in-a-country-meant-for-just-one-religion/articleshow/53700657.cms (accessed 25 August 2023).
5 Ibid.
6 Personal Interview, New Delhi, 12 August 2019.
7 Violette Graff, 'Aligarh's Long Quest for Minority Status: AMU (Amendment) Act, 1981', *Economic & Political Weekly*, 11 August 1990.
8 Lok Sabha Debates, Vol LXI, p. 235.
9 Lok Sabha Debates, Vol LXI, p. 238.
10 M. Mujib, *Dr Zakir Hussain*, New Delhi: NBT, 1992, p. 105.
11 https://indiankanoon.org/doc/161666/ (accessed 28 October 2023).
12 Piara Singh Gill, *Up Against Odds: Autobiography of an Indian Scientist*, New Delhi: Allied, 1992, p. 113.
13 Ibid.

14 M. Mujib, Dr Zakir Hussain, New Delhi: NBT, 1992, p. 163.
15 Ibid., p. 164.
16 Rajya Sabha Proceedings, Vol LXI, p. 204.
17 https://www.scribd.com/document/123074361/Maulana-Azad-s-Convocation-Address-at-Aligarh-Muslim-University-20-02-1949 (accessed 25 March 2022).
18 https://www.thenehru.org/2017/11/nehrus-speech-at-amu-convocation-1948.html (accessed 25 April 2022).
19 H.Y. Sharda Prasad and A.K. Damodaran (editors), *Selected Works of Jawaharlal Nehru* (Second Series), Vol. 29, 1 June–31 August 1955, New Delhi: OUP, 2005, p. 325.
20 Salman Khurshid, *At Home in India: A Restatement of Indian Muslims*, New Delhi: Vikas, 1986, p. 50.
21 https://indianexpress.com/article/education/amu-to-govt-idea-to-drop-muslim-from-name-preposterous-5338265/ (accessed 25 March 2021).
22 Badr-ud-Din Tyabji, *More Memoirs of an Egoist*, New Delhi: Roli Books, 1988, p. 203.
23 Personal Interview with Professor V.S. Rekhi, Aligarh, 15 September 1997.
24 Badr-ud-Din Tyabji, *More Memoirs of an Egoist*, p. 105.
25 Personal Interview, New Delhi, 20 October 1997.
26 Personal Interview, Aligarh, 15 September 1997.

Chapter 8: An 'Ugly Aberration'

1 Personal Interview with P.V. George, Aligarh, 15 September 1997.
2 Interview with Dr Basir Ahmad, convenor of the Students Action Commitee and a former president of the AMU Students Union on 25 October 1997
3 Personal Interview, Aligarh, 25 January 2024.
4 Ibid.
5 M.C. Chagla, *Roses in December*, Bombay: Bharatiya Vidya Bhawan, 1973, p. 215.
6 M.C. Chagla, *Roses in December*, Bombay: Bharatiya Vidya Bhawan, 1973, p. 380.
7 Ibid.
8 https://eparlib.nic.in/bitstream/123456789/3115/1/lsd_03_12_02-09-1965.pdf#search=Aligath%20Muslim%20University%20Bill%201965 (accessed 20 January 2024).

9 Ibid.
10 M.C. Chagla, *Roses in December*, Bombay: Bharatiya Vidya Bhawan, 1973, p. 387.
11 The Aligarh Muslim University (Amendment) Bill, 1965/ 1965-09-15, https://sansad.in/rs/debates/officials/ (accessed 6 February 2024).
12 Ibid.
13 Ibid.
14 Ibid.
15 https://eparlib.nic.in/bitstream/123456789/2513/1/lsd_05_04_01-06-1972.pdf (accessed 6 February 2024).
16 https://rsdebate.nic.in/bitstream/123456789/464434/2/ID_80_02061972_20_p8_p202_11.pdf (accessed 6 February 2024).
17 https://www.ghazalikhan.com/talking-to-badar-kazmi-the-last-soldier-of-dr-abdul-jalil-faridi-a-forgotten-selfless-muslim-politician-in-independent-india/ (accessed 6 February 2024).
18 S.A.H. Haqqi, *National Herald*, 15 March 1973.
19 *Hindustan Times*, 16 January 1977.
20 *Hindustan Times*, 25 March 1977.
21 Personal Interview with Professor V.S. Rekhi, the then President of the AMUTA, Aligarh, 25 October 1997.
22 Opinion of the Minorities Commission, December 1978.
23 H.M. Seervai, *Constitutional Law of India*, 4th edn, Gurgaon: Universal Law Publishing, 2007, p. 305.
24 https://sanjeev.sabhlokcity.com/Misc/minoo-masani-at-90-freedom-first-1995.pdf (accessed 6 February 2024), p. 86.
25 https://eparlib.nic.in/bitstream/123456789/1986/1/lsd_06_07_03-05-1979.pdf#search=null%20[1970%20TO%201979]%2006 (accessed 6 February 2024).
26 https://eparlib.nic.in/bitstream/123456789/838858/1/06_VII_03-05-1979_p144_p186_PII.pdf#search=%20Motion%20to%20Consid (accessed 6 February 2024).
27 Ibid.
28 https://rsdebate.nic.in/bitstream/123456789/422935/1/PD_107_15121978_19_p142_p189_15.pdf (accessed 6 February 2022).
29 https://eparlib.nic.in/bitstream/123456789/834008/1/07_VII_22-12-1981_p192_p231_PII.pdf#search=null%20Part%202(Other%20than%20Questions%20And%20Answers)%20Somnath%20

Chatterjee%20Indrajit%20Gupta%2007%20Aligarh%20 Muslim%20University%20(Third%20Amendment)%20Bill%20 Chandrajit%20Yadav%20G.%20Lakshmanan%20Arif%20 Mohammed%20Khan (accessed 6 February 2024).

30 Ibid.

31 https://rsdebate.nic.in/bitstream/123456789/395706/1/PD_120_24121981_24_p354_p504_47.pdf (accessed 6 February 2024).

32 Ibid.

33 Ibid.

34 Ibid.

35 Salman Khurshid, *At Home in India: A Restatement of Indian Muslims*, New Delhi: Vikas, 1986, p. 53.

36 Iftikhar Alam Khan, *Sir Syed: A Private Life* (unpublished English translation of Urdu book), p. 120.

Chapter 9: Hindu and Muslim Bigots Join Hands

1 Mirza Saeed-uz-Zafar Chaghtai, *Memoirs of Three Continents: Tell you the Truth and Nothing but the Truth*, 2015, iUniverse, p. 776.

2 Mirza Saeed-uz-Zafar Chaghtai, *Memoirs of Three Continents: Tell you the Truth and Nothing but the Truth*, 2015, iUniverse, p. 778.

3 Ibid.

4 Ibid.

5 Salman Khurshid, *At Home in India: A Restatement of Indian Muslims*, New Delhi: Vikas, 1986, p. 61.

6 Salman Khurshid, *At Home in India: A Restatement of Indian Muslims*, New Delhi: Vikas, 1986, p. 63.

7 *Indian Express*, 14 January 1981.

8 Romila Thapar, *Academic Freedom and the AMU Crisis*, The Radical, Humanist, April 1981.

9 Personal Interview, Aligarh, 25 January 1983.

10 https://www.rediff.com/news/slide-show/slide-show-1-what-ails-aligarh-muslim-university/20091118.htm (accessed 21 March 2022).

11 M.N. Farooqi, *My Days at Aligarh*, Delhi: Idarah-i-adabiyat-i-Delhi, 1998, p. 32

12 Personal Interview, 20 June 1996

13 Personal Interview with Professor H.A.S. Jafri, Aligarh, 15 October 2019.
14 https://timesofindia.indiatimes.com/city/agra/eminent-historians-rally-behind-suspended-amu-prof/articleshow/39059106.cms (accessed 20 August 2022).
15 Ibid.
16 https://timesofindia.indiatimes.com/city/agra/amu-dumping-ground-for-retired-generals-bureaucrats/articleshow/46944968.cms (accessed 20 August 2022).
17 https://timesofindia.indiatimes.com/city/agra/no-mixing-work-with-facebook-anymore-at-amu/articleshow/45007129.cms assessed (accessed 15 August 2022).
18 Personal Interview, Aligarh, 20 September 2013.
19 https://timesofindia.indiatimes.com/city/agra/amu-vc-justifies-wider-consultation-for-appointing-successor/articleshow/51605018.cms (accessed 15 August 2022).
20 https://timesofindia.indiatimes.com/home/education/aligarh-muslim-universitys-vc-selection-process-in-muddle/articleshow/56990817.cms (accessed 20 April 2023).
21 https://timesofindia.indiatimes.com/city/agra/amu-vc-rejects-ugcs-inbreeding-charge-says-panel-has-said-same-thing-for-33-yrs/articleshow/60903539.cms (accessed 20 April 2023).
22 Mirza Saeed-uz-Zafar Chaghtai, *Memoirs of Three Continents: Tell you the Truth and Nothing but the Truth*, 2015, iUniverse, p. 770.
23 https://theprint.in/ground-reports/amu-vc-naima-khatoon-is-facing-questions-from-bearded-elite-smashing-glass-ceilings-daily/2067951/

Chapter 10: Tussle over Admissions

1 Dr Jasim Mohammad, *Aligarh Muslim University's Minority Character: A Comprehensive Study*, Alisha Publications, 2016, p. 95.
2 Ibid., p. 99.
3 https://www.courtkutchehry.com/Judgement/Search/AdvancedV2?s_acts=Postgraduate%20Medical%20Education%20Regulations,%202000§ion_art=regulation&s_article_val=9%20(IV) (accessed 4 February 2024).

4 Personal Interview, Aligarh, 30 September 1989.
5 Badruddin Tayyabji, *More Memoirs of an Egoist*, New Delhi: Roli Books, 1988, p. 108.
6 https://timesofindia.indiatimes.com/india/hc-quashes-minority-status-of-amu/articleshow/1252474.cms (accessed 20 November 2023).
7 https://indiankanoon.org/doc/1963676/ (accessed 20 November 2023).
8 https://archives.peoplesdemocracy.in/2005/0605/06052005_irfan%20habib.html (accessed 20 November 2023).
9 Personal Interview, New Delhi, 20 October 2022.
10 https://thewire.in/law/governments-view-on-minority-character-of-aligarh-muslim-university-is-unconstitutional (accessed 25 March 2023).
11 M.N. Farooqi, *My Days at Aligarh*, Delhi: Idarah Adabiyat-I Delli, 1998, p. 124.

Chapter 11: Minority Status: A Matter of Life and Death

1 https://timesofindia.indiatimes.com/city/agra/minority-status-matter-of-life-and-death-amu-vc/articleshow/50536874.cms (accessed 24 March 2017).
2 https://indiankanoon.org/doc/1804721/ (accessed 20 January 2024).
3 https://frontline.thehindu.com/the-nation/article30207026.ece (accessed 24 March 2017).
4 https://indiankanoon.org/doc/1963676/ (accessed 24 January 2024).
5 https://www.dailypioneer.com/2016/india/amu-not-a-minority-varsity.html (accessed 24 January 2024).
6 https://timesofindia.indiatimes.com/india/government-shifts-stand-against-minority-tag-for-aligarh-muslim-university/articleshow/50539503.cms?from=mdr (accessed on 5 February 2024).
7 https://eparlib.nic.in/bitstream/123456789/2079/1/lsd_07_07_22-12-1981.pdf (accessed 24 January 2024).
8 Ibid.
9 Ibid.
10 Report of the Aligarh Muslim University Enquiry Committee, Aligarh 1961.
11 Personal Interview, Noida, 28 July 2023.
12 Ibid.

13 https://scroll.in/latest/893064/amu-says-proposal-to-drop-muslim-from-its-name-is-preposterous-the-indian-express (accessed 10 August 2021).
14 https://timesofindia.indiatimes.com/edit-page/say-no-to-amu-reservations/articleshow/1261600.cms?from=mdr (accessed 6 February 2024).
15 https://scroll.in/article/801890/attorney-general-rohatgi-has-got-it-all-wrong-about-aligarh-muslim-university-former-registrar (accessed 6 February 2024).
16 Personal Interview, Aligarh, 20 September 2016.
17 https://archives.peoplesdemocracy.in/2005/0605/06052005_irfan%20habib.html (accessed 6 February 2024)
18 Ibid.
19 https://www.rediff.com/news/column/history-backs-amus-claim-as-a-muslim-university/20160216.htm (accessed 25 May 2022).
20 Personal Interview, Noida, 26 September 2016.
21 M.N. Farooqi, *My Days at Aligarh*, Delhi: Idarah-i-adabiyat-i-Delhi, 1998, p. 19.
22 https://www.quotemaster.org/Rights (accessed 25 March 2023).
23 Veer Savarkar, *Indian War of Independence 1857*, New Delhi: Abhishek Publications, 2019, p. 278.

Chapter 12: Tradition Trap for Second Sex

1 Quoted in Sadaf Jaffer, Ismat Chughtai, Progressive Literature and Formations of the Indo-Muslim Secular, 1911-1991, Doctoral dissertation, Harvard University, Graduate School of Arts and Sciences, 2015.
2 'Sir Syed and Women's Education' lecture, January 2015, Aligarh, AMU: Publication Division, 2016, p. 12.
3 Gail Minault, *Secluded Scholars: Women's Education and Muslim Social Reform in Colonial India*, New Delhi: Oxford University Press, 1997, p. 115.
4 https://timesofindia.indiatimes.com/city/agra/sir-syed-opposed-equal-rights-for-women-lelyveld/articleshow/45957615.cms (accessed 20 October 2022).
5 Quoted in https://www.outlookindia.com/national/remembering-sheikh-abdullah-legacy-on-muslim-girls-education-how-he-saw-

it-differently-than-sir-syed-weekender_story-275376 (accessed 20 October 2022).

6 Quoted in https://www.outlookindia.com/national/remembering-sheikh-abdullah-legacy-on-muslim-girls-education-how-he-saw-it-differently-than-sir-syed-weekender_story-275376 (accessed 20 October 2022).

7 https://kashmirlife.net/another-sheikh-abdullah-issue-34-vol-12-252530/?fbclid=IwAR1H5sMYOSPj8KjMROIFq1_59Ph-43N3u0OqpJ8uRMC7sAeDnertw9DmkGQ (accessed 21 March 2023).

8 *The Hindu*, Aligarh Memories, 26 June 2005.

9 Nasreen Ahmad, Muslim Leadership and Women's Education, 1886–1947, New Delhi: Three Essays Collective, 2013, p. 38.

10 https://www.newsclick.in/Khwaja-Altaf-Husain-Hali-Our-Times?fbclid=IwAR3uHbDu_Zwytb86wpbnSxtrcWEKMowUl8oulN-dFI5jxGckGFq9RGvYWIk (accessed 18 February 2021).

11 https://thewire.in/women/jamia-aligarh-muslim-university-women (accessed 30 March 2023).

12 The 'relationship' between Kashmir-origin poet Allama Iqbal and the Mumbai-born Bohra Muslim intellectual Atiya Fyzee (1877–1967), the first Muslim woman who studied at Cambridge. Born to Hasnally Feyzhyder, a Mumbai cloth and spices trader connected with the Ottoman Empire, and his second wife, also his cousin, she was born in Istanbul. She studied at a Catholic English School and later was enrolled at Maira Grey College England. In 1905, Iqbal visited Europe to study philosophy at Cambridge and law at London's Lincoln Inn. His dissertation on Persian metaphysics earned him a doctorate from Munich University. It was during this stay that he started knowing Atiya Fyzee, then a sensation in the academic circles of the subcontinent. Her correspondence with Allama Shibli Nomani is also well-known.

13 Quoted by Rahat Abrar in *Muslim Female Education: Veil to Moon*, New Delhi: Reference Press, 2014, p. 90.

14 Mohammad Alimuddin, Rasheed Ahmad Siddiqi ki Khaka Nigari ka Tanquidi Jaiza, Unpublished Doctorate Dissertation, Aligarh, 1995.

15 Quoted by Rahat Abrar in *Muslim Female Education: Veil to Moon*, New Delhi: Reference Press, 2014, p. 158.

16 https://old.amu.ac.in/emp/studym/100000548.pdf (accessed 25 March 2022).

17 Ismat Chugtai, *In Her Own Words: Letters & Interview*, translated by Tahira Naqvi, New Delhi: Women Unlimited, 2023, p. 34.

18 Ishrat Mustaq and Sajad Hassan Khan, https://mainstreamweekly.net/article10315.html (accessed 23 October 2022).

19 https://thecompanion.in/struggle-of-dissent-of-the-female-students-of-aligarh-muslim-university (accessed 25 March 2022).

20 https://www.ndtv.com/india-news/why-some-women-cant-enter-the-aligarh-muslim-university-library-691874 (accessed 5 February 2024).

21 https://thewire.in/women/jamia-aligarh-muslim-university-women (accessed 25 March 2022).

22 Ibid.

23 https://old.amu.ac.in/emp/studym/100000548.pdf (accessed 25 March 2022).

24 Lubna Kazim (editor), *A Woman of Substance*, New Delhi: Kali/Zuban, 2005, p. 135.

25 https://thesite.in/nasa-scientist-dr-hashima-hasan-thanks-amu-for-helping-her-materialise-her-dreams (accessed 25 March 2023).

26 Ammad Aqdas Alvi, linkedin.com/posts/ammad-aqdas-alvi-ab659b15_this-legend-is-a-professor-at-karachi-university-activity-7142154294270607360-RdCy (accessed 20 January 2024).

Chapter 13: A VC Faces Tantrums from Six Masters

1

2 https://indianexpress.com/article/opinion/columns/prakash-javadekar-vice-chancellors-amu-allahabad-university-3067335/ (accessed 25 March 2023).

3 Ibid.

4 Salman Khurshid, *At Home in India: A Restatement of Indian Muslims*, New Delhi: Vikas, 1985, p. 63.

5 Saiyid Hamid, AMU and Discontentment, *Asian Age*, 5 September 1995.

6 Personal Interview, Aligarh, 1 October 1989.

7 Badruddin Tyabji, *More Memoirs of an Egoist*, New Delhi: Roli Books, 1988, p. 245.

8 Personal Interview, New Delhi, April 1991.

9 https://indianexpress.com/article/opinion/columns/ugc-aligarh-muslim-university-vc-appointment-supreme-court-3049943/ (accessed 20 January 2024).
10 What Ails our University, *The Hindustan Times*, 4 March 1991.
11 *The Hindustan Times*, Aligarh VC Selection Reached a Piquant Situation,18 Feb 1995.
12 Bibulous Rites of a Full Mussalman, *The Times of India*, 1 January 1995.
13 M.K. Kaw, An Outsider Everywhere: Everywhere Revelations by an Insider, New Delhi: Konark, 2012, p. 203.
14 Lt Gen. Zameer Uddin Shah, *The Sarkari Mussalman: The Life and Travails of a Soldier Educationist*, New Delhi: Konark 2019, p. 132.
15 Ibid.
16 Ibid.,
17 Ibid.,
18 https://www.hindustantimes.com/cities/lucknow-news/eyebrows-raised-as-panel-headed-by-amu-acting-v-c-shortlists-wife-for-post-101699037189494.html- (accessed 3 February 2024).
19 Why is the AMU so Vulnerable to Controversy, *The Hindu*, 20 March 1995.
20 https://www.tribuneindia.com/news/archive/comment/a-minister-and-a-vice-chancellor-210762 (accessed 20 January 2024).
21 https://theprint.in/opinion/amu-can-be-indian-national-university-not-remain-allah-miyans-university-in-ashraaf-hands/1421030/ (accessed 24 March 2022).

Chapter 14: Feuding Feudal of AMU

1 Personal interview with Prof. V.S. Rekha, Aligarh, 25 September 1997.
2 Ibid.
3 Ibid.
4 Mirza Saeed-uuz-Zafar Chaghtai, *Memoirs of Three Continents: Tell You the Truth and Nothing but the Truth*, iUniverse, 2015, pp. 790–91.
5 Ibid.
6 Badruddin Tayyabji, *More Memoirs of an Egoist*, New Delhi: Roli Books, 1988, p. 246.
7 Personal interview, Chandigarh, November 2011.

8 Saiyid Hamid in Syyed Mansoor Agha, *Memorium*, New Delhi: Indian Education Foundation, 2019, p. 64.
9 Interview with Prof. V.S. Rekha, Aligarh, 25 September 1997.
10 Interview with Prof. V.S. Rekha, Aligarh, 25 September 1997.
11 Lt Gen. Zameer Uddin Shah, *The Sarkari Mussalman*, New Delhi: Konark Publishers, 2019, p. 157.
12 Ibid., p. 158.
13 Personal interview, Aligarh, 27 January 2024.
14 M.N. Farooqi, *My Days at Aligarh*, Delhi: Idarah-i-adabiyat-i-Delhi, 1998, p. 35.
15 https://www.ummid.com/news/2013/June/03.06.2013/dr_aziz_ur_rehman_amu.html#:~:text=This%20'tale'%20is%20about%20Dr,in%20Chemistry%20in%20that%20country (accessed 26 March 2022).
16 https://www.academia.edu/15980108/Prof_Ahsan_Jan_Qaisar_1929_2011_Obituary_of_a_Renowned_Historian (accessed 20 March 2023).
17 Ibid.
18 Personal interview, New Delhi, January 2021.

Chapter 15: Are Families Holding AMU to Ransom?

1 Personal interview, Gurgaon, 25 October 2022.
2 M.N. Farooqi, *My Days at Aligarh*, Delhi: Idarah-i-adabiyat-i-Delhi, 1998, p. 38.
3 M.N. Farooqi, *My Days at Aligarh*, Delhi: Idarah-i-adabiyat-i-Delhi, 1998, p. 17.

Chapter 16: *Shagirds*

1 Personal interview with Syed Hashim Ali, Aligarh, 20 September 1987.
2 Akhtar ul Iman, *Is Aabaad Kharaabey Mein*, Urdu Akademy, 1996, p. 112.
3 J.L. Nehru, *Autobiography*, New Delhi: Oxford, 2002, p. 303.
4 Personal interview, New Delhi, 19 August 1996.
5 M.N. Farooqi, *My Days at Aligarh*, Delhi: Idarah-i- adabiyat-i-Delhi, 1998, p. 32.
6 Lt Gen. Zameer Uddin Shah, *The Sarkari Myussalman*, New Delhi: Konark Publishers, 2019, p. 160.

7 Ibid.

Chapter 17: When Jackals Ruled the Roost

1 https://www.indiatoday.in/magazine/nation/story/20010402-dust-settles-on-kanpur-week-of-violence-but-spectre-of-simi-youth-remains-775409-2001-04-01 (accessed 20 March 2023).
2 Personal interview, Noida, 10 April 2019.
3 *The Pioneer*, 4 December 2000.
4 High-powered committee, 1994, report placed before the Executive Council of the Aligarh Muslim University, 25 Feb 1997.
5 https://indianexpress.com/article/news-archive/print/you-are-being-watched-2/ (accessed 20 March 2022).
6 https://indianexpress.com/article/india/india-news-india/amu-law-and-order-deteriorating-say-teachers/ (accessed 3 February 2024).
7 Ibid.

Chapter 18: Fake Morality Finds a Scapegoat

1 https://www.epw.in/journal/2010/09/editorials/gross-misconduct-aligarh-muslim-university.html (accessed 10 April 2023).
2 https://timesofindia.indiatimes.com/city/agra/five-years-after-gay-amu-profs-death-lover-breaks-silence-on-affair/articleshow/50224046.cms (accessed 10 April 2023).
3 https://www.hindustantimes.com/india/harassed-amu-girl-hunts-for-justice/story-6oRnPZh6BHSHqLBvz9b01M.html (accessed 10 April 2023).
4 https://timesofindia.indiatimes.com/city/lucknow/another-amu-girl-alleges-sexual-harassment/articleshow/1499608.cms (accessed 10 April 2023).
5 Ibid.
6 https://mumbaimirror.indiatimes.com/news/india/ex-amu-girl-student-on-hunger-strike-to-protest-molestation/articleshow/15635569.cms (accessed 3 February 2024).
7 https://www.hindustantimes.com/cities/others/sexual-harassment-amu-prof-s-acquittal-quashed-sentenced-to-one-year-s-ri-101650737375623.html (accessed 20 May 2023).
8 https://timesofindia.indiatimes.com/city/agra/no-foreigner-should-come-to-india-to-study-says-iranian-scholar-at-amu/articleshow/59363864.cms (accessed 20 January 2024).

9 https://timesofindia.indiatimes.com/city/lucknow/sexual-harassment-case-cops-to-issue-notice-to-amu-professor/articleshow/27548958.cms (accessed 20 May 2023).
10 https://www.telegraphindia.com/india/aligarh-axe-on-harassed/cid/739209 (accessed 3 February 2024).
11 https://indianexpress.com/article/lucknow/at-aligarh-muslim-university-malappuram-girls-protest-all-male-panel-to-probe-harassment/ (accessed 20 May 2023).
12 https://elegalix.allahabadhighcourt.in/elegalix/WebShowJudgment.do?judgmentID=6979679 (accessed 20 May 2023).
13 Lt Gen. Zameer Uddin Shah, *The Sarkari Mussalman: The Life and Travails of a Soldier Educationist*, New Delhi: Konark, 2019, p. 135.
14 Ibid. The university preferred to forget that its first chancellor was a veiled woman Her Highness Sultan Jahan Begum, Ruler of Bhopal (December 1920–14 May 1930).
15 https://scroll.in/article/748241/irfan-habib-the-indian-variant-of-secularism-opens-the-door-to-majority-communalism (accessed 20 May 2023).
16 Personal Interview, New Delhi, March 2021.
17 Quoted in https://www.firstpost.com/politics/travels-of-a-political-pilgrim-is-rise-of-religiosity-on-amu-campus-a-precursor-to-another-partition-3284388.html (accessed 20 May 2023).
18 Ibid.
19 Ibid.

Chapter 19: The Luxury of Enquiries

1 https://www.telegraphindia.com/india/probe-costlier-than-scam-rs-82-lakh-spent-on-inquiry-into-alleged-rs-5-lakh-misuse/cid/369759 (accessed 20 August 2016).
2 https://timesofindia.indiatimes.com/india/new-panel-formed-to-probe-allegations-against-amu-vc/articleshow/5540361.cms?utm_source=contentofinterest&utm_medium=text&utm_campaign=cppst (accessed 20 August 2016).
3 Altaf Husain Hali, *Hayat-i-Javed* (A Biography of Sir Sayyid), translated by David J. Mathews, New Delhi: Rupa, 1994, pp. 334–340.
4 Ibid.
5 Iftikhar Alam Khan, *Sir Syed: A Private Life* (English translation), unpublished, p. 54.

6 Sir Syed Ahmad Khan, *Seerat-i Faridi*, edited by Mahmood Ahmad Barkati, Karachi: Pakistan Academy, 1964, p. 130.

7 Altaf Husain Hali, *Hayat-i-Javed* (A Biography of Sir Sayyid), translated by David J. Mathews, New Delhi: Rupa, 1994, pp. 354.

8 Iftikhar Alam Khan, *Sir Syed: A Private Life* (English translation), unpublished, p. 194.

9 https://www.jstor.org/stable/44147222 (accessed 6 February 2024).

10 https://dn790004.ca.archive.org/0/items/dli.ministry.19823/2647.pdf (accessed 6 February 2024).

Chapter 20: Fading Wit, Humour and Graciousness

1 Khushwant Singh, *The Big Book of Malice*, New Delhi: Penguin, 2024, p. 280.

2 Ibid, p. 281.

3 Personal Interview, Aligarh, September 1993.

4 Ibid.

5 Ibid.

6 Mohammad Zakir Ali Khan, *Riwayat-e-Aligarh*, AMU Old Boys Association of Pakistan, Karachi, 1993, p. 156.

7 Mohammad Zakir Ali Khan, *Riwayat-e-Aligarh*, AMU Old Boys Association of Pakistan, Karachi, 1993, p. 276.

8 Ibid., p. 205.

9 Personal interview, Aligarh, August 1965.

10 Personal interview with Dr Rahat Abrar, PRO, AMU, July 2001.

11 Ibid.

12 Personal Interview with Prof. Tariq Jilani, at his residence, October 1995.

Chapter 21: Aligarh's Historic Cafés

1 http://twocircles.net/2009oct29/tale_amu_s_two_upsurges.html (accessed 10 August 2023).

Chapter 22: Nascent Fascism Targets AMU

1 https://www.hindustantimes.com/lok-sabha-elections/ideological-conflict-takes-centre-stage-at-aligarh-muslim-university/story-70hVdVW1HwOATL8YibHV4N.html (accessed 20 January 2024).

2 https://www.newslaundry.com/2019/02/21/aligarh-muslim-university-republic-tv-sedition-bjp (accessed 20 January 2024).
3 Dr Aishwarya Pandit, *Claiming Citizenship and Nation: Muslim Politics and State Building in North India 1947–1986*, New Delhi: Routledge, 2022, p. 79.
4 https://economictimes.indiatimes.com/news/politics-and-nation/muhammad-ali-jinnahs-portrait-at-amu-sparks-row/articleshow/63987397.cms?from=mdr (accessed 20 January 2024).
5 Personal Interview with Mashkoor Ahmad Usmani, Aligarh, 15 May 2018.
6 https://scroll.in/article/878367/opinion-hindutva-groups-assault-on-amu-was-never-about-jinnah-it-had-a-more-sinister-motive (accessed 10 August 2023).
7 https://www.dawn.com/news/1709519#:~:text=Spread%20over%20three%20hand%2Dwritten,the%20%E2%80%9Cexecutrix%20and%20executors.%E2%80%9D (accessed 3 February 2024).

Chapter 23: 'Secular Controversy' over 'Marxist Raja' in 'Muslim University'

1 https://timesofindia.indiatimes.com/city/agra/bjp-wants-donors-birth-anniversary-celebration-amu-says-no/articleshow/45300276.cms (accessed 10 August 2023).
2 Quoted in https://swarajyamag.com/politics/the-secular-controversy-over-a-marxist-raja (accessed 10 August 2023).
3 https://timesofindia.indiatimes.com/city/agra/bjp-mp-slams-amu-for-not-celebrating-jat-kings-birth-anniversary/articleshow/72322544.cms (accessed 10 August 2023).
4 F.M. Bailey, *Mission to Tashkent*, New Delhi: Oxford University Press, 2002, p. 301.
5 https://swarajyamag.com/politics/who-was-raja-mahendra-pratap-singh-the-jat-hero-pm-modi-and-yogi-adityanath-are-taking-steps-towards-in-uttar-pradesh (accessed 10 August 2023).
6 Humayun Ansari, 'Maulana Barkatullah Bhopali's Transnationalism', in *Transnational Islam in Interwar Europe: Muslim Activists and Thinkers*, edited by Götz Nordbruch and Umar Ryad, Palgrave Macmillan, 2014, p. 28.

7 Raja Mahendra Pratap, *Indian Independence*, Asian Solidarity, World Federation, 1930, chapter 9. https://ebin.pub/pan-asianism-a-documentary-history-1920-present-2-1442205997-9781442205994.html (accessed 2 Feb 2024)
8 Ibid.
9 *Illustrated Weekly of India*, 25 July 1971.
10 https://scroll.in/article/692459/with-row-in-aligarh-bjp-is-diminishing-legacy-of-hindu-king-who-helped-create-university (accessed 10 August 2023).
11 https://swarajyamag.com/politics/the-secular-controversy-over-a-marxist-raja (accessed 10 August 2023).
12 Lt Gen. Zameer Uddin Shah, *The Sarkari Mussalman*, New Delhi: Konark, 2019, pp. 159–60.
13 https://timesofindia.indiatimes.com/city/agra/amu-city-school-renamed-after-raja-mahendra-pratap-singh/articleshow/90023320.cms (accessed 2 February 2024).

Chapter 24: The Conflict over AMU Satellite Centres

1 https://awaam.net/political-narrative-amu-satellite-centres-anwar-khursheed/ (accessed 20 March 2023).
2 https://amu.ac.in/amucentres (accessed 20 March 2023).
3 https://www.milligazette.com/news/1-community-news/8271-amu-wins-legal-battle/ (accessed 20 February 2022).
4 https://www.milligazette.com/news/4-national/4372-pros-and-cons-of-amu-centres/ (accessed 20 February 2022).
5 https://www.indiatoday.in/education-today/news/story/smriti-irani-education-311088-2016-02-29 (accessed 3 February 2024).
6 Lt Gen. Zameer Uddin Shah, *The Sarkari Mussalman*, New Delhi: Konark, 2019, p. 158.

Chapter 25: Unlearning Harmony

1 https://www.rediff.com/news/column/when-aligarh-remained-mute-to-a-crime-in-its-midst/20170929.htm (accessed 20 January 2023).
2 Ibid.
3 Devika Sethi, *Banned & Censored: What the British Raj Didn't Want Us to Read*, New Delhi: Roli Books, 2023, p. 203.

4 Ibid.
5 Ibid.
6 Ibid.
7 Devika Sethi, *Banned & Censored: What the British Raj Didn't Want Us to Read*, New Delhi: Roli Books, 2023, p. 236.
8 https://scroll.in/article/926425/how-nehru-reacted-to-violent-protests-in-1956-demanding-withdrawal-of-a-book-about-religious-leaders (accessed 3 February 2024).

Chapter 26: *Majaz: Mera Chaman AMU*

1 https://twitter.com/iamrana/status/253536037719121921 (accessed 10 January 2022).
2 https://mohsinazizblog.org/tag/aligarh-muslim-university/ (accessed 10 January 2022).
3 *Kohsaaron,* also spelt *Khorasan*, is a historical region and realm comprising a vast territory in northeastern Iran, southern Turkmenistan and northern Afghanistan. The Muslim conquest of Khorasan was the last phase of the heavy war between the Rashidun Caliphate and the Sassanid Empire. Recently, it came into the limelight as Islamic State Khorasan (IS-K).
4 https://aligarhnama.blogspot.com/2005/12/aligarh-tarana.html (accessed 20 January 2024).

Chapter 27: Bridge Course

1 Lt Gen. Zameer Uddin Shah, *The Sarkari Mussalman*, New Delhi: Konark, 2019, p. 162.
2 Quoted in https://www.firstpost.com/politics/travels-of-a-political-pilgrim-is-rise-of-religiosity-on-amu-campus-a-precursor-to-another-partition-3284388.html (accessed 10 January 2021).
3 Ibid.
4 Personal interview, New Delhi, August 2020.
5 Quoted in https://www.firstpost.com/politics/travels-of-a-political-pilgrim-is-rise-of-religiosity-on-amu-campus-a-precursor-to-another-partition-3284388.html (accessed 10 January 2021).
6 Ibid.
7 Quoted in https://www.firstpost.com/politics/travels-of-a-political-pilgrim-is-rise-of-religiosity-on-amu-campus-a-precursor-to-another-partition-3284388.html (accessed 10 January 2021).

8 Personal interview, New Delhi, August 2020.

Chapter 28: 'We Have a Rich Past Which Needs to Be Preserved'

1 https://www.telegraphindia.com/india/aligarh-muslim-university-time-capsule-update/cid/1790983 (accessed 15 August 2023).
2 https://www.hindustantimes.com/cities/to-mark-centenary-celebration-amu-to-bury-time-capsule/story-rb8ZLK3VUwYKHJZqfnwO0N.html (accessed 3 February 2024).
3 Ibid.

BIBLIOGRAPHY

Abbas, Asghar, *Print Culture, Sir Syed's The Aligarh Institute Gazette* (translated by Syed Asim Ali) (Delhi: Primus Books, 2015).

Abrar, Rahat *Sir Syed Ahmed Khan aur Bhartiya Navjagran* (New Delhi: 2017).

———. *Sir Syed Ahmad Khan's Writings on 1857 Revolt : A Documentary Record* (New Delhi: Manak Publications, 2022).

Abrar, Rahat, and Shehnoor Shan, *Sir Syed's Legacy of Pluralism and Composite Culture* (Aligarh: Publications Division AMU, 2022).

Ahmad, Aijaz, *Aligarh Muslim University: An Educational and Political History* (Ghaziabad: Lalit Sahitya Sadan, 2005).

Ahmad, Ali, *Sir Syed Ahmad Khan on Education* (Aligarh: Aligarh Muslim University Press, 2006).

Ahmad, Mohammad Syed, *Sayyid Ahmad Khan: An Annotated Chronology* (Aligarh: Public Relations Office, 1995).

Ahmad, Safi, *Selected Documents from Aligarh Archives, Vol. II* (1988).

Ansari, M. Hamid, *By Many a Happy Accident: Recollections of a Life* (New Delhi: Rupa, 2021).

Ashraf, Javed (trans.), *Causes of Indian Rebellion (Asbab-e- Baghawat-e-Hind by Sir Syed)* (New Delhi: Asha Jyoti Publication, 2007).

Asif, Manan Ahmed, *The Loss of Hindustan: The Invention of India* (Harvard University Press, 2020).

Bakshi, Sri Ram, *Sir Syed Ahmad Khan: The Man and His Works* (Faridabad: Om Publication, 2002).

Begum, Rehmani, *Sir Syed Ahmad Khan: The Politics of Educational Reforms* (Lahore: Vanguard Books, 1985).

Bhatnagar, S.K., *History of MAO College* (Bombay: Asia Publishing House, 1969).

Brass, Paul, R. *The Production of Hindu–Muslim Violence in Contemporary India* (New Delhi: OUP, 2003).

Chand, Tara, 'National Integration and Secularism': The First Sir Syed

Memorial Lecture, 1986.

———. *History of the Freedom Movement in India Vol. 2* (New Delhi: Publications Division, 2016).

Dar, Basheer Ahmad, *Religious Thoughts of Sir Saiyyid Ahmad Khan* (Lahore: Institute of Islamic Culture, 1957).

Farooqi, M.N., *My Days at Aligarh* (Delhi: Idarah-i-Adabiyat-i-Delli, 1998).

Farouqui, Ather, *Muslims and Media Images* (New Delhi: OUP, 2011).

Faruqi, Shamsur Rahman, *From Antiquity to Social Revolutionary: Syed Ahmad Khan and the Colonial Experience*, Sir Syed Memorial lecture 2006.

Gauri, Jayakumar, *Comparative Analyses of Films: Aligarh and Boys Don't Cry* (Alapuzza: Self Publication, 2023).

Guha, Ramachandra, *A Corner of a Foreign Field: The Indian History of a British Sport* (New Delhi: Penguin, 2014).

Graham, G.F.I, *The Life and Works of Sir Syed Ahmad Khan, CSI* (London: William Blackwoodand Sons, 1885).

Hali, Altaf Hussain, *Hayat-i-Javed* (translated by Rafi Ahmad Alavi) (Aligarh: Sir Syed Academy, AMU, 2008).

Hali, Altaf Husain, *Hayat-i-Javed (A Biography of Sir Syed)* (translated by David J. Mathews) (New Delhi: Rupa, 1994).

Hameedullah, Mohammad (ed.), *Selected Essays of Sir Syed: Vol. 1* (Aligarh: Sir Syed Academy, 2004).

Hardy P., *The Muslims in British India* (Cambridge University Press, 1972; South Asia Edition, 1998).

Hasan, Mushirul and Zaidi, Nishat (ed. and trans.), *A Voyage to Modernism (Musafiran-e- London by Sir Syed)* (New Delhi: Primus Book, 2011).

Hasan, Tariq, *The Aligarh Movement and the Making of Indian Muslim Mind: 1857–2002* (New Delhi: Rupa & Co., 2006).

———, *Colonialism and the Call to Jihad in British India* (New Delhi: Sage, 2015).

Husain, Mir Wilayat, *Āp Bēti* (Aligarh: 1970).

Husain, M. Hadi, *Syed Ahmad Khan: Pioneer of Muslims Resurgence* (Lahore: Institute of Islamic Culture, 1970).

Husain, Surayya, *Sir Syed Ahmad Khan aur Unka Aihad* (Aligarh: Educational Book House, 1993).

Hussain, Iqbal (ed.), *Documents of Muslim Educational Conference* (Aligarh: Sir Syed Academy, 2004).

——— (ed.), *Justice Mahmood Papers* (Aligarh: Sir Syed Academy, 2005).

Ilahabadi, Akbar, *Pratinidhi Shairi* (New Delhi: Radhakrishan Paperbacks, 2001).

Iman, Akhtarul, *Autobiography: In this Live Desolation* (Translated by Baidar Bakht)(New Delhi: Anjuman Taraqqi Urdu, 2023).

Iraqi, Shahabuddin (ed.), *Sir Syed Ahmad Khan: Vision and Mission* (Delhi: Manohar Publication, 2008).

Jain, M.S., *The Aligarh Movement* (New Delhi: Icon Publications Pvt. Ltd, 2007).

Jalil, Rakhshanda, *A Rebel and Her Cause: The Life and Work of Rashid Jahan* (New Delhi: Women Unlimited, 2014).

Jasim, Mohammad, *Golden Thoughts of Sir Syed* (Aligarh: Alisha Publications, 2016).

———. *AMU's Minority Character: A Comprehensive Study Vol. 1* (Aligarh: Alisha Publications, 2016).

Gupta, Juhi and Kidwai, Abdur Raheem, Oxfor*d of the East, Centenary Commemorative Volume Viva* (New Delhi: 2020).

Kakorvi, Shafi Ahmad, *History of The MAO College Aligarh* (Lucknow: Markaz-e-Adab Urdu, 1988).

Kazim, Lubna, *A Woman of Substance: The Memoirs of Begum Khurshid Mirza* (New Delhi: Zubaan, 2015).

Khan, Arif Mohammad, *Text and Context: Quran and Contemporary Challenges* (New Delhi: Rupa, 2019).

Khan, Gulfishan, *Essays on Sayyid Ahmad Khan and Shaikh Abdullah* (Aligarh: Publication Division AMU, 2017).

Khan, Iftikhar Alam, *Sir Syed: A Private Life* (Unpublished English translation of Urdu book).

Khan, Javed Ali, *Muhammad Shibli Nomanii: Life and Contributions* (Azamgarh: Darul Musannefin Shibli Academy, 2004).

Khan, Syed Ahmed, *The Causes of the Indian Revolt* (New Delhi: OUP, 2000).

Khan, Zeyad Masroor, *City on Fire: A Boyhood in Aligarh* (New Delhi: HarperCollins, 2023).

Khan, Yusuf Hussain (ed.), *Sir Syed's Correspondence, Selected Documents from the Aligarh Archives* (New Delhi: Asia Publishing House, 1967).

Khurshid, Salman, *At Home in India: A Restatement of Indian Muslims* (New Delhi: Vikas, 1986).

Kidwai, Abdur Raheem (trans.), *Sir Syed's Concept of Western Education and its Implementation at Aligarh* (Rasheed Ahmad) (Aligarh: The Aligarh Heritage Publication, 2010).

Kidwai, Shafey, *Cementing Ethics with Modernism: An Assessment of Sir Syed's Periodicals* (New Delhi: Gyan Publication, 2010).

Gayer, Laurent and Jafferelot, Christopher, *Muslims in Indian Cities: Trajectories of Marginalisation* (New Delhi: HarperCollins, 2012).

Laurence, Gautier, *Between Nation and Community: Muslim Universities and Indian Politics after Partition* (New Delhi: Cambridge University Press, 2024).

Lelyveld, David, *Aligarh's First Generation: Muslim Solidarity in British India* (New Delhi: Oxford University Press, 1996).

Madani, Maulana Hussain Ahmad, *Composite Nationalism and Islam* (New Delhi: Manohar, 2007).

Malik, Hafeez, *Sir Syed Ahmad Khan and Muslim Modernisation in India and Pakistan* (Lahore: Royal Book Company, 1988).

Mangalori, Tufail Ahmad, *Towards a Common Destiny: A Nationalist Manifesto* (translated by Ali Ashraf) (New Delhi: Peoples Publishing House, 1994).

Manzar, Mustafa Husain, *Muraqqa-i-Tareekh: Muslim University Aligarh* (Aligarh: Union Book Depot, 1983).

Meer Vilayat Husain, *Aap Biti*, edited by Syed Mohammad of Tonk (Aligarh: 1970).

Mohammad, Nasir, and Ahmed Samreen, *Syed Mahmood: Colonial India's Dissenting Judge* (New Delhi: Bloomsbury, 2022).

Mohammad, Shan (ed.), *All India Muslim Educational Conference Selected Presidential Address 1886–1947* (New Delhi: APH Publishing Corporation, 2003).

——— (ed.), *Glimpses of Muslim Education in India Peeping through the Convocation Address at the Aligarh Muslim University* (Delhi: Anmol, 2006).

——— (ed.), *Sir Syed Ahmad Khan, Memorial Lectures* (New Delhi: Viva Books, 2017).

——— (ed.), *Sir Syed on Education, Society and Economy* (Delhi: Idara-e-Adbiyat, 1995).

——— (ed.), *Sir Syed's Correspondence: Selected Documents from Sir Syed Archives* (Aligarh: Sir Syed Academy, 1995).

——— (ed.), *Writings and Speeches of Syed Ahmad Khan* (Bombay: Nachiketa Publications, 1972).

———, *Education and Politics from Sir Syed to the Present Day (The Aligarh School)* (New Delhi: APH Publishing Corporation, 2002).

———, *Secular Tradition at Aligarh Muslim University* (Aligarh: AMU, 1991).

———, *Sir Syed Ahmad Khan: A Political Biography* (Meerut: Meenakshi Publications, 1969).

———, *Sir Syed's Vision of India and Its People* (New Delhi: Zenith Books International, 2008).

Muhammed, K.K, *An Indian I Am* (New Delhi: Prabhat, 2023).

Hasan, Mushirun and Zaidi, Nishat, *A Voyage to Modernism: A Trip to London; Syed Ahmed Khan* (New Delhi: Primus, 2011).

Naqvi, Noorul Hasan, *Mohammadan College se Muslim University Tak* (Aligarh: Educational Book House, 2001).

Nasreen, M.B., *Khutoot-i-Sir Syed* (Urdu) (Aligarh, Educational Book House, 1995)

Nizami, Khaleeq Ahmad, *Education and Politics: From Sir Syed to Present Day* (New Delhi: APH Publishing Corporation, 2002).

———, *History of Aligarh Muslim University: 1920–1945* (Delhi: Idara-e-Adbiyat, 1995).

———, *Syed Ahmad Khan* (Delhi: Publication Division, Government of India, 1966).

Nizami, Z.A., Ghulam, Umar and Mazhar Ali Khan, Arif, *Reflections on Sir Syed and the Aligarh Movement* (Karachi: Fazlee & Sons, 1998).

Page, David, *Prelude to Partition: The Indian Muslims and the Imperial System of Control 1920–32* (New Delhi: OUP, 1999).

Pande, B.N., *Basic Oneness of all Religions with Special Reference to Hinduism and Islam*, Sir Syed Memorial Lecture, 1987, New Delhi: AMU.Pasha, Mohamed Abdullah, *Sir Syed Ahmad Khan: His Life & Times* (Rawalpindi: Feroze & Sons, 1998).

Panipati, Mohammad Ismaeel, *Makubat-e-Sir Syed* (Lahore: Majlis-e-Taraqqi-e-Adab, 1976).

Qadri, Khalid Hasan, and David J. Matthews (trans.), *Hayat-e-Javed* (by Khwaja Altaf Hussain Hali) (Delhi: Idara-e-Adbiyat, 1979).

Qadri, Khalid Hasan, *Sir Syed Ahmad Khan: An Assessment of his Personality, his Contribution and Achievement in the light of Musalmon ka Raushan Mustaqbil* (London: Books International, 2002).

Qasmi, Al Usman, and Robb, Megan Eaton, *Muslims Against the Muslim League: Critiques of the Idea of Pakistan* (New Delhi: Cambridge University Press, 2017).

Qureshi, Ishrat Ali, *Aligarh Past and Present* (Aligarh: AMU, 1992).

———, *Sir Syed's Relevance Today* (Aligarh: Sir Syed Academy, 1992).

Ray, Niharranjan, 'Nationalism in India: An Historical Analysis of its Stresses and Strains', AMU, Sir Syed Memorial Lecture, 1972.

Ray, Siddarth Shanker, *Sir Syed Ahmad Khan: His Relevance to Present Day India* (Aligarh: Sir Syed Academy, 2004).

Robinson, Francis, *Separatism Among Indian Muslims: The Politics of the United Provinces Muslims 1860–1923* (New Delhi: OUP, 1993).

Russell, Ralph, and Khurshidul Islam Ansari (trans.), 'The Satorical Verse of Akbar Ilahabadi', in Asloob Ahmad (ed.), *Sir Syed Ahmad Khan: A Centenary Tribute* (Delhi: Adam Publishers, 2001).

Sadiq, M., *The Founder of Aligarh* (Karachi: Oxford University Press, 1968).

Sami Ahmad, Syed, *Sir Syed Ahmad Khan: The Saviour of Muslim India* (Lahore: Pak Book Corporation, 2002).

Shackle, Christopher, and Javed Majeed (trans.), *Hali's Musaddas: The Flow and Ebb of Islam* (New Delhi: OUP, 1997).

Shabbir, Shahnaz, *Religious Thoughts of Sir Syed Ahmad Khan: A Critical Study* (Aligarh: Publication Division, 2015).

Shah, Lt Gen. Zameer Uddin, *The Sarkari Musasalman: The Life and Travails of a Soldier Educationist: The Memoirs* (New Delhi: Konak, 2019).

Shamsul, Islam, *Muslims against Partition of India* (New Delhi: Pharos, 2017).

Sheik, B., *A Leader Reassessed: Life and work of Sir Syed Ahmad Khan* (Mysore: Sultan Shaheed Education Trust Publication, 1999).

Shervani, H.K., *The Aligarh Movement* (Aligarh: AMU, 1994).

Siddiqi, Rasheed Ahmed, *Sir Syed's Concept of Western Education and Its Implementation at Aligarh* (translated by Abdul Raheem Kidwai) (Aligarh: The Aligarh Heritage Publications, 2010).

———. *Aashufta Bayani Meri*, https://archive.org/details/AashuftaBayaniMeriRasheedAhmadSiddiqui

———. *Sir Syed ka Maghribi Taleem ka Tasawwur aur Uska Nifaz Aligarh Main*, edited by Meher Ilahi Nadeem, Maktaba-e-Daniyal (Karachi: 1993).

Siddiqui, Mohammad Yasin Mazhar, *Shah Waliullah Dehlavi: An Introduction to his Illustrious Personality and Achievements*, Institute of Islamic Studies, AMU, Aligarh.

Sundus, Juvariya, *100 Years of Aligarh Muslim University: Through the Eyes of Women* (New Delhi: The2am Thoughts Publication, 2022).

Suroor, Aale Ahmad, *Khwab Baqi Hain* (Aligarh: Educational Book House, 1991).

Tyabji, Badr Ud Din, *Memoirs of an Egoist: More Memoirs of an Egoist* (New Delhi: Har-Anand, 1988 and 1994).

The Zajir Husain Memorial Lecture, 1992–2004 Zakir Husain College, University of Delhi (New Delhi: Tulika, 2007).

Troll, Christian W., *Saiyyid Ahmad Khan: A Reinterpretation Muslim Theology* (New Delhi: Vikas Publishing House Pvt. Ltd, 1978).

Varshney, Ashutosh, *Ethnic Conflict and Civic Life: Hindus and Muslims in India* (New Delhi: OUP, 2002).

Wajihuddin, Mohammed, *Aligarh Muslim University: The Making of the Modern Indian Muslim* (New Delhi: HarperCollins, 2021).

William, Sir Muir, *The Life of Mahomet* (New Delhi: Voice of India, Indian Reprint 1992).

BOOKS AND TRANSLATED WORKS (RASYAL) BY SIR SYED AHMAD KHAN

1. *Tassheel fee Jar a Saqeel*, 1844
2. *Aasar us Sanadeed*, 1846
3. *Kalmat ul Haq*, 1850
4. *Rah e Sunnet wal Biddet*, 1850
5. *Silsatul Malook*, 1852
6. *Aayan e Akbari*, 1855
7. *Tareekh e Sarkashi e Bajnor*, 1858
8. *Asbab e Bagawat e Hind*, 1858
9. *Lafz Tehqeeq e Nasara*, 1859
10. *Loyal Mohammadans of India*,
11. *Tabayan ul Kalam*, 1862
12. *Tuzk e Jahangheeri*; *Asal kitab ke tashreeh*, 1864
13. *Aligarh Institute Gazette*, 1866
14. *Ahkam Taam Ahal ul Kitab*, 1868
15. *Khutbat-e-Ahmadiya*, 1870
16. *Tehzeeb-ul-Ikhlaq*, 1870
17. *Safarnama Musafran e London*, 1870
18. *Review of Indian Muslims*, William Hunter, 1872
19. *Tafseer e Quran*, 1878
20. *Safarnama-e-Punjab*, 1884
21. *Al Izzatul Ghane An Zulqarnain*, 1889
22. *Khalq ul Insaan Al Mafi Al Quran*, 1891
23. *Al Dua ul Istajabah*, 1892
24. *Abtalai Ghulami*, 1893
25. *Seerat e Freedia*, 1896

INDEX

ABOUT THE AUTHORS

The septuagenarian Anil Maheshwari segued through the rough and tumble of journalism for five decades before superannuating from *Hindustan Times* as a special correspondent. He has twice been a short-term fellow at Aligarh Muslim University. He has written about a dozen books and is proficient in English and Hindi with a smattering of Urdu. He has contributed to various magazines and newspapers, including the *Economic and Political Weekly* and *Frontier*.

Anil lives in Noida with his wife, two sons, two daughters-in-law, a granddaughter, Anya, and a grandson, Ayan.

Arjun Maheshwari is an Aligarian and a serial entrepreneur. He has founded several startups in various industries. Alongside his entrepreneurial pursuits, he writes articles on technology, entrepreneurship and business strategies for multiple publications. Arjun is based in Noida, Uttar Pradesh, where he is involved in the local startup community, providing advice and mentorship to new entrepreneurs.